D1598995

❖ Puritans and Predestination

Grace in English Protestant Theology,

1525–1695

❖ Puritans and Predestination

Grace in English Protestant Theology,

1525–1695

Dewey D. Wallace, Jr.

The University of North Carolina Press

Chapel Hill

For Marion, Mark, and Paul

© 1982 The University of North Carolina Press

Manufactured in the United States of America

Library of Congress Cataloging in Publication Data

Wallace, Dewey D.
  Puritans and predestination.

  (Studies in religion)
  Bibliography: p.
  Includes index.
    1. Grace (Theology)—History of doctrines—
16th century. 2. Grace (Theology)—History of
doctrines—17th century. 3. Theology, Puritan—
England. I. Title. II. Series: Studies in
religion (Chapel Hill, N.C.)
BT61.2W32   234'.09'032   81-11563
ISBN 0-8078-1499-7   AACR2

Contents

Acknowledgments

A great many debts were accumulated in the research and writing of this book, and in a short preface I can hope to repay only the most important of them. A grant from the University Committee on Research of The George Washington University facilitated the completion of this project. The staff of the Folger Shakespeare Library, where most of the research was done, was unfailingly helpful. Robert W. Kenny, Lois G. Schwoerer, and Harry E. Yeide, Jr., my colleagues at The George Washington University, read portions of the text, called attention to shortcomings, and made many beneficial suggestions. Jackson C. Boswell of the University of the District of Columbia provided many references to passages in early English books relevant to my topic. John Fines of the West Sussex Institute kindly allowed me to use his manuscript "Register of Early British Protestants, 1520–1558." I would also like to acknowledge the skillful typing done by Elnora Carter and the many indispensable tasks in preparing the final manuscript undertaken by Eileen Arthurs. It goes without saying that none of these persons is responsible for such mistakes as remain.

Portions of chapters 3 and 4, particularly material dealing with John Owen, had an earlier form in my 1965 Princeton University dissertation directed by Horton M. Davies. Part of chapter 1 is reprinted in revised form with permission from *Church History* 43 (June 1974):201–15, copyright 1974, The American Society of Church History.

I have abbreviated the titles of many early printed books. Where necessary for clarity, a very few changes in the spelling of material quoted from early printed books have been made. The *Dictionary of National Biography* has been cited as *DNB*.

Introduction

English Puritanism has in the past decades been thoroughly studied as a social and political force, with detailed attention given to its ideas about polity, ritual, and the state, as well as to its activities as a reforming movement. But Puritanism was deeply theological, and theological concepts were important to the other involvements of Puritans. One scholar has complained of a masterful treatment of the Elizabethan Puritan movement that it says too little about Puritan theology.[1] Clearly, Puritanism needs to be studied as a theological movement as well as a social, political, and ecclesiastical one, and the relationship of its other concerns to its theological outlook needs to be analyzed. Certainly many previous scholars were aware of the theological dimension of Puritanism: William Haller noted the importance of the preaching of grace and predestination in Puritanism; Alan Simpson's discussion of the importance of conversion in Puritanism firmly rooted that experience in theology; the works of Perry Miller dealt with Puritanism as an ideological phenomenon and analyzed many aspects of Puritan theology; a more recent study of Puritan theology was made by John S. Coolidge.[2] One of the purposes of this book is to continue the examination of Puritan theology begun by these and other scholars.

But Puritan theology cannot properly be studied in isolation from the thought of what is usually distinguished from it as "Anglicanism." Several attempts have been made to discuss Puritan and Anglican theology together, and these naturally concentrate on the theological differences separating the two parties that long shared the common dwelling of the Church of England. Perhaps the books by John F. H. New and J. Sears McGee are the most significant attempts of this sort.[3] Numerous studies have dealt with Anglican thought in the sixteenth and seventeenth centuries. The weakness of many such treatments, whether comparative or of Anglicanism alone, is that they assume that Anglicanism was a fixed entity, and that there was a classically Anglican *via media* theological perspective of which any particular study but brings out certain ramifications.[4] But the assumption that the terms Anglican (and, for that matter, Puritan) designate fixed entities appears more and more questionable, and therefore I have studied together what is sometimes treated separately as Anglican and Puritan theology, convinced that in some periods they can hardly be separated at all and that at other times they are separated only in the subtlest of ways. In this respect the title of this book is less accurate than the subtitle, for the aim is to examine the English Protestant theology of grace without assuming too easily that it falls into Puritan and Anglican categories.

The focus of this study of English theology from the Reformation to the era of the Glorious Revolution is on the doctrine of grace. This doctrine was central to the Protestant Reformation, and it loomed large not only in controversy between Protestant and Roman Catholic but within Protestantism itself, perhaps more so in England than in some other Protestant lands. The doctrine of grace was central to the Protestant Reformation because it dealt with the basic Protestant notion that salvation was a divine gift, thus bearing on the very heart of the religious revolution wrought by the disputes of Martin Luther with his antagonists. In Protestant theology, God's gracious gift to mankind was the gospel of salvation in Christ, a free gift to those who believed. Grace was the declared word of pardon (forensic grace) by which, for the sake of Christ, the sins of men were blotted out by a merciful creator, in contrast to the Roman Catholic view that grace was a quality inherent in those who cooperated with the divine offer made in the sacramental system of the church.

For the purposes of this study, the doctrine of grace embraces a constellation of ideas and formulations that both sprang out of and revolved around the essentially Protestant piety of salvation as God's gift to faith. The essence of this Protestant piety was a vision of the divine-human relationship as based on the gratuitous mercy of God in the absence of human deserving, with humankind the object of a supernatural renovation worked only by the divine favor. Within the constellation of theological formulations connected to this apprehension of God's free grace were such ideas as the bondage of humankind to sin and a consequent inability to initiate a relationship with God; justification by the imputed righteousness of Christ appropriated instrumentally by faith, rather than by human merit; the irresistibility of grace; regeneration and sanctification by the Holy Spirit operating upon the human soul, leading to an actual holiness of life; the indefectibility of salvation, or the perseverance of the saints; Christ's atoning death as an effectual gift to the redeemed only; and the doctrine of predestination to eternal life whereby the will of God alone is the ultimate cause of salvation. At times and in accordance with the shifting focus of controversy, some of these elements received greater stress than others, but more and more the doctrine of predestination came to the fore as the touchstone of how grace was regarded, and thus special attention is given to it. Increasingly in the period under review, adherence to the doctrine of unconditional predestination came to mean in English theology the acceptance of the whole scheme of redemption as it was understood in this Protestant theology of grace. Attitudes toward predestination thus serve as a convenient measure of the degree of theological unanimity as well as an important index of theological change. Yet the doctrine of predestination is not properly understood in isolation, apart from the whole theology of grace with which it is integrally related, serving as it did as the ultimate guarantor of the absolute freeness of God's salvific benefits. Thus this study is mainly a survey of the vicissitudes of the doctrine of predestination in English Protestant theology from the Reformation to 1695, but predestination is not separated from other aspects of that theology of grace of which it was a crucial part.

In focusing on the theology of grace through emphasis on the doctrine of predestination, a word should be said about the assumption running through this analysis of English theology that a particular theology is an indication of a certain type of piety, or "way-of-being-religious." Such an assumption seems borne out by the different English theologies of grace. These different theologies were not mainly different solutions to intellectual puzzles, carried on by dint of the ineluctable curiosity of the human mind, but were formulations that expressed, enshrined, and stimulated particular pieties. Theological formulations function in relation to religious experience, but that latter phenomenon is the soil out of which they grow and in which they thrive. Regarded in such a fashion, theological dispute loses some of its aridity and detachment and comes into focus as dealing with disparate attitudes about how life is to be understood and carried on. One consequence of such an approach is to minimize extremely technical bits of theological debate that seem tangential to living piety and to maximize theological differences that seem to be related to significant shifts in religious outlook. It should quickly become apparent that in the present study the doctrines of grace in general and predestination in particular are thought to belong to the second of these categories, standing in a very close relationship to a "way-of-being-religious."

This study has been conducted through an analysis of the published theological literature of the period under consideration as it related to the problem and question of grace, and especially to predestination. Basil Hall has suggested that patient attention to the published theology of the period might be one way of casting light on many of the vexed questions in the study of the religion of that time,[5] and such is my intention. Some of this published theological literature has been examined before, but much of the material, especially from the later Elizabethan and early Jacobean periods, has received little or no modern attention. Recognizing how little mined have been veins of Elizabethan theological controversy, a recent book satisfies itself with painstaking bibliographical reconstruction of the material.[6] That I have worked almost entirely with published materials is one of the limitations of this study: conclusions should be taken as inferences from an examination of published books, although occasionally other evidence has been used where it was useful in illuminating controversies carried on in writing. Perhaps another limitation is that because the nature of the study required a very extensive reading of published materials, some of the nuances that might have been discovered by a more concentrated examination of a few writings or of a single theologian have been overlooked.

The aim in studying this theological literature concerning grace and predestination has not been narrowly theological. The main purpose is to use analysis of published theological literature to illuminate problems concerning the character of English Protestant religion and the nature of the English church, its conflicts, and its gradually forming parties. Delineation of the vicissitudes of the theology of grace in English Protestantism should clarify the nature of the English religious struggles from the 1520s to 1695. Among questions that have been of particular concern are the relation of English theology to the theology of the Continental Reformation, the origins and character of Puritanism, the nature of the theological distinctions, if any, separating Puritan from Anglican, and the impact of religious conflict upon social stability.

I have found reason to stress the close relationship of English Protestant theology to that of the Continental Reformation. Not only did the English Protestant movement and its theology develop under the direction and compelling impact of the Continent, but later innovations in English theology can be seen as reflections of issues agitating the Protestant world as a whole and as the pitting of one Continental Protestant tradition against another. In understanding the Continental influence, it is important to be aware of the differences between Lutheran and Calvinist theology, and this comes up at various points in the narrative. The term "Reformed" has been preferred to "Calvinism" as having wider implications, naming a particular kind of theology in the construction of which Calvin was but one figure among many. In English theology the influence of Martin Bucer, Peter Martyr, Heinrich Bullinger, and others was of great importance, and to refer to this strain as "Calvinism" can be misleading.

The importance of the Reformed theology of grace is emphasized as shaping the nature and origins of the Puritan movement. To be sure, not only Puritans saw such a theology as important, but there was a fervor, intensity, and warmly personal character to the Puritan use of this theology of grace that must not be overlooked in any attempt to understand the mainsprings of the Puritan consciousness. Their piety of conversion and holiness and their theology of the grace of God as the sole cause of salvation may have been shared with many in England and abroad, but nonetheless, the story of the English Puritans is in one of its most important aspects the story of the vicissitudes of a group attempting to draw out all the implications of their piety and theology and to apply them to the English church and nation. Puritanism then would seem not simply to have emerged as an effort to purge the church of various abuses, but also as a movement for the explication and cultivation of a vision of what Christianity in its essence and as a way of life truly was. Although many features of Puritanism are apparent in the extensive literature, these features may be seen as radiating outward from an inner and deeply existential core of Puritan piety. Puritan concern with discipline and church polity was a way of realizing in community the consequences of a gracious election and the joys and demands of holiness. The Puritan emphasis upon the moral and spiritual welfare of individuals and of the whole English nation was an aspect of their insistence upon making God's transforming grace triumphant in society. Their preoccupation with eschatology was a witnessing to the triumph of divine grace in the destiny of men and nations. Basic to their position was the central Reformed affirmation that salvation was by grace alone, without cause in man. In Puritanism this evangelical insight was particularly highlighted both in the insistence that salvation by grace alone be a lived experience of every Christian individual and in the way it was hedged about, ensured, and guaranteed through a particularly unyielding theology, but a theology that nonetheless enshrined a vital and vigorous religious experience.

Ironically, perhaps, for a study that maintains the distinct importance of theology for Puritanism, another important theme of this study is the theological closeness of Puritan and Anglican to one another and the very great difficulty of separating them by theological means, at least before the reign of James I. When differences do appear, the Nonconformist Puritans seem most faithful to the earlier theological traditions of the Church of England, and the Anglican conformists are most likely to be the innovators. Thus in addition to being a study in the influence of the Continent upon English theology and of the nature of Puritan theology, this work is an essay in the problem of distinguishing the theology of Puritan and Anglican. Trying to avoid the twin errors of running their theological differences back into too early a period and of denying any theological differences at all,[7] I have sought to show, at least with respect to the doctrine of grace, precisely when and how Anglican and Puritan came to differ theologically and with what consequences.

The more specific conclusions of this study can best be anticipated by a quick summary of the intentions of the five chapters. Chapter 1, covering the doctrine of grace in English theology before the Elizabethan settlement, seeks to establish the point that a pattern of theology centering on a Swiss Reformed order of salvation that included predestination became the outlook of England's first Protestant generations; this pattern of theology laid the basis for the later theology of the Puritans, but it also set the basic shape of theology for almost all of English Protestantism through the Elizabethan period and beyond. The second chapter describes the further refinement of this theological pattern in the Elizabethan and early Jacobean periods, dealing in particular with how that theology was widely assumed at the Elizabethan settlement, defended as essential Protestantism against sectarian and Roman Catholic opponents, articulated especially but not exclusively by Puritan Nonconformists in highly personal terms focusing on assurance, hardened into a more rigid scholasticism by university theologians, and, finally, late in the period, dissented from at various points by English theological writers attuned to other than Reformed strains within Protestantism, such as Renaissance humanism or Lutheranism. Chapter 3 relates the story of the Arminian controversies in England, beginning with the condemnation of Dutch Arminianism in the Jacobean church and proceeding on to the development of a school of English Arminians, eventually to be patronized by Charles I and Archbishop William Laud, who entered into sharp theological conflict with those who upheld the older traditions of English Reformed theology while regarding the new upstart Arminianism as surrender to Rome. The bitterness and alienation of this theological struggle was not unrelated to the coming of civil war. Chapter 4 continues the story of conflict over grace and predestination, depicting a struggle between the defenders of the Reformed theology of grace and their new opponents, sectarian Arminians and a more purely moralistic Anglican breed of Arminians. Reacting to the catalyst of the Antinomian movement, the "Calvinists" themselves began to divide into "moderate" and "high" parties. The final chapter aims to show how these theological differences in the course of vigorous argument came to divide church from Dissent theologically and Dissenters from one another as the specter of Socinianism haunted religious discussion and as the Reformed theology of predestinarian grace became more and more an alien presence in an "enlightened" age. This study will be complete only with another volume, a full treatment of the theology of grace in colonial America in relation both to the English theological heritage that preceded it and to the developing New World environment that unfolded before it.

❖ Puritans and Predestination

Chapter 1 ❖ The Theology of Grace in the Early English Reformation

An understanding of the doctrine of divine grace in redemption and a pattern in the development and explication of that doctrine that was indebted to the Swiss or Rhineland reformers was established in English Protestantism before the reign of Elizabeth and continued long after her accession to provide the central elements in the English Protestant theology of grace. These Swiss reformers influenced England not only with regard to the doctrine of grace. If anything, their influence was even more clearly to be seen in Eucharistic theology, where the differences between the Swiss and the Lutherans were more sharply defined and their respective influences accordingly simpler to identify.[1] The purpose of this chapter is to note some characteristic features in the Swiss or "Reformed" understanding of the grace of God and to locate these features in the theology of the English Reformation before 1558. The distinct features of the Rhineland teaching about grace emerged among England's earliest Protestants, were more fully developed and expressed in the reign of Edward VI, when all restraint on such teaching was removed, and were clung to tenaciously by both exiles and Marian martyrs in the years between the death of Edward and the accession of Elizabeth.

The Swiss and Rhineland reformers include not only the early group of reformers, Ulrich Zwingli, Johannes Oecolampadius, Bucer, Bullinger, and their associates who broke with Luther over the presence of Christ in the Eucharist, but others from outside the Rhineland such as the Italian Pietro Martire Vermigli (Peter Martyr), the Frenchman John Calvin, and others active later in the century, including Jerome Zanchi, Theodore Beza, and Zacharius Ursinus. In short, this is the group of reformers and theologians who created and shaped "Reformed" as opposed to Lutheran Protestantism, sometimes mistakenly but conveniently denominated "Calvinist." These theologians sometimes differed from one another in matters of emphasis and interpretation, and occasionally significant differences between the earlier and later ones can be noted. With respect to the theology of grace, however, they shared certain central emphases, and the theology of grace they launched underwent vicissitudes that allow considering them as representing a distinct viewpoint, even if that viewpoint was sometimes in transition. The effort is sometimes made, especially by students of the English Reformation, to separate out earlier, more moderate strands in this tradition from later, more "rigid" Calvinistic ones,[2] but it is doubtful that Calvin introduced anything distinctly harsher into the tradition than already existed. As John Patrick Donnelly remarks, "The influence of the theologians of Calvin's and Martyr's generation on the following generation was mainly cumulative and overlapping rather than distinct and idiosyncratic."[3] One suspects in such efforts to separate earlier Reformed theology from later Calvinistic theology that there is an underlying motive of clearing some favored movement or thinker of any imputation of "Calvinism."[4] In any case, this chapter chiefly deals with the Reformed tradition before the dominance of Calvin within it.

The significant influence of the Swiss reformers upon the English Reformation in its early and formative years is by now generally acknowledged. In an important article written a generation ago, Leonard Trinterud called attention to the impact of the Rhineland reformers upon English Protestantism, arguing that under their influence a distinct school of theology took shape prior to 1553. But Trinterud clouded the issue both by identifying this theological school with Puritanism alone and by conceding that in spite of such influence "the controlling element" in Puritanism was "the heritage from medieval English thought and life."[5] But it was not just Puritan theology, if there was such an entity in the middle sixteenth century, that was so shaped, but the theology of the English Protestant movement as a whole. It is by now commonplace to remark that the Elizabethan Church of England was "Calvinist" or Reformed in its theology.[6] But the same can be said of the Edwardian Church of England and of most of the Protestant activists of Henry VIII's reign (excluding, of course, the chronologically impossible specific influence of Calvin himself from the earlier part of that period).[7] It is certainly an exaggeration to restrict the influence of the Rhineland reformers to the development of a unique Puritan theology; Trinterud has since commented that "to repeat the all too common observation that the Puritans attempted to introduce 'Calvinism' into England, whereas the defenders of officialdom championed 'patristic theology,' is to misunderstand a very great deal."[8] As to the medieval influences upon Puritanism or English Protestantism as a whole, there was a notable English tradition of

Augustinian theology prior to the Reformation, of which Thomas Bradwardine was the best representative, and there was also an earlier English
tradition of moralistic anticlerical protest against the corruptions of the
church, exemplified mainly by the Lollards, and both of these forces had
something to do with the coming and especially the success of the English
Reformation. Still the English Reformation, especially on its theological
side, was primarily an extension into England of the religious revolution
under way on the Continent, the Henrician schism for marital and dy-
nastic purposes being more its occasion than cause. English Protestants
cited the earlier Augustinians to buttress the antiquity and respectability
of their opinions, and they claimed John Wyclif as a forerunner, but the
English Augustinians had not used the theology of grace as a means for
radical protest as Luther had, and the Lollards, in spite of Wyclif's predestinarianism, seem not to have built their protest upon theological
doctrine so much as on outrage at abuses of ecclesiastical power. Thus
the leaders of English Protestantism had a common inspiration in Luther's
revolt, and, more to the present purpose, whether exiles on the Continent
in the 1520s or 1530s or bishops and their chaplains in the decade before
1553, they passed beyond that initial Lutheran phase to come under the
influence of the Swiss Reformation as they formed their opinions about a
great variety of controverted matters, including their understanding of
divine grace. Continental influence was abetted by the presence in England during the reign of Edward of major Reformed thinkers, especially
Martin Bucer and Peter Martyr, though there were many others,[9] and it
was further increased by the influx of Marian exiles early in the reign of
Elizabeth.[10] Not that the English theological writers were entirely pas-
sive, though some do appear to have been no more than the transmitters
and popularizers of the ideas of their Continental mentors. The major
English theological writers must be given some credit for helping to
shape this common Reformed theology along with the theologians of the
Continent.

The theology of grace found among the Swiss theologians began, as it
did for Luther, with justification by faith alone. That such a justification
was God's gift of grace, a declared or "forensic" word of pardon excluding all human merit and a pure act of the divine sovereignty excluding
all human pride and self-reliance, was as central to the Swiss reformers as
to Luther. But the men of the Rhineland Reformation developed the
theology of grace beyond that of Luther and Lutheranism in their distinct
emphases on predestination and sanctification and their stress on the

assurance and comfort to be derived thereby for the redeemed. Luther may have implied the strictest predestination in his answer to Erasmus on *The Bondage of the Will*, but later Lutheranism was reticent about the topic and came to regard a doctrine of unconditional predestination as characteristic of the Swiss sacramentarians whom they resisted. Those Rhineland reformers who parted company with Luther over the Eucharist, on the other hand, regarded predestination as a very important teaching: Zwingli had a clear predilection for predestinarian and Augustinian theology, and Bullinger, though moderate in his expressions, followed him;[11] for Guillaume Farel and Pierre Viret predestination was central to the gospel;[12] a recent investigation of Bucer's theology concludes that "the doctrine of predestination or election is one that shapes the whole of Bucer's theology" and that "the doctrine of election plays a central part in Bucer's theology";[13] a more recent study of Peter Martyr says predestination was the most important doctrine in his theology.[14] Calvin is notorious for his teaching on predestination; if anything, he is usually regarded as making it more central to his theological system and expressing it more harshly than he actually did.[15] As will be discussed in more detail later, the Reformed theology of the late sixteenth and seventeenth centuries gave predestination an increasingly important place in its systems. Further, this Reformed theology of predestination carried along with it the corollary of reprobation to damnation as the reverse of election to blessedness.

Though the importance of predestination in Reformed theology need hardly be argued, this importance did not result from a fixation upon the attributes of absolute divine sovereignty and the implacable consequences of such sovereignty, but was rooted in the Protestant theology of grace. Because salvation is entirely by grace, and not of human striving nor deserving, God's mere will is alone the cause of all who turn to him in faith and are justified; thereby predestination is made the protector and guarantor of the more important point that justification and redemption are by God's grace alone. Thus predestination is rooted in soteriology. As Peter Martyr clearly stated, "Free justification also should perish, except we be rightlie taught of predestination."[16] A polemical purpose to the doctrine was also put with straightforward clarity by Peter Martyr: without a solid doctrine of God's predestination, the "grace of God" cannot "be sufficientlie defended against the Pelagians," those errorists (especially the theologians of Rome) who taught people to rely on their own merits.[17]

Equally distinct with predestination in the Reformed teaching about grace was the emphasis upon sanctification. Nor was sanctification unrelated to predestination among the Reformed theologians: Peter Martyr, commenting on the need to teach predestination to the "godly," says, "Let them understand also, that they are predestinate, to be made like unto the image of the Sonne of God . . . and to walke in good workes."[18] This formula of election to holiness, of sanctification as at least the earthly penultimate goal and purpose of God's predestination (the ultimate goal, of course, was the state of blessedness, or glorification), was foreign to Luther's outlook and has been regarded as the specific contribution of Martin Bucer,[19] but it is certainly echoed in Calvin.[20] The purpose, then, of God's electing and justifying sinners is that they might become a holy people doing his will on earth, individually and collectively. Hence the Reformed stress upon what was termed "the third use of the law," the need for biblical rules to guide believers in the process of sanctification, and upon Christian discipline, which sometimes appeared among the Reformed theologians as a third mark of the visible church, alongside word and sacraments. But it was always insisted that this sanctification was itself a work of God's grace in the believer, an operation of the Holy Spirit to renew and regenerate the sinner. And at this point sanctification was connected to justification: the Holy Spirit effected a gratuitous regeneration in the justified sinner, and this regenerating work connected the faith and good works of the believer. For Bucer, Martyr, and others, this was called "vocatio," "calling."[21] Thus distinct within the Reformed teaching about grace as predestination, and related to predestination as its end, was an emphasis upon sanctification by the regenerating force of the Holy Spirit.

Both Bucer and Peter Martyr, who were of seminal importance in the development of the form of theology under discussion, integrally related predestination, justification, and sanctification to a whole *ordo salutis*, or "order of salvation," that was a series of sequential steps in the ordering of the theology of grace, proceeding from predestination to calling, justification, sanctification, and, finally, glorification.[22] This formulation was to become a distinctive part of Reformed theology, and it was vastly influential on Reformed future development, especially in England.

Peter Martyr also said that predestination was a profitable doctrine to the godly, bringing them the assurance that their salvation was reliable, being in the hands of God, and certain, perseverance in it depending not on their efforts but on God's election.[23] Calvin frequently reiterated the same thing.[24] Thus another distinctive characteristic of the Reformed teaching about grace was comfort and assurance in predestination and its consequence of the indefectibility of the elect.

England's Earliest Protestants

The discussion of grace found in the theological literature of early English Protestantism reveals how important these distinctive elements of the Reformed teaching were. Not only in that literature was the common Lutheran-Reformed doctrine of justification by grace through faith taken for granted, but there appeared also an acceptance of predestination. Also evident was the noting of the connections between predestination and free justification; its reverse of the reprobation of the damned, or the double decree; a rebuttal of opposing views as Pelagian; a marked emphasis upon sanctification, including the formula of election to holiness; beginnings of the use of predestination for assurance and comfort; and an occasional acknowledgment of perseverance as indefectible in the elect.

Henry VIII never accepted the Protestant teaching about grace. On such questions his thought continued to move in the world of late medieval "semi-Pelagianism." One recent book on the second Tudor monarch recognizes his opinions as "merit-theology,"[25] and another comments that "although he was willing to change Catholicism until it was beyond recognition, he never stepped into the Protestant camp on the two crucial doctrines of good works and free will."[26] Henry therefore never intentionally helped to promote the Swiss theology of grace. But the many movements that converged during his reign to launch a Reformation in England—humanist reformism, anticlerical protest, Lutheranism, and Swiss sacramentarianism—encouraged those who found an opportunity for reform in the king's drive to create a national church under the royal will. Henry's schism provided an opportunity for the appearance in England of the teachings about grace that were central to the Continental Reformation and were being developed by Rhineland theologians. These teachings first came into England with a group of more or less proscribed Protestant writers, among whom William Tyndale and John Frith were preeminent, and only gradually became a commitment of those Henrician church leaders who became the Protestant leaders in the time of the boy king Edward VI. Yet other Henrician church leaders, among whom Stephen Gardiner was principal, opposed the new teaching on grace, and those who with Gardiner lived to see the day of Marian reaction greeted it warmly.[27]

Most of the principal elements of the Swiss theology of grace appeared in the writings of England's earliest Protestants, sometimes as the main thrust of their argument. Following Luther as well as the Rhineland reformers, these early English Protestants agreed that true Christian piety began with justification by grace through faith, as David Broughton Knox has demonstrated with massive evidence.[28] These English Protestants stressed faith and justification as a free gift of God's grace. William Tyndale declared that "the right faith springeth not of man's fantasy, neither is it in any man's power to obtain it; but it is altogether the pure gift of God poured into us freely, . . . without deserving and merits, yea, and without seeking for of us."[29] Many other passages in Tyndale reinforce the same point.[30] John Frith's treatise *A Mirrour or Glasse to Know Thy Selfe* (ca. 1533) is built entirely around the theme of the gifts of God's grace.[31] In Robert Barnes,[32] George Joye,[33] Miles Coverdale,[34] and Simon Fish[35] is found the same insistence that faith and justification are gifts of grace.

The distinctly Reformed emphasis on sanctification also appeared among these early English Protestants, and it was closely connected to justification by the idea so prominent in Bucer that the Holy Spirit gratuitously regenerates those who have the gift of faith, that they might do the good works of the sanctified. Sanctification was also connected to predestination as its end. Tyndale's concern with holiness and the Christian life recurs throughout his writings.[36] As he expressed it, "God hath created and made us new in Christ, and put his Spirit in us, that we should live a new life, which is the life of good works."[37] George Joye believed that the elect and justified are renewed and regenerated by the Spirit.[38] To William Turner, those whom God chose "he instilled" with "the grace of his spirite" so that they might fulfill his commandments.[39] The same theme pervades an early work of Coverdale.[40] Elsewhere Tyndale states more forcefully the predestinarian background of sanctification: "In Christ God chose us, and elected us before the beginning of the world, created us anew by the word of the gospel, and put his Spirit in us, for because that we should do good works."[41] Similarly, George Joye said, "We be predestined saith Paul to this ende that we shulde here be faithful holye and blameless before god by love"; and John Frith repeated that "Christ chose us in hym before the begynnyng of the worlde, that we might be holy and without spotte in his sight."[42]

Current interpretations have concluded, as Luther himself might have, that this emphasis on sanctification and upon keeping God's commandments introduced a thoroughgoing moralism into English Protestanism that is significant in understanding the growth of later Puritanism. Trinterud, for example, has said that these early English Protestants borrowed from the Continent a strongly covenantal mode of thinking that stressed obedience to God's will and law and had much to do with the later creation of a distinct Puritan movement preoccupied with reform based on supposed biblical models. In an article on Tyndale, he finds that early reformer to have been moralistic in his outlook.[43] In the most well-known discussion of covenant theology, Perry Miller implied that such thinking compromised a theology of free grace by its accentuation of the obligation of obedience.[44] Coming to the problem from a different angle, William A. Clebsch has seen the emphasis upon sanctification by the early English Protestants as a matter of indigenous English moralism being reinforced by contact with Swiss theology, the mixture of the two then eventually giving rise to a moralism that was a chief ingredient of later Puritanism. Like Trinterud he sees this as related to covenant theology, and he finds the evidence particularly in what he calls their doctrine of double justification, the second being a justification *before men*, through works, subsequent to justification by grace through faith.[45]

There is no question that the covenantal thinking and the focus on keeping God's commandments detected by Trinterud and Clebsch are truly characteristic of these early English Protestants. But to observe these motifs in their theology from the angle of the Reformed theology of grace places such motifs in proper perspective and avoids exaggerating their significance. For covenant theology never really compromised the theology of grace (nor did Trinterud suggest that it did) but was a way of explicating and making intelligible from the human side what from God's side remained always a simple act of free mercy. Covenant theology did not materially "soften" the insistence on God's free grace; God was regarded as initiating the covenant and enabling persons to respond to its terms. Indeed, its late flowering in England was among the most predestinarian of theologians.[46] The key to understanding the putative moralism of these early English Protestants is to be discovered in the Rhineland doctrines of regeneration and election to sanctification: the sanctification of the believer is always the work of divine grace, occurring in those whom the Spirit regenerates and whom God in his free grace has predestined. What appears to be moralism is a sanctification by grace, obedience of believers to God's will being nothing other than a gift of God. The underlining by these early English Protestants of a sanctification that was in form an obedience to the divine commandments was also in substance an insistence upon an inner spiritual transformation, a new spiritual life, and a redirection of the person toward God that made such obedience not only possible but a joy. And this was the work of divine electing and regenerating grace. Clebsch is right in saying that, in highlighting obedience, these English Protestants had a different outlook from Luther, but to describe this as "moralism" is to miss its spiritual and gratuitous content, and, even more important, is to miss the source of its fervent piety, which was the experience of inner renewing grace.

In sanctification and predestination Reformed theology also found sources of comfort and assurance, and this relating of assurance to these doctrines began to appear among England's early Protestants. Indeed, the double justification of which Clebsch writes would seem to be that the good works of the sanctified believer may be taken as evidence of election and justification. Tyndale, for example, argued, "Not that our works make us the sons of God, but testify only, and certify our consciences, that we are the sons of God; and that God hath chosen us."[47] The discussion of predestination by these early English theological writers also returned to the matter of solace, predestination being to them a "sweet" and "consoling" doctrine for the saints of God, an assurance that their salvation was built upon a rock that could not fail and that the elect ought to be both comforted and encouraged to good works by the recognition that their salvation was indefectible.[48]

Although it has sometimes been disputed,[49] there is considerable evidence for the appearance of the doctrine of unconditional predestination among the earliest English Protestants. They were greatly indebted to the Rhineland theologians for that doctrine, and for them, too, predestination was soteriological in significance. David B. Knox, in his study of the doctrine of faith in the early English Reformation, concluded, "All the English Reformers in this period regarded the doctrine of unconditional predestination as essential to the doctrine of justification by faith only."[50] There is no doubt that the English Protestants, like Zwingli and Calvin on the Continent, were much influenced by St. Augustine in this regard.

Again let us begin with William Tyndale, who frequently affirmed unconditional election: "In Christ God loved us, his elect and chosen, before the world began"; "By which predestination our justifying and salvation are clean taken out of our hands, and put in the hands of God only"; the believer "in Christ was predestinate, and ordained unto eternal life, before the world began"; "In Adam we are all . . . wild crab-trees, of which God chooseth whom he will."[51] Tyndale also implied the doctrine of reprobation: "Now may not we ask why God chooseth one and not another; either think that God is unjust to damn us afore we do any actual deed; seeing that God hath power over all his creatures of right, to do with them as he listeth."[52]

John Frith gave more sustained attention to predestination in his *A Mirrour or Glasse to Know Thy Selfe*. The entire treatise was an assertion of predestination and a description of its effects in the elect. The gifts of grace around which the treatise is built were in fact the elements of the order of salvation that received great attention from Bucer: election followed by vocation and justification. Frith adds that predestination does not have any reference to foreseen good works.[53] Reprobation was clearly asserted: "And thys are we sure of, yt whomsoever he chuseth, them he saveth of his mercy: and whome he repelleth, them of his secrete and unsearchable judgement he condemneth. But why he chuseth the one and repelleth the other, enquire not (saythe S. Austine) if you wilt not erre."[54] Other works of Frith gave an important place to predestination. In his large book against purgatory, the argument based on predestination was one of Frith's favorites: salvation is by an election of grace, and God justifies his elect—can he then cast them into purgatorial fire? The elect will be glorified, not tormented in purgatory.[55] Even in discussing baptism, Frith mentions predestination.[56]

Robert Barnes, who has been described as the most "Lutheran" of the early English Protestants,[57] in fact stated double predestination more starkly than either Tyndale or Frith, referring to "the vessels of wrath, ordeyned to dampnacion," contrasting them with the "vessels of mercy," "elected unto glory," and further noting that "there be certayne open places of scripture, yt gyve onely the cause to God, alonely of election, and also of reprobacyon." God hardens the hearts of the reprobate, "he indurateth them, and blyndeth them & gyveth them no grace to amende," as he did with Esau, who was reprobated before he had done either good or evil.[58]

This Reformed doctrine of predestination was present in the writings of many other early English Protestants. William Roy published a translation in 1527 of a Continental theological work in which appeared an assertion of double predestination.[59] Simon Fish, an active propagandist among the early English Protestants, published a similar treatise affirming predestination.[60] George Joye also affirmed double predestination: "God wil have mercye of whom he lyst, and harden whom it lyketh him."[61] John Bale referred to "the lambes boke of lyfe," in which appear the names of those predestined.[62] William Turner translated a work by the Lutheran theologian Urbanus Rhegius, which he supplemented with material on predestination and declared that God, to show his wrath and make known his power, "brought foorth with great pacyence the vessels of wrath, which are ordeyned to damnacyon, that he myght declare ye ryches of his glory on the vessels of mercy, which he hath prepared unto glory."[63] Lancelot Ridley, cousin of the more famous Nicholas, published a biblical exposition in 1541 in which he commented that God's choice of the elect preceded the foundation of the earth and was of God's mere will, grace, and pleasure.[64] Gerard Garrett offended Bishop Stephen Gardiner in 1540 with a strongly predestinarian sermon at Paul's Cross in London.[65]

These same English Protestant writers attacked as "Pelagian" the enemies of their teachings about grace, particularly Roman Catholics. For them, denial of this doctrine of gratuitous justification and sanctification was Pelagian "works-righteousness," and they used the doctrine of predestination against such heresy. In his *Answer to Sir Thomas More's Dialogue*, Tyndale argued that the pope and his followers could not be the true church for they sought to be saved by trusting in good works: "They say that every man hath . . . power in his free-will, to deserve that power should be given him of God to keep the law. But the scripture testifieth that Christ hath deserved for the elect, even then when they hated God." Elsewhere Tyndale identified Pelagianism and Catholicism, saying that, although formally the theologians of Rome might condemn Pelagianism, in fact they preached the same doctrine.[66] Barnes claimed that Bishop John Fisher was a Pelagian when he taught that God gave commandments to men because they had the power to fulfill them.[67] Coverdale also accused a Catholic opponent of being Pelagian, and George Joye attacked the Henrician Bishop Stephen Gardiner for Pelagianism in 1546;[68] Gardiner's later defection to Rome confirmed the worst suspicions of such Protestant critics. Thus a polemical sword that was to be used continually against Rome for well over a century and also against those Protestants who seemed to be hedging their commitment to the Swiss or

Calvinist theology of grace was unsheathed early in the English Reformation.

Official doctrinal formularies and semiofficial publications throughout the reign of Henry VIII reflected little of the ideas about grace so far examined. These ideas were probably adopted by leading Henrician bishops before Henry's death to a greater extent than the published evidence suggests, for they were discreet about such ideas during the king's lifetime. The Ten Articles of 1536 made few steps in a Protestant direction so far as grace was concerned, speaking only of justification by a faith that included charity and obedience, a typical medieval Catholic formulation that would have been at least "semi-Pelagian" to advanced Protestants.[69] *The Institution of A Christian Man*, or "Bishop's Book" of 1537, never officially sanctioned by the king, attacked the papacy, but its discussion of purgatory and justification remained fairly conservative. It referred incidentally to predestination, defining the church as the company of the elect, a frequent Protestant definition, and it also affirmed that the elect of God could not finally fall away from salvation.[70] *The Necessary Doctrine and Erudition for any Christian Man*, or "King's Book" of 1543, preceded an article on justification with one on free will, but its tone was still semi-Pelagian. Man after the fall was said still to have some free will so that he could understand and obey God's commandments, albeit assisted by grace; with such assistance, free will works with grace to perform good works and avoid sin. Persons may fall from grace. Justification was treated as a "making righteous," with stress upon man's willing cooperation.[71] Lacey Baldwin Smith comments of this book that, although aiming to clarify the proper belief about free will and good works, it dealt with them by expanding human responsibility.[72] Thomas Cranmer apparently expostulated with Henry VIII over the "Pelagianism" of the book, but to little avail.[73] Among his literary remains are some manuscript annotations that may have been his suggested revisions; they state that election comes only from the grace of God and not from any human merit.[74]

After the yet more "Catholic" Six Articles Act of 1539, Nicholas Shaxton, one of the more "Protestant" of Henry's episcopal appointees, resigned his see and was in 1546 compelled, at the burning of Anne Askew for sacramentarian heresy, to recant several of his too radical Protestant notions and to affirm that predestination did not take away free choice of the will.[75] Hugh Latimer also resigned his see after the Six Articles Act; he had apparently adopted the Lutheran view of justification by 1530, as well as preached against reliance on merit.[76] "Matthew's Bible," in notes beginning with the 1537 edition, several times affirmed predestination; much of the annotation was derived from the Swiss reformers.[77] The "postils on the Epistles and Gospels," produced under the editorship of Richard Taverner in 1540, apparently as an aid to preaching and instruction in the Henrician church, had at least semiofficial character.[78] Without being entirely consistent (which one would not expect of such a composite production), these "postils" frequently affirmed redemption by grace apart from merit and in at least two places taught predestination, referring to the "electe" of God being named "before the foundation of the world was layde."[79] And finally, many echoes of the Reformed understanding of grace and even a mention of the doctrine of reprobation appeared in the devotional work of Henry's last wife, Catherine Parr, who wrote that to "wicked men, . . . it semeth" that "God is parcial, because he hath elected sum, and sum reproved."[80]

The Edwardian Reformation

With the accession of Edward VI, the restraints on explicit expression of Reformed doctrine were removed. The belief that the heart of the Christian gospel was the proclamation of a gratuitous salvation that moved from justification to sanctification and was to be defended by means of the doctrine of predestination and the branding of opposition as Pelagian was basic to the Edwardian reformation. Thus during the reign of Edward VI the Reformed theology of grace that was to be dominant in the Elizabethan Church of England as well as central to later Puritanism became firmly embedded in English Protestantism.

Continental theologians who had been major figures in the development of Reformed theology were now invited to England, where they provided theological leadership in the universities as well as acting as advisers to the English bishops. Martin Bucer, perhaps already the most influential of the Rhineland reformers on England, was now granted the Regius professorship of divinity at Cambridge; Peter Martyr was made professor of divinity at Oxford. In their wake came many other Continental theologians who had been in various ways associated with the Rhineland reformers: Bernardino Ochino, Paul Fagius, Emanuel Tremellius, Jean Veron, and John à Lasco. Bucer and Martyr were much preoccupied while in England with the burning issue of the Eucharistic presence, but no doubt also expressed their theology of grace in university lectures.

While in England, Bernardino Ochino, an Italian exile who had spent some time in Geneva, published in English translation some sermons first preached in Geneva on the subject of predestination. Ochino, who later changed his mind about unconditional predestination as he drifted off into the ambience of the Radical Reformation,[81] affirmed in these sermons that predestination was important because it assured the believer of the free grace of God and was crucial to the preaching of the gospel—"he that is offended wyth predestination . . . is also offended wyth the Gospell." The goal of predestination, he further stated, was holiness and sanctification. Nor was he reluctant to affirm the doctrine of reprobation, for God "is not holden nor bound to geve us this grace, he may harden & mollify after his own pleasure." Even Christ, he added, cannot "save a reprobate, nor damn an elect"—certainly an incautious formulation of the matter.[82]

The English divines of the Edwardian Reformation echoed the theology of grace taught by the foreign theologians resident in England, both in the official doctrinal statements they provided for the instruction of the English church and in their sermons and tracts.

The Edwardian Book of Homilies, without specifically developing the doctrine of predestination, everywhere treated faith and salvation as a divine gift apart from any human merit. This view is especially notable in those portions written by Thomas Cranmer.[83] Justification, the Homilies taught, must be completed in sanctification and holiness, something possible only for those who have been regenerated by divine grace.[84] But most of the distinctly Reformed motifs concerning grace, which would separate them from the Lutherans, were not conspicuous in the Homilies.

The Forty-two Articles, drawn up under the supervision of Cranmer and officially circulated in 1553, reflected more specifically the Swiss influence: as in Protestant thought as a whole, justification by faith was affirmed, as was the bondage of man in his fallen state to sin, the act of turning to God being possible only by a gift of God's grace.[85] An article "Of Grace," omitted in the Elizabethan version of the articles, followed Augustine, as did the Continental Reformed theologians and the English Protestants generally, in arguing that in determining whether the will does good or evil God does not compel the will but rather draws it "willingly."[86] Article seventeen taught the doctrine of unconditional election held by the Rhineland reformers: predestination was related to the free grace of justification and also to sanctification when it was said that the elect "be made lyke the image of his onely begotten sonne Jesus Christe: they walk religiously in good works"; the perseverance of the elect is also implied.[87] Because the article omitted reprobation and spoke of predestination as a "comfort to godly persons," it has been claimed that it is more moderate than the Reformed view,[88] but several early Reformed confessional formulations, including the Geneva Catechism and the Confession of Faith of Geneva, passed over the double decree in silence, and it has already been seen that the assertion of the comfort to be found in the doctrine came from the Swiss teaching. John P. Donnelly has claimed that article seventeen came primarily from Peter Martyr.[89]

A catechism published with the Forty-two Articles in 1553, which was the work of John Ponet, Edwardian bishop of Winchester, went beyond the Articles in following the Swiss outlook on grace. Not only teaching predestination and relating it to sanctification, it also used the *ordo salutis* sequence of election, calling, justification, and sanctification by the operation of the Holy Spirit.[90]

A recent analysis of Reformed theology in the Edwardian *Book of Common Prayer* notes that many of its collects required little change because they had been shaped in ancient times in the wake of the Pelagian controversy and had a very Augustinian tone that could easily be put to Protestant uses. Some changes in these older prayers were made by Cranmer, however, to remove from them any hint of merit or synergism in regard to the doctrine of justification.[91]

In less official sermons and tracts, major Edwardian reformers expressed the same Reformed theology of grace. Thomas Becon, a chaplain to Cranmer and an important publicist during the Edwardian Reformation, declared that faith and salvation come from God alone, with faith bringing justification and regeneration in its train.[92] The formula of election to holiness appeared also in Becon. He accepted predestination before Edward's reign,[93] expressed it more fully during that reign,[94] and, surviving into Elizabeth's reign, reaffirmed it then.[95]

Hugh Latimer, back in episcopal office under Edward VI, proclaimed in his sermons that justification and salvation were by grace through faith, that God had predestined those who believe in Christ, and that he watches over his elect. But predestination seems to have been of less than central importance to him, and several passages in his sermons perhaps imply the possibility of falling from grace, a position unthinkable to strict Reformed theology.[96] Incautious as a theologian on other subjects,[97] he was also more of a moralist than the other early English reformers and was concerned, without denying unconditional predestination, lest the wrong conclusions be drawn from it:

Here we may learn to keep us from all curious and dangerous questions: when we hear that some be chosen and some be damned, let us have good hope that we shall be amongst the chosen and live after this hope; that is, uprightly and godly; then thou shalt not be deceived. Think that God hath chosen those that believe in Christ, and that Christ is the book of life. If thou believest in him, then thou art written in the book of life, and shalt be saved. So we need not go about to trouble ourselves with curious questions of the predestination of God. But let us rather endeavour ourselves that we may be in Christ; for when we be in him, then are we well, and then we may be sure that we are ordained to everlasting life.[98]

The commitment of John Hooper, another Edwardian bishop, to the theology of the Swiss reformation has long been acknowledged, especially insofar as he has been taken as a precursor of the Puritans. For Hooper salvation was the work of God, who moves the will by grace so that it can respond to Christ. The cause of this election is, to Hooper, "the mercy of God in Christ," and he also thought that those elected were united to Christ by faith and sanctified. The elect cannot finally fall away from grace.[99] But Hooper wanted to explain that men are damned only for the sins they actually commit (a formula generally acceptable to Reformed theologians because it meant that at the day of judgment those reprobated to damnation will be punished for the sins they committed as a result both of their fallen nature and of the grace to do otherwise that was withheld from them, and not merely for the fact that they were reprobated from eternity)[100] and that reprobation followed the foreseen fall. In arguing particularly this last point, Hooper was following Bullinger and not Calvin and was singled out in correspondence by Bartholomew Traheron for not entirely agreeing with Calvin.[101] The quarrel among some of the English Protestants over this point was eventually patched up.[102] If cautious with respect to reprobation, Hooper nonetheless affirmed, "I believe that the Father in Jesus Christ his Son through the Holy Ghost hath elected and chosen those that are his own, according to his good will, before the foundations of the world were laid, whom he hath predestinate unto eternal life."[103]

Several publications of the Edwardian years developed the doctrine of predestination more fully than did these leading English reformers. In an introductory epistle to the translation of a treatise by St. Augustine titled

A Worke of the predestination of saints wrytten by the famous doctor S. Augustine byshop of Carthage, Nycholas Lesse, a London layman acquainted with the Protestant propagandist John Bale, insisted on the importance of the doctrine of predestination in protecting grace as the free gift of God. Lesse attacked opponents of the doctrine, whom he called "the anabaptists and frewyl masters," as poisonous creatures for their denial of predestination.[104] Another publication of 1550, *Of Pre-destination and Election made by Iohn Lamberd minister of the church of Elham*, also dealt polemically with the issue, attacking opponents of the doctrine. Lamberd's viewpoint was straightforward in its doctrine of reprobation: God chose the elect before the world was made, but he also "ordeyned the vessells of wrath to dampnacion." Even "the passion of Christe can not save a reprobate." God has "predestinate some to be chyldren of perdition."[105] Robert Crowley, later a well-known Puritan leader, in 1548 affirmed double predestination in the course of refuting the recantation of Nicholas Shaxton, the Henrician bishop who was forced to recant Protestant opinions in 1546.[106] Crowley was unguarded in his statement of reprobation, asserting without hesitation that God predestined some to be wicked, a way of expressing the doctrine the more theologically astute avoided.[107] Last among these publications is an apparently lost work of Anthony Gilby, later, like Crowley, to be known as a Puritan stalwart. Gilby was an exile in Geneva during the Marian years and wrote on predestination then and later, teaching unambiguously the double decree. He is sometimes cited as a prime example of the predestinarian influence of the Genevan exiles. According to his own testimony, however, he affirmed reprobation as early as 1553, before his exile, in a commentary written upon the biblical prophet Malachi.[108]

The Marian Years—Martyrs and Exiles

The untimely death of the boy king Edward VI brought the English Reformation to a sudden halt, and Mary's accession seemed to jeopardize all the gains made by Protestantism in England. But although those leaders who had adopted a Reformed theology of grace (as well as of other matters) could no longer freely express their views in England, most continued to maintain them, whether as prisoners for heresy in their own land or as exiles abroad.

The importance of the issue of grace and predestination for the English reformers is evident from a lively dispute that broke out among the imprisoned Protestants over these points. Incarcerated at the King's Bench Prison along with notable leaders of the official Edwardian Reformation was a group of independent Protestant laymen led by Henry Hart and John Trewe, who denied predestination altogether, as did the Anabaptists and many others representative of the Radical Reformation on the Continent.[109] The Edwardian leaders imprisoned with them were Robert Ferrar, whose Protestant activity stretched back to 1528 and who was made a bishop by Edward VI; John Bradford, protégé of Ridley and royal chaplain to Edward VI, who had studied under Bucer at Cambridge and was his devoted follower; and John Philpot, who had been the Edwardian archdeacon of Winchester and who, when examined by Queen Mary's Catholic theologians, defended Calvin and his doctrine of predestination.[110] To this distinguished company the views of the "freewillers," as they called them, were nothing less than the denial of the gospel of salvation by God's grace in Christ. In the long dispute between the two groups, Bradford emerged as the leader among the defenders of predestination, composing a treatise against its deniers and corresponding about the problem with Cranmer, Latimer, and Ridley, imprisoned elsewhere, to enlist them in the same cause. Ridley apparently responded with a written defense of predestination, but it has been lost.

These Marian freewillers had roots in an unofficial lay Protestantism that can be detected much earlier in the English Reformation. Probably their ideas can be explained partly by the long presence in England of lay anticlerical protest of the type represented by the Lollards. Such protest was further stimulated by the years of Protestant propaganda against mass, images, purgatory, and other elements of the old Catholic order and perhaps even touched by currents of the Continental Radical Reformation coming into England.[111] In any case, it is certain that the freewillers rejected the fully developed Reformed theology of grace held by learned theologians as unscriptural and a violation of common sense. Joseph W. Martin, in an article analyzing Henry Hart, has convincingly suggested that Hart's heterodoxy could have resulted from the "impact of the English Bible" on a relatively untutored but "sensitive and articulate layman," who was not interested primarily in predestination or any other elaborate dogma but "in a few basic affirmations derived from the Bible and a simple code of right conduct." Martin sees the religious activities of such persons as part of the long story of English Separatism.[112] The view of O. T. Hargrave, on the other hand, seems wide of the

mark in regarding these freewillers as forerunners of later English Arminianism[113]—they were far closer to Lollards, certain representatives
of the Continental Radical Reformation, and later English "freewilling"
Separatists than to seventeenth-century Laudians.

The presence in England of dissenters who rejected the Protestant
theology of grace while denying transubstantiation and other Catholic
dogmas has been noted as early as the reign of Henry VIII.[114] A general
fear of radical Protestant ideas loosely dubbed "Anabaptist" existed in
the time of King Edward VI, and a conventicle of such persons at Bocking
in Essex supposedly led by a certain Thomas Upcharde was accused,
among other things, of denying predestination.[115] Another conventicle of
freewillers was found at Faversham in Kent. The group imprisoned at the
King's Bench included leaders of both these groups. Spokesmen for these
groups were reputed to have said that theological error was to be blamed
on learned men, that children were not born in original sin, and that "the
doctryne of predestynation was meter for divilles than for christian men."
[116] As early as 1550 the introduction by Nicholas Lesse to a translation
of a work on predestination by St. Augustine mentioned the exponents of
free will as enemies to the gospel, who like the "papists" are Pelagians,
but unlike "ye superstitious and arrogant papystes" pretended to a great
holiness of life, making them yet more dangerous.[117]

All the details of the prison debate over predestination need not be
repeated here, having been recounted elsewhere,[118] but analysis of the
way the freewillers were answered further reveals the commitment of the
English reformers to the Swiss theology of grace and also suggests the
very practical and personal way these themes were being developed in
England. Ridley's lost answer apparently drew together and appended
comments to a number of scripture passages dealing with predestination.[119] John Careless, a layman imprisoned with the others, after "much
conference" with the freewillers, prepared a confession of faith directed
against them, also now lost.[120] Augustine Bernhere's treatise against
them, which survived in manuscript, argued in typical Reformed fashion
that God elected some persons that he might regenerate them by an
operation of the Holy Spirit in their hearts.[121] John Philpot, in several
letters against the freewillers, affirmed that the elect cannot finally fall
away and denied that predestination was a license to sin because the very
purpose of election was the ordaining of the elect to "walk in righteousness and holiness."[122]

The most important writings directed against the freewillers came from

John Bradford. In the letter that he, along with Ferrar, Philpot, and the others, sent to Latimer, Ridley, and Cranmer, and of which he was the principal author, Bradford made clear how important he thought the issue of free will was and why: Christ's glory and grace will lose their brightness if all good is not "attributed only and wholly to God's grace and mercy in Christ," apart from any human merit or willing. The free-willers, he said, "so mingle and confound" the effects of salvation with the cause of salvation that they cause more damage to the gospel than the "papists" ever did, "inasmuch as their life commendeth them to the world more than the papists." (Bradford, no mere moralist, was far more concerned with the root of the Christian life than with mere deeds.) "In free-will," Bradford continued, "they are plain papists, yea Pelagians."[123]

Bradford took a pastoral stance toward the freewillers, trying to win them from their errors by love. He wrote to them, assuring them of his concern for them; it was only because of such love, he told them, that he sought to bring them from error—indeed, he could say to them, "Though in some things we agree not, yet let love bear the bell away; and let us pray for one another, and be careful one for another; for I hope we be all Christ's."[124] He sent them money to relieve their sufferings in prison.[125] After he had been condemned to death at the stake, Bradford wrote to them:

Although I look hourly for officers to come and have me to execution, yet can I not but attempt to write something unto you, my dearly beloved (as always you have been, howsoever you have taken me), to occasion you the more to weigh the things wherein some controversy hath been amongst us, especially the article and doctrine of predestination, whereof I have written a little treatise. . . . Only by the doctrine of it I have sought, as to myself, so to others, a certainty of salvation, a setting up of Christ only, an exaltation of God's grace, mercy, righteousness, truth, wisdom, power and glory, and a casting down of man and all his power.[126]

Nothing could make clearer the real purpose and function of predestination than these deeply personal statements of Bradford.

Besides these personal letters are two short treatises by Bradford, "A Defence of Election" and "A Treatise of Election and Free Will," and two other letters, more argumentative than pastoral, both called simply in the collection of his writings, "To a Free-Willer." In addition, there is a sermon of Bradford on repentance that comes from the period before his imprisonment and several other relevant letters and manuscript fragments. All strike the same chord of a piety built around the sense of

divine grace that elects and regenerates, bringing men to holiness. In the
early sermon on repentance, Bradford says that to repent comes from
God, for faith is "far from the reach of man's free-will."[127] God chooses
some to have faith so that they might be made holy and given "newness
of life"; such "newness" is a fruit of justification, "a demonstration of
the justifying faith" of believers. Nor can such believers ever be finally
separated from God's love.[128] Against the freewillers, he argued that the
will of God is immutable and totally without respect to any deeds in the
elect; otherwise redemption is not by grace—"Now, if you will say that
salvation dependeth partly on ourselves, and not simply, wholly and
altogether on God's mercy and truth in Christ and his merits, you deny
salvation to come of grace. . . . And hereof I half suspect you all, that
indeed you are adversaries to grace by maintaining free-will."[129] Yet
there is no compulsion in this election, for under sin a person freely sins
and under grace is free to the extent that he does good.[130] The purpose of
this doctrine is for piety: it gives confidence that the world is not ruled by
fate, but that God is in control and that his promises are sure: "It
overthroweth the most pestilent papistical poison of doubting of God's
favour, which is the very dungeon of despair and of the contempt of
God."[131] Nor can predestination mean license, for it is an election to
holiness, taking away pride in merits, provoking piety and "a true desire
of our home in heaven," and encouraging contempt for worldly things as
well as service of the neighbor and care for God's glory.[132]

Those elected to regeneration and sanctification are "to increase from
virtue to virtue," even though it means striving, by God's grace, against
the old nature. Spiritual warfare is the keynote of the Christian life; the
elect may be known to themselves precisely by this inner mark of spiritual
struggle, for none but they undergo it.[133] In what can only be described
as letters of spiritual counsel, Bradford turned these thoughts to pastoral
purposes, evidence again that ideas about grace were closely related to
vital piety and not mere matters of speculation. For example, he wrote to
a correspondent with this spiritual direction:

I doubt not but that your ladyship considereth often with yourself, that you are
the child of God, and a citizen of heaven by Christ, in whom God the Father,
before the world was made, hath chosen you of his own mere mercy, and not of
your deserts done or to be done.[134]

And the cause why we are so faint in fleeing evil and diligent doing good is the
wavering of this certainty of God's election.

If he had not chosen you (as most certainly he hath), he would not have so called you; he would never have justified you; he would never have so glorified you with his gracious gifts, . . . he would never have so exercised your faith with temptations, . . . if, I say, he had not chosen you. . . . Ah! mine own dear heart, Christ only, Christ only, and his mercy and truth, in him and for him is the cause of your election. This Christ, this mercy, this truth of God, remaineth for ever, is certain for ever: and so is your election certain for ever.[135]

All of this obviously has the tone of the later English Protestant and Puritan writings on the spiritual life and, like them, concentrates upon assurance. Piety is here also firmly connected to the Reformed order of salvation. In Bradford the ideas about grace under examination find full expression, especially on their practical and experiential side.[136]

That the arguments and "loving concern" of such men as Bradford had at least some effect upon the freewillers is indicated by a letter from one of them recanting his former errors. This convert rather preposterously maintained that God was punishing England with the present persecution because of the sin of those Protestants who were not "sound in the predestination of God; but we were rather enemies unto it." There followed an exposition of teaching very much like that of Bradford: to teach free will is to be a Pelagian errorist, and it derogates from God's grace and glory in redemption. Rather, unconditional election is the fountain of all grace, the source of assurance, and the basis for the knowledge that God will preserve the elect to the end. The former freewiller continues: "I, for my part, repent that ever I was so bitter unto them that were the teachers of this undoubted truth. Verily, I am not able to express the sorrows that I have in my heart, most especially in that I went about by all means to persuade others, whereby they might be one with me in that error of freewill."[137]

During the same years of the Marian persecution when the imprisoned reformers debated the freewillers before sealing their faith with their lives (Ridley, Bradford, Ferrar, and Philpot all went to the stake, and John Careless died in prison), other English Protestants in exile on the Continent became ever more thoroughly versed in the developing Reformed theology of grace. Most of the exilic writings that dealt especially with the Reformed ideas about grace and predestination came from the group resident in Geneva, specifically from Anthony Gilby, John Knox, John Scory, and William Whittingham. Knox and Gilby each wrote a theological treatise on predestination; Scory and Whittingham worked as translators, Scory translating Augustine on predestination; and Whittingham translated a work on the same subject by Theodore Beza, a Genevan theologian who was a younger colleague of Calvin and later became his successor. Whittingham and Gilby also had special responsibility in the preparation of the *Geneva Bible*, and although others aided in the work, including Christopher Goodman and Miles Coverdale, the general theological line developed in its annotations reflected especially Gilby's outlook.[138] Together, these writings, translations, and biblical annotations continued and sharpened the doctrine of grace as taught by the earlier English reformers. If there is among them a greater emphasis on defending grace through appeal to the doctrine of predestination, this was no more than a logical development out of the previous theology that needed only time and further theological controversy to reach that point—there is no need to interpret this development as a Genevan influence injecting something altogether new into English theology.[139] Exiles not in Geneva were also committed to the doctrine of predestination.[140]

John Scory, Edwardian bishop of Chichester, while in exile translated writings of St. Augustine on predestination and perseverance. The tone and purpose of his work is indicated on the title page, which described these works as "very necessary for al tymes, but namely for oures, wherin the Papistes and Anabaptistes have revived agayne the wycked opinions of the Pelagians, that extolled mans wyll & merites agaynst the free grace of Christe." In an introductory epistle, Scory developed this point further: the papists corrupt "the true doctrine of the gospel touchynge remission of synnes, eleccion, vocation, and justification" with the leaven of their false doctrine. Those who read St. Augustine, however, will see that the Protestants teach the ancient catholic doctrine of grace, which is that man's will is too weak either to come to God or to "continue in hym" and that man is redeemed, not by "the merites of dedes, but by grace frely geven." Scory frequently employs the categories of the Reformed order of salvation.[141]

William Whittingham, while in Geneva, translated and published a short work by Theodore Beza on predestination, originally written in Latin. Although this work was better known in the later translation of John Stockwood, published in 1576 as *The Treasure of Trueth*, Whittingham had translated an earlier version during his exile as *A Briefe declaration of the Chiefe Poynts of Christian Religion*. This work treated the steps in Christian redemption as a sequence related closely to the doctrine of predestination, the latter serving as the superstructure by which the doctrine of free grace was to be guaranteed and defended.[142]

Printed in the same year (1556) and place (Geneva) as was in all probability Whittingham's Beza translation, Anthony Gilby's *A Briefe Treatyse of Election and Reprobacion wythe certane answers to the objections of the adversaries of this doctryne* also indicated how the Reformed teaching about grace could be defended through predestinarian doctrine. The doctrine of predestination, Gilby argued, was essential, because "so wonderfully appeareth in this his rych mercy towards us, whom he chewseth from the fylthe of syn," and because at the same time that it humbled man it gave him a true basis for assurance: "Because that wythoute some tayste of thys divine providence in predestination, there can be no faithe, but either a doubtful waveringe, leading to dispare, whyche we have felte in the papistrye whyles we looked to our owne weaknes and infirmitie, not able to endure one howre in the waye of ryghtousnes; or els a vane presumption of fained holiness, whyls we beholde our owne beliefe, and good works, or the perfection that we do ymagyn in our own selves, as do the Anabaptistes." Moreover, Gilby insisted that predestination was to and for holiness; those lifted out of sin were redeemed that they might "serve him in righteousness."[143] For Gilby such election related closely to the action of the Holy Spirit "worckynge in the hartes of the electe and chosen by faythe and trust in God hys promyses throwghe Chryste, teaching us that we are the chyldren of God, chosen to hymself by Jesu Christ, frome the beginninge, and therefore preparynge us to an holye and blamelesse lyfe to the laud and prayse of the grace of God."[144] Gilby proceeds with a long discussion of reprobation as the execution of God's judgment on sin. No man is condemned but for his actual sins. But even reprobation is related to grace, for God in his mercy included all men under sin that he might show his free grace and mere favor in redeeming some.[145]

John Knox's treatise on predestination was written during his exile in Geneva, probably in 1558, but not published until 1560.[146] It was directed specifically against an "Anbaptist" denier of predestination, Robert Cooche, or Cooke,[147] whom he included with "papists" and various other heretics in denying that redemption is by "the eternall love and undeserved grace of God alone." Such people, Knox said, are the enemies of God's free mercy. The doctrine of predestination, he continued, was important because it humbles man, shows him God's grace, and gives him a firm basis for faith.[148] Predestination, too, must terminate in the charity and holiness of the elect.[149] The beginning of the work established the importance of the doctrine of predestination and its relationship to the divine grace and piety. The task of refuting the charges against predestination by its opponents took up most of the book and is very uninspiring reading, but through the complex argumentation there occasionally shines forth the experiential rooting of the doctrine in a piety of divine grace.

The annotations of the *Geneva Bible* bear out the same theology of grace and must have therefore acted as an important disseminator of it. Among the exiles, Whittingham and Gilby were especially involved in preparing this version of the Bible. The annotations on portions of the New Testament directly related to the doctrine of grace, such as the Pauline letters to the Romans and the Galatians, show that the Reformed theology of grace was embedded there. No works of men can save them, but only that faith which apprehends Christ as one's justification and sanctification;[150] faith is the only condition of the gospel, and that faith is a gift of God in Christ;[151] regeneration and sanctification are the work of the Holy Spirit;[152] election and reprobation have their ultimate cause in the mere willing of God, the mercy of God being the cause of election, and God's hardening of the sinner the cause of reprobation.[153] The same themes are also developed in some of the Old Testament annotations. The comment on Exodus 33:19, for example, reads: "For finding nothing in man that can deserve mercie, he wil frely save his."[154]

There emerged and developed among England's Protestant leadership from the beginnings of the English Reformation through to the end of the reign of Queen Mary a Swiss or Reformed theology of grace emphasizing predestination. This doctrine of predestination was rooted in the more basic Protestant belief in justification by faith alone and was used to defend that latter doctrine. To reject this complex of ideas about grace, whether done by Roman Catholics or Separatist freewillers, was seen as Pelagian "works-righteousness." This same doctrine of predestination was connected to regeneration and sanctification by the Holy Spirit and to a whole order of salvation and was also regarded as a source of assurance for the believer that those once renewed in Christ would not fall away. These notions first appeared among the earliest English Protestant theological writers, among whom Tyndale and Frith were preeminent, were given explicit expression by the leaders and in the official statements of the Edwardian Reformation, were confirmed by the Marian martyrs, among whom John Bradford in particular brought out the practical side of this doctrine of grace, and received further reinforcement in the labors of English Protestant exiles, especially those resident in Geneva. In all of this, a pattern of theology took shape that was to dominate the Elizabethan and Jacobean Church of England in general and the Puritan movement in particular. That the English Reformation was a series of acts of state is well known; that it was also a thoroughly Protestant religious revolution, is recognized in a general fashion, but needs to be continually accentuated. And clichéd remarks about the English Reformation as a *via media*, if anything more is meant by this than that the English church retained something more of the fabric and structure of medieval Catholicism than did most other Protestant churches, should be abandoned. With respect to the central matter of the theology of grace (and other crucial doctrines, such as the Eucharist), the English Reformation was uncompromisingly Protestant.

Chapter 2 ❖ Trends in the Elizabethan and Jacobean Theology of Grace

A Reformed theology of grace, deeply indebted to Continental thinkers and long to be identified with those designated as Puritans, became the fundamental theology of English Protestantism in the generation preceding the reign of Elizabeth I. It was a theology that sought above all to magnify the role of divine grace in the process of salvation by stressing gratuitous regeneration and sanctification as well as predestination. With a variety of modifications, undercurrents, and even some countercurrents, this Reformed theology of grace continued to be the prevailing pattern in English Protestantism until nearly the end of the reign of James I. This chapter in the story of grace in English theology will treat the period 1560–1620 as being sufficiently united in its theological literature dealing with grace that the basic currents can be discovered. Such periodizing of English theological history runs some risk of oversimplifying the currents of English theology during that time, but gains the advantage of forcefully showing that the direction Anglican theology took after 1620 was a radical reversal of previous trends in the theology of grace. To be sure, there were some signs of such a theological shift before 1620, but only hindsight gives them the significance many modern books have given them. At the time, they would have seemed minor discordances in a larger picture of concord. Overall, it is difficult to disagree with the judgment of Nicholas Tyacke that "Calvinist predestinarian teaching was . . . a crucial common assumption, shared by a majority of the hierarchy and virtually all its nonconformist opponents, during the Elizabethan and Jacobean periods."[1]

Not all was perfect unanimity in Elizabethan theology, however, and several important theological currents developed from 1560 to 1620. The period began with the acceptance of the earlier Reformed theology in the official formularies of the Elizabethan settlement, and the leadership of the Elizabethan church was comfortable with this Reformed or "Calvinist" theology. But it would appear that those who came to be identified as Puritans differed from many conformists in the intensity with which they held and promoted that theology. Furthermore, the

Reformed theology of grace moved toward practical application in a piety of regeneration, sanctification, and assurance. Many ministers covering the entire spectrum of the Elizabethan church shared in that development, but the most active were those Puritan pastors who have been identified by William Haller and others as mainly interested in preaching and pastoral care. As the Elizabethan period progressed, academic and scholastic Reformed theology, like the Protestant scholasticism of the Continent, emerged with an ever more rigid version of the doctrine of predestination. This led to another current, the gradual appearance of several converging theological streams that called into question elements of Reformed theology and can, though not without some exaggeration, most broadly be denominated as "anti-Calvinist." Finally, this theological era ended with a high output of anti-Roman Catholic polemic that stressed the Protestant-Catholic differences over the theology of grace, denouncing Roman views as "Pelagian." Each of these currents will be examined in turn.

Official Theology in the Elizabethan Church

The theological standards of the Elizabethan settlement clearly were grounded in Reformed theology and reaffirmed the pattern of the theology of grace that had emerged in earlier English Protestantism. At most points where Lutheran and Reformed views differed, as, for example, the theology of the Eucharist, the Thirty-nine Articles, which were little changed from the Forty-two Articles of the reign of Edward VI, took the Reformed side.[2] The older articles had been revised in 1563 and were given additional authorization in 1571, confirming the theology of grace in the earlier version.

There had been some controversy about the doctrine of predestination in the few years before 1563. In quick response to the impugning of Protestant views by remaining Marian clergy, Protestant spokesmen, led by the returned exile Edwin Sandys, soon to take up his duties as bishop of Worcester and later to be the archbishop of York, presented a "Declaration of Doctrine" to the queen in 1559. Appended to the statement was a long explanation of the article on predestination, which affirmed that although predestination is a doctrine some "godly men" think may be passed over in silence lest it be misunderstood and lead to licentiousness, in reality it is "fruitful and profitable to be known," especially because "some men of late are risen, which do gainsay and oppugn this truth."[3] The "oppugners" of this doctrine could, of course, be Roman Catholic controversialists, to counter whom the declaration was prepared, it being a continuing commonplace of Catholic polemic that the Protestant teaching about predestination was fatalism and led to licentiousness,[4] but the suggestion that such misbelievers had "lately arisen" points to the freewill men of the prison controversy and their possible successors, about whom returned exiles and other Protestant writers continued to be worried.[5] An echo of those earlier freewillers appeared in 1562 when a London minister named Thomas Talbot presented a petition to the bishops asking that he and his associates no longer be reviled as "Pelagians, papists, epicures, anabaptists, and enemies unto God's holy predestination" because they did not believe that God predestined some to do evil.[6] But these petitioners seemed to accept a predestination to life and did not deny that salvation was by grace alone—the formulation to which they objected was not really a proper expression of Reformed theology, though at least one English theological writer did express reprobation in that way.[7] Whether these petitioners had any connection to the earlier freewillers or were simply "mainstream" English Protestants reacting negatively to some extreme formulation of the doctrine of predestination and had been upbraided accordingly cannot be determined, though these protesters did refer to some among their number who had suffered imprisonment under Queen Mary, pointing to possible connection with the earlier freewillers.

The final version of the Articles only slightly modified the article on predestination, and although some have regarded these changes as moderating the original assertion of unconditional predestination,[8] I cannot agree. The 1563 version of the Articles taught that predestination was "in Christ" by inserting that phrase in article seventeen. But this qualification does not really moderate the doctrine of predestination; it was a commonplace of Reformed theology and appeared in Calvin.[9] That predestination was "in Christ" was a corollary of a soteriologically rooted doctrine of predestination indicating that God's purpose to elect was not an act of providence irrespective of the Redeemer, and thus this formula has the effect of connecting predestination to the order of salvation central in the Swiss Reformed theology. The Elizabethan article on predestination also omitted the phrase "although the Decrees of predestination are unknowen unto us," an omission that may be related to the growing

Reformed use of predestination for providing assurance—in a certain sense one may know one's election and receive assurance thereby, though such assurance is far from that carnal curiosity about the mysteries of the decrees of God against which article seventeen also warns.[10]

Several other changes from the Forty-two Articles of 1553 bore on the theology of grace. The article on original sin was brought more in line with Reformed theology with its clarification that sin remained in the "regenerate," not just in the "baptized," which would be obvious. The article on free will made clear that the inability of persons to do the good works of which it spoke referred to the time after the fall. Article ten of the earlier version, "Of Grace," was omitted: it was an explanation, along Augustinian lines, of how the will is moved by the Holy Spirit but without compulsion.[11] Perhaps this was thought an unnecessarily abstruse point for short articles, although its substance continued to be a commonplace of English Protestant theology.[12]

The Edwardian Book of Homilies was reinstated by the Elizabethan Injunctions of 1559, and to it was added a second Book of Homilies, drawn up by the bishops and authorized by Convocation in 1563. In 1571 one more homily, on obedience, was added to the second book.[13] Thus the splendid expositions of the Protestant theology of grace to be found in Cranmer's sermons on salvation, faith, and good works were again the official teaching of the Church of England. The new homilies contained a good deal of fairly routine moral exhortation, but kept in mind that good works were done by God's grace and did not constitute merit before God;[14] justification by faith apart from any human merit was also reasserted in these new homilies.[15]

Not to be classed with the Articles and Homilies as a statement of the doctrine of the Church of England, the catechism of Alexander Nowell nonetheless received a "minor official status" when the episcopal canons of 1571 ordered schoolmasters to use it, in both its Latin and English versions, in the instruction of the young. Nowell was one of the Marian exiles and, upon his return to England in 1559, was appointed dean of St. Paul's in London. His catechism, as William P. Haugaard has demonstrated, is basically indebted to the teaching of Calvin.[16] The catechism strongly asserted predestination and related it to grace and sanctification in typical Reformed fashion.[17]

Though without official authorization, many catechisms and theological compendiums published in the Elizabethan and Jacobean periods expressed the same theology as Nowell's catechism: redemption as a gracious work of God, holiness as the end of God's election, and the underlying importance of predestination.[18] Some of these compendiums and catechisms went further than Nowell's and asserted the decree of reprobation.[19] Such writings as these, often not easily separated into Puritan or Anglican in their character, must have had considerable influence in shaping belief for several generations.

Important among such compendiums, though in its later editions considerably longer than most, was *The Catholic Doctrine of the Church of England* by the unimpeachably conformist Thomas Rogers, eventually chaplain to Archbishop Richard Bancroft. This work, published in several considerably different forms before reaching its final shape in 1607, was an explanation of the Articles. Uncompromisingly Protestant in its treatment of justification, and repeatedly identifying "popery" with Pelagian works-righteousness, Rogers's work was thoroughly predestinarian, specifically teaching reprobation as well as election to life. And it is noteworthy that although Rogers abandoned Calvin's interpretation of the Descent of Christ into Hell in the later edition, his predestinarian teaching underwent no parallel falling away from Calvin.[20]

Not only does the Reformed theology of grace appear to have been deeply ensconced in the doctrinal standards of the Elizabethan church, but it also provided the theological framework within which the leaders and bishops of the English church lived and moved. Many of these leaders had been exiles on the Continent during the years of Marian persecution, where their Reformed theological formation was strengthened: Bishop Scory and Miles Coverdale had been at Geneva, Bishops Richard Cox, Robert Horne, John Jewel, John Parkhurst, and Sandys all spent some of their exile in Zurich, Bishops Thomas Bentham and James Pilkington were in both places, and Edmund Grindal, eventually to be Elizabeth's second archbishop of Canterbury, spent part of his exile in Strasbourg. Other future Elizabethan bishops had been Continental exiles, too: Gilbert Berkeley, Nicholas Bullingham, Richard Davies, and Thomas Young. Sandys and Jewel had both been closely associated with Peter Martyr while that theologian was in England, and Grindal has recently been regarded as a protégé of Bucer.[21] Heinrich Bullinger, Zwingli's successor at Zurich and a very influential Reformed theologian, befriended the English exiles at Zurich, who after their return to England maintained a lively correspondence with him, often deferring to his advice. As John M. Krumm has commented, "Almost all of the earlier Elizabethan bishops knew the leaders of the Reformation abroad from personal contacts established in the time of their extremity as refugees from the Marian reaction."[22]

During the period of the Marian persecution and the few years follow-ing, the differences between the Reformed and Lutheran theologians on the Continent erupted into controversy, not only over the Eucharistic presence but also concerning predestination and the indefectibility of the elect. At the accession of Mary, Peter Martyr went to Strasbourg, where he joined another exiled Italian Protestant, recently come from Geneva, Jerome Zanchi, and both maintained Reformed views against the Lu-theran theologians who, however, were gaining the upper hand with the Strasbourg magistrates. Zanchi's lectures on predestination, with regard to which he regularly consulted Peter Martyr, were rebutted by the Lu-theran theologian Johann Marbach, who had previously been something of a mediator among theologians but had now gone over entirely to the Lutheran side. J. P. Donnelly considers this dispute an occasion when predestination became a much greater matter of Lutheran-Reformed divi-sion, commenting, "The Strasbourg quarrel marks an important stage in the gradual retreat of later Lutheranism from Luther's *De Servo Arbitrio* to a milder position."[23] In 1556, Peter Martyr left Strasbourg for Zurich, where Bullinger was now won over to a stronger position on predestina-tion, but Zanchi continued his polemical role in Strasbourg for several more years. A recent study of the dispute between Zanchi and Marbach concludes that "the critical theological issues between the two men cen-tered upon predestination and perseverance of the faithful, rather than the Lord's Supper";[24] the latter issue has usually been taken as the most divisive. By 1576 the Lutheran Formula of Concord rejected any decree of reprobation and declared that God willed the salvation of all men. Only a predestination to life was acceptable. Lutheran theologians also refused to accept the perseverance of the saints as a logical extension of predestination.[25]

These disputes were echoed among the English leaders, who clearly took the Reformed side. Bishops Jewel, Cox, Parkhurst, Grindal, and Horne all expressed concern in their correspondence with Continental Protestants over the ubiquitarian error of the Lutheran teaching on the Eucharist.[26] In 1562, Grindal commented of the Lutherans that "it is astonishing that they are raising such commotions about predestination" inasmuch as Luther had taught it in his *On the Bondage of the Will*, which Bucer, Calvin, and Martyr had simply followed in their predestinarianism. The next year Zanchi wrote to Grindal complaining of his trouble with the Lutherans over predestination. Bishop Horne wrote Bullinger in 1563 that the Church of England had the same doctrine as Zurich, though differing in some ceremonies. And writing to Bullinger in 1571, Bishop Cox referred to the Lutheran theologian Johann Brenz as "a man who is gone crazy through a variety of error."[27] The only Elizabethan bishop who was known as a "Lutheran," Edward Cheyney, who rejected the Reformed doctrine both of predestination and the Eucharist, was deposed from the episcopate for his refusal to sign the Articles of Religion in 1568.[28]

While predestination was a matter of Lutheran-Reformed debate on the Continent, these same English church leaders were teaching it in its Reformed version. James Pilkington wrote that God had chosen the elect before the foundation of the world, and in a short Latin treatise, *De Praedestinatione*, written earlier when a student at Cambridge, he affirmed that God by a mere act of will hardens the hearts of the reprobates.[29] Bishop Jewel similarly asserted a decree of election from the beginning of time that was simply of God's mercy, and added what the Lutheran theologians denied—that election meant that the one chosen in Christ could not fall away.[30] The Reformed doctrine was asserted by some bishops who had not been exiles on the Continent. James Calfhill, nominated in 1570 to be bishop of Worcester (he died before taking office), asserted an election in Christ "before the foundations of the world."[31] Two later members of the Elizabethan episcopate, Matthew Hutton (bishop of Durham, 1589; archbishop of York, 1595) and Gervase Babington (bishop of Llandaff, 1591; Exeter, 1595; Worcester, 1597), showed considerable interest in predestination. Published posthumously was Hutton's *Brevis & dilucida explicatio, verae, certae, & consolationis plenae doctrinae De Electione, Praedestinatione ac Reprobatione*, which strongly asserted unconditional reprobation.[32] Babington appeared to be an uncompromising predestinarian in a 1591 Paul's Cross sermon in which he said predestination must be taught to all and was denied only by "madmen." As for reprobation, Babington averred that God decreed the damnation of some who were "vessels of wrath prepared to destruction."[33] The Elizabethan bishop of Exeter, John Woolton, similarly affirmed an unconditional predestination.[34] No less a Church of England theologian than Richard Hooker was to say that he did not doubt that Lutherans would attain salvation in spite of their holding an error so serious as that the elect could fall from grace.[35] And the Jacobean bishop of St. Davids, Anthony Rudd, accepted the name "Calvinists" as indicative of the theological position of the Church of England.[36]

The leaders of the English church did not focus on the doctrine of predestination for its own sake but rather as a very visible sign of their commitment to the Reformed theology of grace as a whole. Predestination was stressed because it exalted grace alone and was part of a theology that insisted that "Faith, piety, holiness, and religion, come not by nature, but by grace," as Sandys put it. Also for these English leaders, as for the Reformed theologians of the Continent and for their predecessors within English Protestantism, "holiness is the end of our election," and a life of faith and sanctity are evidence of election and a source of assurance.[37]

Predestination Strongly Asserted

It is evident that the bishops and leaders of the Elizabethan church did not consider that their views of the theology of grace differed from those of more radical nonconforming Protestants who were eventually dubbed Puritans and "precisians." Bishop Thomas Cooper, the object of barbed attacks from the Puritan "Martin Marprelate," insisted that although the differences between Rome and Canterbury were fundamental, relating to the central points of salvation, those between the bishops and dissenting Protestants concerned such indifferent items as vestments and were not theological at all.[38] William Barlow, made bishop of Lincoln in 1605 by King James I, said in 1601 that the differences between the bishops and the Nonconformists were "onely for ceremonies externall, no points substantial."[39] Anthony Wotton, speaking perhaps more from the Puritan side, echoed Barlow's words in 1605.[40] Archbishop John Whitgift, in his quarrel with the Puritan leader Thomas Cartwright, taxed the latter for saying that the Greek fathers were saved even though they believed in free will; Whitgift commented that "he that dieth in the opinion of free-will" could not truly hold to a faith in Christ. Whitgift included among Cartwright's errors that the Puritan held that "the doctrine of free-will is not repugnant to salvation," whereas, Whitgift added, this was a teaching "clean contrary to free justification by Christ."[41] One conformist went so far as to accuse the Puritans, because of their legalism and moralism, of teaching justification by works, "the very justification of Romanists, Anabaptists and Familists."[42] The most frenzied anti-Puritan of all, Richard Bancroft, who charged the Puritans with all kinds of fanciful errors, never included anything to do with the theology of grace—their errors in his view were all Donatist and "Anabaptisticall" falsehoods about government and discipline.[43]

Only when the great extent of the conformist and Nonconformist agreement on the Reformed theology of grace is acknowledged and taken as a starting point is it proper to point out that differences of emphasis, of intensity of feeling, and of urgency about the need to proclaim the doctrine of predestination did appear in Elizabethan Protestant theology, suggesting a slight divergence between Puritan and Anglican (as they are somewhat anachronistically called) about matters of grace. In an apt phrase, Patrick Collinson has alluded to "differences of theological temperature" as separating Puritan and Anglican, and Roger B. Manning has written that "the creed of Puritanism could be distinguished from the reigning Calvinist theology among the Anglican upper clergy only by the enthusiasm with which these beliefs were preached." Such differences of degree and emphasis could be significant, however, as J. Sears McGee has reminded us in his recent analysis of Puritan and Anglican differences and could be reflections of larger divergences in piety and religious style.[44]

With proper caution, then, it is possible to suggest that there was a rough correlation between Puritan Nonconformity and enthusiasm for the doctrine of predestination, although some conformists continued to be just as enthusiastic and probably (though it is difficult to document anything in an argument from silence) some Nonconformists lacked such enthusiasm. O. T. Hargrave has spoken of a "predestinarian offensive" mounted by the former Marian exiles in the early years of Elizabeth's reign,[45] and certainly returning exiles and other English Protestants allied to them, some of whom became Nonconformists, produced a considerable literature in defense of predestination. They also wanted to include a more detailed statement of that doctrine within the English creedal standards.

Many polemical treatises dealing with predestination were printed in the early years of Elizabeth's reign. While still in exile, John Knox had answered an attack on predestination by the English Anabaptist Robert Cooke, and the defenses of the doctrine in the early part of the queen's reign were mainly directed against similar radical opponents, variously reviled as "Anabaptists" and "freewillers," though Roman Catholic enemies of the doctrine were not forgotten. Nothing in these treatises would suggest that their authors feared the leaders of the Church of England placed too little stress on predestination. The quarrel of the free-will men with Bradford and his prison associates during the Marian years was no doubt part of the background for this literary output, but the reappearance of these views in the person of the obscure John Champneys prompted much of the furor. Champneys had been an advanced Protestant, probably tainted by Anabaptist influences, during the Edwardian years and had been compelled to abjure the perfectionist heresy that the truly regenerate cannot sin in April 1548.[46] He had published a rather garbled theological book in 1548 in which he described himself as "an unlearned laye mane borne in the countie of Somerset," who preferred the simple reading of scripture to the "sophistry" of "clerks,"[47] words that point toward the ambience of the earlier freewillers, though there is no evidence to connect Champneys to Henry Hart and the others. Apparently, Champneys printed and distributed privately an anonymous attack upon predestination a bit before 1561.[48] An anonymous work reproduced in the course of refutation by Robert Crowley has been identified as that of Champneys,[49] but Crowley does not acknowledge Champneys as author. Jean Veron earlier recognized Champneys as the author of an anonymous work against predestination: this was thus probably a second and slightly later anonymous book against the doctrine. In any case, the first Elizabethan refutations of deniers of predestination were aimed at radical sectarian Protestants.

The first and the largest number of these Elizabethan defenses of predestination came from the pen of Jean Veron. Born in France, Veron had settled in England in 1536 and studied for a while at Cambridge. He received preferment during the Edwardian Reformation and established himself as a controversialist by attacking purgatory and the mass. Imprisoned at Mary's accession, he was for a time incarcerated with John Bradford and thus presumably aware of the debate with the free-will men. One of the few foreigners who remained in England during Mary's reign, he was rewarded by Queen Elizabeth, who saw that he was cared for until his death in 1563.[50] Within the single year 1561, four works by Veron directly related to predestination appeared.

First was *A Fruteful treatise of Predestination and of the divine providence of god*. In the introduction, he said that his purpose was to defend the church against "the pestiferous sect of the free will men of our time" who were "enemies unto the most comfortable doctrine of predestination," and he proceeded to the heart of the issue, from the perspective of

Reformed theology, that these persons "wyll have part of our salvation to be attributed unto oure selves, and to the merites of oure owne workes, and not the hole glorye thereof to be geven unto Christ." Predestination is defined as a double decree, by which God did "Appoynt and ordayne unto death and condepnation, and too be the vessels of his wrath" some from among humankind. He argued against any thought that predestination might be based on divine foreknowledge, which, if the case, would nullify the main purpose of the doctrine of predestination, which is to magnify God's grace.[51]

Issued with this first treatment of predestination was *A Moste Necessary treatise of free will, not onlye against the Papistes, but also against the Anabaptistes*, in which the epistle dedicatory informed the reader that in order to reinforce the work on predestination it was necessary to deal with free will in such a manner as to obviate any denial of salvation by free mercy alone. Again, two enemies of predestination were singled out, "pope pelagians" and "the viperous broode of the fre wyll men," who, even though they would be accounted "most earnest favourers of the gospel," are, like "papists," enemies of God's free grace.[52] With many quotations both from scripture and St. Augustine, Veron used a dialogue method to explain that the will moves as God energizes it by grace, yet without compulsion.

Apparently within a few months, Veron reissued his earlier work on predestination and included with it *An Apology or defence of the Doctrine of Predestination*, intended to meet objections to his earlier book. In this work he alluded to "Champnies" as his opponent, dubbing him "the blind guide of the fre wil men," who, though unlearned, mocked the doctrines of election and reprobation, thereby showing himself to be "A verye Pelagian."[53]

Veron's outpourings of 1561 were completed with *The Overthrow of the justification of workes and of the vain doctrine of the merits of men*, which built on the previous works. The introductory epistle announced that justification by faith, predestination, and the right understanding of free will were doctrines that "do so depende one of an other, that they can in no wyse by separated." Again, he denounced those who "storme" against the "comfortable" doctrine of predestination, whom he now identified as, besides "papistes," "a sort of Atheistes and swinyshe Epicures," who substitued human works for true faith.[54]

Robert Crowley, whose affirmation of the decree of reprobation during the Edwardian Reformation was discussed in chapter 1, was in exile in

Frankfort during the Marian years and then in trouble with the Elizabethan church authorities during the 1560s for nonconformity in the matter of vestments.[55] In 1566, he vindicated the predestinarian theology of Veron and Knox against an anonymous challenger whom he continually referred to contemptuously as "Cerberus." The refuted work, which Crowley reproduced in the act of assailing it, remonstrated against the charge of Pelagianism merely because one denied the "shamefull Doctrine" of predestination currently being taught in the Church of England.[56] Against this opponent, Crowley argued that the decree of reprobation preceded man's fall, the fall itself having been decreed by God.[57]

John Foxe, the famed martyrologist, also wrote on predestination in the early years of Elizabethan England, and though he was not an outspoken Nonconformist like his friend Crowley, he apparently resigned as a prebendary of Durham because of scruples over vestments and was at least on the margins of Nonconformity.[58] He, too, had been an exile, at Strasbourg, Frankfurt, and finally Basel. Two writings by Foxe bear directly on predestination. The first was a set of notes appended to the "godly letters" of John Bradford in the 1570 edition of *Acts and Monuments*. Bradford, of course, had defended the doctrine against the prison freewillers, and predestination was therefore a recurrent theme in his correspondence. Foxe's other contribution to the doctrine of predestination, his completion of Walter Haddon's response to the Roman Catholic challenge of the Portuguese bishop Jerome Osorio, was published posthumously. Haddon, a lawyer who had been active in the Edwardian reform, died in 1572, and Foxe finished his defense, which appeared in Latin in 1579 and in the English translation by James Bell in 1581. In his part of the work, Haddon had accused his opponent of Pelagian error for denying the free mercy of God, so Foxe's lengthy addition, which dealt mainly with predestination, was appropriate. Foxe clearly affirmed both election and reprobation according to the mere will of God, related predestination both to justification and sanctification, and above all treated it as a reinforcement of the gratuitous nature of redemption.[59] The fact that he dealt with predestination in connection with the letters of Bradford, with their rich, warm piety, suggests, as does his whole treatment of the matter, that for Foxe predestination was soteriological and related to piety.

Not a former exile like Crowley or Foxe, John Field surfaced in the later 1560s as a leader of radical Nonconformists and continued to be a troublemaker for those in authority in the church until almost the end of the reign.[60] Also concerned about predestination, Field translated some sermons of Calvin on the subject and published them in London with a polemical introductory epistle that referred to the earlier defenses of the doctrine by Knox, Veron, and Crowley and roundly condemned deniers of "the everlasting predestination and election of God, the most comfortable doctrine that can be, being the foundation of all the rest." Predictably, these deniers are "papists," but also "counterfeite professours," such as Anabaptists, libertines, Pelagians, Arians, and the "Familie of Love."[61] Field does not hint in his preface that he considered the Church of England lax in this doctrine, but when he drew up a confession of faith with Robert Wilcox, which they presumably deemed better than the Thirty-nine Articles, it contained the doctrine of reprobation.[62] Other Nonconformists besides Crowley and Field stressed predestination, including former exiles Gilby, Whittingham (Whittingham's translation of a treatise on predestination by Theodore Beza appeared in 1575),[63] and Thomas Cartwright.[64]

Some efforts were made to get the Church of England officially to affirm predestination with greater precision. Some churchmen wanted Nowell's catechism, which gave a detailed version of predestination, made a binding formulary, but it is impossible to say if this was because of predestination.[65] A Puritan petition of 1584, raising the question of desired alterations in the doctrinal standards of the English church, asked "whether the 17th article, speaking of election be well put downe, that maketh no mention of reprobation, seeing Paule, speaking of the one, speaketh of the other? And whether the doctrine of predestination of it self is daungerous, and maie cause a daungerous downfall to any, as is put down in the article?"[66] Later, at the Hampton Court Conference, the Puritan petitioners asked that the strongly predestinarian Lambeth Articles be made one of the official standards of the church.[67] A dialogue written by a Nonconformist attacking the bishops had a "godly" spokesman say that the only learned man he ever heard who asserted free will was a bishop in his sermon; the speaker added that this was blasphemy because predestination is a part of the scriptural gospel that must be preached.[68] And a reported story about Archbishop Matthew Parker claimed that he had warned a certain Richard Kechyn, whom he had preferred to a living near Bocking, that he was not to preach too often on "the divine counsels"; thus Kechyn thereafter but "lightly touched the topic of predestination in his discourses" and was for that moderation denounced by a licensed preacher named Holland, who insisted that predestination "should and ought to be preached in every sermon, and in every place, before all congregations, as the only doctrine of salvation" and that those who believed it but did not everywhere preach it were as much enemies of God as those who denied it. According to the same account, this Holland also denounced various ceremonies, thus identifying himself as a sympathizer with Nonconformists.[69] The conclusion to be drawn from such evidence is not that bishops and Nonconformists held different theologies, but that at least some inclined to Nonconformity felt an uneasiness about the lack of enthusiasm of some bishops for predestination and about the failure of the Articles of Religion to be explicit on the decree of reprobation.

It might be expected that if the Nonconformist Puritans who remained within the Church of England were strongly predestinarian, similar and even stronger affirmations would come from the Separatists. Examination of the Separatist materials, however, does not so indicate. The Separatists were so completely taken up with disciplinary matters, questions concerning the true nature of the church, and the need to realize the true fellowship of Christians in a small group that they apparently ignored this theological issue. One reason could be that, just as the early Puritans had little to complain of in the theology of the Church of England, the Separatists had little to complain of in a church whose theology of grace was firmly Reformed. But it is also possible that a legalistic and moralistic version of Christian piety prevailed so strongly among the Separatists that the theological concerns of the "preaching and pastoral" Puritans did not concern them. The true church for them involved pursuing the right kind of Christian discipleship in a gathered fellowship. Edmund S. Morgan has shown that their requirements for membership were quite different in their attention to external "walking" from those of Church of England Puritans,[70] whose concern was with the experience of grace; and their understanding of the covenant, as their recent historian B. R. White shows, has strongly legalistic overtones.[71] It is possible, too, that the Separatist tradition was more deeply rooted than is usually thought in sectarian and biblical "commonsense" religion, with its distance from the learned Reformed tradition, thus making them more akin to earlier freewillers than might be supposed.[72] In any case, the early Separatists showed scant interest in predestination, the definition of the church as the elect being the closest they got to the subject.[73]

The Piety of Predestinarian Grace

The Reformed theology of predestinarian grace, which had been adopted by the leadership of the Church of England and emphasized by many Nonconformists, was increasingly hardened into a scholastic theology of the divine decrees, a process already well along in the writings of Veron and Crowley. But it must be remembered that this theology gained its strength from the nourishing springs of piety from which it was continually drawn. The theology of grace was not merely a school doctrine or an official theology useful in assailing the Roman Catholic enemy, but a theology related to the everyday religious experience of a growing lay clientele who were continually instructed in it by zealous Protestant preachers. Much of the earlier English Reformation was merely official or touched only limited circles in London or other centers where new ideas could quickly circulate. During the Elizabethan age, Protestant teaching was effectively brought to many areas and classes of the English populace hitherto largely untouched by it. Ministers of that period, fresh from the universities and under the impact of the Reformed theology of grace they had learned there, fanned out through England carrying their message. Protestant propaganda was often spread by those who are considered Puritans, although, as Patrick Collinson reminds us, it is hard on this level to "distinguish absolutely between Puritanism and, so to speak, mere Protestantism."[74] Thus an ever larger body of lay opinion wedded to a piety of grace alone was built up, and the continuing development of the theology of grace ought to be seen against that background.

There thus grew up a school of popular preachers and devotional writers who mediated the Reformed theology of grace to a lay clientele by means of sermons and treatises. They were practical theologians who focused on the recognizable signs of grace in religious experience, dealing mainly with questions of conversion, comfort, and assurance. These were the "godly affectionate divines" of Puritan lore, the "physicians of the soul" brought to the fore by the research of William Haller,[75] the preaching and pastoral Puritans of Trinterud's typology,[76] or those Puritan ministers whose main function was as spiritual directors.[77] But, as shall be seen, many of these "affectionate divines" were by no means Nonconformists and some were even bishops of the Church of England.

That the Reformed theology of grace was rooted in and related to piety is evident in the enthusiasm with which it was preached as an essential part of the gospel, indeed as the gospel itself. The preaching of the gospel of God's grace in Christ has with some justice been regarded as the central motif of the Puritan movement, the inner spring from which various reform impulses radiated outward.[78] What must not be forgotten is that this centrality of preaching the gospel included the preaching of the doctrine of predestination, a teaching that was important in establishing that salvation was entirely the gift of God's grace. As Thomas Tuke put it with impeccable logic, Christ commanded the gospel to be preached, but predestination belongs to the gospel, "and therefore is to be preached."[79] Other theologians and preachers repeated this theme: Jean Veron replied to the objection that predestination was too abstruse for the common people that, quite the contrary, "it ought to be thoroughly preached"; for John Field, it was necessary that predestination be "published and preached to the people"; to John Knox "the doctrine of Gods eternal predestination is so necessarie to the Church of God" that without it faith cannot be truly taught nor "surely established"; Bishop Babington declared that it was to be taught to all.[80] Preaching the gospel was, moreover, the outward means by which the predestined would be called.[81]

The Reformed theology of grace was preached and developed in practical treatises chiefly through the structure of the order of salvation that was earlier noted as characteristic of the theology of Bucer and other important teachers and of the English reformers. John Bradford, a close pupil of Bucer, had given elements of that order—election, vocation, justification, sanctification, and glorification—a very warm and personal tone as he employed them as instruments of conversion, comfort, and assurance, a use to which it was the declared intention of the Reformed theologians that they should be put. Thus not only did the Reformed theology of grace follow the pattern of this *ordo salutis*, but the piety of grace shaped by English preachers and devotional writers put the same *ordo* to the everyday uses of pastoral instruction and the direction of souls.

In the development of this piety and theology of the order of salvation, the different elements were seen as integrally related. Thus, in the words of Anthony Maxey, "Predestination, Calling, Justifying and Glorifying are so coupled and knit together, that if you hold fast one lincke, you draw unto you the whole chaine; if you let goe one, you loose all."[82] The precise elements in this order sometimes differed, and in some very practical expositions there was a tendency to simplify them, but they unanimously began with predestination (or rather election, the decree of the salvation of some; predestination also included reprobation). As John Downame explained it, the various elements of the order of salvation were "effects" of God's election, the "degrees and meanes" of it, all of which were contained in the decree of election.[83] These elements of the order were the unfolding steps that proceed out of the decree of election by which the elect came finally to God. Following election, the usual list gave vocation or effectual calling, justification, sanctification, and glorification.[84] John Downame followed election with "Christ our Mediatour" as the first effect of election and added "adoption" before vocation. John Foxe's list omitted sanctification and placed vocation after justification,[85] but it is clear that a basic pattern to this *ordo* was continually repeated by the "spiritual writers" and was closely related to Paul's statement in Romans 8:30.

The unfolding of God's decreed purpose to redeem in the elements of the order of salvation, was, in the words of Thomas Wilson, "no mere speculative thing" but "tendeth to practice."[86] Bishop Babington managed to compress the relationship of the links in the chain of the order of salvation to practice in one rich sentence: "Our fruits [sanctification] show our faith, our faith [justification] showes our comming to Christ [effectual calling], and our comming to Christ in this sort showeth our election by God to eternall lyfe." Thus Babington makes it clear that each element in the order of salvation was related to the problem of assurance of salvation. Arthur Hildersam later insisted that it was a Christian's duty to seek such assurance.[87] Baird Tipson has written that "the problem of assurance dominated early Puritan theology," and it soon becomes apparent that the spiritual and "affectionate" literature produced by many preachers and devotional and theological writers of the Elizabethan and Jacobean periods was pervaded by the issue of how one was to be assured of God's gracious favor. Ian Breward has further commented that the whole focus on the problem of the certainty of salvation in relation to the order of salvation brought "questions of predestination into the forefront of pastoral care." Perhaps with some exaggeration, Ernst Troeltsch long ago commented, "In the interest of assurance of salvation the doctrine of Predestination becomes the central doctrine of Protestantism."[88] As applied to Reformed piety and theology in England in the period being investigated, this judgment seems accurate, especially if it is qualified so that predestination includes certain related doctrines that also emphasized grace alone, although predestination still remains central as the preeminently useful doctrine in the search for assurance. Such a consideration again reinforces the point that the doctrine of predestination was far from being a merely speculative and structurally unifying point in theology, but was deeply embedded in very practical religious concern.

All these spiritual writers agreed with Samuel Hieron that the assurance that one was among God's children was "a priviledge of all beleevers" and with William Cowper that "a Christian may be assured of his salvation in this life." Cowper added that such an assurance was "contrary to the doctrine of papists,"[89] and it was a continual refrain of this literature that "papists" err "who teach that none are to think or persuade themselves that they are of the number of the predestinate unto salvation, but to be ever doubtful thereof."[90] Such doubting, it was argued, led wavering persons to desperation.[91] "But," Downame asked, "what peace can we have, if wee be not assured of our election, but have our mindes distracted and racked betweene faith and doubting, hope and despaire?"[92] Nor was such an "assured confidence" considered presumption, for it was dependent on God's grace;[93] rather, the Roman Catholic "proud perswasion that they have of their own merites and deserts" was presumption.[94] To wrongly think that one could not attain assurance of salvation was a great hindrance to the Christian life, and therefore, the spiritual writers agreed, the doctrine of assurance must be taught to all, so that they might know themselves to be "beloved of God, and that they shall be saved."[95] Nevertheless, these writers often cautioned against a false assurance that could be mere rashness and recommended that one must examine oneself by means of a right understanding of the order of salvation in order to gain a well-grounded certainty.[96]

For all the theologians and spiritual writers during this period, the order of salvation began with predestination or, more precisely, election to life as the positive side of God's predestinating decree. Thus these writers strongly affirmed unconditional election,[97] not in the least inhibited from doing so by pastoral concerns but, rather, considering it an important part of their everyday preaching of the gospel. It was agreed that unconditional election meant that salvation was by grace alone, apart from any human merit,[98] and this was taken to be cause for thanksgiving to God as well as for humility before God.[99] If one depended upon oneself for salvation, declared John Prime, there would be no hope or assurance, for then would "we cast the anker of our hope in an unstable place."[100] Predestination was therefore clearly connected to assurance.[101] Richard Rogers defined the pastoral work of assurance as teaching "how men may know that they are the elect of God."[102] Thus the spiritual writers agreed that predestination was a "comfortable" doctrine,[103] as Bradford and others had stressed before, which, as Bishop Babington said, brought to God's "true servants sweete comfort."[104] In election, said William Cowper, we may "marke the certaintie and solidite of our salvation"; for Thomas Tuke it protected faith against diffidence; for Anthony Maxey, predestination was comfortable because it showed that salvation depended upon God's infallible purposes; for Samuel Gardiner it made the faithful "throughly [sic] perswaded that we shall one day come to Heaven." Veron had argued at the beginning of the Elizabethan period that to take away the right understanding of predestination was to take away all comforting assurance.[105] Clearly, the teaching of unconditional election was a means of providing comfort.

Though reprobation was obviously not an element in the order of salvation, it was nonetheless frequently dealt with by the spiritual writers alongside of election,[106] and it, too, had uses in the search for assuring evidences of salvation. One must undergo self-examination to make sure that faith was not a mere "carnal securitie," an outward call only, without true signs of grace.[107] One should not rashly judge of another's reprobation,[108] but remember that there is no one who might not turn out finally to repent and be numbered among the godly. Sinners were exhorted to repentance and righteousness and reminded that they were condemned for nothing but their own sins, although it was at the same time acknowledged that "the purpose of God in the reprobate cannot be altered."[109] Nor were spiritual writers averse to using the doctrine of reprobation to instill fear: Richard Rogers thought it godly advice to be reminded that no reprobate could be converted, and Samuel Gardiner considered it helpful to piety to tell his auditors that God reprobates some, for "we are thereby stroken with no small fear."[110]

But, although assurance was to be found in the consideration of election, the spiritual writers warned against those who sought to pry into the mysteries of God's decrees.[111] Rather, one was to gain assurance by looking to Christ, for election was "in Christ,"[112] a formulation that had recurred frequently in the English reformers. John Bowle, the Jacobean bishop of Rochester, connected Christ to the different steps of the order of salvation when he rhetorically proclaimed, "Looke in every linck of the chaine of Heaven: How are we predestinated to the adoption of children? By Jesus Christ. . . . How are we called to glory? By Jesus

Christ. . . . How are we justified? By Jesus Christ. . . . How are we sanctified? By Jesus Christ."[113] But the work of Christ was especially connected to the order of salvation by placing it right after election, signify-
ing that election was in Christ, but perhaps more strongly proclaiming
that Christ was the means by which election unfolded and that his work
was a necessary step in the order prior to vocation and justification. As
Thomas Tuke put it, "For God did not elect us, because Christ was to die
for us: but on the contrarie, Christ did therefore die for us, because God
had elected us in him." Thomas Wilson stated more clearly, "The purpose of a Saviour was subordinate to the purpose of election."[114] The
placing of Christ's work in the order of salvation at this point had the
effect of emphasizing that the work of Christ, particularly his atoning
death, was directed specifically for the elect, "whom he had chosen to
everlasting life."[115] Christ's death, a sufficient payment for the sins of all,
in fact becomes an efficient payment for the sins of the elect only.[116] Thus
the doctrine of limited atonement appeared in the spiritual writers, but
was not used much polemically, as it was to be in the later Arminian
controversies, but directed toward the creation of comfort: Christ's
death was not a mere offer of salvation but an effectual salvation for the
elect. And assurance of election was also an assurance in Christ, being
"only proper to the elect, whereby thorow faith . . . I am assured that my
salvation is wrought by Christ."[117]

If assurance was to be found in the recognition that election was in
Christ and that Christ's redemptive work was for the elect only, the
sufferings of Christ take on a special place in the assurance inculcated by
such a piety. For Christ's sufferings become a very personal matter to the
elect and a strong incentive to devotion, considering that they were
undergone in place of what the elect themselves should have suffered.
Accordingly, the practical writers of the period tended to meditate very
personally and affectionately on Christ's sufferings and to heighten the
extent of those sufferings. Toward the end of the Elizabethan period,
Puritan writers argued not just that Christ died on behalf of the elect, but
that he underwent the very same pains due to the elect and suffered, on
the cross, the weight of the full wrath of God against sinners.[118] Thus
some Elizabethan writers and preachers, mainly of Puritan ambience,
followed Calvin's interpretation of the clause in the Apostle's Creed that
affirmed the descent of Christ into hell; by Calvin's interpretation the
descent bore the meaning of the pangs of soul endured by Christ while on

certain that they will not finally fall away. Faith itself, looked at in this aspect, is the assurance of perseverance to the end.[149] As Downame wrote, "Surely being assured that we are in the state of grace, and in Gods love and favour, there is no doubt but we shall be saved, and persevere in the meanes which are inseparably joyned with our salvation."[150]

"When sanctification endeth in this life, then glorification entreth," according to John Prime, and the elect shall then all be glorified by the grace of God. "Predestination is unto glory," wrote Cowper.[151] Glorification is also a source of comfort and assurance and helps to ensure perseverance, for how could those elected in God's immutable will to glory fail in their final end? The right understanding of glorification, the last element in the order of salvation, provided believers with the last hope of their assured salvation, that glorification was the final end to which the work of God begun in them tended. Even eschatology thus becomes an element in the theology of grace.[152]

Examination of the background of the various individuals who participated in the development of this "affectionate divinity" of assurance and the order of salvation leads to several conclusions about its relationship to English Protestantism and the Church of England. First, the themes espoused by these spiritual writers appeared before the Elizabethan period, especially in the writings and letters of spiritual advice of John Bradford, and the character of this writing was dependent upon the Reformed theology and its order of salvation, which had been earlier established in English Protestantism.

Second, bishops of the Church of England were prominent in this group. Among those who were or became bishops are John Jewel (whom Haller considered a precursor of the brotherhood of Puritan preachers[153]), Edwin Sandys, Richard Curteys, Thomas Cooper, Gervase Babington, John Woolton, Thomas Morton, William Cowper, Robert Horne, and John Bowle. Some merely echoed or alluded in passing to the major themes of the spiritual writers, but others gave voice to a wide range of these ideas. In a Paul's Cross sermon that has been frequently cited in this chapter, Babington provided a compact statement of the range of the themes of these spiritual writers. Bishop Thomas Cooper, a major focus for radical Puritan attacks and a staunch defender of conformity, must be counted among the spiritual writers on the basis of his published sermons. John Woolton, who became bishop of Exeter in 1579, was a major figure among the authors of Elizabethan writers of practical divinity. Although not bishops, other churchmen who were impeccably conformist contributed to the genre, for example, John Prime, a fellow of New College, Oxford, who had a considerable reputation as a preacher,[154] Anthony Maxey, dean of Windsor and later a chaplain to James I, and Elnathan Parr, a Suffolk rector. Samuel Gardiner was the author of a dialogue aimed at recovering Nonconformists for the church.[155] Thomas Tuke lived long enough to be a decided royalist in the civil war. Richard Cavendish and Thomas Palfreyman were prominent laymen of the Church of England.

A third conclusion might be that the distinction between Puritan and Anglican becomes blurred with respect to these spiritual writers. Writing and preaching that stressed the personal application to the question of assurance of the elements of the order of salvation, all the while strongly emphasizing grace alone in the process of redemption, cut a wide swath across the Church of England. One of the confusions that has clouded the picture is that individuals are often named as Puritans merely because they wrote books of practical divinity of the type examined here. Thus the *Dictionary of National Biography* says that Anthony Anderson wrote books of a "puritanic character" and cites Nicholas Byfield, William Attersol, and John Randall as "Puritan divines" without mentioning any specific nonconformity. Remarkably, of Samuel Hieron it declares, "He was inclined to Puritanism, though he strictly conformed to the Church of England."[156] Often what was in fact the majority opinion of the Elizabethan Church of England is taken as specific evidence of Puritanism!

A final conclusion must be, however, that, if Puritanism is defined narrowly as actual Nonconformity or substantial sympathy for or connection with Nonconformists, it is apparent that such Nonconformists were disproportionately involved in spiritual writing and preaching, that they were exceptionally enthusiastic over it and most likely to make extensive practical application of doctrines that all accepted as orthodox. It is a matter of degree: although many English churchmen who were impeccably conformist and even anti-Puritan were also spiritual writers, it was the more identifiably Puritan writers who were generally the most emphatic about the piety of the order of salvation and who most deeply and thoroughly probed the problems of predestination and assurance and who, through time, produced the largest amount of "affectionate divinity." Thus, of the spiritual writers discussed in this chapter, John Field was a leader in the Puritan disciplinary movement,[157] Thomas Wilson, lector of Canterbury, was "complained of" for Nonconformity, Christopher Shutte has been called a leading Puritan of York diocese,

Bartimaeus Andrewes was disciplined by Archbishop Bancroft,[158] and Cambridge theologians William Fulke and William Perkins had important connections with the leaders of Puritan Nonconformity.

But most important of all were a group of preachers and writers who, though occasionally in trouble for Nonconformity, were most concerned with preaching and pastoral activities. Patrick Collinson has convincingly identified Edward Dering as a fountainhead of this impulse, and with him should be included George Gifford, John Dod, John Downame, Richard Rogers, Richard Greenham, Laurence Chaderton, Arthur Dent, William Negus, and the Cambridge theologian Perkins, whose work can be regarded as basically practical.[159] A large number of Puritan figures of the next century should be added to the list: Richard Sibbes, Arthur Hildersam, John Rogers, Ezekiel Culverwell, and Paul Baynes, for example. These eager preachers believed that taking the gospel of grace to the common folk throughout England was of the greatest urgency. Much of their Nonconformity, especially participation in the "prophesyings" and in lectureships, may have derived more from their desire to place able preachers in every English parish than from doctrinaire notions of the right biblical polity. These preachers frequently stated their aim to uproot the rude and mistaken religious notions of the "ignorant sort," which they often identified as a kind of residual "popery."[160] They also wanted to provide spiritual direction for the growing groups of lay people who were avidly responding to their tutelage.[161] In any case, published sermons and other books detailing the spiritual life with special attention to assurance, predestination, and the order of salvation long continued to flow from the presses of England.[162]

Protestant Scholasticism in English Theology

At the same time that Reformed theology in England was giving rise to a practical piety focusing on the seeking of assurance of predestinating grace, it was also being cast in the mold of a hard and fast theological system of the type usually designated as scholastic. That a religious writer could be of signal importance in both of these developments is well attested by the case of William Perkins, one of the most important of the spiritual writers as well as an English theologian of European reputation,[163] who may well have been the most important figure in the emergence of Reformed scholasticism in England. Alongside of Perkins as a scholastic theologian, however, must also be classed two prominent theologians, William Whitaker, the Regius professor of divinity, and Robert Some, master of Peterhouse. Other theological writers before and after this Cambridge trio were important in the development of Reformed scholasticism in England, including such theological giants of the next century as William Ames and John Owen.

The Reformed orthodoxy and scholasticism of these theologians was an English version of a development of theological definition, consolidation, and elaboration that had long been under way on the Continent, often in response to polemical needs. Though usually described as "Calvinism," caution should be exercised in so naming it, because it constituted the tendency of a large school of theologians, many of whom at crucial points departed from Calvin's views and methods. A recent study of Protestant scholasticism asserts that the Reformed scholastics seldom referred to Calvin and that, ironically, recent studies tend to minimize the "role played by Calvin in the development of Calvinist thought."[164] Peter Martyr, Jerome Zanchi, and Theodore Beza are generally conceded to have been crucial in the development of Reformed scholasticism. Donnelly, in his study of Martyr, says, "Jerome Zanchi was the most thoroughgoing and influential in pioneering Calvinist scholasticism, Theodore Beza was the most prolific, but Peter Martyr Vermigli was the first and the inspiration of all who came after."[165] To these should probably be added the Heidelberg theologian Zacharias Ursinus. Theological compendiums and other works by these and other less important Continental theologians, often in translation, were published in England,[166] and their major works, published on the Continent and usually in Latin, would also have been available to English students of theology.

The particular elements of this Reformed scholasticism that were evident in its English practitioners and bear upon the present inquiry into the theology of grace may be identified as the use of a scholastic method depending on logic and perhaps even on metaphysics, the use of the doctrine of predestination as the center of a theological system, the close connection of predestination to the divine decrees considered generally, and a militantly defensive posture with reference to a number of points corollary to predestination, such as reprobation, limited atonement, the indefectibility of the elect, and other matters recognizable along with these as the primary issues of the Synod of Dort.

The employment of a logical method as one of the features of Reformed scholasticism had the effect of giving Reformed theology a rigid and precise character and led to the treatment of theological assertions as deductions from given premises leading to yet other deductions. This approach also entailed the use of philosophical terms and distinctions in order to sharpen theological concepts. Such a highly articulated theological method often meant reliance on Aristotle, but sometimes involved instead the employment of the revisionist logic of the French Protestant Petrus Ramus. Luther had fulminated against "that pagan rascal" Aristotle, and Calvin in common humanist fashion preferred Plato,[167] but the study of Aristotle was too firmly embedded in the educational curriculum to be easily displaced, and Protestant theologians were becoming increasingly interested in the more humanistic Aristotelianism of Padua and Pietro Pompanazzi. Melanchthon, especially in his later years, was responsible for a continuing interest in Aristotle in the Protestant educational curriculum, and the Italian exile theologians Peter Martyr and Jerome Zanchi, both of whom had had direct contact with Paduan Aristotelianism, made Aristotelian method and distinctions crucial to their theology. Thomas Aquinas's Aristotelian approach was an important model for Zanchi. At Geneva, Theodore Beza gave the logic of Aristotle a central place in the study of theology, and the dual influence of Beza and the two Italians was exerted strongly on the important new center of Reformed theology at the University of Heidelberg.[168]

This Aristotelian hegemony, however, was vigorously challenged by Ramus, whose influence was significant among French and English Protestants. But his logic of dichotomies and classifications hardly made theological expression less "scholastic," if anything giving it a yet more intricate structure of divisions and subdivisions. Insofar as Ramist logic lacked a metaphysic, however, and was practical in its intent through its basically rhetorical nature, it opened fewer doors to abstruse speculation than did Aristotelianism.[169]

Of the Protestant Aristotelians, the influence of Peter Martyr in England was of long standing, but Zanchi, too, was often cited by English theologians, and Beza, as Calvin's successor at Geneva, also had considerable influence. But more distinctive of English Reformed scholasticism was the use of Ramist method. Perkins has been frequently cited as an example of the English use of Ramist method, and his attempts to "chart" theology bear the earmarks of Ramist dichotomizing. William Ames, a Puritan Nonconformist who had a distinguished theological career in the Netherlands, was a more thoroughgoing Ramist than Perkins; in a recent study of Ames, John D. Eusden says that only Perkins exerted more influence on him than Ramus![170] The extensive influence of Ramist logic on the Puritan movement as a whole has by now become a commonplace.[171]

The second element of Reformed scholasticism was the controlling place given to the doctrine of predestination within the theological system and the treatment of it under the topic of God's decrees and in connection with divine providence. According to John S. Bray, "Predestination became the keystone of Protestant scholasticism."[172] For Calvin, with his biblical-humanist orientation, predestination was related to soteriology and connected with the problem of assurance in the Christian life, its treatment in the *Institutes* being widely separated from the doctrine of God and his providence.[173] Whether the doctrine of predestination was the organizing principle of Beza's theology has recently been questioned, but it clearly had a very great importance for him, and he treated it in connection with the nature of God and his decrees alongside of the providential decrees of creation and preservation. Beza also espoused predestination in its supralapsarian form. Predestination was central for Martyr and Zanchi, and they, too, linked it to God's attributes and providence.[174]

This connection of predestination with the divine attributes and providence, giving it thereby a more central role in a system of theology, appeared fairly early in English theological writings. Jean Veron, in *A Fruteful treatise of Predestination and of the divine providence of god* (1563), as the title indicates, treated predestination in the context of providence, as did also Robert Crowley, whose attack upon the "free-willing" Cerberus included long discussions of fate and providence.[175] Other theological writers continued such an approach: *The Treatise of Heavenly Philosophie* by Thomas Palfreyman, published in 1578, was composed mainly of quotations following theological headings but predestination was placed under the doctrine of God, parallel to providence.[176] Dudley Fenner's *Sacra Theologia* of 1586 began with God's attributes and then proceeded to God's acts, including predestination in relation to God's general decrees.[177] Thomas Wilson's 1611 *Jacob's Ladder*, a brief statement prefatory to longer treatises on justification and sanctification, also placed predestination at the beginning of its system, in the context of God's decrees as a whole.[178] Wilson's approach, though, keeps predestination closer to the other elements of the *ordo salutis*, so that its soteriological rooting was not completely obscured. But in the 1616 work of John Forbes, *A Treatise Tending to Clear the Doctrine of*

Justification, there is an apparent tendency to swallow up the order of salvation in the abstract consideration of the divine decrees.[179] A more extreme example of this kind of scholasticism appeared in Robert Hill's *Life Everlasting: Or the True Knowledge of One Jehovah, Three Elohim, and Jesus Immanuel*, published in 1601 at Cambridge, where Hill was a fellow of St. John's. The book purports to be a discussion of the divine names or attributes, but its nearly seven hundred pages devoted much space to a number of problems related to providence and predestination and dealt with them as "questions" in the mode of medieval scholasticism, answering the questions through propositions and syllogistic deductions from such propositions. Among the matters of concern to the author were such questions as "Whether there be any power in God?" "Whether providence be truly in God?" "Whether Predestination, Election, and Reprobation be properly attributed to God?" "Whether God were moved to reject any, by any other means, than his good pleasure?" "What is the final cause of reprobation?"[180] Thus predestination was related to abstruse metaphysical speculations about the being of God, and a metaphysical interest, something common but not universal in Reformed scholasticism, became paramount.

Most important of the Elizabethan English scholastics was no doubt William Perkins, whose scholasticism was significantly modified by very practical spiritual concerns, a characteristic of many Puritans that enabled them to be both spiritual writers and scholastic theologians. Indeed, many of these Puritan writers show that scholastic theology and concern with the devout life were by no means mutually exclusive. In his *Armilla Aurea* of 1590, translated into English the next year as *A Golden Chaine* and subsequently revised and enlarged in both its Latin and English versions, Perkins followed Beza and Zanchi (Zanchi's views were quoted often and widely disseminated by this work of Perkins) in linking predestination to the doctrine of God. As did Peter Martyr and his followers, Perkins treated the doctrines subsequent to predestination as succeeding links in an order of salvation—paralleled, in Ramist dichotomizing fashion, by an "order of Damnation," leading from the decree of reprobation to the actual suffering in hell of the damned, just as election led to the glorification of the blessed. For Perkins, all of the works of God fell either under his decrees or the execution of his decrees, a distinction derived from Beza, with every topic related to predestination. Thus the work of Christ is one of the means of predestination, creation and the fall are considered means of accomplishing predestination, the church is defined as the body of the predestined, and the efficient cause of the church is identified as predestination.[181]

In addition to the use of logic to achieve precise definitions and to the great importance given to predestination, a third element of Reformed scholasticism was a defensive posture regarding a number of corollaries of predestination. Such logical consequences of a theology of unconditional predestination as the decree of reprobation, limited atonement, and the inevitable perseverance of the elect needed to be asserted with greater force than before insofar as predestination was becoming the central point of an airtight theological system. The need to defend this system in controversy not only against its longstanding Catholic enemies but also against the newly arisen Arminian enemies within the Protestant camp made ever more pressing the task of upholding not only predestination but also its logical outerworks. Both in the Netherlands and in England there were some criticisms of strict predestinarian theology of which Perkins was aware, calling opponents of his theology "New Pelagians." He published his *De Praedestinationis Modo et Ordine et de Amplificatione Gratiae Divinae* to vindicate "the Calvinists doctrine, of those reproaches which are cast upon it."[182] In 1602, with *A Treatise of Gods free Grace, and Man's Free-Will*, Perkins continued the assault. His fellow Cambridge theologians William Whitaker and Robert Some also made contributions in defense of points related to predestination. Robert Some defended limited atonement and the saints' perseverance in *Questiones Tres: De Merito et Efficacia, Remissionis Paccatorum Per Fidem Certitudine ac Iustificantis fidei perseverantia* and *The Perpetuity of Faythe*.[183] Whitaker defended the will's total inability to turn to grace apart from divine help in his *Tractatus de peccato originali*, published posthumously.[184]

But the corollary of predestination most strikingly defended by these Reformed scholastics was the decree of reprobation. Beza had been more interested in stressing this than Calvin,[185] and Perkins devoted considerable attention to its defense. Reprobation for Perkins was a distinct decree of God, defined as "that part of predestination, whereby God, according to the most free and just purpose of his will, hath determined to reject certaine men unto eternall destruction, and miserie, and that to the praise of his justice."[186] Reprobates are, then, in Ramist fashion, subdivided into infants and adults, the former "being left in Gods secret judgment unto themselves, they dying are rejected of God for ever," while the latter, "Reprobates of riper age," are sometimes called "by an ineffectual calling" and then fall away to damnation, and others, not called at all, such as infidels, add "hardness of heart" to natural "ignorance and vanitie of minde," from which ensues the "committing of sinne with greedinesse," to which is added the just reward of "fearful condemnation."[187] Such reprobates "are wholly in body and soule tormented with an incredible horrour, and exceeding great anguish, through the sense and seeing of Gods wrath, poured out upon them for ever." This, Perkins concluded, "is the full execution of Gods decree of reprobation, whereby appeareth the great justice of God in punishing sinne: from whence also commeth Gods glorie, which he propoundeth to himselfe, as the last and chiefest end in all these things."[188]

Perkins had explained that God's hatred of the reprobate was really a hatred of their sin and was an effect, not a cause, of their reprobation. "Hatred of God" became one of the divine attributes in Robert Hill's *Life Everlasting*, where the decree of reprobation was dealt with in great detail and subdivided into various questions. This divine wrath was variously defined by Hill as God's "misliking, detesting, abomination, or abhorring of a thing" and as "the execution of his decree of punishing and destroying the wicked."[189]

It might appear that the theological outerworks thrown up to defend God's grace had ended up obscuring that merciful commodity. It is certainly clear that a logically stated theology centering on the doctrine of predestination and eager to defend its every consequence, however harsh, was built up in Reformed scholasticism. But it must not be forgotten, and Perkins's own pastoral concern is a reminder, that this theology was not only a function of the need to be precise and logically consistent for polemical purposes, but also continued to protect and enshrine, however distortingly, a living and warmly personal religiosity by means of the strong outer walls of a grim fortress.

The Doctrine of Grace in the Polemic against Rome

From the beginning of the English Reformation many Protestant shots had been fired at the Church of Rome. The barrage continued in the early Elizabethan period, with Jewel's exchange with Harding a major example, though there were many others.[190] The controversy between Protestant and Roman Catholic roamed over a wide range of issues, inevitably pausing at such obvious matters of difference as images, the mass, indulgences, pilgrimages, and the invocation of saints. Where the dispute was more focused, it often related to the question of authority, dealing with scripture, tradition, and the papacy. But the question of the nature of God's grace had also long been involved in this controversy, and quite early in the English Protestant theological literature it had become an established point that Catholic theology was Pelagian in its doctrine of grace,[191] an assertion that became a common refrain in much of the spiritual and theological writing of English Protestants.[192]

By about 1590, both the quantity and the length of attacks against Rome increased, and the doctrines related to grace became more prominent. Many factors help to account for these trends. By that time, the influx of Jesuits and Seminarists had begun to cause considerable alarm. Rome was no longer something to be routinely attacked in passing, but required a full counterattack. Furthermore, the papacy was no longer the easy target it had been earlier in the Reformation: now revitalized, it was less vulnerable to attack over abuses, and Protestant polemic accordingly took a more theological cast. This tendency also resulted from the "scholasticizing" of Protestant thought, as a reinvigorated Catholic enemy called forth a more precise and finely nuanced Protestant theology. Conversely, such dispute had probably been a significant factor in the development of Protestant scholasticism in the first place. Other factors particular to the English situation also contributed to the many Protestant attacks upon Rome after 1590. For one, the threat of Puritan Nonconformity seemed to decline in the early years of the reign of James, and disputes related to Nonconformity waned. As documented by Nicholas Tyacke, "From 1611 until 1618 no work directed specifically against Puritanism, either in its nonconformist or presbyterian guises, is recorded in the Stationers' Register as being licensed for the press." Additionally, by 1611 the strongly Calvinist George Abbot presided over the church as archbishop of Canterbury, and this encouraged refutation of the papal opponents of the English church.[193]

However explained, English Protestants eagerly vied for the honor of refuting Rome. John Rainolds, a major theologian at Oxford, disputed the questions of church and scripture with Catholic opponents, but his arguments included reference to the differences over grace. At Cambridge, William Fulke, Puritan activist and master of Pembroke from

1578 until his death in 1589, joined Whitaker and Perkins in the task of refuting Rome. Both Fulke and Whitaker disputed the Catholics primarily over the authority of scripture, but neither ignored the subject of grace. Perkins concentrated more strongly on the question of grace in his anti-Roman writings. A major writer against Rome, greatly reputed for his learning, was Andrew Willet, who once remarked that he wished Protestants would stop arguing with one another and concentrate on the common enemy. Willet's *Synopsis Papismi*, published in 1592, devoted major attention in its 626 pages to the theology of grace and, against Catholicism, provided an uncompromising version of the scholastic theology of predestinating grace. A similar emphasis on the theology of grace appeared in *The Survey of Popery* (1596) by Thomas Bell, a former Seminarist, in the anti-Roman writings of William Barlow, bishop of Lincoln after 1605, and in the numerous books of other lesser practitioners of the polemic art. Robert Abbot, brother of the archbishop of Canterbury and himself eventually a bishop, was particularly prominent in the assault against Rome; something over one-half of the twelve hundred pages of his *Defence of the Reformed Catholicke* dealt with topics related to grace. Some conformists notorious as opponents of the Puritans joined the fray against Rome most enthusiastically. For example, Matthew Sutcliffe passed beyond theological discussion to the wildest kind of invective: "Popery in many points is more absurde and abominable, than the doctrine of Mahomet."[194]

The main themes of this argument with Rome respecting God's grace were the same elements of the Protestant doctrine of grace already examined as the theology of the English Reformation. But the needs of theological controversy gave them a particular shape, as, against Catholicism, it was insisted that justification was an imputed, not an inherent righteousness, that faith involved some assurance of salvation, and that salvation was by the free favor of God's grace, with no respect to human merit, the reliance on merit being seen as the very essence of popish falsehood.[195] Bishop Barlow pointed out, for example, that in Catholic theology grace was an inherent righteousness, not the free favor of God, thus "annihiliating" faith "by merite of worke." Nor is there "hope" in Roman theology either, for it is taken away "by doubtfulness of salvation."[196] Thomas Bell believed that papists "dishonour God, while they seek to establish their owne righteousnesse." Accordingly, added Anthony Wotton, "Our Papists, that are sett upon magnifying themselves, more than glorifying God, cannot abide to heare of any imperfection in their workes, which may impeach or impaire the merite of them." "No marvaile" continued Willet, that Catholics "doubt of their salvation, because their confidence is built upon their workes."[197]

Predestination in Protestant anti-Roman Polemic was therefore used emphatically to assert *sola gratia* and often appeared along with the assertion that the will was in total bondage to sin, without freedom to choose the good, prior to grace. If anyone was to be saved, it must be through the grace of God irresistibly and effectually calling those whom God had predestined to life. Not otherwise can the grace of God in salvation be truly vindicated against Roman "works-righteousness." Specifically, then, Protestant polemicists declared that man has no free will to choose the good,[198] and that predestination can in no manner depend upon foreseen merit. Thus Josias Nicholls argued that according to Roman theology "free will is made author of some things and God onely foreknoweth it"; by this error, he continued, they "make not God the cause of causes," but picture his "eternal counsel" as "determined according to works foreseene." Against such a Catholic view (real or supposed), Anthony Wotton replied that without God's grace no one has power "to do anything acceptable unto God, or to procure this grace to himselfe, or to receave it when it is offered." Robert Abbot used the doctrine of a limited, effectual atonement to the same purpose: Christ is a savior, he argued, "by saving us immediatelie himselfe, not by giving us power to save ourselves." Andrew Willet developed the doctrine of predestination at great length to counter any thought of human cooperation with grace, claiming that "our election is a worke of Gods meere mercie: there then is no respect at all to be had to our workes, for then were it not of Gods meere and sole mercie."[199] Roman Catholic controversialists were willing to see the issues in these terms of the doctrine of grace and frequently stressed free will as against predestination.[200] A recent investigator of the period comments, "It is not too much to say that for many people in the early seventeenth century the basic issue as between Protestantism and Catholicism was that of divine determinism versus human free will."[201]

The Protestant polemic against Roman Catholicism concerning grace was most frequently and easily summed up, as it had been earlier in English Protestant thought, in the formula that "popery" equaled Pelagianism. Thus William Attersol declared that "the Church of Rome" maintained "the ragges & reliques of the old Pelagians, & refuse [sic] to have the grace of God freely bestowed upon them." For Matthew Sutcliffe, the "papists" agree with the Pelagians in being "the enemies of Gods grace."[202] This was a constant refrain throughout the Elizabethan period and beyond. Simple identification of Catholicism and Pelagianism was relevant for the future because even as it was being reaffirmed, a party of theologians within the Church of England were abandoning Calvinism for a theology that gave greater scope to human freedom and that, if it did not altogether deny predestination, certainly tended to minimize it. Such a theological turn would inevitably appear to strict predestinarians as not only Pelagian but also smacking of Catholicism. For if "popery" was Pelagianism, then Pelagianism was also "popery," and to Puritan and conformist alike, those in the Church of England who seemed to be wavering on the Reformed theology of grace were understood to be betraying the essential Protestant character of the English Reformation settlement. The strength of this perception must be recognized in order to understand the fury involved in the religio-political issues of the decades after 1620.

Rumblings of Opposition to the Predestinarian Theology of Grace

Even as the Reformed theology of grace was undergoing scholastic solidification late in the Elizabethan period, theological assertions that called in question some of its elements were beginning to be made. It has already been demonstrated that there was little overt opposition to the predestinarian theology of grace in the early years of Elizabeth's reign, apart from the obscure "Pelagians" and freewillers whom Veron, Crowley, and others refuted. But such opponents of Reformed theology as these were located on the "left" of the Church of England, being mainly Lollardlike "folk" radicals whose protests against the old religion took a more extreme form than adoption of Swiss theology. There was at most a possible lack of enthusiasm for the doctrine of unconditional predestination among some leaders of the Elizabethan Church of England, including perhaps Archbishop Matthew Parker.[203]

Later in the reign of Elizabeth, some persons of standing in the Church of England began to question the Reformed orthodoxy of grace, principally by the denial of unconditional predestination. One of the first incidents revealing this change concerned Antonio de Corro, a Spanish monk who converted to Protestanism, fled to France in 1558, and then made his way to England. He was for a while pastor to exiled Spanish Protestants in London and reader at the Temple and lecturer in divinity at Oxford. At the Temple he was criticized by the master, Richard Alvey, a former Marian exile, for teaching "not wisely on predestination."[204] At Oxford, John Rainolds complained to the vice-chancellor that he held serious errors concerning justification and predestination.[205] In one of his writings dealing with such questions, Corro stated that God wished the salvation of all and spoke ambiguously on the question of whether predestination depended upon foreseen faith. Generally, however, his writings bear the marks of an independent and humanistically inclined approach that treated biblical texts in a devout and straightforward manner with little concern for the standardized categories of Reformed theology, though such categories are by no means absent and salvation by grace is frequently affirmed. It could be described as an "Erasmian" approach and as such was not uncharacteristic of other Spanish exiles.[206]

A more dramatic incident of overt opposition to the doctrine of predestination as held in the Church of England occurred in the 27 October 1584 sermon of Samuel Harsnett at Paul's Cross. Harsnett, eventually to be a leader at Cambridge and then archbishop of York, preached on Ezekiel 33:11, "I delight not in the death of the wicked," declaring, "There is a conceit in the world (beloved) speakes little better of our gracious God, then this: and that is, that God should designe many thousands of soules to Hell before they were, not in eye to their faults, but to his own absolute will and power, and to get him glory in their damnation. This opinion is growne huge and monstrous (like a Goliath) and men doe shake and tremble at it; yet never a man reacheth to David's sling to cast it downe."[207] Harsnett did reach for David's sling, however, and although he failed to appreciate the argument of Reformed theology that reprobation could be both of God's absolute power and for the sins of the reprobate, he accused the predestinarians of making God the author of sin, denying human liberty, and perverting scripture. Positively, Harsnett claimed that God wished all to be saved, that none are damned except those who refuse God's grace, and that God sent his son to die not just for the elect but to offer saving grace to all.[208] For this breach of the regnant teaching, he was commanded by John Whitgift, the archbishop of Canterbury, to preach no more on such subjects.[209]

The main incidents of opposition to the predestinarian theology of grace in the later Elizabethan period occurred in connection with William Barrett and Peter Baro and were the occasion for the drafting of the Lambeth Articles.[210] In a sermon to the University of Cambridge preached in April 1595, William Barrett announced that there was no certain assurance given by faith and that perseverance in grace was dependent upon the effort of the individual, accompanying these conclusions "with most bitter railing upon those worthy men Calvin, Peter Martyr, Beza, Zanchius, and others, to the great offence of the godly." The university leaders were outraged by this denial of that doctrine "which hath been always in our memories both here and elsewhere, taught, professed and continued, and never openly impugned amongst us"[211] and compelled Barrett publicly to recant his opinion, but this did not bring quiet. Not only did Barrett appeal to the archbishop, but Whitgift himself had some misgivings about the proceedings against Barrett and, even though agreeing with Barrett's opponents that the latter should not have attacked worthy divines like Calvin and that one may have assurance of salvation, he felt the recantation imposed upon Barrett had gone too far. Heartened, Barrett renounced his recantation, but eventually Whitgift lost patience, concluding that "Barrett had erred in divers points . . . some of his opinions being indeed popish."[212] To Whitgift, the views of Barrett's opponents were those approved by the Church of England, and so it was determined that Barrett must again recant. Within a few years, Barrett had gone abroad where he defected to Roman Catholicism.

From this turmoil came the Lambeth Articles, which grew out of discussions at the archepiscopal palace between Whitgift, the Cambridge theologian William Whitaker, and others. The final articles, approved on 20 November 1595, powerfully set forth the predestinarian theology of grace, making clear that election is simply by the will of God, without any reference to foreseen good works, and that the elect, who cannot fall away, can have "full assurance" of their salvation. The reprobate, the Lambeth Articles proclaimed, are condemned on account of their sins and "are not drawn by the Father to come to the Son."[213] Although in the final version, the description of reprobation from the first draft of the articles drawn up by Whitaker was somewhat mollified, the Reformed character of the final articles is obvious enough.[214] Their official standing was that of a statement of correct teaching for the University of Cambridge, promulgated by the archbishop of Canterbury. The other Archbishop, Matthew Hutton, expressed to Whitgift his strong assent to the articles.[215]

The next stage in the Cambridge dispute centered on Peter Baro, Lady

Margaret professor of divinity at the university. A Frenchman ordained at Geneva by Calvin in 1560, Baro had come to England in 1572 and taken up residence at Cambridge. Earlier suspicion concerning his theological soundness was revived by the Barrett incident because Barrett was considered his disciple.[216] In an earlier Cambridge discussion of the problem of reconciling human freedom and God's decrees, Baro had referred to Protestant differences on the subject and had wondered whether any satisfactory answer could be found.[217] In the wake of the issuance of the Lambeth Articles, Baro declared in a sermon that God only reprobated those who rejected his grace and that Christ died for all, not just the elect. A posthumous publication makes it evident that Baro rejected the views of the scholastic Reformed divines on predestination.[218] Baro was not reelected to his professorship in 1596 and retired to London, where he died a few years later.

Echoes of these Cambridge disputes continued for some time, and it was apparent that a party was emerging in the Church of England that found little that was objectionable in the claims of Baro and Barrett. Those at Cambridge who sympathized with Baro included John Overall, who succeeded Whitaker as Regius professor of divinity, Lancelot Andrewes, successor of Fulke as master of Pembroke, and Samuel Harsnett, who followed Andrewes at Pembroke in 1605 when the latter was elevated to the episcopate.[219] Andrewes had long cautioned reticence about predestination, Harsnett, as mentioned above, had publicly attacked the decree of reprobation, and Overall had several times been complained of for teaching a universal atonement.[220]

It was inevitable that the shadow of the Arminian conflict in the Netherlands should be cast over these discussions. Overall later opined that the Church of England should follow a middle course between the two Dutch parties,[221] but Richard Thompson, considered a disciple of Overall,[222] was nicknamed "Dutch" Thompson for his Arminian proclivities, and his Calvinist enemies said that "he was a man of most debauched conversation, and confirmed himself in his debauchedness, by his Arminianism."[223] Thompson affirmed that Christ died not for the elect only and was answered by the bishop of Salisbury, Robert Abbot.[224] John Richardson, master of Trinity and longtime Regius professor of divinity after his election in 1607, was another reputed Arminian sympathizer, for which he was "publickly reproach'd in St. Marie's Pulpit in his own University, by the name of a Fat-bellied Arminian."[225]

At Oxford University as in Cambridge, staunch predestinarians found their hegemony challenged. Prominent among them were John Rainolds, who spoke for the Puritans at the Hampton Court Conference with King James I, Henry Airay, head of Queens College until 1616, and John Prideaux, rector of Exeter College and Regius professor in the university, where he succeeded two earlier staunch predestinarians, Thomas Holland and Robert Abbot. John Buckeridge, the tutor of William Laud at St. John's, sympathized with the antipredestinarians, and in 1611 his protégé William Laud became head of that college and gathered a group around him, including William Juxon and Richard Baylie, that was unfriendly to the prevailing Reformed theology of grace. As Mark Curtis notes, the disputes of 1595 "implanted in the English Universities the seeds of a theological system which came to rival orthodox Calvinism."[226]

Richard Bancroft, Whitgift's successor as archbishop of Canterbury in 1604, had affinities with this antipredestinarian party. Although he never explicitly rejected predestination, he was hysterically anti-Puritan and at the Hampton Court Conference advised care in the discussion of predestination lest there be too much presumptuous certainty about election. In the revised canon law of his archepiscopate there appeared a warning against preaching too forwardly on "the deepe points" of predestination and reprobation.[227] But, as will be discussed in chapter 3, the newer generation of supporters of such views went considerably farther in their rejection of the predestinarian theology of grace than did the generation of Andrewes, Overall, and Bancroft.

Alarm about these doctrinal innovations was felt by defenders of the hitherto regnant theology. Whitaker, in a sermon just before his death, sounded it,[228] as did Perkins and Some by their defensive works concerning the disputed points,[229] and Andrew Willet.[230] Hugh Ince, identifying himself as "preacher of the word of God," as early as 1598 worried about the denial of predestination because to do so struck at "the maine grounds of our Religion."[231] Archbishop of York Hutton, staunchest of predestinarians, sent a treatise to Whitgift to further clarify the subject.[232]

Puritan nervousness about this issue is especially evident from the desire of the Puritan spokesmen at Hampton Court to have the Lambeth Articles appended to the Thirty-nine Articles as part of the doctrine to be subscribed by the clergy of the church. When this suggestion was made, the king did not at first know what the articles were,

but when it was informed his majesty, that by reason of some controversies, arising in Cambridge, about certain points of divinity, my lords grace assembled some divines of especial note, to set down their opinions, which they drew into nine assertions, and so sent them to the university for the appeasing of those quarrels; then his majesty answered; first that when such questions arise among scholars, the quietest proceeding were, to determine them in the universities, and not to stuff the book with all conclusions theological.[233]

At the same conference, John Rainolds of Oxford suggested that article sixteen of the Thirty-nine Articles be amended to state explicitly that one may "neither totally nor finally" fall from grace, but both Overall and Bancroft objected that this might lead to dangerous presumption, and the king agreed.[234]

Anxiety over these issues continued. William Sclater, a fellow of King's, Cambridge, preached at Paul's Cross on 17 September 1609 in vindication of the biblical basis of the decree of reprobation, and Samuel Gardiner in a sermon the next year warned that if election were denied, the whole foundation of faith would be destroyed. The new preface to the 1613 republication of a work by Perkins commented that it was now quite needful to study predestination because it was being impugned "as a frivolous and forged invention of mans braine."[235] In a sermon of 1614, Miles Mosse expounded the Reformed theology of justification, election, and assurance and then proclaimed ominously that those who "secretly whisper otherwise, doe greatly wrong our church" and "jumpe close with the Papists against us." And Henry Airay, writing in 1618, noted that all English Protestants agreed in essentials, differing only in some ceremonies, but nonetheless cried out with alarm at the "Cockatrice egges" of Pelagian error being presently hatched in the Church of England, mentioning free will, universal grace, and "other like damnable errours."[236]

Thus there emerged a new theological spirit and a strain of opposition to the predestinarian theology of grace as it had come to be expressed in a piety of assurance and a scholastic Reformed system. How should the appearance of this new outlook be interpreted? It has commonly been taken for granted, particularly within the Anglican tradition, that a normative Anglicanism, moderate and "middle way" and retaining many "catholic" characteristics, persisted as the basic "Anglican" substratum through the vicissitudes of the English Reformation. Temporarily eclipsed by the Protestant extremism of the reign of Edward VI or the Calvinist veneer of the Elizabethan period, according to this view, it eventually resurfaced and became established as "classical" Anglicanism. Even

H. C. Porter's account of the controversies leading up to the Lambeth Articles interprets them as the "rear-guard" action of a temporarily ascendant Calvinism and assumes that Cranmer, Jewel, and even Bradford represented an Anglican tradition on matters like predestination that was distinct from the "Calvinists."[237] The basic problem with this approach is that it begs the most important question, assuming the existence of a clear-cut entity identifiable as "Anglicanism," as opposed to such other clear-cut entities as "Puritanism," whereas the theological literature might be understood to suggest that Anglicanism did not, through most of the sixteenth century, designate a fixed entity at all, but rather a shifting phenomenon of state-sponsored religious reform and establishment, gradually defining itself only in relation to alternative approaches that were themselves also in process of change. And in the Elizabethan period, it is possible to consider that Puritanism took shape earlier than "Anglicanism" and that Anglicanism arose as a defensive response to the Puritan challenge. Indeed, Puritanism has also often been misunderstood in this way, by the assumption that it had a completely defined shape from its first appearance to its legacy in the various dissenting denominations. Patrick Collinson has noted: "On the issue of definition and relationship, Puritanism is too often treated in contradistinction to Anglicanism or conformism as Nonconformity and minority opposition, which is to say that it is defined negatively, with respect to supposed norms, and peripherally, in relation to a supposed center." Instead, Collinson continues, it is possible "to consider Puritanism as embodying the mainstream of English Protestantism" in a situation in which "Anglicanism was equally emergent."[238] But if the notion of longstanding and defined Anglicanism is abandoned, how is the appearance of the new theological spirit of Overall, Andrewes, and others such as Richard Hooker to be accounted for? It might be suggested that a number of elements played some role in the eventual and gradual shaping of something distinctly "Anglican" in the theology of grace in the last part of the Elizabethan era: a continuing humanist strain, a residual and revived Lutheran influence, the Erastianism of the established church reacting to Nonconformist pressures and gaining appreciation of its own inherited fabric, and the conservatism and perhaps even indifference of the ordinary folk.

Among some Anglicans, continuing humanist elements and impulses in English theology were a factor in the emergence of a theology of grace that differed from the Calvinist theology of grace as it had developed in the Elizabethan period. Erasmian humanism, in stressing a simple piety relying on Christ and the gospels, did not need a doctrine of predestination, and of course Erasmus had disagreed with Luther over the bondage of the will. But although much Erasmian and humanist influence continued in the Protestant Reformation, it was seldom clear and distinct in bequeathing an understanding of grace different from that of the Protestant mainstream. After all, Reformers such as Zwingli and Calvin, who taught predestination, represented one aspect of the legacy of humanism in the Reformation. Perhaps Bibliander at Zurich, philologist and biblical scholar, who objected to the extreme predestinarian formulas of Zanchi, represented the continuation of a more purely Erasmian and humanist strain in Protestanism. In the second half of the sixteenth century, humanist impulses were evident among scholars who continued a devout exegetical and philological biblical study with increasing emphasis on patristic study, and among some of the more radical "free spirits" of the Reformation, often and typically exiles from southern Europe.[239] These impulses frequently came together in the same individual. Although it has often been argued that the English Reformation was a bearer of humanist impulses in a distinct fashion, in the Elizabethan period wandering exile divines apparently were the leading bearers of this humanist strain in England. Among these were Antonio de Corro, with his devout exposition of scripture and Erasmian moderation in the doctrine of grace, and Peter Baro, whose Erasmian moderation on the decrees of God he himself rooted in the theology of the ancient fathers. To them may be added Francesco Pucci, Italian exile and acquaintance of Corro at Oxford, who was suspected of Pelagianism, and Hadrian Saravia, half Spanish, half Flemish, who came to England in 1587 and as a chaplain to Whitgift counseled moderation in the Barrett affair, or considerably later, Isaac Casaubon, befriended by Lancelot Andrewes. Jacobus Arminius himself, Carl Bangs has argued, represented a resurfacing of such moderation in contrast to Reformed scholasticism in the Netherlands, and Brian Armstrong has seen the same continuing humanist strain in the moderate Calvinism of Moise Amyraut later in France.[240] This more humanist approach to the doctrine of grace was often accompanied by a great interest in the ancient church fathers and was abetted by an increasingly able scholarship concerning them.[241] A more moderate theology of grace than that enshrined in Reformed scholasticism, then, arose in the Church of England at the end of the sixteenth century, partly under revived humanist impulses emanating from the Continent and partly from a renewed patristic interest. This view, however, was not distinctly

English but represented English participation in a general movement of international Protestantism, with parallels in Dutch Arminianism and elsewhere.

Lutheran influences had been very important in the earliest English Reformation, but the English reformers had gradually come more under the influence of the Swiss Reformation, whose doctrines on the Eucharist and predestinating grace they followed. But among religious conservatives in the Elizabethan establishment, there continued to be a strain of what might be called "residual Lutheranism." Bishop Cheyney had been deposed for his Lutheran view of the Eucharist, but there may have been other conservative churchmen who quietly preferred the more traditional Lutheran approach. By the end of the Elizabethan period, a group of English theological writers led by bishop Thomas Bilson were showing a clear preference for the Lutheran rather than the Calvinist interpretation of Christ's descent into hell,[242] and Barrett's point that one could fall from grace was acceptable to Lutheran orthodoxy, as was moderation on predestination. Baro corresponded with the Danish Lutheran theologian Niels Hemmingius and claimed his support for the view that predestination was based on God's foreknowledge.[243] Samuel Ward in his diary referred to the Cambridge disputes as being over "Lutheranism."[244] Nor is it surprising that as time went on leaders in the Church of England would feel an affinity for Lutheranism, which like the English church was Erastian in its governance and held matters of vestments, ceremonies, and ritual to be "adiaphora," as did conformist opponents of the Puritans.[245] Reference to Lutheran theologians, especially to Melancthon, became common among Anglican authors in the next century.

A humanist strain and residual and revived Lutheranism could be sources for an understanding of grace different from that of Reformed piety and theology, but what would cause leaders of the Church of England to turn to another theological viewpoint? One reason must be sought in the Erastianism of the Church of England and the conflict with Nonconformity. A basic fact about the English Reformation was that it began as an act of state, and religious and theological changes often occurred in the context of a church first changed for other reasons. Henry had attempted a very personal *via media*, and though that middle way was shown in the next reigns to be an unstable compromise, the only real possibilities being either Protestantism or Roman Catholicism, his daughter Elizabeth seems to have preferred or at least accepted a moderate Protestantism. Thus the Protestant Church of England retained in its government and fabric such characteristics that were usually swept away in the Continental Reformation as episcopacy, ecclesiastical courts, cathedral chapters, archdeaconries, some of the traditional vestments, and a bit more ritual and ceremony than usual in Continental Protestantism.[246] Having done so, the Church of England required persons to staff and defend this establishment, and though many of those called upon were hardly distinguishable at first from their Nonconformist opponents and defended practices they thought were only temporary or at least inessential, the habits of conformity and Nonconformity gradually drove a wedge between those who had earlier shared much. And where possible, Queen Elizabeth relied more and more upon moderate Protestants who had not shared the exile experience, such as Matthew Parker and later John Whitgift, both of whom had less enthusiasm for Reformed theology than did such other Anglican leaders as Sandys, Jewel, or Grindal. What has sometimes hitherto been regarded as a distinctly Anglican viewpoint may have been no more than the compliance of Erastian churchmen with Tudor despotism. Such Anglicanism began as little more than the defense of the crown's ecclesiastical policy by career clergy.

In any case, the controversies over vestments and the adoption of a "more godly" discipline drove a wedge between conformist and Nonconformist: the latter took up positions more uncompromising than those even of their Continental mentors, and the former came in time to value what they were defending more than they originally had. Certainly a later generation of spokesmen for the status quo in the church—Whitgift, Bancroft, and Andrewes, for example—seemed to place a more positive value on the liturgy and episcopacy they were upholding than did earlier defenders of this outer dress of the Church of England. The government, ritual, and fabric originally kept for no better reason than monarchical conservatism were now valued by these churchmen for their own sake, and it ought not to be surprising that those who so valued these aspects would cast about for a theology that might distinguish them from their iconoclastic opponents while allowing greater scope for the appreciation of such things. If such were the case, it would be logical to turn in the direction of more moderate humanist and Lutheran strains within Protestantism. Probably also a reverse mechanism was at work: what the Puritan Nonconformists questioned, their opponents praised, thus driving both sides to take stands more distant from each other than originally. Not that Calvinism and Reformed theology were at once abandoned in the English church, but only that conformists might now tend to be more moderate in their espousal of Calvinist positions, more open to humanist and patristic interests, and less afraid of Lutheran error.[247]

Perhaps another factor in the complex that led to Anglicanism can be discovered by examining the question of a popular basis for Anglicanism. Puritan preachers found the ordinary Englishman a recalcitrant subject for gospel tutelage, and there is plenty of evidence to suggest that Puritanism and even Protestantism grew very slowly in many areas of England. Although Puritan preachers built up an enthusiastic following of godly laity, a great number of the common folk probably resisted their militant Protestantism and found comfort in many of the old Catholic religious practices and attitudes that were being swept away. Puritans complained that among the "common sort" or the "ignoranter sort" nostalgia for the old religion and a sort of common-sense resistance to the precise theological formulas of Protestant preachers were rife.[248] Complaints about "church-papists," persons who went to the services of the parish church but held opinions closer to the old church, were common. Such people, scattered throughout the parishes of the Church of England, and probably predominant in many, would have been more comfortable and less threatened with a more moderate Protestantism and could have exerted pressures upon those who served them as pastors. But possibly equally influential could have been unreformed and unreconstructed local clergy, often undereducated, often left over from earlier reigns (including that of Mary!), and relatively uninformed about the new religious order, perhaps even explicitly resistant to it, though not sufficiently in opposition to abandon the church for recusancy.[249]

In any case, there is some evidence that members of this new Anglican school of theology were, like the Puritans, concerned with pastoral questions and, like them, introduced theological modifications partly dictated by pastoral need. John Overall, for example, found members of his parish at Epping distressed because "they could not be persuaded that Christ died for them," a result presumably of the preaching of election and limited atonement. In response, Overall preached a sermon teaching that Christ died for all.[250] Similarly, John Downe in 1601 found a "godly Matron" of Bristol afflicted, feeling she lacked faith because she did not have assurance of salvation, and when he told her that was not necessary, she responded that "hitherto I have been taught, Faith is no other than Assurance." Downe therefore preached in Bristol on the subject and declared that assurance is distinct and follows faith. A conformist, Downe also defended kneeling at communion.[251] Pastoral concerns, then, could have been in the minds of those in the Church of England who resisted some of the more extreme formulas of piety and theology concerning grace.

This emerging "Anglican" school of theology needs more precise definition. John Overall and Lancelot Andrewes were out of step with the strict and scholastic predestinarianism of the Cambridge theologians Some, Perkins, and Whitaker in the combat of the latter with Baro and Barrett. But Richard Hooker must be accounted the outstanding theologian among this group. These three defenders of the established religion against Puritan dissenters can be distinguished from their opponents not by any substantial abandonment of Reformed theology but by certain subtle but in the long run important matters of tone and emphasis. A different tone can be sensed in their preaching, which was partly a matter of style, partly a failure to stress those themes of the *ordo salutis* that so engaged Puritan preachers, and partly a residual traditionalism. In their greater emphasis upon sacramental piety, greater reliance upon patristic sources, and defense of ritual and tradition there breathes a different spirit from what had previously prevailed in the Church of England among both conformists and Nonconformists. But their specific theological formulations continued to move within the general arena of Protestant and even Reformed theology, with no wavering on the Protestant position of justification by faith or in their emphatic rejection of Roman Catholicism, contrary to attempts to portray their theology as somehow more "catholic" than Protestant.[252]

Examination of their views on predestination will provide greater precision concerning where these "Anglican" thinkers stood with respect to the theology of grace. Andrewes was very reticent to express his views on the subject, but he did comment on predestination in connection with the censure of the views of Barrett. Andrewes found predestination too great a mystery to be disputed about; the reprobate, he wanted it carefully stated, were so on account of their sins and not merely by the divine decree.[253] Overall dealt with predestination by making a distinction between the "particular absolute decree" of God and God's "general and conditional will" by which he set forth the promise of grace to all. Thus Christ may be said to have died for all, though this grace offered to all is resisted by some, whereas by his particular decree God gives effective grace to some, for whom alone the death of Christ is efficacious.[254]

But of this trio, Richard Hooker had the most to say about predestinating grace. After he became master of the Temple in 1585 he ran afoul of the militant Puritan Walter Travers, who found Hooker's preaching about assurance and predestination unsound. Hooker's views, Travers proclaimed, smacked too much of "that wherewith Corranus [Antonio de Corro] sometime troubled this Church." He added that it was an error on Hooker's part to regard the assurance of faith as lesser than the assurance gained of physical things by the senses,[255] surely an unduly picayune point on the part of Travers!

In his classic *Of the Laws of Ecclesiastical Polity*, Hooker treated predestination at length. He was uncomfortable with any formulation that claimed that the will of God had no reason for what it chose beyond the mere act of willing itself, preferring the assumption that God wills in accordance with his own wise counsel and reasons even if these are unknown to humans. Again, even though acknowledging that some have been chosen for eternal life while others are "vessels of wrath to whom God will never extend mercy," Hooker argued that prayers for the salvation of all should be offered. Hooker also maintained that election was in Christ and that therefore one was not truly included among the redeemed until actually incorporated into Christ by adoption, a formula consonant with Reformed theology. Hooker regarded this point as an important one, for some, he thought, relied too much on "the bare conceit of that eternal election" without reference to the means subordinate to it, which for Hooker included sacramental incorporation into Christ.[256] In manuscript fragments not published until the nineteenth century, Hooker showed himself much concerned with the problem of reconciling divine prescience and predestination with human freedom. He also agreed with Overall in distinguishing two wills in God, one more general and one more particular, a discussion that seems occasioned by the need to interpret the Lambeth Articles.[257] In sum, Hooker's departures from scholastic predestinarian Calvinism were more significant in tone than they were in departing from prevailing formulations.[258]

Overall, Andrewes, Hooker, and their allies clearly were the first representatives of a more distinctly Anglican theology that in the next generation of "Laudians" was to carry the criticism of elements of the Reformed theology of grace much farther. Nonetheless, these three English theologians mainly sought only to mollify some of the harsher aspects and expressions of predestinarian theology and by no means carried out a wholesale rejection of Calvinism. Another of their number, the poet and renowned preacher John Donne, who spoke similarly about the divine will, affirmed that Calvin was "A later Divine, worthy to be compared to the Ancients, for the exposition of Scriptures."[259] The viewpoint of Andrewes, Overall, and Hooker on grace probably appears more important by hindsight than it would have at the time, given that the theological complexion of the English church changed dramatically after 1620.

Chapter 3 ❖ The Arminian Controversies, 1610–1650

The predestinarian theology of grace that took root in England early in the Reformation was further developed in the Elizabethan period by preachers and spiritual writers, scholastic theologians, and anti-Roman polemicists. Broadly accepted by the Church of England as a whole, this theology was espoused with special enthusiasm by advanced Protestants who were dissatisfied with the extent of reform in the English church. But clear signs of unhappiness with the prevailing Calvinist theology appeared at the very end of the Elizabethan period among the supporters of the episcopal leadership of the established church. In its rejection of the harsher aspects of predestinarian theology, this counter-current against the predominant theological fashion paralleled other movements of Protestant reaction against strict Calvinism, most notably that of the Dutch Arminians. These breaches in the Reformed theology of predestinarian grace at the end of the Elizabethan age were in the half-century after the death of Richard Hooker in 1600 to be greatly widened by the successive assaults of those who from the analogy of the Dutch conflict were dubbed "Arminians." A series of stages in this assault and the corresponding responses constituted several different Arminian controversies: first, there was the English participation in the international Reformed condemnation of the Dutch Arminians, accompanied by strictures against the English breed; there followed a reversal of this official condemnation of Arminianism as King Charles I and the churchman William Laud patronized the opponents of predestinarian theology; then that, too, was reversed with the meeting of the Long Parliament and the defeat of the king's ecclesiastical policy, only to be followed in the 1640s by a further Arminian dispute between Calvinists and their radical sectarian opponents. Different parts of the story of the rise of the English Arminians have been told before,[1] though only recently has the great impact of the conflict on English life been rightfully assessed.[2] The focus here will be on tracing the ramifications of the dispute as they were disclosed mainly by the theological literature it produced.

English Reaction to a Dutch Conflict

Granted the predominance of the Reformed theology of grace in the English church at the time when the Arminian conflict raged in the Netherlands, it is not surprising that the most obvious English response was to join in the arraignment of those who assaulted predestination, a response in keeping with the outlook of Archbishop Abbot and the Scottish-educated king. In chapter 2 it was shown that alarm was caused by the rise of Arminianism at the beginning of the century, but this attitude became official in the actions of the king against the Dutch heretics.

The royal feeling against the Dutch Arminians first became apparent in the role played by James I in the affair of Conrad Vorstius. In 1610, Vorstius was invited to be Arminius's successor at the University of Leyden, but was soon dismissed by the government because of his reputation for unsound theology. The Arminians considered Vorstius to be their ally, and the Counter-Remonstrants sought the aid of the English king in preventing his appointment. Although earlier, both at the Hampton Court Conference and in some remarks he had made about the Dutch dispute, James I had revealed no great desire to emphasize predestination, he strongly approved the condemnation of Vorstius, who had been discredited also by suspicion of his Socinianism.[3] The king declared Vorstius to be a "wretched Heretique" who deserved burning, but the Dutch theologian's books were publicly burned at Paul's Cross and the two universities instead.[4] In his statement on Vorstius, the king added that he had intervened in the dispute because not only was the Netherlands aflame with heresy but it was beginning "to creep into the bowels of our owne Kingdom." He referred to the "corrupt seed which that enemie of God Arminius did sowe amongst you some few yeares ago," whose heresy he would himself have refuted but that it "was Our hard hap not to heare of this Arminius before he was dead." James also reviled Peter Bertius, one of Arminius's Dutch sympathizers who had earlier sent his *De Apostasia Sanctorum* to the archbishop of Canterbury as being consonant with English teaching, only to be excoriated by the monarch as the author of a book, "the title whereof onely, were enough to make it worthy the fire."[5] Additionally, the English king's appointee to the see of Canterbury, Archbishop Abbot, a staunch Calvinist, reported that James I was opposed to the view of the Arminian Grotius that one could fall totally from grace.[6]

And when in 1616 a fellow of Trinity, Cambridge, Edward Sympson, maintained in a sermon before the king that "the committing of any great sin doth extinguish Grace and Gods Spirit for the time in a man," he was forced to make a public recantation, even though the opinion sounds very much like the doctrine John Overall had explained before the king at Hampton Court.[7]

Soon King James I was urging the Dutch to call a synod to condemn Arminianism,[8] and when such a meeting convened at Dort in November, 1618, English delegates participated. The delegation sent by James I included George Carleton, bishop of Llandaff, Joseph Hall and John Davenant, soon to be bishops of Exeter and Salisbury, respectively, Samuel Ward, master of Sidney Sussex College, Cambridge, and Walter Balcanqual, a Scotsman. When Hall became ill and returned to England, he was replaced by Thomas Goad, one of Archbishop Abbot's chaplains. Of these six, the three who were or became bishops were Calvinists who continued to hold the positions taken at Dort after those positions had become unpopular. Ward was a follower of Perkins whose expression of alarm over heterodoxy at Cambridge was discussed earlier. Only Balcanqual lacked enthusiasm for the doctrinal decrees of Dort, though many years later Goad may have defected.[9]

The English delegates at Dort agreed that predestination was unconditional, that atonement was limited to the elect, and that grace was irresistible and perseverance final. A joint statement drawn up by the English divines and presented to the synod shows how thoroughly committed they were to the Reformed predestinarian theology of grace. As befits bearers of the English Reformed developments, their statement pressed the motif of the order of salvation as the subordinate means of carrying out the decree of election and discussed the problem of assurance at length, echoing many familiar themes of the spiritual writers.[10] Balcanqual, the first to express misgivings, later said that while approving the substance of the doctrinal articles they nonetheless gave advice concerning "some incommodious phrases."[11] Apparently, he objected to the harshness of the expression of limited atonement and reprobation. In one of the major debates of the synod, that between supralapsarians and infralapsarians, the English delegates took the latter, more moderate, position, although in the discussion the Dutch theologian Franciscus Gomarus noted that the Church of England in the persons of its theologians Perkins and Whitaker had taught the former position.[12] But the synod as a whole did not canonize the more extreme views, most of the delegates apparently being content with the formulation that predestination had as its subject humankind after the fall.

The Synod of Dort and the support its decisions received from the English king temporarily silenced the English anti-Calvinists and emboldened the predestinarians. King James I approved the use of "all legal means to put down the Arminians," comparing them to "the Pelagians of old."[13] Bishop Carleton, on returning from the Netherlands, found some "murmuring in corners" against the decisions of the synod, but was confident that the king would silence such dissent.[14]

Meanwhile, books refuting Arminianism poured from English presses. In a 1615 publication, John Yates, an Ipswich minister identified by Kenneth Shipps as the most prominent Puritan preacher of Norfolk, attacked Arminianism in a thoroughly scholastic work that reproduced much of what William Perkins had earlier written. Yates considered Arminius a grievous sinner who had derogated the divine majesty.[15] A posthumous book by Paul Baynes published in the same year the synod met charged Arminius with destroying predestinating grace by making it subsequent to foreseen faith.[16] That same year, there was published, under the authority of Archbishop Abbot and with a dedication to the king, an anti-Pelagian treatise by the medieval predestinarian Thomas Bradwardine, who, like the volume's sponsor, had been archbishop of Canterbury. Robert Abbot, brother of the archbishop and an Oxford theologian, died in 1618, leaving uncompleted a treatise against Arminianism. In 1620, an English translation of a work against Arminianism written by the Huguenot theologian Pierre Du Moulin appeared under the title of *The Anatomy of Arminianisme*. The patron of the translation was Sir Henry Mildmay, and it was an ardent defense of the Synod of Dort and an attack upon the Remonstrants. A few years later, Joseph Hall, one of the delegates to the synod, sought to obviate the influence of Arminianism in England by restating the five points of Dort in as mild a manner as possible, while remaining thoroughly predestinarian.[17] Many publications— sermons, biblical commentaries, theological compendiums, and polemical works against Rome—continued to assume the predestinarian theology of grace that was the opposite of Arminianism without necessarily addressing themselves to the explicit refutation of the Dutch heresy.[18]

The English pulpit, too, rang out against Arminian error, at home and abroad. One of the spiritual writers who was at least suspected for Nonconformity, Richard Crakanthorpe, preached his sermon on predestination, he claimed, to refute those who spoke or wrote against the doctrine of unconditional election. Griffith Williams, unlike Crakanthorpe an enemy of the Puritans who was made an Irish bishop in 1641, had a sermon printed in 1622 in which he assaulted the "Arminian broode" for following Pelagians and Lutherans (he mentions the Lutheran theologian Hemingius, to whom Baro had appealed) in falsely teaching both a universal atonement and an election based on foreseen faith. Humphrey Sydenham preached a sermon in that same year (published later) that referred with alarm to the revival of Pelagianism, blaming it on "a troope of Arminians" who have made "our election mutable"; these "new sprung Sectaries" resulted from the "mud and corruption" of those Lutherans who falsely held that Christ died for all. Sydenham, like Williams, was to be on the Royalist side in the civil wars. A sermon preached by Robert Harris in 1622 alluded to disputes over reprobation.[19]

The Arminian Controversy in England

But in spite of attacks and setbacks, English Arminianism was gradually gaining ground both in the two universities and in the episcopate. Despite his condemnation of the Dutch Arminians, James I advanced to the English episcopate churchmen who sympathized with the heretics he denounced, largely because they were the staunchest upholders of his prerogatives. Lancelot Andrewes entered the episcopate in 1605 and as bishop of Ely during the conflicts in the Netherlands was regarded by the Dutch Arminians as a sympathizer through whom they might mollify the king. Harsnett, controversial long before for his denial of reprobation, was made bishop of Norwich by James I. Buckeridge, one of the founders of Oxford anti-Calvinism, was also a Jacobean appointment to the episcopate, and John Howson, whom Robert Abbot at Oxford had censured for impugning the annotations of the *Geneva Bible*, was made bishop of Oxford in 1619.[20] Richard Neile, another Jacobean bishop, has been called "the most powerful member of this early Arminian leadership."[21] By the end of his reign, and in spite of his Calvinism, King James was coming to identify Puritanism with Calvinism and both with opposition to his prerogative. But it was with his son and successor Charles I, who had had no indoctrination in Calvinism as a youth similar to that of his father, that the royal favor swung decisively to the Arminians. The new king was in theological, liturgical, and political sympathy with these churchmen.[22] In the words of Tyacke, "King Charles became the architect of an Arminian revolution which had at most been dimly foreshadowed in the last year of his father's reign."[23] Under Charles, William Laud, bishop of London and eventually archbishop of Canterbury, became the architect of an "Arminian" church renewal in theology, liturgy, and administration that was to attempt a drastic alteration in the character of the Protestant Church of England. Thus a second phase of the Arminian controversy occurred: not the condemnation of foreign deniers of predestination and the ferreting out of their English sympathizers, but a great reversal in which the Arminian position became favored by church and monarch and was assaulted by predestinarians, who increasingly saw themselves as dissenters in the Church of England.

At the beginning of this phase of the Arminian controversy in England the chief *cause célèbre* was the case of Richard Montague, an anti-Puritan rector in Essex whom Charles I made bishop of Chichester in 1628. A book ostensibly written by Montague against Catholic missionaries active in his parish that sought to define the real differences between Rome and Canterbury was published in 1624. According to Tyacke, the book's passage through the censors was engineered by Bishop Neile and his allies[24] though it contained many departures from conventional English Protestant views. In it, Montague not only denied that the pope was Antichrist, but maintained that fallen man had sufficient free will to concur with God's assisting grace, that with such grace God's commandments could be kept, and that justification included good works. In addition, Montague denied that either unconditional election or the perseverance of the elect were teachings of the Church of England.[25] In a letter to the sympathetic John Cosin, he attributed such notions to the Puritans and claimed they opened the door for the Roman adversaries of the English church to "impute the frantick fitts and froth of every Puritan paroxysme to the received doctrine of our Church."[26] Opposed by Archbishop Abbot, Montague appealed to the king the next year with *Appello Caesarem* and was soon appointed a royal chaplain.

Meanwhile, a torrent of theological fury was unleashed against Montague. Two Ipswich ministers, John Yates, who had previously attacked Arminius in print, and Samuel Ward (not to be confused with his namesake who attended the Synod of Dort), supplied information against Montague to Parliament in 1625.[27] Yates entered the fray the next year in print, with an answer to Montague's *Appello Caesarem*. Henry Burton, soon to be a famous opponent of the bishops, also answered Montague in 1626, accusing him of overthrowing the gospel of free grace. Also in that same year, Bishop Carleton, a former delegate to Dort, published *An Examination of those Things Wherein the Author of the late Appeale holdeth the Doctrines of the Pelagians and Arminians, to be the Doctrines of the Church of England*, declaring that humanity faced two great menaces to body and soul, plague and Pelagianism, the latter identified with Montague's beliefs. England, Carleton added, must hold firmly to what she had learned from Martin Bucer and Peter Martyr and not falter in asserting unconditional election and the perseverance of the saints, neither of which had been denied by English Protestants until the appearance of Baro, Barrett, and Dutch Thompson at Cambridge. Another onslaught against Montague in that same year came from Daniel Featley, rector of Lambeth and former chaplain to Archbishop Abbot, entitled tellingly *Pelagius Redivivus*. In parallel columns, Featley outlined the views of Pelagius and Arminius to prove that the latter had "raked" the heresies of the former "out of the ashes"; another series of parallel columns evidenced the agreement of Montague and Arminius, enabling the completion of the syllogism that because Pelagianism is heresy and Arminius is a Pelagian, Montague's agreement with the Dutchman made him a heretic. For Featley, both of these make grace so general that it is no different from nature, and thus salvation is made a matter of human merit. Anthony Wotton's attack on Montague, still in 1626, stressed another ingredient in the mixture of the Essex rector's misbelief: that Montague's views were nothing less than "poynts of the Popish Faith" and their author a promoter of the interests of Rome. The last of the year's attacks on Montague came from the staunch parliamentarian and ally of John Pym, Francis Rous, whose *Testis Veritatis* consisted of testimonies taken from earlier theological writers to prove that the doctrine of the Church of England was Calvinistic. Finally, Puritan nervousness in that year of Montague's appeal is apparent from Ezekiel Culverwell's *A Briefe Answere to Certaine Objections against the Treatise of Faith*, in which that accomplished spiritual writer strongly affirmed that he followed Dort and abominated Arminius. The *Answere* resulted from criticism of the innocent Culverwell for seeming to speak too loosely in an earlier book of salvation being offered to all.[28]

The next year witnessed two more assaults upon Arminianism. One of these was by the lawyer William Prynne, no friend of Charles I, whose *The Perpetuity of a Regenerate Mans Estate* piled precedent upon precedent to prove that the Church of England was opposed to Arminian teaching. Greatly enlarged in subsequent editions, with the title changed to *Anti-Arminianisme*, Prynne's treatise amassed an astonishing number of citations from earlier writers showing that the views of Dort on predestination and perseverance were of long standing in English Protestantism. But Prynne did not rely wholly on precedent; he also summarized the various theological arguments in use against Arminianism to conclude that Arminianism denied grace, subordinated God to man, spoiled God of his glory, and baptized "the naturall power and freedome of mans will, with the very name of Grace." Prynne also excelled in the argument *ad hominem*, rounding off his theological conclusions with the judgment that Arminians, not relying on divine grace, live wickedly, being "generally the very proudest; the slothfulest, the most ambitious, envious, lascivious, voluptuous, vitious, and prophanest of our Clergie; making no conscience either to seeke Christ's glory, or to feed their flockes."[29]

A more reasoned but in some respects more extreme answer to Montague and the English Arminians was William Pemble's *A Plea for Grace*. Originally Oxford lectures, Pemble's arguments were posthumously made available in print, according to both an introductory epistle by Richard Capel and a preface by George Walker, in order to rebut the Arminians, "the wolves of this age," who join with the "Romish religion" in obscuring God's "powerfull worke of grace in the effectual calling, conversion, and regeneration of the elect."[30] Pemble's lucubrations following such introductions consisted of a very scholastic and quite extreme version of the Reformed predestinarian theology of grace. In conjunction with the usual Calvinistic assertions about predestination, Pemble reasoned that God "hates forever" the reprobate, that the justification of a sinner precedes the sinner's actual believing, and that the grace of sanctification is entirely supernatural, "without the concurrence of any abilities of our corrupted nature."[31]

Other printed responses to Arminianism suggest different ramifications of the debate on English religious life. Adam Harsnet, clearly to be classed as one of the spiritual writers, was distressed by the effect of the new Arminianism when he plaintively commented that "with too many (who follow the fashions of the world) grace is out of fashion." And John Doughty, who eventually sided with the Laudians, expressed what must have been the doubt and hesitancy of many when he reflected, in printed sermons, that among the numerous problems that were too mysterious for endless probing was the question of the decrees of God, about which both those who taught reprobation and those who upheld the Arminians err when they delve too nicely into the secrets of God.[32]

But the controversy over Montague was conducted not only in theological tomes; it also became an immediate ecclesiastical and political issue at the York House Conference of 1626. The story of this clash between Montague's opponents and supporters has been told before, but it needs examination in the context of the entire Arminian dispute. A group of Puritan lords, led by Brooke, Say, and the earl of Warwick, sought a conference with leading churchmen in order to press their attack upon Arminianism. Those who sympathized with Montague feared such a conference as a step in the direction of making the definitions of the Synod of Dort binding on the English Church.[33] Montague apparently feared such a development at the convocation of 1626.[34] Lancelot Andrewes reportedly cautioned against any challenge to Calvinism at that convocation because it would bring the wrath of the archbishop and many bishops down upon the Arminians.[35]

When the York House Conference finally convened on 11 February, Bishop Morton of Lichfield and the leading Puritan John Preston were pitted against Bishop Buckeridge and Francis White, the dean of Carlisle, with the duke of Buckingham presiding. Morton began by presenting seven charges against Montague's two books and their defenders, foremost among which were the accusations that Montague had departed from the Articles of the English church and overthrown the grace of Christ, opening the door for "popery." Buckingham, an erstwhile supporter of some Puritan leaders, including Preston, openly took Montague's side, and when he was about to dismiss the meeting because he felt Morton's charges had not been substantiated, Lord Say rose to object that "the chiefest matter" of the possibility of falling from grace and the establishment of the decrees of Dort in England had not yet been broached. Then Bishop Morton remarked that Montague's supporters would surely not defend anything so heinous as falling from grace, but Dean White rose to the challenge and said that if a justified man lived in great sin, he was fallen from grace; Morton replied that such a man had never been justified, and White responded with the case of David, which somewhat nonplussed Morton. At this point, Preston was called upon for the first time, and he asserted that though God's children may sin they do not cease thereby to be his children: "As a father cannot make an ill son to be none of his child, no more can God; if they be once His children . . . they must be his children for ever." Here it was demanded of Preston if a man living in great sin though he had been justified was not thereby "in the state of eternal guiltiness until he did forsake his sin?" Preston boldly answered with a simple "no." After some argument over baptism, Lord Say interposed that "All these matters would be quieted . . . if the Synod of Dort might be established here in England." White and Buckingham then spoke against the decrees of Dort, White insisting that Christ died for all men and concluding that "we of the Church of England be not put to borrow a new faith from any village in the Netherlands." Buckingham added, "We have nothing to do with that synod; it is all about the hidden and intricate points of predestination, which are not fit matters to trouble the people withal." At that, Bishop Morton cried out, "Our own articles speak of predestination; and it is a very comfortable doctrine to the elect people of God!"[36]

Montague attended a second meeting of the conference six days later. Now John Preston took a larger role in pressing the predestinarian position, arguing that unless election is unconditional it is no election at all, that election entails perseverance, and that the elect alone benefit from Christ's death.[37] But it was clear from both meetings that Charles I and his favorite, Buckingham, were solidly behind the Arminian faction and that the conference could not pressure the monarch into any steps against Montague and his friends.

Thus the attempt to silence the Arminian supporters of Montague through a conference failed, but opponents also availed themselves of the forum of Parliament. In doing so, they were resorting to a tactic long favored by the more Nonconformist Calvinists. In 1626 a subcommittee of Parliament had considered the errors of Montague. Reporting for this committee, John Pym claimed that Montague's Arminianism consisted of doctrines repugnant to the teaching of the Church of England and to parliamentary authority over the church and was similar to "popery."[38] But Parliament was dissolved before both houses had an opportunity to act on this report.

When the Parliament of 1629 met, one of the chief grievances was Arminianism. The attack upon it began in earnest in January 1629, with the speech of Francis Rous, who had earlier written against Montague. Rising in the House of Commons, Rous declared:

I desire first that it may be considered what new paintings are laid upon the old face of the whore of Babylon to make her seem more lovely, and to draw so many suitors to her. I desire that it may be considered how the see of Rome doth eat into our Religion and fret into the banks and walls of it, . . . I desire that we may consider the increase of Arminianism, an error that maketh the grace of God lackey it after the will of man, that maketh the sheep to keep the shepherd, that maketh mortal seed of an immortal God. Yea, I desire that we may look into the belly and bowels of this Trojan horse, to see if there be not men in it ready to open the gates to Romish tyranny and Spanish monarchy. For an Arminian is the spawn of a Papist; and if there come the warmth of favour upon him, you shall see him turn into one of those frogs that rise out of the bottomless pit. And if you mark it well, you shall see an Arminian reaching out his hand to a Papist, a Papist to a Jesuit, a Jesuit gives one hand to the Pope and the other to the King of Spain. . . . Yea let us further search and consider whether these be not the men that break in upon the goods and liberties of this Commonwealth, for by this means they make way for the taking away of our religion.[39]

Other parliamentarians echoed Rous, Mr. Kirton adding, "It is apparent to every man that new opinions are brought in by some of our Churchmen to disturb the peace that our Church was formerly in; the meaning of it can be no other but to bring in the Romish religion amongst us. . . . This proceeds from some of the clergy that are near his majesty."[40] More rhetorically, Mr. Sherland said:

We have a Religion that is worth the loving with all our hearts. It was sealed with the blood of martyrs, and kept by miracles. To have our noses wiped of this would grieve any heart; much more to see our Religion quite taken away and designs made on it, and Arminianism still to increase as it doth. . . . it is the desire of some few that labour to bring in a new faction . . . and so suggest that those that oppose them oppose his Majesty, and so they put him upon designs that stand not with public liberty, and tell him that he may command what he listeth and do what he pleaseth with goods, lives, and Religion. And so they involve all true-hearted Englishmen and Christians under the name of Puritans.[41]

The next days saw more attacks upon Montague, until on 3 February, Sir John Eliot suggested that the Lambeth Articles represented the true faith of the Church of England on the disputed questions and that Arminian books and sermons should be suppressed.[42] Just before an irate king dissolved Parliament, resolutions upon the religious question were agreed upon, which included the burning of the books of Montague and Cosin,[43] exemplary punishment for the authors and abettors of "Popish" and Arminian teachings, and the firm establishment and free teaching of the orthodox faith, meaning predestinarian Calvinism, as the sole viewpoint of the Church of England.[44]

Important assumptions run through this parliamentary attack. It was taken for granted that the Reformed predestinarian theology of grace was the teaching of the Church of England; that Arminianism was not only innovation, but conducive to Roman Catholicism; and that all this was a prelude to Spanish domination and the destruction of English liberties. Without minimizing the political overtones of the debate and the inevitable intertwining of religious and other issues, it is indisputable that a particular kind of Christian piety and the theology that enshrined it were also at stake and mattered dearly to some of these parliamentarians. It is clear, too, that the strong identification of essential Protestantism with a certain theology of grace challenged by Arminianism, lay behind the charge that Arminianism led to Rome and not just the ceremonial and sacramentalist notions that accompanied it. How long and thoroughly the differences between Rome and the faith of the English Reformation had been defined in terms of the theology of grace has been noted in the preceding chapters.

But the English Arminians had not been idle; they had long urged the monarchy to adopt a policy of silencing dispute over predestination and related subjects. In 1622, to stifle controversy and Puritan protests, King James had issued injunctions decreeing that instead of afternoon sermons there should be catechizing and that in such exercises preachers should meddle neither with political matters nor with the "deep points of predestination." That tortured subject was to be handled by bishops and deans only, except that in the universities learned men might discuss it "moderately and modestly."[45] In 1626, the year of the torrent of published attacks upon Montague and of the York House Conference, Charles I deplored the prevalence of theological dissension and forbade any discussion of the disputed topics of predestination and falling from grace that went beyond the words of the Articles of Religion.[46] An attempt was also made to suppress books against Montague, and at least one, by Matthew Sutcliffe, dean of Exeter and ironically a longtime foe of the Puritans, was stopped while in the press. The reprinting of others was forbidden.[47] A new edition of the Articles in 1628 was accompanied with a royal order to refrain from curious contentions about the divine decrees.[48] Nonetheless, in that same year an anonymous English poem published on the Continent attacked Cosin and Laud by name as abettors of an Arminianism that was nothing more than a plot to subvert English Protestantism, and beginning in 1626 the agreement of the English delegates at Dort with the opinions of that synod was printed four times, once in an English translation of the original Latin.[49]

The Arminian party argued that the edicts against the discussion of predestination were a proper and fair means of concluding the debate, especially because the arguments were over minor points. Montague called the question of falling from grace unimportant.[50] Christopher Potter, an Oxford sympathizer, felt that the controversy touched nothing essential.[51] But upholders of the predestinarian theology of grace could not allow such minimizing of the subject—to them predestination was a central part of the gospel of grace and must be preached far and wide. To forbid its discussion was to forbid discussion of the gospel and was thereby an assault upon the heart of the Christian faith and the Protestant character of the Church of England. Late in the 1630s, a group of London clergy petitioned the king, contending that his declaration had placed them in the dilemma of either disobeying their earthly ruler or incurring the wrath of God for failing to proclaim the gospel. They went on, "Your Majesty's said edicts are so interpreted as we are deterred from preaching those saving doctrines of God's free grace in election and predestination which confirm our faith,"[52] a reference to the importance of predestination in the piety of assurance. Later the unsympathetic Royalist and Arminian Peter Heylyn indignantly remarked, "Much was the noise which those of the Calvinian party were observed to make on the publishing of this last order as if their mouths were stopped thereby from preaching the most necessary doctrines tending towards mans salvation,"[53] which was, of course, exactly how they felt about the edict. Meanwhile, as a disgruntled Puritan later remembered, "the new upstart Arminians were suffered to preach and print their heterodox notions without any controule."[54]

Though hardly overwhelming in number, several works advocating the Arminian position were printed in spite of the directive to leave such subjects alone. Some of these came from the pen of Thomas Jackson, an Oxford theologian patronized by Laud, who in a major publication considered it presumption to deny the possibility of falling from grace, referred to the doctrine of reprobation as "an idolatrous and blasphemous imagination," and asserted that Christ died for all.[55] In *A Treatise of the Divine Essence and Attributes*, published in 1628, Jackson described being censured as an Arminian as not unusual for him and called the opinion that God decreed all things ahead of time an error.[56]

In 1633, Samuel Hoard made a strong but reasoned attack upon the doctrine of reprobation in *Gods Love to Mankind. Manifested, by Disproving his Absolute Decree for Their Damnation*. Hoard attacked one of the more vulnerable points in the Calvinist armor, a doctrine he termed without basis in antiquity, "abhorred" by Lutherans and "odious to the Papists, opening their foule mouthes against our Church and Religion." Furthermore, Hoard considered it a fatalism like that of the Manichees, which dishonored God by making him the cause of sin, thus subverting "holy endeavours." More significantly, he argued that such a doctrine thwarted the goal of the sacraments, making baptism, for example, of no effect.[57]

Five Pious and Learned Discourses by Robert Shelford, a Suffolk rector who died in 1627 but whose posthumous lectures were clearly a round fired in the Arminian battle, exposed other aspects of the English Arminian outlook. Shelford argued, in contradistinction to Puritans and Calvinists, that God's laws could be fulfilled in this life. He denounced those who ran eagerly to sermons and then became puffed up with the claim to great knowledge of mysteries; instead of such pretended knowledge, what was needed for salvation was attention to the sacraments, which infused grace into persons, making them thereby acceptable to God. Charity as well as faith was needed for justification. This clear rejection of Protestant forensic justification was followed by the argument that too much emphasis on faith leads to license. Those who "soar into points of predestination" were condemned, and free will and universal grace were straightforwardly affirmed.[58]

William Milbourne, who tellingly identified himself on his title page simply as "priest," criticized the predestinarian theology of grace in a scholastic work later in the decade. Challenging a favorite text of his opponents, Milbourne argued that Pharoah was not absolutely damned or "hardened" from his birth but simply received a just condemnation for his crime.[59]

Also to be counted among these Arminian writings during the reign of Charles I should be the publication *An Historicall Narration of the Judgement of some most Learned and Godly English Bishops, Holy Martyrs, and Others . . . Concerning God's Election*, which, like the work of Prynne on the other side, sought to amass testimonies on behalf of a more or less Arminian viewpoint. Much of the tract consisted of a reprinting of the book of an earlier anonymous antipredestinarian writer who had been excoriated by Robert Crowley as "Cerberus"; the author also compiled some very much misunderstood quotations from Cranmer, Latimer, and Hooper.[60]

Among the books supporting Arminianism, one was the work of a Roman Catholic, published abroad, and can hardly have pleased the English Arminians or aided their cause. Its author smugly congratulated the leaders of the English Protestant church for having adopted the views of Arminius, which the treatise defends by way of dialogue against "Enthusiastus," "a great Precisian."[61]

As might be expected, the theological struggle between the Arminian innovators and the upholders of the old Reformed theology was intense at the universities, where greater latitude was given in discussing controverted matters than was given to preachers generally. Nonetheless, the king's declaration against discussion of the disputed points was enforced first at Cambridge when the duke of Buckingham became its chancellor in 1626[62] and then at the other university. But even four years before that, when a certain William Lucy of Caius College had "preached a sermon totally for Arminianisme, wonderfully boldly and peremptorily, styling some passages of the contrary by the name of blasphemie," the Cambridge Calvinists had protested to the authorities to no avail, a result very different from the censure of Barrett long before. Obviously, the seeds planted in the university by the influence of Andrewes, Overall, and others, coupled with recognition of the direction in which the royal will was tending, had borne considerable fruit. Ten years after the unavailing protest of Lucy's Arminian sermon, Nathaniel Bernard of Emmanuel was required to recant a sermon preached in St. Mary's, Cambridge, in which he had upheld unconditional election.[63]

At Oxford, the influence of its Calvinist chancellor, the earl of Pembroke, prevented the silencing of anti-Arminians until a few years later than at Cambridge,[64] but in 1630, William Laud became chancellor, elected over a Calvinist opponent by a very small margin in the university convocation.[65] With Laud in authority, a new strictness prevailed at the university, accompanied by ceremonial innovations highly offensive to Puritans and attempts to enforce silence respecting the disputed points began.

The anti-Arminian leadership at Oxford centered on John Prideaux, Regius professor of divinity until 1641. Prideaux had long harried those of Arminian sympathies: in 1622 he censured Gabriel Bridges for an offensive sermon and then required him to defend publicly, to Prideaux's satisfaction, the anti-Arminian theses that "Decretum praedestinationis non est conditonale" and "Gratia sufficiens ad salutem non conceditur omnibus."[66] Three years later, Prideaux rebuked George Palmer of Lincoln College for allying himself with Montague's opinions. In 1631, Prideaux compelled one Rainsford of Wadham College to recant the opinion that election was based on foreseen faith.[67] But in 1633 the order of silence became too much for Prideaux, for when disputing with the Arminian Peter Heylyn, at the mention of the decrees of God, Prideaux "brake into a great and long discourse, that his mouth was shut by authority, else he would maintain that truth *contra omnes qui sunt in vives*, which fetched a great hum from the country ministers that were there." Warned for this offense, Prideaux protested his loyalty to the Church of England.[68]

Prideaux was not without Oxford allies, who included Ralph Kettell, president of Trinity, and Degory Wheare, principal of Gloucester Hall,[69] but the Laudians and Arminians were in the ascendant at the older university, led by Richard Baylie, Brian Duppa, Accepted Frewen, and William Juxon, the last of whom became archbishop of Canterbury at the Restoration. And some erstwhile anti-Arminians now changed sides, notably Samuel Fell, who succeeded the strong predestinarian Sebastian Benefield as Lady Margaret professor of divinity in 1626,[70] and Christopher Potter. Potter became provost of Queen's, also in 1626, and after preaching a sermon at the consecration of Barnaby Potter as bishop of Carlisle in March 1628, it was necessary for him to defend his remarks on that occasion against Calvinist calumny. In a letter of vindication, Potter denied he was a Pelagian, but admitted that as an untutored youth he had railed against the Arminians, though he avowed that he now felt that the Church of England's position was closer to that of the Arminians than to the Synod of Dort. He also thought both Lutherans and the ancient fathers agreed more with the Arminians.[71]

With those opposed to Prideaux's predestinarianism increasingly in control, the tide of battle turned at Oxford. When Thomas Hill denounced Arminians in a 1631 university sermon as defenders of Pelagianism and Rome, describing their tenets as "Popish darts whet afresh on a Dutch grindstone," he was forced to make a humiliating public recantation in which he admitted that he "did let fall divers scandalous speeches" in defiance of the king's order not to discuss such matters by "imputing Pelagianisme and Popery" to one faction in the church (obviously the

Arminians), "besides private glances against particular persons concerning some speeches delivered in their late Sermons."[72]

Emboldened by this suppression, the Arminians, according to a contemporary, now became more open in their views, begetting yet more denunciations of them as Pelagians. The university authorities sought to control three anti-Arminians in particular, Thomas Forde of Magdalen, Giles Thorne of Balliol, and William Hodges of Exeter, but they disobeyed the vice-chancellor. For their contumacy they were summoned before the court of Charles I at Woodstock and royally expelled from the university; but when they left Oxford, they were accompanied out of town by a crowd of sympathizers. Hodges was eventually reinstated after a public recantation from which we learn something of what he had earlier claimed, namely, that Arminian heresy had become the way to preferment. In 1640, two fellows of Magdalen were required to publicly recant their criticism of universal grace as heresy.[73]

Oxford predestinarians found other means to strike back at their persecutors. In 1632, an anonymous satire was scattered about the university, entitled "The Academicall Army of Epidemicall Arminians, to the Tune of the Soldier." Retaliating, the authorities decreed that any scholar found with a copy would have his degree postponed one year.[74] A letter of Laud indicates that those now unable to attack Arminianism in their sermons began to do so in their public prayers, written copies of which were not required to be submitted to the authorities, so that proof of disobedience to the injunctions was difficult to establish—Laud complained that "the fashion is now to turn the libellous part into a prayer."[75]

The case of Richard Kilbye of Lincoln College best points up the transition regarding acceptable theology at Oxford. In 1637, Kilbye preached a sermon at St. Mary's in which he attacked Arminianism, and though forced to make a public disavowal, in his recantation he plaintively recalled that he had preached the same sermon in the same pulpit sixteen years earlier, "and then it was well approved of."[76]

The predestinarians justifiably regarded William Laud, bishop of London and then archbishop of Canterbury, as the ringleader of the Arminian conspiracy against the faith of the English Reformation (the Scot Robert Baillie claimed that Puritans and bishops had not disagreed theologically until Laud "began to blow upon these unhappy seeds of Arminius"). The archbishop said and wrote little for public consumption that dealt with the points disputed between Arminians and their opponents, but his sympathies were obvious. Whether as bishop, archbishop, or chancellor of Oxford, he strove to silence the predestinarians. Laud apparently agreed with the remark made to him by Dr. Brooke of Cambridge that predestination was the "root of Puritanisme," and thus of all disobedience, "schisme and sauciness in the country."[77] From his letters it is clear that he hoped silence on the matter at Oxford would lead to the withering away of the predestinarian position and that he felt the study of Calvin's *Institutes* was inimical to the peace of the Church.[78] In 1630, he silenced a London lecturer for speaking on election;[79] in 1635, Cornelius Burges received the same treatment for attacking Arminianism. At his trial, Laud was accused of depriving many "godly" ministers through the Court of High Commission, including a Mr. Bernard, whose only offense had been "Words about Pelagian Errors and Popery."[80] Bishops sympathetic to his cause used the visitations he encouraged to silence Calvinism in their dioceses, as one of the visitation queries of Richard Montague, after he became bishop of Norwich, shows: he asked, "Doth your Minister commonly or of set purpose in his popular sermons fall upon those much disputed and little understood doctrines of Gods eternall Predestination?"[81]

Seeking also to control the press, Laud prevented the publication of some anti-Arminian works, while, as was charged against him at his trial, winking at the publication of Arminian books.[82] William Prynne, under a pseudonym, attacked Laud's suppression of an anti-Arminian publication and the imprisonment of the printer involved.[83]

Even during incarceration and undergoing trial, Laud did not dissemble his views: he admitted distinguishing between clergy as either orthodox or "doctrinal Puritans," and though denying that he was a follower of Arminius, he affirmed that the doctrine of universal atonement was the "constant Doctrine of the Catholic Church in all Ages, and no Error of Arminius." That God reprobated from eternity the greater part of mankind he called an "Opinion my very Soul abominates."[84]

Laud promoted Arminianism, not through the expression of theological opinion, but by preferring to high positions those who held such opinions. Many of his English allies received such favorable treatment, including, of course, Montague and Cosin. Nor did his tactic end with the borders of England. To Ireland he sent William Chappel, described by Prynne as "the most notorious seducing Arminian in the whole University of Cambridge,"[85] and John Bramhall, who in 1634 became bishop of Derry. In the Irish church, Laud had to contend with the well-entrenched

Calvinism of James Ussher, the archbishop of Armagh, whose thoroughly predestinarian Irish Articles, which had been based partly on the Lambeth Articles, Laud attempted to suppress, while Ussher still resolutely defended them in 1634.[86]

The injunction to silence on predestination was outwitted by Ussher when in 1631 he issued a book about the medieval monk Gottschalk (and Pelagianism in Britain long before), who had been persecuted in the ninth century for his belief in unconditional predestination. In the guise of a historical study, Ussher marshaled all the arguments against Pelagianism and, tacitly, Arminianism.[87] Laud was displeased, but could strike at Ussher only through his colleague in the Irish episcopate, George Downame, who was officially silenced after writing on behalf of the certainty of the perseverance of the elect.[88]

The correspondence of Archbishop Ussher during the years of the Arminian dispute in England shows him to have been very much in touch with the debate and involved in the planning of strategy to counter the Arminians. He was in correspondence with Samuel Ward at Cambridge and John Prideaux at Oxford, from whom he received reports on the progress or setbacks of Arminianism there. Samuel Ward could still tell him in 1628 that Arminianism had made little headway at Cambridge although "preferments at Court" were causing some to turn in that direction. In that same year, Prideaux complimented Ussher on a recent publication and hoped that it would put a stop to some who were tending toward the views of Pelagius. By 1639, Ward was acknowledging that he was being opposed by some who thought he had violated the monarch's declaration of silence respecting predestination.[89] Meanwhile, Ussher took time in his letters to explicate such matters as limited atonement, recommend that Ward make sure that there existed a "fair copy" of his lectures on grace and free will for the use of posterity, and discuss his book on Gottschalk and Downame's on perseverance as part of an assault on Arminianism. By 1635, he was exclaiming to Ward, "how cometh it to pass that you in Cambridge do cast such stumbling-blocks in our way? by publishing unto the world such rotten Stuff as Shelford hath vented in his five Discourses?" a book that he adds is clearly Jesuitical.[90]

If Ussher made the progress of Arminianism difficult in Ireland, Laud found even more resistance to his efforts to alter religion in Scotland. That nation, of course, had long been nourished by the milk of predestinarian theology, but Laud hoped through a small group of bishops and university professors to feed the Scots on Arminianism. In 1634, the

Scottish Parliament indignantly petitioned King Charles I about Arminians who were teaching their views with impunity there, but obviously to no avail, because the king was supporting such innovation in doctrine. When in 1638 the English yoke was thrown off and the Scottish church's General Assembly again met, one of the chief charges against the Laudians in Scotland was that they had labored to bring Arminianism and "popery" into the kingdom. James Wedderburn, Thomas Sydserf, John Maxwell, and William Forbes among the episcopate, Dr. Panter, a university professor, and two ministers, John Creighton of Paisley and David Mitchell of Edinburgh, were all accused, the latter specifically, of teaching "Arminianisme in all the heads and sundrie poynts of Poperie." Mentioned also among the doctrines of these men were universal grace, falling from grace, and freedom of the will.[91] William Guild's treatise of 1639, *An Antidote agaynst Poperie*, defended the Calvinist position and treated the Arminian opinions as nothing more than the doctrine of Rome.[92]

The nature of this Anglican Arminianism, its relationship to the Dutch movement, and its role in the English political and religious conflicts that led to civil war all call for extended analysis. English Arminianism included elements that gave it a theological character quite different from Arminianism in the Netherlands, most notably its sacramentalism and ceremonialism, which have often received more attention than the theology of grace.[93] For the English Arminians can be described as "high church" or even "Anglo-Catholic," emphasizing the sacraments as channels of divine grace and desiring to surround sacramental worship with elements of ceremony that quickly became focal points of controversy, such as the use of candles and crosses and the substitution of altars and altar rails for holy tables. Laud brought strife into many localities by his enforcement of the king's order that communion tables should be put "altarwise" at the east and railed in. Consecration and decoration of churches were other matters for Puritan protest.[94] Sacramentalism meant the exaltation of priesthood and episcopacy, and for Laud episcopacy was of divine origin[95] and needful for a rightly ordered church. And in the case of the Laudians, divine right episcopacy was closely related to divine right monarchy. Without entirely repudiating the reformers, patristic inspiration and authority were central to the Laudians; Montague appealed to the church fathers, and Potter claimed them as the source of his "supposed" Arminianism.[96] That the movement constituted something of a national English Counter-Reformation, as Roland G. Usher long ago thought,[97] is evident especially from their attitude to the Reformation: to Laud it was a "deformation"; to Cosin the English reformers were "ignorant and unlearned Calvinisticall bishops." Laud's chaplain Heylyn expressed his hatred of Calvinists innumerable times.[98]

But though differing from Dutch Arminianism in its more "catholic" character, English Arminianism shared with it a general reaction against strict predestinarianism. Nor was it merely accidental that with the English Arminians sacramentalism and rejection of predestinarian theology converged: the doctrine of predestination had often been a radical dissolvent of a churchly and sacramental outlook, as John Wyclif long before had illustrated, for redemption when totally a matter of God's mysterious choice cannot be at the disposal of a church hierarchy with its sacramental prerogatives. Thus, though the Arminian theology could entail a more liberal, ethical, and moralistic viewpoint, as it mainly did with the Dutch Remonstrants and with such Anglicans as John Hales and William Chillingworth,[99] it took on a quite different character for those Anglicans seeking a theology more suitable to a church that had retained more of the old structure, liturgy, and ceremonial than typical of most Reformed churches and who had long been engaged in defense of those elements from the attacks of Protestant extremists. As Tyacke says, "English Arminians came to balance their rejection of the arbitrary grace of predestination with a new found source of grace freely available in the sacraments,"[100] and it may be added that the very nature of that grace began to change. For it is evident that the Laudian Arminians began to reject the Protestant understanding of grace as forensic and to substitute for that conception formulas that spoke of grace more as quality or substance to be infused into the individual in the sacramental life of the church. Montague wrote to Cosin that one of the chief differences between himself and his opponents concerned justification, which he understood not as forensic pardon but as a making just by infused grace.[101] C. F. Allison has detected something of this in the changing way in which some Laudians understood justification as compared to Reformed orthodoxy.[102] It is apparent that these Laudian Arminians had moved beyond the hesitant and tentative steps toward a different theological outlook taken by the earlier generation of Hooker, Overall, and Andrewes, whose discussions of grace still moved within the ambience of Reformed theology. In short, the Laudian Arminians seem to have introduced theological innovations of the most startling sort, which were to have the most violent repercussions.

The Laudian Arminians, then, minimized the differences between

Rome and the Church of England (it was a point of some significance to them that the pope was not Antichrist)[103] and had definitely departed from the predestinarian theology of grace that had long prevailed in the Reformed churches, including the Church of England. The opponents of the Laudians, who included many more than those usually considered Puritans, thus rightly blamed them for innovation and subversion of the Protestant religion in England as it had been known up to that time. The anti-Arminians agreed that the main issue between the two parties was the very nature of Christian salvation—no peripheral matter. They interpreted Arminianism as the assertion of salvation by human merit and therefore as the total overthrow of the Reformation gospel. Salvation by merit, of course, made Arminianism in their view no different from the religion of Rome. As Bishop Morton declared concerning Montague at the York House Conference, "All his discourse about justification tends to the justifying of the popish doctrine, and to the making of Good Works a part of our justification."[104] Anthony Wotton claimed that Montague was teaching the "popish" doctrine of justification, and George Downame, Ussher's colleague in the Irish episcopate, wrote in 1633, in a work that must have had one eye on the English Arminians, that the Christian gospel was the belief in free justification by the merit of Christ alone, without any human preparation or disposition to receive it.[105] When the Laudian effort collapsed, the idea that the Laudians had subverted the Protestant doctrine of justification was frequently reiterated: the Scottish General Assembly accused one of Laud's agents of holding Roman Catholic views on justification;[106] Robert Baillie was more precise in claiming that the Laudians held the Tridentine doctrine of justification; a London minister complained to the Long Parliament that he had been harassed for teaching "the true doctrine of justification by the imputed righteousness and satisfaction of Christ"; and at his trial Laud was charged with promoting William Chappel, though the latter had maintained "justification by works."[107]

No charge could have been more damaging to the Laudians or more inflammatory of English opinion. It will remain problematical to what extent abstruse points of theology mattered to ordinary folk (to many they clearly did), but almost everyone understood the cry of "popery," and now the Laudians had rendered it not implausible and given it by their ceremonial changes the most tangible objects of Protestant outrage. An article by Robin Clifton has recently made a strong case for the importance of the "fear of popery" as a major element in alienating people from the king's cause by the time of the outbreak of civil war,[108] and in that sense (as well as others soon to be examined) the Arminian conflict cannot be overlooked as one of the major factors leading to breakdown in English society and to civil war.

The charge that the Laudians were denying the Protestant and Reformation tenet of justification by faith shows where Calvinists felt that the attacks upon perseverance and predestination were leading. Bishop Carleton echoed a familiar charge when he reproached Montague for "defacing" the whole doctrine of grace in his denial of predestination.[109] For the Arminians had not only attacked certain predestinarian formulas dear to their opponents, but they had also introduced theological innovations that jeopardized the heart of Reformation teaching. They had threatened the essence of Protestant religious experience, a point missed by concentration only on the theological niceties of the conflict. That the issue finally came back to piety is evident in an autobiographical remark of Thomas Shepard, who remembered that after his conversion by the intervening grace of God he was "never tempted to Arminianism, my own experience so sensibly confuting the freedom of the will."[110] But that a basic issue of differing religious sensibility underlay the conflict is most apparent in the words of the Puritan preacher Richard Sibbes: "But some others there are amongst us, that regard not Christ and his satisfaction alone, but join faith and works together in justification; they will have other priests, and other intercessors than Christ. Alas! beloved, how are these men fallen from Christ to another gospel, as if Christ were not an all-sufficient Saviour, and able to deliver to the uttermost! What is the gospel but salvation and redemption by Christ alone?"[111]

The effect upon the Puritans of the Arminian control of the English church was accordingly staggering. Disputes that had previously been between those who accepted a common Protestant faith while differing over matters of discipline and church order were now transformed into a far more basic struggle. A larger group of Protestant religionists were more totally alienated from the leadership of the state church than had yet been the case since the Reformation. Now was time for desperate persons to emigrate while their embittered confreres at home battled tenaciously with a regime perceived as subverting the entire Protestant Reformation in England.

Moreover, for the first time since the Protestant Reformation, Puritan theological views could be distinguished from a regnant "Anglicanism," though many non-Laudian Anglicans agreed with the Puritans. For the first time to other Puritan grievances could be added a theological one, fanning into flame an earlier Protestant dissidence that had waned in Jacobean times. The Puritans themselves, feeling that they were fighting for the very substance of the faith, played down their criticism of lesser matters and concentrated on the theology of grace. Mark H. Curtis noted as much for university Puritans, whom he described as "forced to soft-pedal their own criticisms of the Church in order to preserve, if possible, fundamental doctrinal positions without which their programme for reforms in ritual and church government would have no solid theological foundations."[112] John Davenport, later an emigrant to New England, told a Scottish correspondent that he was conforming in such matters as episcopacy and the wearing of the surplice because of the greater serious-ness of the theological challenge:

Were it not better to unite our forces against those who oppose us in Fundamen-talls than to be divided amongst ourselves about Ceremonialls? Who can, without sorrowe, and feare observe how Atheisme, Libertinisme, papisme, and Arminian-isme, both at home, and abroad have stolen in, and taken possession of the house, whilst we are at strife about the hangings and paintings of it? and the enemy strikes at the heart whilst we busy ourselves in washing the face of this body. How much better would it become us to combine together in an holy league against the common adversary.[113]

Puritan alarm over Arminianism was predictable, but it was significant that Davenport spoke of making common cause with the episcopalian Calvinists who probably constituted the largest group in the Church of England and who formed a broad middle party between Laudians and Puritans. They represented the continuing Protestantism of the Elizabe-than settlement, and they too were gravely alienated from the new leader-ship of the Church of England. Erastian, and not too concerned about ridding the church of abuses, they nonetheless held to the piety and theology of predestinarian grace in its Reformed version, even if their adherence was less passionate than that of those usually denominated Puritans. These were the men Richard Baxter was to speak of as "the old common moderate sort" of "Episcopal men" "who were commonly in Doctrine Calvinists," who felt a kinship with the Reformed churches of the Continent; Baxter thought these men were a majority who had been outmaneuvered by the Arminians.[114] Such people now found themselves foul-weather friends of the Puritans. One of the Venetian ambassadors observed in 1637 that "many of the Protestants themselves, scandalized by the new institutions, become Puritans for fear of falling into Catholicism" if they followed the Laudians.[115] Such episcopalian Calvinists were now aspersed by the Arminians as "Puritans": the contemporary church historian Thomas Fuller commented that after 1622 all who were anti-Arminian came to be called "Puritan" whereas that name had previously referred only to "such as dissented from the hierarchy in discipline and church-government."[116] The Puritan historian Daniel Neal, writing considerably later than Fuller, observed that "as the new explications of Arminius grew into repute, the Calvinists were reckoned old-fashioned divines" and dubbed "Doctrinal Puritans."[117] How great a reversal this must have been for many such episcopalians Perry Miller underlined when he noted that such figures had in the days before Laud been "hostile or indifferent to Puritanism" but, "shocked by the Popish aroma of the Arminian prelacy," they now joined their erstwhile opponents.[118]

Among such Calvinist episcopalians could be included many who have already appeared in the present story: George Abbot, archbishop of Canterbury until 1633; Archbishop Ussher; bishops Morton, Davenant, Carleton, and Hall, the latter three veterans of the Synod of Dort; university theologians such as Samuel Ward and Prideaux; men active in the ministry like Daniel Featley, later purged from the Westminster Assembly as a Royalist; or a militant layman such as Prynne, an episcopalian in his church views who could never be reconciled to Oliver Cromwell, for all that he lost his ears protesting arbitrary monarchy.

One of these episcopalian Calvinists, Bishop Davenant, preaching before the king in 1630, in a counterattack on the Arminians took the liberty of touching on the forbidden points, maintaining that election precluded human merit and free will in salvation. As punishment, Davenant was forced to appear before the Privy Council on his knees and was berated by Samuel Harsnett, by then advanced to the archbishopric of York. In defense, Davenant insisted that he had preached no more than what all ministers of the English church were obliged to subscribe in the Thirty-nine Articles.[119] In correspondence, Bishop Hall agreed with Davenant's views, declaring he would "live and die" in agreement with the Synod of Dort, and Ussher marveled that the established doctrine of the church could be so questioned.[120] No longer required to be silent after the convening of the Long Parliament, Davenant then wrote against the Arminian Samuel Hoard, defending "the absolute decree of predestination" and "the absolute decree of negative Reprobation" as the official teaching of the Church of England and warning against any setting forth of God's general love to mankind that obscured "the speciall love and mercy of God prepared from all eternitie and bestowed in due time upon elect men."[121] But Davenant showed his kinship with the piety of the spiritual writers when he added that "the doctrine of predestination doth serve to kindle in the hearts of the faithful a most ardent love towards God."[122]

The rise of Arminianism in the Church of England thus had long-range consequences of the greatest importance: creating a totally new religious outlook in the Reformed Church of England, it utterly alienated Puritans from the established church and deeply divided conformists themselves. By raising the specter of "popery" it dangerously inflamed national passions. All chance for a unified national church was dissipated, and it is not an exaggeration to consider Arminianism a contributing factor to the deep divisions in English life that eventuated in civil war.[123] Nor should the seemingly remote and abstruse character of theological controversy over grace mislead the student of seventeenth-century England into assuming that such questions were not a major part of those divisions,[124] for the English Arminians had adopted a theological outlook in many respects redolent of the old replaced Catholicism, awakening a bitterness of religious strife not seen in England since the years of the Reformation.

The Long Parliament and the Rise of Sectarian Arminianism

The Long Parliament began to sit in 1640, and the tables were quickly turned on the Laudian Arminians. Laud and his allies were now in disfavor, with the archbishop himself soon to be a martyr for his cause, to be eventually followed by the royal martyr, Charles I. Clergy suspected of Arminianism were ejected by the Long Parliament and the parliamentary armies throughout the decade.[125]

Lord Brooke and other political leaders now inveighed with impunity against Arminian innovators and their "malignant influence,"[126] and preachers before the Long Parliament vied with one another for the honor of arraigning Arminian heresy. Edmund Calamy lamented that Arminianism had come to be "accounted the doctrine of the Church of England"[127] and called for its extirpation as did such other rising stars among the clergy favored by the Long Parliament as Cornelius Burges and Stephen Marshall.[128] Even John Gauden, whose name became intertwined with the popularization of Charles I as a martyr-king, was distressed by Arminianism in 1640.[129] An analysis of the preachers before the Long Parliament has concluded that "to them church reform meant the substitution of Calvinism for Arminianism."[130] The Root and Branch bill of 1641 cited the role of the bishops in the spread of Arminian falsehood as one of the reasons for the total abolition of episcopacy.[131]

The defeat of the Laudians also removed all restraint on the publishing of anti-Arminian books, and several appeared in the wake of the Laudians' fall. The *Animadversions* of John Davenant directed in 1641 against the universalism of Samuel Hoard was followed by others. A short satirical poem by Thomas Harbie attacked the Arminians the next year; an early form of the Scotsman Robert Baillie's arraignment of Arminianism appeared in 1641; and John Ball's posthumous *A Treatise of the Covenant of Grace* was described on the title page as written against the Arminians.[132]

Auguring his later enormous theological output to crush the Arminians was an early work of John Owen, *A Display of Arminianism*, issued in 1642. As did the other anti-Arminian writers, Owen blamed his opponents for striving to bring "popery" into England, maintaining that they did not represent the established doctrine of the English church. But, characteristically for Owen, the chief issue was theological, whether or not "the chief part in the several degrees of our salvation is to be ascribed unto ourselves" or to God. For Owen the answer was clearly the latter, and he sought to establish it by discussion of the major theological points of original sin, atonement, predestination, and the irresistibility of grace. Humankind, after the fall, is unable to call upon God until grace intervenes, something Owen felt the Arminians had denied, as they labored "to clear human nature from the heavy imputation of being sinful." The atonement, he further argued, was efficacious only for those elected to life; otherwise there is "a predestination, and none predestined." He declared the root of Arminianism to be the exaltation of human self-sufficiency, an effort like that of old in building the tower of Babel. The theme of the spiritual writers, that a true teaching about predestinarian grace provided "a sure anchor of hope" and "a firm ground of consolation," was also prominent in Owen's argument.[133]

The Long Parliament authorized a convening of an assembly of clergy, which began to sit in 1643 and completed its Confession of Faith in 1646. This famous assembly of divines included most of the leading Calvinist and anti-Arminian theologians of the realm, with the strongly anti-Arminian William Twisse serving for a while as its prolocutor, and it sought to provide a statement of faith that would prevent any further ingress of Arminianism into the Church of England. Its treatment of the theology of grace was accordingly detailed and careful and certainly must have fulfilled the desires of those English theologians who had earlier wanted the Lambeth Articles and then the decrees of the Synod of Dort incorporated into the standards of the English church. The Westminster Confession of Faith, sometimes cited as an example of the incorporation of covenant theology into a creed, might also be regarded as a confession built around the order of salvation as it had developed in English theology from Bucer to Perkins and on up to the 1640s. It enshrined the theological formulas dear to spiritual writers and scholastic Calvinists alike. Although the strongly anti-Arminian Scotsman Baillie could write that "we had long and tough debates about the Decrees of election," he concluded that "all is gone right according to our mind,"[134] for the confession affirmed straightforwardly not only election but reprobation and limited atonement, though like the Synod of Dort it avoided some of the harshest formulations of these matters, including supralapsarianism. As commonly recognized, the Confession sets everything, in scholastic fashion, within the context of God's decrees[135] and labors everywhere to exalt the grace of God in redemption.

No sooner had the prelatical Arminians been struck down, however, than new representatives of that heresy popped up on the Puritan left, among the sectarians who had long nourished heterodoxies of various sorts in their separatist conventicles but who became more numerous and visible with the ferment of the 1640s. The sectarian Arminians paralleled the earlier freewillers and, like them, were often drawn from common folk who found in scripture a simple and direct appeal for men to choose Christ and who scorned tutelage by their betters in the arcana of proper orthodoxy. Late in the sixteenth century there were several references to an obscure Edward Glover, who was considered by those who attacked him an ally of the Brownists. Apparently a minister with a personal and local following, he was charged with teaching heretical perfectionism as well as making election dependent on obedience and with denying the perseverance of the saints. Coming to the attention of Archbishop Whitgift, this Glover was imprisoned for his opinions.[136]

The Puritan sectarians who took refuge in the Netherlands early in the seventeenth century were by no means inclined to Arminianism, but were staunch predestinarians. One of them, Henry Jacob, considered separatism a fitting response to the growing Arminianism of the national church.[137] Nonetheless, Arminianism made headway among some of the Puritan extremists who turned Baptist in the Netherlands during the reign of James I. Rejecting unconditional predestination and insisting upon a universal atonement, they came to be called General Baptists. The leaders of this direction among Baptists were John Smith, whose 1609 statement of his belief denied original sin and reprobation and declared that the grace of God was offered to all and that all were able to repent, predestination meaning nothing more than that those who believe are then chosen by God,[138] and Thomas Helwys, who wrote *A Short and Plaine proofe by the Word and Workes of God that Gods decree is not the cause of anye Mans sinne or condemnation*, printed in 1611 probably in the Netherlands. This short tract argued that no particular persons were elected or reprobated. Helwys considered predestination to be presumptuous, making God the author of sin.[139] Opinions differ as to whether this Arminianism of sectarian Baptists was derived from the Dutch Mennonites,[140] but it should be noted that there was a long though disconnected English tradition of the rejection of predestination by simple followers of the Bible.

With the death of Helwys in 1613 or 1616, leadership of these General Baptists passed to John Murton, and the little congregation returned to London. In 1620, in the wake of the excitement of the Synod of Dort, Murton published a book setting forth his Arminian position and rejecting the conclusions of Dort.[141] Murton was quickly answered by two individuals who had had extensive experience among Puritan separatists and radicals on the Continent, Henry Ainsworth and John Robinson. Ainsworth's rejoinder came out in 1623, after the author's death, and directed its arguments against Anabaptist deniers of Calvinism, vindicating predestinarian theology from the aspersions they cast on it.[142] Robinson, the Pilgrims' pastor who never made the journey to New England, the next year marshaled the usual anti-Arminian arguments against those he also dubbed Anabaptists and bemoaned, "Oh, that any made partakers of this free grace of Gods spirit dwelling in them, should deny the powerfull work of it, to establish their own freewill," an argument clearly directed at the sectarian type of Arminian, who could be regarded as having shared something of the Puritan piety of grace.[143]

Several General Baptist congregations pursued a clandestine life until the 1640s, when their brand of Arminianism became more public.[144] In 1645, the London General Baptists published a statement of their doctrinal position titled *The Fountain of Free Grace Opened*, which included assertion of their now favorite theme of universal atonement.[145] Baptists of Arminian outlook began to appear in other places as well as London.[146]

As alarmed heresiographers testified, these Arminian sectarians were becoming aggressive in spreading their notions, many of them managing to get their heterodoxies into print. Such was the case with Francis Duke, author of *The Fulnesse and Freenesse of Gods Grace in Jesus Christ*, which argued that all persons may attain eternal life by Christ if they apply the truths Christ taught to their lives, John Horne, who decried the notion that Christ died for only a few, Thomas Moore, who declared that Christ died for all, and Henry Denne.[147]

Most notorious and vocal of these Arminian sectarians was John Goodwin, who for at least a while was counted among the Independents. Late in the 1630s, he had begun to broach Arminian ideas on the atonement and the will[148] and came under vigorous attack from the tireless heresy hunter George Walker, who had been among the first to detect heretical danger among the Puritans themselves. As early as 1611 Walker had accused Anthony Wotton, no slight anti-Arminian himself, of Socinianism because of his version of the doctrine of the imputation of Christ's righteousness.[149] Debating Walker and giving vent to Arminian views, Goodwin published *Impedit Ira Animum* in 1641 and *Imputatio Fidei or A Treatise of Justification* the next year.

These sectarian Arminians clearly presented a very different challenge to Calvinist orthodoxy than had the Laudian Arminians. They shared something of the piety of the predestinarians and could outdo them in calling for the remedy of abuses in the national church. They were at the very opposite end of the spectrum from Anglican Arminian sacramentalism. With the radical and dissenting conventicles of the Protestant left as their environment, they must have been as distressing to Laudian bishops as to scholastic predestinarians. But in the 1640s these radical sectarian Arminians became the problem not of the bishops but of those who were struggling to bring the Church of England back to its original doctrinal purity while continuing earlier Puritan efforts to reform the church in ritual and government.

The anti-Arminians, who had risked so much in the struggle against the prelatical Arminians, were distressed by such defections from within Puritanism. An anonymous lampoon accused sectarians of Arminianism. Richard Baxter complained that such sectarians abounded in the parliamentary army. John Owen, then an Essex minister, wrote that he and neighboring ministers were conferring in alarm over the spread of sectarian Arminianism in their locale.[150] An important example of their outraged counterattack was that of Francis Cheynell, who perceived that the Calvinists were being attacked from two sides and who linked the Laudians and Sectarians, as his fantastic title of 1643 indicates: *The Rise, Growthe, and Danger of Socinianisme. Together with a plaine discovery of a desperate design of corrupting the Protestant Religion, whereby it appears that the Religion which hath been so violently contended for (by the Archbishop of Canterbury and his adherents) is not the true pure Protestant Religion, but an Hotchpotch of Arminianism, Socinianisme, and Popery. It is likewise made evident, That the Atheists, Anabaptists, and Sectaries so much complained of, have been raised or encouraged by the doctrines and practices of the Arminian, Socinian, and Popish Party.* Cheynell detected a grand conspiracy of Arminians, papists, and Socinians to reduce the nation to Rome. He acknowledged, however, that Laud did not really accept all the points of these factions, but united them to himself in order "that all three might joyn with him to suppresse Calvinisme." He identified the Anabaptists and sectarians with Socinianism and thus blamed the prelatical Arminians for the current of unlearned and irregular "tubbe-preachers."[151]

The heresiographers devoted considerable space to the description and refutation of Arminians. Ephraim Pagitt, episcopalian as well as Calvinist, who finally joined the king's side in the civil war, found the sum of their error in the denial of free justification—Arminianism is Pelagianism.[152] The greatest heresiographer of them all, Thomas Edwards, bemoaned in 1646, "O how is the scene changed within these few years! Those Doctrines of Arminianism and Popery which in Episcopall men we cryed out so of . . . are delivered and received with great applause."[153]

Indicative of renewed alarm over Arminianism, three anti-Arminian books focusing on atonement and redemption appeared within the space of little more than one year. The Independent John Stalham's *Vindiciae Redemptionis* sought to provide exegetical basis for the anti-Arminian view of the atonement and concluded that "the Arminians, in making Christ a general Saviour, make him none at all," that "the freenesse of grace is magnified and manifested the more, by Christ's dying for a certain number," and that the Arminians meant something altogether different from the Calvinists by grace, making it not efficacious, but "an ability given to men to be saved 'if they would.' "[154] Samuel Rutherford, one of the Scottish commissioners who sat in the Westminster Assembly, made many of the same points in his *Christ Dying and Drawing Sinners to Himselfe*: "It was no blind bargain that Christ made; hee knew what he gave, hee knew what he got. Christ told downe a definite and certaine Ransome, as a told summe of money, every penny reckoned and layed, and he knew who was his own, and whom, and how many, by the head and name he bought." Rutherford also remembered that at root a question of piety was being argued, declaring that to believe in an ineffectual atonement was to be bereft of comfort.[155] The third work was the next foray of John Owen into the Arminian controversy, *The Death of Death in the Death of Christ*, written to answer the argument of the obscure Thomas Moore of Lincolnshire, described by Edwards as "a great Sectary and Manifestarian." Moore had forcefully asserted that Christ died for all men,[156] basing his appeal upon a simple reading of scripture and rejection of theological subtlety. Owen lamented that these new heretics surpassed in abomination the former prelatical Pelagians and stated that they must be defeated by a clear and thorough exposition of the orthodox doctrine of redemption. Owen then explained that God's grace was by its very nature effectual and that anything that denied or compromised that efficacy destroyed the Christian gospel of grace alone.[157]

Owen, Rutherford, and Stalham chose to oppose Arminianism by stressing the doctrine of redemption as an effectual application of grace to the elect. By focusing on the atonement, they managed to keep the discussion centered on the question of salvation by grace, which was, after all, its "existential" core, the point at which dogma most obviously intersected with piety. But in so defending it, they employed rather strong statements of limited atonement that became increasingly characteristic of the direction in which Calvinism was moving in the 1640s and 1650s. Proponents of this strict Calvinism not only did not hesitate to speak in extreme ways about limited atonement but also chose to defend orthodox Calvinism against Arminianism by stressing God's decrees, including the decree of reprobation, and by introducing the Antinomian language of justification before actual faith, thereby pushing justification itself back into election. Thus at the end of the several phases of Arminian controversy that occurred through the middle of the century, there emerged the clear outline of a school of extreme Calvinists, fond of speaking of the supralapsarian decrees and incautious about Antinomianism, who were gradually being separated from more moderate Calvinists. These extreme Calvinists were reacting to a sectarian Arminianism that seemed to go farther than even the Laudians in dismissing predestinarian grace and also to Anglican Arminians whose connections were closer to Chillingworth and the Dutch Arminians than to the Laudians and whose formulas went farther in negating free grace than the Laudians had. As these Anglican and sectarian Arminians converged, their opponents raised the alarm of a Socinian specter.

Chapter 4 ❖ The Antinomian Catalyst and the Further Formation of Theological Parties, 1640–1660

In the era of civil war, Commonwealth, and Protectorate, theologians and religious writers continued to dispute over the role of divine grace and the part played by predestination in the all-important matter of Christian salvation. Gradually such conflict resolved itself into a three-cornered match among those who tended to attenuate earlier meanings of grace while forwarding an increasingly frank moralism, those who regarded such a view as a graceless Socinianism and responded with more extreme formulations of the place of grace in redemption, and those who sought to retain the core of the Reformed theology of grace without offensive overstatement and with some moderating qualifications. Under the shadow of earlier theological arguments, including the Arminian controversy, in the midst of the social and ecclesiastical turmoil of the Cromwellian years, and not without some relation to newer tendencies in the mood and spirit of the age that in later and more fully formed shape are designated by the term "Enlightenment," these three theological parties followed out the logic both of their ideas and their ecclesiastical needs. Anglican Arminians became "moralists" stressing the will's freedom, thus distinguishing themselves from those Calvinists whom they regarded as the architects of the king's downfall and of a nonepiscopal church establishment. Some Calvinists, in a burst of enthusiasm over what God's grace was achieving in "new-modelling" England and reacting against such moralism as a denial of the Reformed faith altogether, became "high Calvinists" in their magnification of God's grace, eventually retreating into an arid theological isolation. Other Calvinists, fearful of what seemed the ecclesiastical and theological extremes to which some of their erstwhile Puritan brethren were going and eager to leave the way open for rapprochement with moderate episcopalians, were more open to new intellectual currents and moderated their predestinarian theology of grace. Several episodes in theological discussion were catalytic in the drawing of theological battle lines in this fashion, and none more so than the controversy over Antinomianism.

Antinomianism

As discussed in chapter 3, Arminianism had not been crushed with the defeat of the Laudians but had continued as a theological force, finding new life among some of the radical sectarians. Also in the period of civil war and Interregnum, many Anglican opponents of Cromwell and the Puritan regime nourished and developed their anti-Calvinist theology, not least because to do so was to reject the new order and its predestinarian confession of faith. On the other hand, the furor over the Arminian denial of effectual redemptive grace gave rise to extreme formulations of predestinarian theology, and perhaps Antinomianism is best seen as such a formulation. In any case, the Antinomian controversy burst upon the English scene in the 1640s and continued to have repercussions until the end of the century and even beyond.[1]

Much of what has been written about this subject has not interpreted Antinomianism as a new extremism concerning predestinarian grace. It has proved tempting to understand Antinomianism as yet another manifestation of a longstanding tendency in Christian life and thought to throw off orderly structures of restraint and control in the name of a spiritualistic inner freedom that disdains all law and to connect it with earlier spiritualists of Radical Reformation ambience, or even with the ancient Montanists, or with the later Quakers. The temptation to so regard it has found reinforcement in the strictures against it, both in old and New England, by those contemporaries who in condemning it saw it as a dangerous disruption that would lead straight to all the excesses of Munsterite Anabaptism. It has also had a usefulness to historians of the development of freedom as an example of lay religiosity in which the religious component is seen as a thin veneer over other social and political motives.[2] But of the seventeenth-century critics it must be said that to draw the worst conceivable consequences from an opponent's doctrine was a very hoary ploy in religious controversy, and though a real sense of the fragility of public order in New England or England in the 1640s was no doubt a factor in the fear of Antinomianism, the excitement of heresiographers ought to be taken with a grain of salt. Indeed, when considering the dispute, it is easy to get the impression that Antinomianism was often decried because to decry it was useful. For Anglican opponents of the Puritan and Cromwellian leadership it served as an example of where Calvinism and Puritanism led, whereas to Puritan defenders of the establishment it was a convenient whipping boy whereby to indicate one's commitment to and the desperate urgency of creating an orderly society, as well as an apologetic means to disavow those more extreme possibilities which Anglicans claimed to be endemic to Puritanism. In short, the Antinomian menace may have been blown up out of all proportion by its enemies; like Voltaire's God, had there been no Antinomianism, it would have been necessary to invent it. It might also be wondered if modern historians, in transposing Antinomianism into its "real" social and political meaning have not found it as useful as Stuart heresiographers did.

Others, acknowledging Antinomianism as a movement inspired by religious needs, especially the need for assurance, rather than a theological covering cast over a libertarian spirit (though without denying its very significant social and political ramifications), have nonetheless differed as to exactly what the religious issue was that begot it. Following Perry Miller, students of New England Antinomianism have interpreted it as a reaction to the growing emphasis on "preparation" for grace which they see building up among religious writers both in old and New England, an emphasis that, though in more subtle ways than outright Arminianism, nonetheless similarly brought into theology a greater role for human response.[3] Yet other authors, approaching it more from a theological standpoint, have regarded Antinomianism as a phase of extreme Calvinism.[4] Thus its predestinarianism can be seen as a reaction to "preparation," but more plausibly, granted the somewhat earlier pedigree for the movement in England than sometimes thought, as a reaction to Arminianism as a whole and a continuing if aberrant defense of a piety of grace alone. In any case, many of the so-called Antinomian writers asserted that they were reacting to Arminian error and in some cases appealed to Luther as the proponent of the kind of thoroughly "gracious" piety they exalted. William K. B. Stoever has recently illuminated the phenomenon of Antinomianism by depicting it as emphasizing grace to such an extreme that nothing of "nature" could be allowed to play a part in the redeemed individual.[5] This conclusion seems to be plausible and correct: it fits the Antinomian insistence on imputed rather than inherent righteousness, and it would also make the putative misbelief of those Antinomians, including Anne Hutchinson, who denied the soul's natural immortality and that the resurrected body could be the same natural body of earthly life, consistent with other Antinomian views—if grace were to be truly magnified, both soul and body must be new ones of grace alone.[6]

John Eaton was frequently cited by contemporaries as the father of English Antinomianism.[7] While preaching at Wickham Market, Suffolk, he was vehemently attacked by Peter Gunter for "libertinism" as early as 1615. Gunter charged him with maintaining that after justification God no longer saw the sin of the justified, a doctrine his detractor thought smacked of Familism and Anabaptism and which he feared had "stirred up a rabble of miscreants." Gunter introduced a method of argument of guilt by association and blame for the worst possible consequences of one's teaching that anti-Antinomian writers would long continue. Gunter saw Eaton's view as a blasphemy worthy of death, in accordance with the rule of Leviticus.[8] Although Eaton had a university education, he was described by Archbishop Abbot as "simple" and "ignorant" and was deprived of his Suffolk vicarate in 1619.[9]

Eaton died in 1641, but a book by him appeared posthumously the next year, *The Honey-Combe of Free Justification by Christ alone,* which makes possible the examination of his views apart from what his detractors said of him. The book does not so much evince an inordinate longing for freedom as it is a passionate protest against legalistic piety, which for Eaton was but a "cold apprehending of Christ."[10] Apparently, a "warm" piety of grace for him entailed a rejection of all legalism with respect to justification as well as a setting forth of the "excellency" of free justification in the manner of Luther and the beginning of the Protestant Reformation. Indeed, much of what Eaton said was simply a reiteration of Luther, whose works, especially his *Commentary on Galatians,* are cited on almost every page, often with ample quotations. Thus, frequently in Luther's very words, Eaton protested against legalism in Reformed theology. Here apparently was someone who discovered a Luther freed of the categories of later Protestant Scholasticism and marveled afresh at the glories of free grace. For Eaton, a true theology of justification must be grounded in Luther's distinction of law and grace; sanctification may serve to show justification to the world, but to rely on sanctification for assurance was to confuse law and grace; assurance for the Christian must come from believing that Christ's righteousness had been imputed to the believer in place of sin, apart from any works. And as did Luther, Eaton insisted upon the importance of remembering one's baptism in order to find assurance. Running through the highly rhetorical pages of Eaton's work is a recurring image that sums up his spirit: men must flee the "menstruous cloathes of their own righteousnes" and cover themselves with "the precious wedding-garment" of the righteousness of Christ.[11]

The heterodoxy of Eaton seems to be compounded mainly of his enthusiasm for Luther and his penchant for incautious rhetoric. As with Luther, law has little place in the life of the believer: the purpose of the law is to drive the sinner to Christ, and thereafter the believer does not need law, for he serves Christ spontaneously and thankfully.[12] Reformed theology, however, had insisted upon the law's necessity as a rule for the life of the believer and placed the purpose of the work of God in redemption in its result in holy living. That sanctification was the evidence, even to the believer himself, of the genuineness of justification was a frequent refrain of the spiritual writers. Here in Eaton, then, there appeared a "heresy" of so exalting grace that he feared its contamination even by sanctification as a means of assurance.

Other heterodoxies of Eaton similarly insisted upon grace alone, using extreme formulations that were obnoxious to others. For Eaton as for some other Puritans who maximized the extent of God's grace in Christ, Christ suffered not only the punishment due the elect for their sins, but was himself made a sinner and suffered the curse and wrath of God against sinners.[13] This heightening of what Christ suffered on behalf of the elect was a feature of the high Calvinism that was developing in the period and will be seen later to have been prominent in the theology of John Owen and others. Many Calvinists could accept this part of Eaton's views, but he went yet further in maintaining that the justified one was so perfectly covered by Christ's righteousness that God no longer saw sin in him at all; therefore God never saw sin in the elect, but only saw Christ's imputed righteousness; even in the necessarily imperfect process of the sanctification of the elect, God sees only their perfection in Christ.[14] Thus, goaded by Luther, and seeking only to heighten to the greatest extent possible the glories of God's grace, Eaton was betrayed into the bold formulation that God saw no sin in the elect, leaving himself open to the charge of teaching moral licentiousness. And from the identification of Christ with the believer in imputation he moved to incautious language about the union of Christ with the believer.[15] Finally, he spoke of the glories of an inner knowledge of justification experienced by the believer united to Christ in such a way as to make him liable to the charge of "enthusiasm," or the claim to a special private revelation, particularly when he affirmed that such knowledge "opens unto us the very closets of heaven."[16]

The lateness of the publication of his views notwithstanding, at least much of Eaton's Antinomianism considerably antedates that of the New

England Antinomians, as Gunter's 1615 rejoinder makes evident. It is surprising, therefore, that this has been so little noted in the literature about Anne Hutchinson and her allies, especially in that so many of the views she was accused of holding were similar to those of Eaton. Anne Hutchinson was, of course, much blamed for denying that sanctification could be an evidence of justification. She, too, thought that assurance came by some more immediate sense of being united to Christ, and she carried that assertion coupled with an extreme view on the imputation of Christ's righteousness to the believer to the point of maintaining that there was such a union of Christ with the Christian as to blur the distinction of Christ and the soul and of nature and grace.[17] John Wheelwright, a New England minister and Mrs. Hutchinson's brother-in-law, gave vent to similar opinions. There are also several hints in the documents concerning Anne Hutchinson that she had brought Antinomianism with her from England where she had learned it from various heresiarchs. She herself, however, claimed that her doctrine had simply come from the sermons of John Cotton, whom she regarded as especially skillful in setting forth the grace of God. Cotton was later much embarrassed by the charge, but it is clear enough that he, along with others to be examined later, was on the road leading to high Calvinism and was consequently far less fearful of the specter of Antinomianism than were other New England Calvinists.[18] Furthermore, the relationship of Anne Hutchinson to Cotton is probably paradigmatic of the rise of Antinomianism altogether; spiritual preachers exalting grace begot in some auditors a taste for ever more extreme formulations of the role of grace in redemption until nature was entirely swallowed up in grace.

Later theological writers in England repeated the excesses of Eaton in the exaltation of grace and added some more of their own, the "horrible" example of New England Antinomianism notwithstanding. Like Eaton, these later English Antinomians also drew strongly on Luther. William Eyre, whose views were sufficiently acceptable to some orthodox Calvinists as to merit a recommendatory preface from John Owen, cited Luther in his *Justification without Conditions* almost as frequently as Eaton had. John Saltmarsh, rather notorious as a parliamentary army chaplain, commented that he could have quoted Luther in support of his views, but that he refrained because Luther "is now lookt on by some" as having "over-writ Free-grace."[19]

Saltmarsh echoed much else found in Eaton. He, too, wished the legalism of conditions and qualifications not to be mixed up with the gospel of free grace, for to do so was little different from Arminians and papists, who also talked of grace but really relied on works. True assurance came from greater "gospel-light," which Saltmarsh expounded in emotive terms as "breathings" of the soul to God, "meltings of heart in prayer," and the "closing" of the heart with Christ. To look for assurance from one's changed external way of life was dangerous, Saltmarsh thought, and might tempt to "works-righteousness." To regard one's repentance or obedience is to neglect God's grace, for under grace one is freed from the law.[20] Saltmarsh was so fearful that some virtue inherent in the believer might derogate from divine grace that he maintained that the blessedness of the redeemed was greater in having the curse of sin taken away than the corruption of sin: "Our justification is more glorious than our sanctification, and our forgiveness from sin, more than our cleansing from sin."[21] Such an assertion would seem, in its eagerness to exalt grace, to belie one of the central motifs of the Puritan and Reformed theology of grace as it had come down from Bucer and Calvin and had been emphasized in the spiritual writers—that the earthly goal of the election of grace was the holiness of the believer. The end of election instead was for Saltmarsh and his fellow Antinomians the glorious sense the believer had that grace was everything, grace not only overcoming nature but virtually replacing it.

Generally predestinarian in their outlook,[22] neither Eaton nor Saltmarsh built their doctrine entirely on predestination (Saltmarsh even rejected limited atonement).[23] But their tendency to push justification back into predestination (both held that God from eternity saw no sin in the elect), making it prior to the actual faith of the believer,[24] gives weight to the interpretation that they indeed were engaged in theological innovation as a consequence of extreme predestinarianism. This notion of justification before actual belief and its consequent regeneration especially troubled critics—this was what seemed to open the door literally to "lawless" behavior.[25]

In a certain respect the charge might appear idle when made by those who themselves believed firmly in predestination and so also maintained that only the elect would be justified. But the Reformed orthodoxy concerning grace had carefully placed predestination within an order of salvation where it stood as one among several steps in an economy of grace, with actual justification coming only when a person was effectually called and actually believed, that calling and belief being also the beginning of holy life, though to be sure it was still all of grace, whether calling, belief, or holiness. By such a formulation, Reformed theology had combined its emphasis upon grace alone guaranteed by predestination with the sense that something real actually occurred at the moment of calling and believing. The Antinomians, fearful that unmerited grace was being compromised in this way just as all Calvinists were fearful that Arminianism compromised free grace, abandoned those formulas that had protected justification by faith from being wholly swallowed up in predestination and concluded that those elected in grace for whom Christ had died had Christ's righteousness eternally imputed to them, thus certainly before they had actual faith. And no wonder that looking for signs of sanctification as assurance of justification was improper to them, for when actual faith did come it was a spirit-given moment of illumination about their eternal justification.

Neither Eaton nor Saltmarsh specifically taught the formulation of justification from eternity.[26] The extremely scholastic anti-Arminian writer William Pemble seems to have done so, however,[27] and John Cotton regarded both Pemble and the prominent English scholastic theologian William Twisse as sound in maintaining that if justification was not from eternity it must nonetheless in some sense precede faith; otherwise faith is made a kind of work or instrument in procuring justification, and free grace would be compromised.[28] Justification from eternity and before actual faith was mentioned among the errors of Anne Hutchinson.[29] But most notorious, especially later in the century, among those who held that justification preceded actual faith was Tobias Crisp, a Wiltshire rector who died at London in 1643 before most of the furor over his views. He believed that faith was transformed into a good work upon which eternal life was conditional unless justification came before it.[30]

John Simpson also taught justification before belief. He followed Walter Cradock (who had left London to preach in Wales in 1647) as the pastor of a London "gathered church" and also followed Cradock as an Antinomian, later compounding his heterodoxy by becoming a Baptist.[31] Simpson published some of his sermons in response to the complaint of fifty-two London ministers that he was guilty of Antinomian error. Answering them, Simpson expressed concern over Arminian error instead and warned that too much stress was being given to good works as preparation for grace to the detriment of free grace: not only were persons not justified by works, but "the presence of good works" was not necessary at all in coming to God for justification. Instead, he asserted that it was the eternal grace of God in predestination by which the elect were saved.

The elect are justified by grace before knowing anything of that grace; to God they are justified from eternity.[32]

William Eyre likewise built more or less Antinomian conclusions on the foundation of predestination. For him the true teaching about justification had been sadly diluted by those who spoke of doing the works of grace or of "new covenant works" as conditions of justification. The true teaching, that justification was without conditions and was a free act of God's grace from eternity, by which Christ's righteousness was eternally imputed to the elect, was being slandered as Antinomianism.[33] Eyre labored to give respectability to his views by connecting them to the great anti-Arminian writers of the preceding generation, but their best endorsement came from John Owen, by then not only a prominent theologian but an important adviser to the Cromwellian church. Owen recommended Eyre's book as needed to stem the rising tide of salvation by works,[34] which concerned Owen and other strict Calvinists more than Antinomianism, although Owen in later writings disavowed justification from eternity.[35] Joseph Caryl, also a stalwart of the Cromwellian establishment, scandalized some by giving his endorsement to the writing of John Crandon, another teacher of justification before faith.[36]

All this leads to some conclusions of importance for the rest of the present story: Antinomianism, reaching back somewhat earlier in English religious history than usually thought, from an excess of predestinarian zeal drew heterodox formulas that frightened establishments both in England and New England. To Calvinist critics, these Antinomians were especially dangerous because they seemed so much to "magnifie the grace of God and Christ" while really "prostituting the Free-Grace of God."[37] Most significantly, however, the Antinomian crisis and controversy acted as a catalyst in the forming of theological parties, on the one hand driving a wedge between moderate Calvinists who abhorred them and high Calvinists who found them incautious allies and, on the other hand, further alienating Arminian Anglicans from all Calvinists.

Continuing Arminianism

The Antinomian movement provided an ideal opportunity for Anglican Arminians to continue their attack upon Calvinism. Their attack was quite different from that of the Laudian years, when Arminians were in control, for now the Arminian Anglicans were an embittered and embattled group who had lost power and who, in disfavor and sometimes exile, nourished their grievances against the Puritan establishment. No doubt this made them yet more eager to find a vulnerable spot in the Calvinist armor. Antinomianism provided not only a theological doctrine to refute, but also could be richly exploited to expose social and political dangers ostensibly inherent in Puritanism and Calvinism.

Neither the first nor the most rancorous of the Anglican Arminians to raise the specter of Antinomianism, Herbert Thorndike was the most persuasive. Thorndike was a biblical and patristic scholar, educated at Cambridge. His royalism led to the sequestration of his benefice by the Long Parliament and his withdrawal from a Cambridge fellowship. He found some patronage at the hands of sympathizers and continued throughout the Interregnum to write in behalf of the royal and episcopal cause. Before and after the Restoration he attacked what he thought to be the inevitably Antinomian consequences of Calvinism. The Antinomians, he declared, held that they uniquely possessed God's spirit and that they were justified by the obedience of Christ *imputed to them from eternity* so that God saw no sin in them. Acknowledging that the "Presbyterians," or more moderate Puritans, did not teach such things,[38] he nonetheless maintained that all Calvinists opened the door to fanaticism and often joined themselves to "fanaticks." The root of these false teachings, Thorndike claimed, was the doctrine of predestination apart from foresight of future obedience and the doctrine that one can be assured of one's election; these positions, taken together, were "downright haeresie." Followers of Calvin who "presume" upon their predestination feel that no matter what they do they cannot be damned, and thus their claim to assurance of salvation leads to Antinomianism and their Antinomianism destroys all Christian morality.[39]

Others joined Thorndike, often speaking in less measured tones. Laurence Womock, who became a bishop after the Restoration, similarly attacked the Antinomian notion of justification from eternity. Thomas Pierce, who, like Thorndike, had been ejected from a college fellowship only to find the patronage of a royalist supporter, regarded the Antinomian teaching as the belief of wild sectarians that they as saints could commit horrible crimes and still remain saints, an inflammatory enough rendition of Antinomianism and a train of logic that he blamed upon the teaching of the doctrine of predestination. For Henry Hammond, writing in 1660, it was an old complaint of "pious and learned men" that the crude treatment of the doctrine of predestination and a "hasty premature perswasion" of "being in Christ" contributed to the final impenitency of many sinners.[40]

Finding ammunition in the bugbear of Antinomianism, Arminian Anglicans set going a concerted offensive against the doctrine of predestination that lasted throughout the 1650s and into the Restoration years. In 1651 a manuscript by John Plaifere, originally written apparently for the author's own satisfaction, was published posthumously with the title *Appeal to Gospel for True Doctrine of Divine Predestination.* Plaifere had been a Suffolk rector until his death in 1632, and to claim him for Arminianism had the benefit of adding further precedent to the cause. In the text, Plaifere roundly declared the teaching of Arminius to be consonant with that of the ancient church fathers.[41]

In the same year there appeared the first of several antipredestinarian satires, a Latin dialogue entitled *Fur Praedestinatus*, issued anonymously but now generally acknowledged as the work of William Sancroft, the future archbishop of Canterbury. The purpose of the dialogue, the reader is told, is to expose the opinion of strict predestination as pernicious and absurd by using the very words of the "doctors" of the doctrine.[42] Among those whose predestinarian views were held up to ridicule were not only the members of the Synod of Dort and William Perkins but also the two foreign divines, Martin Bucer and Peter Martyr, who had been instrumental in the early English Reformation. The burden of the dialogue is that predestinarian theology subverts morality. It was translated into English and printed again in 1658.

Another anonymous satirical dialogue dealing with the same subject appeared in 1658, *The Examination of Tilenus before the Triers; In order to his intended settlement in the office of a publick Preacher in the Common-wealth of Utopia. Whereunto are annexed the Tenets of the Remonstrants touching those five Articles Voted, Stated and imposed, but not disputed at the Synod of Dort.* Its author was eventually known to be Laurence Womock, who, like the other satirist, rose to the Restoration episcopate. The dialogue purports to be the questioning by the Triers, an obvious reference to the boards of examiners set up to admit clergy in the Cromwellian church, of a certain Tilenus, who seeks admission. The name Tilenus may have been chosen for the protagonist after a Daniel Tilenus who had defended the Arminian position among French Calvinists and had visited England during the reign of James I.[43] The names of those who question Tilenus clearly indicate the tone of the piece: among them are Dr. Absolute, Mr. Fatalitie, Mr. Fri-Babe, Dr. Dam-Man, Mr.

Narrow-Grace alias Stint-grace, Mr. Indefectible, Dr. Confidence, and Mr. Know-Little. Someone very like Richard Baxter is introduced as Dr. Dubious. Tilenus's argument with the Triers, shown by a series of examinations he carries on with the "straw-men" Infidelis, Carnalis, Tepidus, and Tentanus, is that the doctrine of the Synod of Dort cannot convert infidels, correct the immoral, quicken the slothful, or comfort the afflicted in conscience. The attack on the maintainers of predestination was embittered: they were portrayed as having no qualms about tossing "innocent babes into Hell"; as leading persons to immoral license; as teaching that God is the author of sin. Tilenus instead argues that God's grace does not work irresistibly and that persons must cooperate with it; everywhere he blurs the distinction of nature and grace. The Triers, complaining that Tilenus has been studying the ancient fathers more than Calvin and Perkins, refuse to admit him to the ministry.[44]

Three years later Womock wrote another dialogue attacking predestinarian theology. Its pages bear such running titles as "Calvinisme a Cloak for the Carnal," "Calvinisme a Sanctuary for the Secure," and "Calvinisme a Scourge to the Disconsolate."[45]

Some of the most furious attacks upon predestinarian theology came from the febrile pen of Thomas Pierce, who admitted having held predestinarian views in his youth.[46] One of Pierce's opponents ruefully commented that because Pierce "can print more Books in two years, than a wiser man would undertake to print in all his life, . . . I may be excused if I have no mind to meddle further with him."[47] Pierce, rector of Brington after 1656 through the intervention of a patron and made a royal chaplain in 1660, continued long after the Restoration to engage in various quarrels with the other fellows of his college, his bishop, and the prebendaries of Salisbury Cathedral after he became dean there.[48] His first work on the subject of predestination, *A Correct Copy of Some Notes concerning Gods Decrees, Especially of Reprobation. Written for the private Use of a Friend in Northamptonshire. And Now published to prevent Calumny,* declared that he preferred silence on this question (a preference his later writings would seem to belie) but that, forced into the open, he must avow that God's decrees of election and reprobation are conditional upon the faith and obedience of the new covenant and that God's grace is not irresistible.[49]

Two years later, Pierce returned to the fray with two large works, *The Divine Philanthropie Defended . . . In Vindication of some Notes concerning Gods Decrees, Especially of Reprobation* and *The Divine Purity*

Defended: Or Vindication of some Notes concerning God's Decrees, Especially of Reprobation. In these responses to a number of attacks upon his earlier work on the subject, Pierce denied the oft-reiterated charge of Pelagianism[50] and repeated the antipredestinarian complaints that God is made the author of sin, that innocent babes are condemned, and that predestination leads to license.[51] His own positive doctrine is set forth again: election and reprobation depend upon man's repentance and are therefore conditional, and Christ died for the sins of all.[52] But Pierce was adept at creating diversions from the main issue, and he raised a number of matters that were to be debated at length in succeeding controversy. King James, he claimed, abandoned his earlier Calvinism; Beza and Peter Martyr were "blasphemers"; Pemble and Twisse taught Antinomianism;[53] Archbishop Ussher changed his opinions and came to accept "universal grace."[54] But most of both works consists of point-by-point refutations of his opponents' arguments, though the refutation is frequently more raillery than argument.

The following year, 1658, saw two more works by Pierce on the same subject, consisting primarily of further refutation of new and old critics. The controversial tone of one of these was set by its long title: αὐτοκατάκρισις, *or, Self-Condemnation, Exemplified in Mr. Whitfield, Mr. Barlee, and Mr. Hickman. With Occasional Reflexions on Mr Calvin, Mr Beza, Mr Zwinglius, Mr Piscator, Mr Rivet, and Mr. Rollock: But more Especially on Doctor Twisse, and Master Hobbs; against whom, God's Purity and his Praescience, and his Eternal Decrees according to Praescience, . . . with the sincere intention and the general extent of the Death of Christ, are finally cleared and made good; And the Adversaries Absurdities . . . are proved against them undeniably.* In these he taxed his critics with fatalism and making God the cause of sin.[55]

Pierce included among his opponents the philosopher Thomas Hobbes, already becoming notorious for determinism and other unorthodox notions, saying that he is "as able a Calvinist (as to these points) as their party hath lately had."[56] The attempt to tar Calvinism with the brush of Hobbesian determinism was rejected by Pierce's opponents (Henry Hickman, for example, complained that "when he hath called me Hobbist, what can he say more, except he should call me Devill?"[57]), but the writings of the Anglican and Arminian John Bramhall[58] against Hobbes can be seen as related to the offensive against predestinarian thinking. His attack upon Hobbes echoed many of the same polemical points as did the Arminian and predestinarian controversies of the preceding decades: Hobbes falsely accuses Arminius of returning to "Popery"; Hobbes makes God the author of sin; Hobbes's doctrine of necessity destroys true religion.[59] But Bramhall recognized differences between the views of Hobbes and the principles of Calvinism and admitted that although Hobbes claimed admiration for Calvin and Perkins he did not really understand them, Calvin being innocent of so total a determinism as that of Hobbes.[60] Bramhall also accused Hobbes of reducing God to nature, and Bramhall attributed this and other extreme views of the philosopher to Hobbes's very personal and idiosyncratic interpretation of scripture.[61]

The decade of the 1650s closed with a last Anglican Arminian sally against predestination from Henry Hammond, one of the most important of the Anglican writers of the period, of whom Robert S. Bosher has written, "It is due in large measure to his efforts and his encouragement of others that the Interregnum became in fact a golden age of High Anglican theology and apologetic."[62] Hammond began his *A Pacifick Discourse of Gods Grace and Decrees: In a Letter, of full Accordance, written to the Reverend, and most learned, Dr. Robert Sanderson* by criticizing both sides in the debate over predestination for engaging in bitter uncharitableness and then offered his correspondence with Sanderson as a means of clearing up some of the difficulties regarding the subject. But Hammond's standpoint was clearly antipredestinarian: God's grace is not irresistible, Christ died for all, the promise of salvation is conditional on human obedience, and it is possible to fall from grace. Absolute decrees, whether of election or reprobation, are called "the meer invention and fabrick of men's brains."[63] Sanderson, however, was perhaps not yet so anti-Calvinist as Hammond.[64]

In rejecting the Reformed predestinarian theology of grace, these Anglican Arminians showed themselves no longer reluctant to defend Arminius himself and did not deny, as earlier Anglican anti-Calvinists had, that they had read the Dutch theologian's writings. For "Tilenus," Arminius was no Pelagian, but a person of "acute wit, solid judgment, and great Learning."[65] Thorndike believed that the views of Arminius were what the church had always taught.[66] It was left, however, to a sectarian Arminian, Tobias Conyers, in a writing dedicated to Oliver Cromwell, to translate a whole work in order to rehabilitate the Dutch heretic, *The Just Mans Defence, or, The Declaration of the Judgment of James Arminius*, which appeared in 1657. The dedicatory epistle by Conyers declared that the views of Arminius should be made known, to show "that Arminius was no such monster in religion as some men have attempted to represent him." Most Protestants, Conyers thought, agreed with Arminius, not holding the rigid views of grace of his opponents.[67] The book is mainly a translation of a long self-defense by Arminius himself. A similar work appeared considerably later, *The Life and Death of James Arminius, and Simon Episcopius . . . Both of them Famous Defenders of the Doctrine of Gods Universal Grace and Sufferers for it.* Here, too, the preface maintained the innocence of Arminius from the unjust reproaches long heaped upon him by English writers.[68] What followed was a translation of the Latin lives of Arminius and Simon Episcopius written by Peter Bertius, who was for a time prominent among the Dutch Arminians.

Thomas Pierce also spoke favorably of Arminius, but connected him with Melancthon and the "Lutherans" as a representative of their version of the Reformation faith.[69] Melancthon, Pierce said, avoided the errors of Calvin and taught with greater moderation concerning grace; Pierce considers himself a "Melancthonian."[70] Thereafter Melancthon was frequently quoted, and also Hemingius, a "disciple of Melancthon."[71] That Danish Lutheran theologian had been claimed much earlier by Peter Baro as one who held his view of predestination and had also been much cited as a source for Anglican teaching about the descent of Christ into hell; thus in the middle of the seventeenth century Anglican writers were still eager to cite Lutherans in their rejection of Calvinist formulations concerning grace. "Tilenus" makes the same claim about the relationship of Melancthon and Arminius.[72] These Anglicans also defended Hugo Grotius from the accusation of Socinianism,[73] and Pierce speaks well of Sebastianus Castellio, one of Calvin's famous antagonists.[74]

Pierce also claimed some English theological writers as precursors of his views: he thought Cranmer and Latimer were more Melancthonian than Calvinist. He mentioned favorably Thomas Jackson and Lancelot Andrewes.[75] But he referred most frequently to John Overall,[76] as did Henry Hammond.[77] Clearly, Overall loomed large as a founder of Anglican Arminianism among the Arminians themselves. In one of the less frequent references to Hooker in the literature of this discussion, he was acknowledged to be on the Calvinist side![78]

Henry Hammond, Herbert Thorndike, Thomas Pierce, and the antipredestinarian satirists rejected the Reformed doctrine of predestination and such accompanying doctrines as limited atonement and perseverance of the saints because these teachings seemed to them to undermine human effort and moral striving. This is the main point of all their polemic and points to the very different religious spirit these theological writers exemplify. Living in the midst of the religious turmoil of the years of civil war and Cromwellian rule, they were the enemies of all fanaticism in religion and of all claims to special graces and revelations, which they associated not only with sectarian religion, but with Calvinism itself as the ultimate source of such excesses. As a consequence, they abandoned not only the predestinarian formulation of the theology of grace, from which the earlier Laudians had also departed, but explicitly rejected the central Protestant and Reformed teaching of justification by faith, substituting for it a clear "moralism." C. F. Allison has documented this "rise of moralism" and the way it departed from the earlier normative teaching on justification with reference to a circle of writers whom he dubs the "holy living divines," a group that included Hammond and Thorndike and also such others as Jeremy Taylor and George Bull. Taylor's theology, Allison says, stressed "God's pardon and eternal life as rewards for and incentives toward obedience and holy living."[79]

These writers rejected justification as a gratuitous taking hold, by faith, of the righteousness of Christ: for Pierce human faith and obedience are conditions of a new covenant that must be fulfilled for salvation.[80] Indeed, these writers used the scheme of covenants to introduce a legalistic moralism into their theology much more clearly than did Puritan writers who have often been accused of doing so. In the words of Thorndike, "God from everlasting determined to give life or death to every man, in consideration of his being found qualified for this or for that, according to those terms which the covenant of grace proposeth."[81] This covenant of grace, or gospel, is "the last law of God,"[82] better than the old law, which could not be fulfilled, in that, by God's helping grace and human cooperation, this new law of Christ can be fulfilled, and such fulfillment is the way to salvation.[83] Thorndike, more objective and honest about the radical departure involved in his views than the others, admitted that he disagreed with the homily on justification and said that he rejected the still frequently held opinion that justification was a trusting in the mercy of God in Christ because that opinion led to extreme views that undermined morality.[84] Henry Hammond was one of the first to explicitly adopt such a moralism when, in his *Practical Catechism* of 1646, he stated that justification, or God's pardon of sins, followed upon believing, repentance, and the firm resolve to lead a new life and that at least the beginning of sanctification preceded justification.[85] Perhaps the most explicit rejection of the not only Reformed but Protestant doctrine of justification came a little later with George Bull.[86] This school of Anglican theology, then, had moved very far from the Reformed theology of predestinarian grace in a very few years. It is less surprising that they sometimes masked their views than that they so often frankly avowed them, speaking as though their views were obvious and commonplace, whereas those of their opponents were fanatical and extremist, even as they departed from the most essential points of the Reformed theology as it had come down from the earliest years of the English Reformation. Accused now by their opponents, not of "popery," which stood for salvation by a gratuitous righteousness albeit one infused by participation in the sacramental system of the church, but of a graceless Socinian moralism, they usually responded by restricting Socinianism to a heresy concerning the person of Christ, and so avoided the issue.[87]

Although the moralism of this school of divines also differentiated them from the Roman Catholic and Tridentine theology of justification by infused and inherent grace, they spoke of that view with less disfavor than they did of the Reformed alternative. It is apparent that to Thorndike, for example, the views of the "fanatics" on predestination and assurance were much worse than anything taught in Roman theology.[88] That this new moralistic theology felt considerable sympathy for some more "catholic" usages and thus continued in the path of the high churchmanship of Laud and Cosin is evident in the irenic tone toward Rome adopted by Thorndike: he argued that the Roman Catholic veneration of the host and of images was not idolatry and that the pope could not be the Antichrist. This tendency was present in other of the "Caroline Divines," and reinforced the alienation between them and the Calvinists.[89] That these same theologians showed a clear preference for patristic over Reformation writers would be a truism.

But to interpret this school of Anglican "moralists" as representative simply of the continuation of the Arminianism and high churchmanship of the Laudians sharpened by polemic with a prevailing Puritanism would be to overlook some important new aspects of the religious situation in the middle of the seventeenth century. For in addition to the earlier Laudian Arminianism, these "moralists" had also inherited the more liberal and anthropocentric outlook of Laudian allies in the previous generation such as Hales and Chillingworth. The greater tolerance in outlook of some of them (Jeremy Taylor, for example) was obscured by their intense conflict with the reigning Cromwellian order and its supporters, but this latter influence probably nudged them toward more frankly moralistic views that opponents stigmatized as "Socinian." Such a more liberal and tolerant outlook was in that generation, however, most apparent in the circle of thinkers commonly referred to as the Cambridge Platonists, a group more or less Arminian in their views, but who nonetheless kept their distance from the more polemical Anglican churchmen already considered.

"With scarcely an exception, the Cambridge Platonists came out of a Puritan background," Gerald R. Cragg has noted.[90] And yet they breathed a spirit quite different from that of scholastic Calvinism, and much in their standpoint would seem to have been at least implicitly Arminian. Something can be said also for the influence of the Dutch Arminians upon them.[91] The quiet Arminianism of the Cambridge Platonists perhaps first was expressed in the correspondence between Anthony Tuckney and Benjamin Whichcote in 1651. Tuckney, earlier a tutor at Emmanuel, Cambridge, and then a rector in Lincolnshire who had been appointed to the Westminster Assembly, became master of Emmanuel in 1645. Suspicious of Whichcote, whom he had long before tutored, he tried through correspondence to draw him out on various issues relative to Arminianism and Socinianism by imputing to him certain errors, including a "moral influence" view of the atonement that slighted imputed righteousness (a view then considered "Socinian"), questioning the decrees of God, and excessively advancing "the power of Nature in morals."[92] Whichcote responded that he had studied Calvin, Beza, and Perkins more than he had Arminius and that what he had said about justification and sanctification had been intended not to derogate from free grace but to preclude grace becoming an occasion of "wantonness." The purport of Whichcote's remarks, however, was a greater reliance on human effort, even where he stated his views about grace with great care. And he explicitly declared his belief in religious toleration, even if such a belief associated him with Socinians.[93]

Similar attitudes characterized others classed as belonging to the group of Cambridge Platonists. At about the same time as the Tuckney-Whichcote exchange, Ralph Cudworth spoke of his differences from Calvinism.[94] Henry More later said that even in youth he could not accept Calvinistic predestination.[95] Nathaniel Culverwel shared many of the leading themes of the Cambridge circle and decried the misuse of free grace in Antinomianism, but remained more wedded to Reformed theology than the others.[96] Peter Sterry, though at least on the fringes of the group of those leading Independent divines whose advice Cromwell sought, nonetheless shared much with the Platonists. His considerably later *A Discourse of the Freedom of the Will* expressed hope for the avoidance of "bitter zeal" in the discussion of that question. His more mystical treatment of the subject was filled with references to Plotinus, Boethius, the Kabbalah, and the "mystical ladder" by which Christ is approached.[97] But Sterry was no Arminian.

Sectarian Arminianism

To be classed neither with Anglicans such as Hammond and Thorndike nor with the Cambridge Platonists were those English Arminians whose connections were with the world of sectarian Puritanism. Foremost among them was John Goodwin, who continued to write on grace in the 1650s. In 1652, his views and those of "the Church of God walking with him" concerning the theology of grace were made known by the publication of a short summary of their opinions, in which predestination, limited atonement, irresistible grace, and the indefectibility of the elect were denied.[98] Goodwin's major work was his *Redemption Redeemed*, which centered on the doctrine of the atonement, advancing the view that the death of Christ was for all, not just the elect. As did Anglican Arminians, he cited patristic sources in support of his approach; unlike them he showed interest in the reformers, too; but in radical Puritan fashion his real authority was that of new light coming forth from scripture. He proudly asserted that he had continually changed his own mind as he studied the matter, having found his earlier opinion of limited atonement to be "gravellesh in my mouth" in spite of the esteem in which he held those who taught it. Admitting that the late "Romanizing" and "tyrannizing" prelates had adopted the doctrine of the Remonstrants, he felt they had done so for "politique" reasons, a case of the wolf putting on sheep's clothing. In any case, he added, a doctrine is not made worse by those who teach it, but must stand on its own. He, too, showed concern with the moral consequences of extreme predestinarian teaching: to claim that the elect were justified from eternity was morally dangerous, the perseverance of the saints led to a false security and moral declension, and the notion that God reprobated some dishonored Him.[99]

Little in Goodwin's argument was new; what so markedly separated him from Anglican Arminians were matters of tone and emphasis. For Goodwin shared much with the Puritans and Calvinists that the Anglican Arminians denied. He had the same piety and spirituality as they and clearly regarded himself as on their side in the ecclesiastical struggle. Thus he has no desire to berate his Calvinist opponents for dangerous opinions but to convince them that the Reformation must be reformed (a Puritan desideratum after all) and that the new light coming forth from scripture must be heeded in order to make the faith more truly evangelical and to summon all men to conversion and regeneration. In short, one finds Goodwin not a moralistic Arminian but an evangelical one. He was very precise in his discussions of grace, clearly intending not to let go of the central Puritan and Calvinist notion that God's grace was a supernatural transforming power, but rather seeking a theological base from which to offer that transformation to all mankind. He frequently complained that his opponents were obscuring the gospel of God's grace in Christ. Defending himself in a later writing, he argued that predestinarian teaching, far from exalting God's grace, minimized it, turning "the unsearchable riches of Christ in the Gospel" into no more than a "morsel of bread." This the predestinarians fail to recognize, and thus they wrongly suppose that those who are offended by their views are offended by the gospel rather than by "a narrow limited or confined redemption."[100] Far more drastic in his conclusions than were moderate Calvinists, Goodwin perhaps had more in common with them than he did with the Anglican Arminianism of Hammond and Thorndike.

The evangelical character of Goodwin's Arminianism should also provide a caution concerning broad generalizations about the tendency of sectarian religion in the period. Christopher Hill has written of "the popular Pelagianism of the sectaries" as constituting an "Arminianism of the left," properly distinguishing it from the more "catholic" Anglican kind, but regarding it as crypto-rationalistic, pointing forward to Deism and rationalism and akin to the protests of the Ranters.[101] But if much of this sectarian Arminianism was evangelical in intent, it may be more important as a precursor of the general "arminianizing" of Reformation religion evident in Methodism and the awakenings than it is of rationalism.

John Goodwin was a leading figure among an array of sectarian Arminians who seemed to be multiplying in the relatively free religious atmosphere of the time. How such sectarian freewillers began to publish their opinions in the decade of the 1640s and how all this hearkened back to a kind of lay person's common-sense "freewilling" religion, of which new examples were not lacking, was discussed in chapter 3.[102] Other Independents besides John Goodwin may have held Arminian views, as did some Fifth Monarchists,[103] but it was the General Baptists and Quakers who as communities became the main bearers of the left-wing Arminian outlook. General Baptist Arminianism by this time had a fairly long heritage; but the Quakers had just burst upon the scene, and George Fox's ministry included denunciation of the predestinarian teaching of the Calvinist clergy.[104] Critics of the Quakers connected them to Arminianism, John Stalham claiming that they had reduced grace to no more than nature,[105] thus making them the logical opposite of the Antinomians, whom Stalham also rebuked. This is a point worth making, for treatments of radical sectarian religion in mid-seventeenth-century England have a tendency to lump all sectarians together under some one generic tendency, overlooking important distinctions. A recent study of the Quakers, however, has argued that their doctrinal affinity was with moderate Calvinists, "preparationists," and Anglican Arminians rather than with Antinomian "spiritualists."[106]

The great Puritan poet John Milton probably should be classed among these sectarian Arminians. Certainly the range of his opinions might allow his inclusion among some of the groups already discussed on one point or another, but a great deal of current opinion stresses his closeness to the radical sectarians.[107] *Paradise Lost* requires some assumptions about human freedom for its vindication of God's ways to men, but it was in the posthumously printed *De Doctrina Christiana* that Milton most explicitly revealed his Arminianism. In that treatise, Milton argued that Arminianism was not a heresy, that predestination was based on God's foreknowledge of the righteous, and that justification is by a faith "not destitute of works" and follows upon regeneration,[108] the last point sounding very much like the treatment of the matter by the Anglican moralists.

Moderate Calvinism

John Goodwin had written that the decree of reprobation "involves so many inextricable difficulties, palpable absurdities (that I say not, intolerable Blasphemies also) that my hope is, it will shortly ... fall and sink with the insupportable weight of its own evil, in the mindes and judgments of men."[109] This doctrine, apparently so plausible to an earlier generation, was a rock of offense to many by the middle of the seventeenth century. Not only radical sectarians such as John Goodwin and moralistic Anglicans such as Herbert Thorndike but also some who were pledged to the theology of predestinarian grace recognized this offense. Thus there emerged a school of "moderated" Calvinism, in which some defenders of the Reformed theology of gratuitous redemption re-acted with sensitivity to the most vulnerable spots in their outlook as they had been uncovered in the Arminian critique and sought to disavow some of the more extreme formulations of predestinarian grace, includ-ing certainly those of the Antinomians. In doing so, some of them, Rich-ard Baxter in particular, came perilously close to the Arminian position. Their aim was to protect the vital core of Reformed theology that related to the life of piety in which salvation was seen as God's gift, while aban-doning some of the more scholastic and offensive outerworks of that the-ology. Such a program was not unlike that at which John Goodwin aimed, but he went about it with such incautious abandon and in such sectarian isolation from these moderate Calvinists that he was never an accepted member of their group. Moderated Calvinism can be seen emerging in a series of theological "moments" from the predestinarian discussions of the Westminster Assembly, to the outcry against Antinomianism, to the controversies surrounding Richard Baxter, and finally to the answers of Henry Hickman to the Anglican Arminians.

In discussing different views of God's decrees, John Goodwin had praised those of John Cameron,[110] a Scottish theologian whose teaching career and influence were mainly exercised among the Protestants of France. And even fierce Thomas Pierce spoke favorably of the most im-portant pupil of Cameron, Moise Amyraut,[111] who developed and spread Cameron's views. Cameron and Amyraut sought to reconcile Calvinism with a universal atonement by speaking of hypothetical universal grace, and they also abandoned some of the starkness of scholastic Calvinism's discussion of the decrees. A recent study of Amyraut by Brian Armstrong has argued that he represented the continuation of humanist impulses in French Protestantism and also that certain of his views were closer to those of Calvin than was much of later scholastic Calvinism.[112]

Earlier reference has been made to Robert Baillie's statement that the Westminster divines had long debates on predestination. A study of these debates by Benjamin B. Warfield showed that the differences that sur-faced pertaining to this matter were between the majority who were strict Calvinists and a few who had moved in the direction of Amyraldism. This group, consisting of Edmund Calamy, Stephen Marshall, Richard Vines, and Lazarus Seaman, argued that though Christ's death was fi-nally effective only for the elect, it was also conditionally effective for the reprobate, although that condition could not be fulfilled because of their nonelection. In this view, the decree of the satisfaction of Christ for sin preceded and was wider than the decree of election. But the final statement of the Assembly's Confession of Faith excluded this possibility by teaching in the scholastic fashion of the order of salvation that the decree of election was prior to the gift of Christ for redemption and that the latter was one of the means for carrying out the former.[113] It was also suggested, but rejected by the assembly, that a clear statement of the doctrine of reprobation ought to be left out of a confession of faith, especially because in any case it was obviously implied by the decree of election.[114]

In the outcry of many Puritans and Calvinists against the Antinomians is to be found another root of moderate Calvinism. The quick reaction of these writers to any suggestion that Antinomianism was an implication of their views shows their sensitivity on the subject. Thomas Gataker, a man of reputation as a scholar who was a member of the Westminster Assembly, wrote against Antinomianism when it was called to his attention that John Saltmarsh had adduced Gataker's testimony for Saltmarsh's Antinomianism. Gataker complained that Saltmarsh "would herein make men believe, that I come a great deal neerer the Antinomian party, . . . than ever I did." Gataker wanted all to know that as far as he was concerned the Antinomians had "miserably corrupted" the gospel.[115] Gataker sounded like an Arminian moralist when he called Antinomianism a "foul abuse" that turns God's grace into wantonness, a "groundless perswasion" that one can be saved in spite of "a lewd and loose course of life."[116] Antinomian opinions are so scandalous, declared Thomas Bakewell, the author of *The Antinomians Christ Confounded*, that once exposed, the Antinomians themselves will "be ashamed to owne them."[117] Stephen Geree thought that Antinomianism appealed to the "carnal"—it was the religion of the "loose libertines of this age."[118]

The nature of the arguments used by these Calvinist opponents of Antinomianism showed that they regarded the Antinomians as extremist in their use of predestination. In particular, they maintained that the Antinomians had gone astray by taking election out of the context of the order of salvation with which it belonged and, by overstressing it alone, had thereby collapsed justification, the work of Christ, and assurance into election. The opponents of the Antinomians agreed that it was improper to speak of sins being forgiven to the elect in Christ prior to the actual work of Christ accomplished in their behalf and that it was false to speak of justification from eternity—justification comes even to the elect only in time and when they believe (even though their believing is God's gift).[119] If justification must not be conflated with election, neither should sanctification. Earlier spiritual writers spoke of election as a comfortable doctrine ministering assurance, but it was never to be alone the source of such assurance; rather, it was to be complemented by sanctification, for it was above all in contemplating the signs of sanctification within oneself that assurance was to be found, moving from God's last and most evident effects to his gracious causation. Gataker felt that it was a mistake to teach that God saw no sin in his justified children;[120] God gave grace to sinful yet regenerate souls that they might mortify sin in themselves. Whereas faith only was "required" for justification, good works and holy living were needed "unto salvation." Assurance was found above all in repentance and holy living.[121] Geree and Bakewell reminded the Antinomians that although holiness was not the cause of gaining heaven, it was the "way" to do so.[122] Another opponent of the Antinomians observed that "Gods free grace in Christ, is as much seene and magnified in our Sanctification as in our Justification" and that sanctification, a real taking away of the "filth" of sin, went much beyond the "bare pardon" of justification.[123]

The controversy over Antinomianism eventually resolved itself into the question of assurance and thus became an issue of pastoral care. Gataker objected that Saltmarsh "describes the dealing of our Ministers with men, for the bringing of them to repentance, as if he were painting out some Popish Priest, pressing men to shrift."[124] An old refrain of the spiritual writers, that assurance must be found by looking to one's sanctification, was frequently repeated by those who warned against the teachings of the Antinomians.[125]

Not all Calvinists who wrote against the Antinomians can be classed as moderate Calvinists, but the very fact of assailing the Antinomians involved at least the admission that one could push grace and predestination too far. Some used the assault to introduce modifications into the Reformed theology of grace that would obviate the Antinomian menace. Gataker and Geree both thought that in some sense faith was required for and antecedent to justification; they stressed the "conditions" required by the grace of the new covenant. Bakewell also spoke of such conditions and of the need to be "prepared" for justification.[126] Up to a point, such language was fairly common in covenant theology. But excessive talk of conditions and of preparation was not only what some

Antinomians had reacted to in the first place but could lead to more cautious formulations concerning the initiatives of divine grace.

Thomas Gataker in particular came under fire for minimizing the imputed righteousness of Christ and for holding that the imperfect faith and repentance of the believer was imputed for righteousness in the process of justification.[127] The latter position was sometimes stated by Anglican moralists, but among Puritans was especially associated with Richard Baxter, the one figure among the moderate Calvinists who came the closest to moralism in his rebuttal of Antinomianism. Benjamin Woodbridge, another writer against the Antinomians, defended Baxter from the charge of Arminian moralism, and both he and Baxter can be considered Amyraldians in their view of the atonement.[128] The Arminian Thomas Pierce cited Baxter as evidence that not all Calvinists held the harsh views he found it necessary to refute.[129] Combating Antinomianism, even some ostensible Calvinists began to sound as if they were moralists.

The theological controversies that revolved around Richard Baxter, mostly in the 1650s, can be seen as another step in the unfolding of moderate Calvinism. To do so avoids treating Baxter as an isolated maverick who embarrassed his fellow Presbyterians and places his admittedly carelessly expressed ideas about justification and grace in the context of the general theological tendency of a religious party.

Baxter later asserted in his autobiography that he was instigated to write on the subject of justification by the prevalence of Antinomianism, particularly in the army.[130] In *Aphorisms of Justification*, Baxter's first published writing, which appeared in 1649, he sought to define justification in order to make clear that humans were responsible for obeying God's commandments and responding to his promises. He argued that Christ's work for the redeemed was that of making satisfaction for Adam's disobedience, but not of obedience as a substitutionary and imputed righteousness; the righteousness of the redeemed is rather their own obedience to the covenant of grace, with which Christ's obedience concurs. Thus Baxter concluded that only those shall have a part in Christ, and "be legally righteous, who do believe and obey the Gospel." He explained: "Our Evangelical Righteousness is not without us in Christ, as our legal Righteousness is: but consisteth in our own actions of Faith and Gospel Obedience. Or thus: though Christ performed the conditions of the law, and satisfied for our non-performance; yet it is our selves that must perform the conditions of the Gospel."[131] Those who opposed this doctrine and taught that new covenant righteousness "is in Christ, and not in ourselves, or performed by Christ, and not by ourselves," Baxter thought were guilty of "a monstrous piece of Antinomian doctrine." Such Antinomians, he added, would no doubt regard his view as "flat Popery, . . . as if we cryed down Christ and set up ourselves," but this was because they failed to understand the distinctions between the different types of righteousness, imputed and that which was truly one's own.[132]

In the attempt to explain himself further, Baxter increased his vulnerability to the strictly orthodox by arguing that faith was taken for righteousness under the gospel covenant and that such justifying faith included in itself all the other parts of obedience, which are known as the works of the gospel, though these works can only be said "secondarily" to justify. Baxter observed that though his views might cause some to cry him down as guilty of "Heresie, Popery, Socinianism and what not," the epistle of James clearly taught "that a man is justified by Works, and not by Faith only."[133] Such an opinion would seem to have been as blatantly "moralist" as that of any of the Anglican Arminians, and it was no surprise that a torrent of Calvinist wrath was unleashed against the unwary Baxter.

Among those who entered the lists against Baxter were distinguished theologians as well as fledgling controversialists. Anthony Burgess, who had been a member of the Westminster Assembly and to whom Baxter had in innocence dedicated his book, accused him of teaching justification by works. John Warren, apparently hitherto a personal friend of Baxter, also wrote against him.[134] John Owen, by then a well-established theologian and religious adviser to the Cromwellian establishment, lamented that it might have been supposed that the end of prelatical persecution would have brought to a close the "unthankfulness" of the "carnal mind" that caviled at the free grace of God, but experience was showing that Satan was again at work seducing persons "to renew the contest of sinful, guilty, defiled nature, against the sovereign distinguishing love and effectual grace of God." Owen limited himself to a rebuttal of what he regarded as Baxter's errors about universal atonement and left it to others to controvert his notions on justification.[135] Those others included William Eyre, to whose book Owen contributed a commendatory preface, and John Crandon. Eyre, himself suspected to be an Antinomian,[136] answered Baxter in a book entitled *Justification without Conditions*. There Eyre held that Baxter had diluted Reformation doctrine with "Popish leaven," making "new covenant works" the condition of justification.[137] A more intemperate attack came from Crandon, who claimed that the sharpest vilification of Baxter was well deserved, for Baxter, worse than the overt misbeliever, "vends" "Popish and Arminian under the name of Protestant tenets." Baxter, he added, had defended justification by works in order to return England to the "Babylon" of "popery" and should cease his dissembling.[138] Baxter later mentioned this with the bemused observation that Crandon, himself nearly an Antinomian, out of "excessive Zeal for his Opinions" and "being an utter stranger to me," "got a deep conceit that I was a Papist," "which moved laughter in many, and pity in others, and troubled his Friends, as having disadvantaged their Cause."[139]

Baxter's chief response to his critics was to accuse them of Antinomian excesses,[140] but he soon recognized that he had wandered too far from acceptable orthodoxy, admitting he had said things that were not "well digested or perfected"[141] and that in particular he had "meddled too forwardly with Dr. Owen."[142] Consequently, he attempted a more careful outlining of his position, though without going back on his strictures against Antinomianism.[143] Thus he wrote in 1665: "Though Faith in Christ be a fruit of God's Eternal Election, and of Christ's meritorious Redemption, and of the Holy Ghost's Effectual, Special, saving operation; yet is it mans Act and Habit, and by the Precept made his duty, and by the Promise made the condition of our first Right in Christ as our Head and Husband, and our Conjunction with him, and consequently of our first Actual proper pardon of our sins."[144] And although he now acknowledged that charity was not a part of this faith, nonetheless it was still "essential to Faith to receive Christ with love" and to understand that faith justified, not only by accepting Christ as a satisfaction for past sin, but also by accepting him as a savior from the tyranny of present sin. Still, Baxter employed phrases that must be regarded as quite close to the contemporary expressions of Anglican moralism or even Tridentine theology, for example, God "regenerateth us, that he may Pardon us."[145]

Baxter spoke moderately on predestination. Not denying God's eternal election, he thought disputes about God's decrees were unnecessary[146] and felt that predestination should be placed in an order of salvation as one item among others, with the clear understanding that there was no actual justification of the elect before their believing.[147] All things considered, Baxter probably should be understood as one nurtured on the Reformed theology of grace who stressed its more moralizing undertones such as covenant conditions and election to holiness rather than one who revolted against it altogether. He took with a special seriousness what Reformed theology had said about sanctification as the goal of election and of Christ's death,[148] and it was from that context that he was led into a number of incautious formulations that brought down the ire of other Puritans upon him.

Perhaps Baxter was for a while an isolated figure, pursuing his own idiosyncratic path, but the Scotsman Baillie, troubled that Baxter was reputed a "Presbyterian," wrote to Simeon Ashe in 1665 about the embarrassment Baxter was causing their party, noting that one of his latest works "highly offends" many because "it seems to be stuffed with grosse Arminianisme." "Why take you no care either to gaine the man from his errors, or yoke with him some able divines to guard against his infection?" asked Baillie.[149] For Baxter's connections were not with Arminian sectarians like John Goodwin, but with the growing party of moderate Calvinists frequently called "Presbyterians," who were also sometimes allied with the Scottish Presbyterians because they were neither episcopalians nor ardent supporters of the Cromwellian church establishment. Baxter did not republish his *Aphorisms* but rather kept trying to explain away his heterodoxy; although reputed an Amyraldian, he was still considered a Calvinist. When examined for his commitment to the whole pattern of Reformed theology, the theology (and especially the piety) of the Bucerian order of salvation, he appears something less of an Arminian moralist and at a greater distance from Hammond or Thorndike than he does when his views on justification are examined in isolation. But there is certainly no denying the extreme heterodoxy of his explanation of justification from a Calvinist or even from a Reformation Protestant standpoint.[150]

By the time of his answer to Thomas Pierce in 1658, *The Grotian Religion Discovered*, Baxter defended the Synod of Dort, although he defended it for what he interpreted as its essential moderation. Thus he argued that Dort had not canonized the supralapsarian version of the divine decrees, had refused to say that only a few would be elected, had affirmed that God reprobated with reference to the sin of the reprobate, and had avoided anything susceptible of Antinomian error.[151] Baxter even sought to reconcile the formulations of Dort with his own Amyraldian view that the death of Christ satisfied for the sins of all, even if effectual only for the elect. The views of the "Presbyterians," not those of his opponent Pierce, Baxter maintained, followed those of the "old Episcopal

Divines" such as Jewel, Pilkington, Hall, Grindal, Carleton, Davenant, Morton, Ussher, and Abbot.[152] Baxter's discussion of free will in this context was especially interesting: free will in the ordinary activities of life was not denied, only that it was adequate for disposing oneself to salvific grace. He wanted the discussion of grace separated from that of free will and determinism, which was to him more properly "a Philosophical controversie." He objected to Pierce mainly because the latter discredited godly persons and was a scoffer.[153] This later work by Baxter shows his affinity to the positions being taken up by the moderate Calvinists more clearly than do his earlier works on justification.

Henry Hickman addressed himself more extensively and directly to the theology of grace in relation to predestination than did Baxter. Hickman was one of the major participants in the controversies of the Puritans with Thomas Pierce and also crossed swords with an Anglican apologist more virulent than even Pierce, Peter Heylyn. Whereas Pierce's other Calvinist opponents sought to match Pierce's vituperation and quibbling with larger amounts of the same, Hickman met invective with persiflage and showed wit, restraint, and a degree of common sense surprising in seventeenth-century theological controversy as he strove to answer Pierce's wild charges against Reformed theology while avoiding the more extreme predestinarian formulas of the strict Calvinists. Hickman had been educated at both universities and became a fellow of Magdalen College, Oxford; ejected at the Restoration, he continued to defend the Puritan and Presbyterian cause though spending much of his time in the Netherlands until his death in 1692. He corresponded with Baxter.

In vindication of Reformed theology and its predestinarian teaching, Hickman wrote three works in 1659 directed against three different opponents, "Tilenus," Pierce, and Heylyn.[154] Hickman denied the accusation that Calvinism taught that God was the author of sin and many other cavils of that sort directed against predestination, but the main line of his argument was not to defend everything said by Calvinists but to insist on the importance of divine grace in Christian salvation as against Pelagianism—he was even willing to admit that not all Arminians had a Pelagian view of grace. He did, however, think that the new Anglican school consisting of Pierce, Hammond, and Thorndike effectively nullified God's grace, and that these men were thereby guilty of Pelagianism.[155] He also considered Jeremy Taylor guilty of that ancient heresy for what Hickman took to be Taylor's rejection of original sin.[156]

In stating his own views on predestination, Hickman conceded that there were "depths in the Controversie, relating to Predestination and Grace," which he was unable to fathom and that he did not understand fully how to reconcile God's "determining grace" with the liberty of persons; nor did he feel that such complicated matters as the divine decrees should be preached from the pulpit.[157] Nonetheless, "Antiarminians" (Hickman's preferred phrase) held that there must be a "determining" divine grace and an election of individual persons if redemption was really to be by the grace of God.[158] Many godly persons, he thought, rejected rigid supralapsarian views, "but that there is no personal election, that conversion is onely by moral suasion, that Gods elect do totally and finally fall away, are dangerous and uncomfortable opinions" and run counter to the experience of those "who have felt the power of converting grace."[159] The religious experience of the believer was for Hickman the heart of the matter, in relation to which the outerworks of theological formulation were secondary. This emphasis appeared again when Hickman asked rhetorically, "Would you therefore know why I hold Absolute, Eternal, Personal Election, Efficacious determining Grace and the certain infallible perseverance of all Believers: Truly because I find these opinions most agreeable to Scripture, to the *communis sensus fidelium*, the instinct and impulse of the new creature in all ages"; and because those doctrines exalt the free grace of Christ.[160]

Even those whom Hickman variously called supralapsarians, "Supracalvinists," or "absolute Predestinarians" did not hold views as extreme as those caricatured by Heylyn. Hickman distinguished such strict predestinarians as a group from those "Presbyterians" who like himself held more moderate views, stressing election to life and, following Amyraut, considering the atonement to be at least conditionally universal.[161] Hickman also employed an Amyraldian distinction (to be found earlier in Richard Hooker) between two divine decrees, one universal, willing that all be saved, and one particular, choosing individual persons.[162] Like Baxter worried about Antinomianism, Hickman argued that justification only followed upon actual believing.[163]

Hickman was most comfortable, however, with the argument from historical precedent and seemed outraged by the dishonesty of his opponents in their refusal to recognize the Reformed formulations of the theology of grace as those that obviously had prevailed in the earlier Church of England. Although it is difficult not to believe that Peter Heylyn engaged in deliberate deception and obfuscation, Hickman complained that Heylyn sought to find evidence that everything Archbishop

Laud ordered was not an innovation, but of long standing in the English church.[164] Hickman thought it quite evident that the first reformers and writers of the Church of England had held a Reformed and Calvinist theology like that of the Continental Protestants and that though some glimmers of a different theology appeared earlier with such individuals as Harsnett and Overall, full-fledged Arminian doctrine did not appear until the time of Laud's hegemony.[165]

Heylyn, once chaplain and later biographer of Laud, cast his arguments against Puritanism and Calvinism in the guise of historical works, one of which, his *Historia Quinqu-Articularis*, first published in 1660, aspersed the doctrine of Dort and the Continental Reformation as the worst kind of folly, even including in his general condemnation many of the early English Protestant heroes, including Wyclif, Tyndale, and Foxe. Hickman responded to Heylyn's tendentious history in 1661, seeking to refute, among other points, Heylyn's ill words about the Edwardian Reformation.[166] But it was in his own *Historia Quinq-Articularis* that Hickman most thoroughly amassed evidence for the prevalence of Reformed theology in the English Reformation, although the work was carelessly published from his notes long after he had drawn it together. Commenting on the evidence brought forward, Hickman admitted that he could not defend every opinion of those whom he had cited on behalf of the Calvinism of the Church of England, but that he wanted to establish the point as a matter of fact about the nature of the English church.[167]

Hickman presented a winsome version of moderate Calvinism, which was more carefully phrased and more theologically astute than that of Baxter, but this kind of Calvinism nonetheless came to be known as "Baxterian." One reason for that naming was that Baxter gradually emerged as an important leader among a group of Puritan clergy whose political and ecclesiastical views were more conservative than those of the Cromwellian divines at the same time that their theological standpoint was in its moderation distinct from the high Calvinism of many of the leading Puritan spokesmen for Cromwell's regime. Collectively, this group has come to be designated as "Presbyterian" though many of them stood more for a mixture of presbytery and episcopacy than they did for the strictly Presbyterian polity of the Scots.[168] During the Interregnum, many of them sought to make common cause with moderate Anglicans on behalf of a better regulated and more conservative state church than that projected by Cromwellian supporters, and after the Restoration they searched for some compromise formula by which they could be "comprehended" within the Anglican establishment.[169] It has even been surmised that one reason for their willingness to modify their Calvinism was the desire for comprehension within a broader established church. Both during the Restoration era and after the Toleration Act they found it difficult to work with their more strictly Calvinist brethren among the Dissenters (the Congregationalists and some Baptists) because they still feared sectarianism, hoped for inclusion in the state church, and suspected that Antinomian potential lurked in strict Calvinism.[170] In the next century, many of these Presbyterians were to become frankly Arminian and even Socinian in their outlook.[171]

In the 1650s and later, these Baxterian "Presbyterians" were the principal source of moderate Calvinism. A quick reckoning of the "membership" of this group would have to begin with those Amyraldians of the Westminster Assembly already mentioned, some of whom were still active much later in the century. Edmund Calamy, who had observed in a sermon of 1641 that "it is not a dispute about Predestination that will turn away God's wrath," but "humiliation and reformation,"[172] worked closely with Baxter on various projects until his death in 1666; his grandson worked with Matthew Sylvester to edit Baxter's papers after his death. Richard Vines, who died in 1656, spoke approvingly even of Baxter's *Aphorisms.* Lazarus Seaman was included in a 1672 list of Baxter's followers.[173] Hickman was abroad much of the time after the Restoration, an irreconcilable enemy to the Restoration episcopate, and his name did not crop up very often among these Presbyterians, but those of several newcomers did, including Thomas Manton, Thomas Jacomb, John Howe, Vincent Alsop, and William Bates. Some of these, including Manton and Howe, had ties to the Cromwellian church, but during the Restoration era all were more or less considered Presbyterians. Among them should also be included Edward Reynolds, whom Baxter helped persuade to accept a bishopric after the Restoration.[174] Worried about Arminianism and Socinianism as early as 1632, Reynolds nonetheless recommended charity rather than theological quarrelsomeness in 1638, as long as there was agreement on fundamental doctrines.[175] From 1661 until his death in 1676, Reynolds should be counted as a moderate Calvinist within the established church.

Examination of the range of those expressing the ideas of what can be identified as moderate Calvinism shows it to have been, however, a wider phenomenon than its special connection to the Baxterian "Presbyterians" of the Interregnum. Not only did there continue to be English Presbyterians who were strict Calvinists, but moderate Calvinism can be found earlier in the century as well as on both sides of the line separating conformists and Nonconformists. The compendium of Elnathan Parr, *The Grounds of Divinitie*, first published in 1614 and reprinted several times, was fully committed to the Reformed theology of grace, but had features of later moderate Calvinism. Chief among these was an argument against the supralapsarian version of the divine decrees espoused by Beza, from whom Parr rather humbly dissented, and a clear belief that predestination to life always came into effect through the "means" of holiness.[176] Anti-Arminian conformists and bishops such as Joseph Hall and John Davenant stressed their sublapsarian interpretation of the decrees and thought caution appropriate in the avowal of reprobation.[177] Archbishop Ussher, who was willing to compromise with Presbyterians in his scheme for "reduced episcopacy," was a sublapsarian also.[178] It would be fairly safe to generalize that moderate Calvinism continued as a significant strain in Restoration Anglicanism.[179] On the other hand, Peter Sterry, whose views have already been considered, might be cited as an example of moderate Calvinism among the Congregationalist clergy of the Cromwellian establishment, though as such he would have been a striking exception to their stricter Calvinism.

High Calvinism and John Owen

Out of the same matrix of theological discussion from which came Arminian moralism and moderate Calvinism came also the high Calvinists of the 1650s and thereafter. Rooted in the Reformed scholasticism of earlier generations and further shaped on the anvil of the Arminian controversies of preceding decades, high Calvinism came to be distinguished from moderate Calvinism by its particular responses to the catalytic events of the rise of moralism, the Antinomian crisis, and the concerted attack of "Tilenus," Pierce, and others upon predestination, until it attained solidity and a finely wrought shape in the theology of John Owen, Thomas Goodwin, and others.

The high Calvinists feared moralism much more than Antinomianism. Though the latter ran into certain excesses in its exaltation of divine grace, the former seemed to destroy the very notion of redemption by grace and to replace it with a dependence on moral effort that was to the high Calvinists no more than Socinian. The specter of "popery" had been raised against "catholicizing" Laudian Arminians, for such Arminians seemed to be asserting a sacramental theology that infused a kind of grace with which persons might cooperate into the receptive believer in order to be pleasing to God. To anti-Arminian writers, this opened the way for Pelagian or at least semi-Pelagian "works-righteousness" that the Protestant Reformation took to be the hallmark of Roman Catholic theology. But the moralistic Arminians seemed to have a new emphasis that high Calvinists saw as little more than the assertion that salvation came by human effort, assisted a bit, perhaps, by grace. In debating the issue, high Calvinists came to focus on the atonement and to accuse the moralists of teaching that the death of Christ was merely exemplary, an encouragement to moral effort or at best the forgiveness of past sins upon an engagement to refrain from further wrongdoing, rather than a fountainhead of effective grace, whether of the Catholic sacramental or Reformed forensically imputed sort. To high Calvinists, Socinianism meant denial that the death of Christ was a satisfaction for sin along with that moralism which would inevitably accompany such a rejection of the substitutionary atonement and imputed righteousness of Christ. Although some Calvinists refuted Socinianism as Antitrinitarianism, especially in the wake of the notorious John Biddle's publication of his views, the high Calvinist opponents of this heresy focused more on the questions of atonement and imputed grace.[180] This was certainly true of John Owen's enormous refutation of Socinianism, *Vindiciae Evangelicae*, published in 1655. In their arguments against Socinianism, such Calvinists often maintained that Christ suffered the exact pains due the sinners for whom he made satisfaction.

The story of the unmasking of moralism as nothing more than Socinianism might well begin with Francis Cheynell, mentioned in chapter 4 as identifying Socinianism as one among several heresies he thought Archbishop Laud was using to undermine the Reformed religion. This same Cheynell found "pure Socinianism" among Anglican moralists, attacking first William Chillingworth and then Henry Hammond for that misbelief. Chillingworth, protégé of Laud and an early Latitudinarian, had conversed extensively with Cheynell on theological subjects, while a royalist prisoner of the parliamentary army. According to Cheynell, Chillingworth believed in a conditional justification dependent upon good works, relying upon "reason" and "obedience" rather than the grace of Christ.[181] A few years after his broadside against Chillingworth, Cheynell published correspondence between himself and Hammond, wherein Hammond is taxed with making "faithful actions" a condition of justification.[182]

George Walker, a London minister who like Cheynell sat in the Westminster Assembly, also had early sounded the alarm of the Socinian menace, but in connection especially with the sectarian Arminian John Goodwin.[183] This was followed by other high Calvinist references to the threat of Socinianism: Richard Resbury discovered John Goodwin to be a "Pelagio-Socinian"; John Owen appended his answer to Baxter's putative moralism to his attack upon the Socinians; and in commending Eyre's work against Baxter, Owen observed that many were welcoming "an almost pure Socinian Justification."[184]

But if the threat of Socinian moralism put strict Calvinists on the defensive, the appearance of Antinomianism drove a wedge between them and moderate Calvinists, as well as further widening the gulf between themselves and the moralists. It has already been noted that strict supralapsarian Calvinists of considerable repute such as William Pemble and William Twisse approached some Antinomian formulations, and both because of this and because of their own principal motive of exalting grace, high Calvinists found Antinomianism to be little more than incautious excess of zeal on behalf of a good cause. This was true of John Cotton's treatment of Anne Hutchinson in New England. Later, when Baxter claimed that John Owen taught justification from eternity, Owen denied it,[185] but he did endorse Eyre's book, which at the very least verged on predestinarian Antinomianism. Several high Calvinist opponents of John Goodwin came perilously close to espousing the formula of justification from eternity.[186] And the question of the acceptability of the works of Tobias Crisp recurred later in the century as a source of conflict between moderate and high Calvinists.

Thus high Calvinism was taking shape in the middle of the century in the midst of theological controversy, coming to be associated with a strong emphasis on Christ's propitiatory satisfaction and imputed righteousness as well as with a willingness to go part of the way with the Antinomians in exalting grace, in spite of Arminian moralists, whether Anglican, sectarian, or Baxterian. But also, and still in reaction to moralists and in the company of Antinomians, high Calvinists inherited and continued to develop the supralapsarian side of earlier Reformed scholasticism, even including a penchant for horrific statements of the decree of reprobation. George Kendall, a strict Calvinist who wrote against both Baxter and John Goodwin, commented in one of his long and dreary books that no doubt "unregenerate" readers would find much to offend them in what he was saying, but that the need to exalt God's sovereignty was more important than concern for such persons[187]—no attempt at winsome apologetics here!

William Twisse, who had been an internationally known theologian, was important in the expression of the supralapsarianism of high Calvinism. Many of his manuscripts were prepared for publication and sent forth with appropriate commendatory prefaces and sometimes defensive apologies directed against those who had controverted him, mainly through the labor of Henry Jeanes. In 1631, Twisse had accused Thomas Jackson of Arminianism; the next year he defended Perkins against Arminius. In 1646, the year of Twisse's death, his examination of a treatise by John Cotton was published; the American colonist was upbraided for neglect of the doctrine of reprobation, which Twisse feared would open the door to the denial of free grace.[188] In 1650 came forth *The Doctrine of the Synod of Dort and Arles, reduced to the practise*, in which predestination was placed in the context of God's general willing of all things.[189] A polemical work, it attacked those who claimed that the theology of Dort was destructive of piety and comfort and was specifically directed against a scoffing manuscript that had been circulating at Oxford.[190] In 1653, Twisse's *The Riches of Gods Love unto the Vessels of Mercy, Consistent with His Absolute Hatred or Reprobation of the Vessels of Wrath*, originally written against Samuel Hoard, was brought up to date and pressed into service against John Goodwin by means of an appended *Vindication of D. Twisse from the exceptions of Mr. John Goodwin in his Redemption Redeemed*; the addition was the work of Henry Jeanes. Twisse, whom Jeanes dubs "the Bradwardine of the Age" and "Ornament of his Nation," pulled no punches in his exposition of reprobation. Proceeding from the supralapsarian assumption that God chose to save some and damn others prior to any consideration of the creation or fall, Twisse explained that "God doth purpose to inflict damnation on them whom he reprobates" out of his mere good pleasure to do so, unmoved by any cause external to himself.[191]

Other high Calvinist polemicists defended predestination against moralists and Arminians. George Kendall added an answer to *Fur Predestinatus* to his previous polemical sallies.[192] Richard Resbury contended against John Goodwin that the doctrine of the divine decree was the foundation of Christian truth and defended the supralapsarian version of the decree of reprobation, which he saw not as directed to fallen man but as part of God's aim in creation. To Resbury, it was a "decree of hatred."[193] William Barlee wrote two answers on predestination to the Anglican Pierce, defending Twisse and acknowledging himself a follower of that formidable Calvinist's supralapsarianism. Barlee declared that Pierce was fed and nourished only by "humane and moral philosophy" and that abandonment of the doctrine of predestination was the first step in making shipwreck of the faith.[194] Kendall had provided a commendatory preface for the first of these two books by Barlee, and among its other "Reverend Prefacers" had been Thomas Whitfield, an Independent divine of advanced age who had eleven years of experience in New England. Whitfield had earlier written against Arminianism,[195] but in 1657, he undertook the refutation of Pierce for the edification of the common people, Barlee, he thought, having refuted him to the satisfaction of the learned.[196] Opposing predestinarian grace to the moralism of Pierce and his friends, Whitfield apparently considered supralapsarianism not too much for the understanding of the common people, as he insisted for their benefit that original sin was not a cause of reprobation, nor Christ the cause of redemption; God, he said, hated the reprobate. In explaining such matters, he opined that "it is no injustice in God to inflict sufferings upon innocent creatures," because there is no injustice in our smashing worms, and we are less to God than worms to us.[197]

Though much later in its date of publication, a major work by Thomas Goodwin that was printed posthumously deserves attention in connection with the development of high Calvinism. Thomas Goodwin, who had been one of the five "Dissenting Brethren" among the Westminster divines because of his Independency, was an important clerical adviser to Oliver Cromwell as well as one of Cromwell's Oxford deputies. Elements of his teaching smacked of Antinomianism.[198] His treatment of predestination, however, showed greater circumspection than was true of many of the high Calvinists and included an attempt at the reconciliation of the sublapsarian and supralapsarian positions, though by incorporating some of the sublapsarian themes into a supralapsarian framework. Even if predestination has some provisional reference to fallen man, he argued, its primary reference is to God's own glory and his sovereign choice in the creation of humankind. Thomas Goodwin also rooted predestination in various "motives" within the Godhead, in connection with his understanding of the interrelationships of the persons of the Trinity. But the intention to exalt God's grace was foremost, as Thomas Goodwin considered grace to be "the most absolute principle" in the divine being.[199]

Frequently coupled with the name of Thomas Goodwin both during the Interregnum and after the Restoration was that of John Owen,[200] whose rapid rise to influence among the staunchly Calvinistic Independents soon eclipsed Goodwin's leadership. And though high Calvinists were to be found outside the circle of Owen and his Congregationalist associates, among the Presbyterians as exemplified by George Kendall and Cheynell (Baxter called this fellow "Presbyterian" the "over-orthodox doctor"),[201] or among Anglican conformists such as Thomas Tully or Thomas Barlow,[202] high Calvinism most flourished in that circle (Barlow, by the way, had once been Owen's tutor).[203] To be sure, high Calvinism also flourished among some of the sectarian Baptists and Antinomians, but they, too, often looked at Owen with considerable respect[204] and found themselves occasionally allied with the conservative Independents against Presbyterians and Anglicans on certain ecclesiastical issues.

These conservative Independents were very important in the councils of the Rump Parliament and of Oliver Cromwell, preaching frequently to the former and playing an active role in the various schemes for church settlement of the latter. Alongside of Owen must be counted other newcomers, including Joseph Caryl and Nicholas Lockyer, who joined with the remaining "Dissenting Brethren," Philip Nye, Thomas Goodwin, William Bridge, and Sydrach Simpson. The erstwhile New Englander Hugh Peter was also connected with them, as were certain of the anti-Arminian writers such as John Stalham, Richard Resbury, Thomas Whitfield, Samuel Petto, William Eyre, and Thomas Brooks.[205]

Owen figured prominently among the theological writers engaged in the explication of high Calvinism. Not only did he contravene Baxter, John Goodwin, and the Socinian threat, but he wrote commendatory prefaces for others who were engaged in their refutation. Thus he recommended Eyre's work against Baxter, both of Kendall's large volumes against John Goodwin, and Twisse's *Riches of God's Love*, noting there that Arminians delighted, in vain, "to try and exercise the strength of fleshly reasonings" against the decree of reprobation.[206] Kendall in turn recommended one of Barlee's works against Pierce and spoke of contacting Owen in connection with the refutation of *Fur Predestinatus*.[207] Joseph Caryl, a close associate of Owen, recommended Crandon's book against Baxter.[208] Prefaces by Owen continued to grace Calvinist theological treatises all through the period of the Restoration.[209]

With the passing of Oliver Cromwell, Owen's public importance underwent an eclipse, only to be offset by his growing prominence as the leader of the English Congregationalists. In the last years before the Restoration he was much occupied with the task of making sure that his group was firmly wedded to orthodox Calvinism, and this was achieved through his leadership in the Savoy Synod of 1658. In the Savoy Confession of Faith of 1658, a modification of the confession of the Westminster Assembly, an unwavering statement of Congregationalist polity and strict Calvinist theology was produced that was to be the authority for English Congregationalists for many years to come, protecting them from the siren song of conformity and Arminianism on the one hand and from the vagaries of sectarian heterodoxy on the other. The degree to which the theological modifications and idiosyncrasies introduced into the Westminster Confession of Faith by the Savoy meeting bear the earmarks of Owen's views is striking.[210] After the Restoration, still led by Owen, the Congregationalists remained faithful to strict Calvinism and found themselves at odds, in a series of acrimonious controversies, with both the moderate Calvinism of the Presbyterians and the moralistic Arminianism of much of the establishment.

John Owen was the foremost expositor of high Calvinism in England in the second half of the seventeenth century, and his reputation as a major international theologian probably protected him in the years right after the Restoration when he certainly must have been among the more vulnerable of the Cromwellian divines. Invited to Massachusetts, he came to be referred to in awe as the "great Dr. Owen."[211] Recent scholarship has concentrated on Owen's ecclesiastical leadership to the neglect of his theology,[212] which constituted a life work of dedication to the exposition of the Reformed predestinarian theology of grace and the refutation of Arminian and Socinian error. Merely to pass cursorily over the topics he dealt with is to see that Owen at one time or another defended every one of the major theological points of the Synod of Dort. And though in the development of his theological system he made few concessions to the moderate Calvinists and intended to keep his theological party separated from anything that smacked of Baxterian Latitudinarianism, he retained his focus on the piety of grace as the living core which it was ever the purpose of doctrine to enshrine. Thus there is in Owen a Christocentrism that protects him from some of the excesses of supralapsarianism and a spirituality that continually brings him back from scholastic argumentation to the springs of vibrant piety.

Owen's theology both defended the main points of the Calvinism of Dort and revolved around the main topics of the order of salvation that has been seen as long dominant in the Reformed theology of England. In his earliest writings, Owen concentrated on the atonement, or Christ as the means by which the elect came to redemption, the subject of his 1648 book against Arminianism, of his answer to Baxter, and of much of his anti-Socinian *Vindiciae Evangelicae.* Long after the Restoration, he gave extensive exegetical attention to this question in his commentary on the Epistle to the Hebrews, which focused on the "priestly" work of Christ. His massive work on perseverance against John Goodwin took him to the other end of the order of salvation to consider sanctification and the indefectibility of the elect. In *Vindiciae Evangelicae* and another work of about the same time, *A Dissertation on Divine Justice,* as well as scattered throughout most of his writings, are to be found many discussions of God's will and decree. Owen's writings against Baxter contain much about justification, the center of the order of salvation. He later returned to this point with a major work, *The Doctrine of Justification by Faith, Through the Imputation of the Righteousness of Christ.* His enormous work on the Holy Spirit[213] was also strongly anti-Arminian and anti-Socinian, aiming to describe the workings of the irresistible regenerating grace that operated effectively in the renewal of the elect. Thus it was chiefly a defense of vocation, regeneration, and sanctification as the work of grace alone, through the instrumentality of the Spirit. Rounding off Owen's defense of divine grace in the order of salvation were smaller works that defended the union of the believer with Christ as a supernatural regeneration as well as many practical and devotional works on grace in the human soul, by which the order of salvation was continually brought back to its role in piety.[214]

The order of salvation began with God and his decrees, and the Synod of Dort had upheld these decrees as unconditional. Owen, following in this tradition, frequently reduced theological problems to their root in God, his nature, and decrees, but with some differences from the usual views of scholastic supralapsarian Calvinism. The English Socinian John Biddle had sought to overthrow the absolute prescience of God in order to assert human freedom. Thus Owen found it necessary in his *Vindiciae Evangelicae* to affirm that God knew perfectly beforehand all the actions of persons and that God accomplished his purposes with and through persons without abolishing their freedom. Freedom was understood here in its Augustinian sense of absence of compulsion,[215] for it was central to Owen's theology to maintain the absolute freedom and sovereignty of God. This freedom of God meant that he did all things of his mere good pleasure and not because moved thereto by a cause external to himself, and it applied to election and reprobation as it did to all his immutable purposes relative to what was external to himself.[216] This absolute freedom of God in election cannot even be said to be the result of any property or tendency in God himself, such as love or mercy.[217]

Different from God's absolute freedom in election, however, is his need by nature to preserve his justice in the decrees against sin. Thus in his *Dissertation on Divine Justice*, Owen pushed the doctrine of Christ's satisfaction back into the very nature of God and in the process found it necessary to disagree with such extreme supralapsarians as Twisse and even to reverse his own earlier position. For in *The Death of Death in the Death of Christ*, Owen had asserted that Arminians took advantage of those theologians who claimed that God can have mercy on persons only if his justice has been satisfied by arguing that if that was the case, then the atonement merely gave God the right to forgive sinners, but did not actually effect the redemption of some. But if God can forgive sins if and when he pleases, and only chose Christ's satisfaction as a decorous means of saving some, then Arminians could not have so argued.[218] But now Owen reversed his earlier position and criticized Twisse for maintaining that God chose to forgive the sins of the elect before he decreed the satisfaction of Christ as the means whereby he would do so. God can only clear the guilty for whom satisfaction has been made,[219] and not otherwise can the grace of God as the grace of God in Christ be kept central —a matter of importance to piety. Owen also now argued that God's justice was in itself "the very rectitude and perfection of the Deity." Thus vindicatory justice is not only metaphorically ascribed to God, but is his very nature: "We affirm the justice by which God punishes sin to be the very essential rectitude of the Deity itself, exercised in the punishment of sins."[220] Therefore, the justice with which God is "endowed" "is not a free act of his will . . . but a habit or excellence at all times inherent in his nature."[221] It is God's nature to punish sinners and not to clear the guilty, to hate sin and not to let it pass unpunished, and he cannot act contrary to this without contradicting his own essential nature. If this be the case, then God cannot forgive sins without the satisfaction of his offended vindicatory justice, which is, of course, what the work of Christ accomplished. That act of satisfaction was required by God's justice, and not otherwise can it be maintained, against Socinian denials, that the death of Christ as a satisfaction for sin was necessary.[222] It is clear throughout Owen's work on divine justice and also in the *Vindiciae*

Evangelicae that for him the Socinian threat began with the denial of Christ's satisfaction[223] and then, rid of an imputed righteousness, proceeded to put a mere moralism in its place. Thus it was in defense of high Calvinism against heresy that he found it necessary to modify the absolute and total freedom of the divine being as it had been exalted by supralapsarians like Twisse and Rutherford, who made the work of Christ merely one possibility among others as a means of carrying out God's decree of predestination.

The redemptive work of God in Christ linked election to the succeeding elements of the order of salvation, and for Owen with his Christocentrism it was a point at which soul-destroying heresy must above all be defeated. Thus redemption in Christ was not only dealt with as related to the nature of God but also to the exact nature of what Christ suffered and for what purpose. Owen is an important figure in the continuation of that *pietas crucis* which maximized the sufferings of Christ in order to exalt the extent of God's grace, noted in chapter 2 as characteristic of some Puritan writers. Owen regarded the atoning death of Christ as a punishment for sin inflicted on an innocent person and as the putting upon Christ of the exact punishment due to the elect for their sins. In developing this view, Owen emphasized the heinousness of sin and the sufferings of Christ by detailing precisely what Christ suffered. He suffered the four possible aggravations of death: "that it be violent and bloody," "that it be ignominious and shameful," "that it be lingering and painful," and "that it be legal and accursed." In the last case, the legality and curse is found in the fact that God laid it upon him. Altogether he experienced the curse of the law and alienation from God.[224] Owen also expatiated on the threefold significance for the redeemed of the death of Christ: redemption, as a price paid, reconciliation, as a sacrifice offered, and satisfaction, as a punishment due. Socinians, he noted, denied all of these, making redemption and reconciliation metaphorical and rejecting the need for the punishment of the innocent on behalf of the sinful.[225] Against Baxter, Owen especially stressed that Christ underwent the exact penalty due for the sins of the elect and thus paid their debt in full, as the righteousness of that act was imputed to them for their righteousness,[226] a viewpoint Baxter considered Antinomian. Such an exaltation of the grace of God in redemption by maximizing the sufferings of Christ on behalf of the elect was characteristic of high Calvinism and was developed further in the hyper-Calvinism of later times.[227]

Owen had much to say about the grace of God in justification. He criticized John Goodwin, Baxter, and the Socinians for teaching that justification came by the merit of faith and obedience.[228] In *Of the Death of Christ and Justification* he traced the Socinian error concerning justification to the rejection of an efficacious atonement.[229] After the Restoration, a major work by Owen was *The Doctrine of Justification by Faith, Through the Imputation of the Righteousness of Christ*, written not to rebut a particular heretic but to set forth the truth in this matter against its great opponents, the "Papists and Socinians," whose views, if unchecked, he feared would end in a triumph for the teaching of justification by morality.[230] Instead, justification must be maintained as a reliance upon imputed righteousness of Christ utterly apart from any self-reliance, however much this went against reason, for such is the radical meaning of God's free grace in Christ. This justification has as its inevitable concomitant a spiritual renewal from which obedience to God flowed.[231] In a sermon, Owen declared that any who denied this are truly Antinomians, not those who relied on faith in the imputed righteousness of Christ alone for justification.[232] Insistence on the importance of the imputation of Christ's righteousness came to be characteristic of high Calvinism.

The process of sanctification as the inevitable renewal and regeneration of the elect person that inevitably accompanied justification was treated by Owen entirely as a work of grace. There was a grace in the process of sanctification that was the "effectual working of the Spirit of God in and upon the minds and souls of believers," consisting of "the actual supplies of assistance and ability given to believers" and of "the effects wrought and produced by this operation of God and his grace in the hearts and minds of them that believe."[233] This meant that infused grace and inherent righteousness were excluded from justification, but not altogether from the process of sanctification. Sanctification by grace in this sense had long been a part of the Reformed theology of grace. Yet Owen and other high Calvinists especially stressed in sanctification two emphases that in more unguarded expression were favorite themes of the Antinomians: the union of the believer with Christ and the indwelling of the Holy Spirit as the agent of regeneration. Before the Restoration, Owen wrote a practical treatise entitled *Of Communion with God the Father, Son, and Holy Ghost*, and later in his career he wrote *Christologia* (1679) and *Meditations and Discourses on the Glory of Christ* (1684) to describe the soul's union and communion with the divine. Owen believed that communion with God was entered only through the door of the "grace and pardoning mercy" of Christ,[234] and that the new spiritual principle within from which sanctification flowed was the union of the soul with Christ. By such communion with the person of Christ, Christian truth gained "living power and efficacy in the souls of men." Owen maintained that the very design of the gospel dispensation was that persons should be formed in holiness by having the image of Christ imprinted within them.[235]

For Owen and the high Calvinists, the purpose of emphasizing the union of the believer with Christ was to evidence the weakness and unspirituality of that moralistic religiosity they saw rapidly gaining ground and which was in effect a denial of God's grace. Owen thought the denial of the Trinity was spreading dangerously, but he was more interested in refuting those who held orthodox views about Christ's person but minimized union with him, those "who expressly deny not his divine person yet seem to grow weary of any concernment therein. A natural religion, or none at all, pleaseth them better than faith in God by Jesus Christ." A consequence of such an attitude was that there are "so many discourses published about religion, the practical holiness and duties of obedience, written with great elegancy of style, and seriousness in argument, wherein we can meet with little or nothing wherein Jesus Christ, his office, or his grace, are concerned. Yea, it is odds but in them all we shall meet with some reflections on those who judge them to be the life and centre of our religion. The things of Christ, beyond the example of his conversation on the earth, are of no use with such persons, unto the promotion of piety and gospel obedience." In addition, "reproachful reflections" fall upon those who "plead the necessity of acquaintance" with Christ; "professed love unto the person of Christ is traduced, as a mere fancy and vapour of distempered minds or weak imaginations"; and the expression of "preaching Christ" has become "a term of reproach and contempt."[236] Thus Owen thought the moralism of the age had gone beyond the old heresies of Arminianism and Pelagianism that had detracted from God's grace to become a religion that needed no grace of God at all and ascribed salvation to "a light within," treating those mysteries of religion that go "beyond the line of nature and reason" as folly.[237] But for Owen religion that was satisfied with "natural discoveries of the Divine Being" without reference to the person of Christ was "the highest degeneracy from the mystery of the Christian religion."[238]

The mystical and gracious union of the believer with the person of Christ, the very antithesis of Socinian moralism, was reinforced by high

Calvinism and its greatest exponent John Owen by an emphasis upon the work of the indwelling Holy Spirit in regeneration. Owen has been long renowed and perhaps best known for his extensive theology of the Holy Spirit. The Puritan interest in the Holy Spirit has come to be regarded as connected with the characteristically Puritan internalization of religion and accordingly has been related to the rise of Quakerism and similar radical uses of the "Spirit."[239] But with Owen the primary focus would seem to have been upon this as another way to defend the Reformed theology of predestinarian grace by highlighting the irresistible grace of regeneration as an operation of God himself in his Spirit. It was also another way to stress grace alone so as to remain near to the needs and categories of piety, compared, for example, with the more remote and abstract question of the divine decrees. Owen's anti-Quaker conservatism certainly puts his treatment of the Spirit at a far remove from their approach.[240] Owen's chief work on the Holy Spirit, *Pneumatologia*, was published in 1674 and was followed by several smaller, more practical treatises further elucidating the subject.[241] Owen directed his *Pneumatologia* against both Quaker mysticism and Socinian moralism; he believed the former caused the latter to heap contempt upon those who spoke of God's Spirit. Owen remarked, "He needs no furtherance in the forfeiture of his reputation with many, as a person fanatical," who shows interest in the work of the Spirit.[242] The first part of the book defended the full divinity of the Holy Spirit against Socinianism. But the central portion was dedicated to explicating and defending the work of the Spirit as the Spirit of grace who operates effectually "in the regeneration or conversion of sinners." Owen called this doctrine of the work of the Holy Spirit in salvation the second great truth of the gospel, after the truth of Christ given for man's salvation; for all the works of Christ would be useless to the believer apart from their application by the Spirit, who *is* the Spirit of Christ. By the Spirit alone is the grace of Christ "communicated unto us and wrought in us," so that all that is partaken of by grace is bestowed by the Holy Spirit.[243] Thus the Holy Spirit was for Owen certainly no inner principle belonging to man, nor a basis for mystical speculation, but an aspect of the divine, effecting salvation by grace.

The enemies of this doctrine of the gracious work of the Holy Spirit were Owen's recurrent enemies, the upholders of human merit. Against them he argued that regeneration by the Spirit meant that regeneration was not a moral reformation carried out by human effort. Nor is regeneration merely a moral way of life, but to be regenerated is to be a "new creature," with a new inner principle, and it is to have undergone a spiritual renovation. Only such a supernatural regeneration by the Spirit of God could redeem fallen man, and in affirming this view Owen claimed that he taught only what had been the constant faith of the church as it had been determined in councils against the Pelagians, "whose errors and heresies are again revived among us by a crew of Socinianized Arminians." The "habit" of sanctifying grace worked in the believer by the Holy Spirit was altogether different from any natural moral habitude—it was a work of grace and a supernatural spiritual principle. The holiness that resulted from this sanctification was not simply moral virtue or outward honesty and propriety of life, but an inner renewal of the soul, whereby one strove to comply with the will of God "in all duties of obedience and abstinence from sin, out of a principle of faith and love," done with "a designation of all the actions of life unto the glory of God by Jesus Christ."[244]

This treatment of Owen has gone beyond 1660, in order to survey the whole system of the greatest of the expositors of high Calvinism after 1650. But a plethora of theological writings from others associated with his version of theology and often also with his Congregationalism testifies to the fact that he was far from alone. Thomas Goodwin, Thomas Brooks, Samuel Petto, and others wrote in the same vein. In the generation after the Restoration, their version of Calvinist orthodoxy came to seem more and more anachronistic in a more anthropocentric age, in spite of its ardent defense in yet further controversies.

Chapter 5 ❖ Divine Grace
Defended in a New Age, 1660–1695

"The second half of the seventeenth century saw many changes in English religious thought, but none more striking than the overthrow of Calvinism," which "fell from a position of immense authority to obscurity and insignificance," Gerald Cragg wrote in 1950.[1] Having recounted the rise of the Reformed predestinarian theology of grace in English Protestant thought and the challenges it faced in the first half of the seventeenth century, it is necessary finally to chronicle its decline as an intellectual force in general culture while noting its persistence in the subculture of the Protestant Dissenters and the ways its transformation in that subculture would have impact in the future. To state the fact of Calvinism's decline in this period is accurate up to a point, but a further question must be asked: for whom did it decline?

The decline of Calvinism in general culture, especially in the world of polite letters, is apparent enough. The generation after 1660 was on the threshold of the Enlightenment, and a new spirit of critical inquiry was rising, while at the same time religious thinking was tending to give more and more scope to nature at the expense of grace. Paul Hazard has claimed that the great clash of ideals between the traditional and the modern occurred before 1700,[2] and the point has considerable validity when applied to the underlying implications of English religious controversy toward the end of the seventeenth century.

In a larger perspective, the decline of Calvinism was but a part of the wider phenomenon of the decline of both the clergy and theology in general culture and intellectual life. C. John Sommerville has observed that in Restoration England, "polite society" was replacing the clergy "as arbiters of intellectual debate,"[3] with the result that many religious questions were simplified by the "common sense" of the lay person. In ecclesiastical and theological policy, the Restoration was not a return to a church of Laudian ideals, but a triumph of Erastian politiques determined not to allow religious zeal again to disrupt the state.[4] Indeed, the Restoration era was a time of nearly universal ecclesiastical disillusionment. Old Puritan visions were belied by events, and new Anglican ones fell short of realization. It was, in the phrase of Leonard Trinterud, the time of the "dying" of "the clerical world."[5]

The rise of the new science was a crucial ingredient in the new outlook,[6] but judging by the participation of clergy in the scientific movement, even that remained a surprisingly "clerical" world. But the scientific concentration on the study of nature, even study of the physical world as an investigation of the ways of God in creation, had the effect of shifting the center of interest from grace to nature,[7] widening the scope of natural religion though without necessarily denying the realm of grace. Anglican clergymen with scientific interests such as Thomas Sprat, Joseph Glanvill, or John Wilkins did not so much controvert Calvinism as ignore it. Wilkins's recent biographer describes him as having been moderately Calvinist before the Restoration but in his later years writing "as if all men held their salvation in their own hands by acting morally," with grace pushed into the background.[8]

The decline of Calvinism after 1660 in English culture at large, then, is clear enough. But how did this broader cultural phenomenon relate to the religious parties of the day and in particular to the three theological factions outlined in the preceding chapter? In a general way, Anglicanism tended to an Arminian rejection of predestinarian theology consonant with the prevailing culture, the Presbyterians sought a middle ground, and the Congregationalists and Particular Baptists held to their high Calvinism however much it isolated them from the larger culture. But to speak of these groups as coherent, organized "denominations" in the modern sense of the word is anachronistic for the Restoration period; denominations and theologies overlapped rather than coincided perfectly. There continued to be staunchly Calvinist Anglicans, for example George Morley[9] or Thomas Barlow; some Presbyterians were high Calvinists, for example Samuel Annesley;[10] sometimes the distinction between Presbyterian and Congregationalist is almost impossible to draw, for example, in the case of Stephen Charnock; and many Baptists were not Calvinistic but Arminian (General) Baptists. But there was a rough coincidence between theological outlook and ecclesiastical party, with the consequence of further separating dissent from church and Presbyterian from Congregationalist.

The restored Anglican clergy were in 1660 less likely to be Calvinist than ever before: Calvinism had been ecclesiastically discredited for them by its close connection to an antiepiscopal regime under which they had suffered. The Restoration Church of England revived much of the fabric and ceremonial of the Laudian church and its concomitant Arminianism, and that type of high churchmanship continued to have representation in the Church of England (John Cosin was back and a bishop until his death in 1672; there were younger recruits in Peter Gunning, Thomas Ken, George Hickes, and William Sancroft, the last three of whom were nonjurors after 1689). But more characteristic in the leadership of the English church were the "High Church Politicians,"[11] such as Gilbert Sheldon, archbishop of Canterbury from 1663 to 1667, who were more Erastian and less theological in outlook than the Laudians had been. The Arminian and moralist views of Henry Hammond, Jeremy Taylor, and Herbert Thorndike grew in influence. The latter two lived into the Restoration era, and new clergy with this bent appeared, among them Isaac Barrow,[12] Robert Sanderson,[13] William Sherlock, and Edward Stillingfleet. With the theology especially of the latter two, Arminianism was becoming Latitudinarianism[14] and was converging with the legacy of the Cambridge Platonists and the scientific divines. The new Anglican style was much more Erastian and moralist than it was Laudian or sacramental, as befitted the new age. Such clergy found themselves out of patience with the theological formulations of predestinarian grace, especially as those formulations had been discredited by high Calvinist extremes by 1660.

Throughout the period between 1660 and 1689, the Presbyterians still hoped to be comprehended within the established church and thus were not yet ready to turn away from the intellectual currents of the larger society. The moderation of their Calvinism kept them in contact with that wider world and also with the Anglican thinkers. Of this group, Richard Baxter, though the most controversial, continued to be the most prominent; Henry Hickman was occasionally heard from, although he spent much of the period an exile in the Netherlands; but most characteristic were four Presbyterians who had first come upon the scene in the Cromwellian era: Thomas Jacombe, Thomas Manton, John Howe, and William Bates. Jacombe, who preached the funeral sermon for the Amyraldian Richard Vines in 1656, was one of the Presbyterians who joined Baxter in seeking comprehension at the Savoy meeting of 1661.[15] John Howe, a friend of the Platonist Henry More and John Wilkins, and who has been described as dependent on the Cambridge Platonists,[16] stressed charity and peaceableness in his writings, disliked controversy and scholastic quibbling,[17] and had some taste for the new vogue of natural theology.[18] Henry Hickman made Howe responsible for the distribution of some of his legacy to needy students for the ministry.[19] Manton had also been with Baxter as one of the Presbyterians at the Savoy conference with the bishops and joined with Baxter in various other projects. William Bates preached the funeral sermons for Baxter, Jacombe, and Manton, praising Baxter for his "middle way" in "some points of modern controversy" and for refusing to interpret "the promises of the gospel in a less gracious sense than God intended them."[20] Bates affirmed single predestination, but in a clearly sublapsarian fashion, and refused to speculate on God's reasons for predestination.[21] Of all these Presbyterians, Bates showed the most interest in natural theology and the use of scientific knowledge in theological discussion and must be counted an early exponent of the "evidences of Christianity" school.[22] Bates's funeral sermon was preached by John Howe. To these may be added Joseph Alleine, whose fervent piety seems closer to that of the strictly Calvinist Congregationalists, but whose ecclesiological views were Presbyterian and who apparently held moderate Calvinist views.[23] But though these Presbyterians promoted a moderate form of Calvinism and evinced touches of moralism and natural theology, their piety, as the case of Joseph Alleine best testifies, remained mainly warmly evangelical, keeping them much closer to the high Calvinist Congregationalists on that level than in doctrinal theology.

Congregationalists and Particular Baptists had neither hope nor desire for comprehension in the established church. By 1660, their churchmanship had developed to such a point that the fellowship of the gathered congregation was essential, and it took no great perception to see that such a view could never find a place in an established English church. John Owen was clearly the leader of the Congregationalists, but Thomas Goodwin, Thomas Brooks, John Stalham, Philip Nye, George Cokayne, George Griffiths, and others equally wedded to strict Calvinism were associated with him,[24] as were new recruits such as Stephen Lobb or, temporarily, Robert Ferguson. The Savoy Confession of Faith, as previously noted, was their touchstone of correct doctrine and a measure of John Owen's ascendancy among them. But especially after the Restoration, the Particular Baptists shared much with these Congregationalists, and sometimes the line between them was vague. These Baptists put out a Confession of Faith in 1677, which was their recension of the Westminster and Savoy Confessions. Expressed by Benjamin Keach, John Bunyan, and John Tombes,[25] their Calvinism was if anything stricter than that of the Congregationalists and certainly less fearful of Antinomianism. Among these Congregationalists and Particular Baptists Calvinism can hardly be said to have declined at all, but to have survived, albeit in isolation from general intellectual life in a particular context, that of the sometimes lively and certainly steadfast ethos of the piety of the persecuted Nonconformist conventicles led by ejected ministers. In that context, a warm evangelical piety, detached from worldliness, and inward looking, could thrive, its leaders from time to time sallying forth to denounce the apostasy of Anglican theology or to question the loyalty of the Presbyterians to the old Calvinist landmarks.

The rest of this chapter will explore the relationships among these three ecclesiastical factions and theological parties as they impinged on the theology of grace, first by detailing the continuing theological debate over grace and then by investigating the direction taken by the piety of predestinarian grace in the latter part of the seventeenth century.

Continuing Debate over Grace

After the Restoration, controversy between conformist and Nonconformist and even sometimes between different kinds of Dissenters focused extensively on ecclesiastical questions, especially on the issues of conformity or the extent of Nonconformity. But theological issues, particularly those related to grace, kept surfacing in these discussions, and in several notable theological debates Dissenter and churchman or Presbyterian and Congregationalist were increasingly pitted against each other on that difficult subject. Though the matter continued to be blurred by the presence of Anglican Calvinists, there were basically four main controversies in which Dissenters charged churchmen with upholding a "Socinian-like" moralism, revolving around George Bull, Edward Fowler, Samuel Parker, and William Sherlock (though they hardly exhaust the list of Anglicans so accused),[26] and three loci of conflict between Presbyterian and Congregationalist, focusing on Richard Baxter, John Howe, and Antinomianism.

George Bull has been classed with Taylor, Thorndike, and Hammond as a "moralist" by C. F. Allison, whose analysis of Bull's views on justification shows that Bull believed that the doing of the good works commanded by Christ was necessary for justification.[27] But Bull, in his well-argued and fair-minded *Harmonia Apostolica*, first published in 1669–70, went beyond those earlier moralists in his straightforward assertion of justification by good works. Bull, educated at Oxford and made bishop of St. Davids in 1705, refuted in print both anti-Trinitarians and Roman Catholics and sought in his *Harmonia Apostolica* to show the harmony between the views of St. Paul and St. James on faith and works. He took it as theologically self-evident that "no one is justified in the sight of God by faith alone, without the other virtues," and even though he maintained that the good that persons performed "towards the obtaining justification" was done with the aid of grace,[28] that grace was not at all an infused sacramental grace like that of Roman Catholic theology[29] but merely a divine help to morality.

Anglican criticism of Bull's harmonization of Paul and James was plentiful. The Calvinist bishop of Winchester, George Morley, issued a pastoral charge against Bull's book; Thomas Barlow, eventually to be bishop of Lincoln, lectured against Bull's views at Oxford;[30] and Thomas Tully, made a royal chaplain by Charles II, though according to the Oxford antiquarian Anthony Wood hindered in his career by his strict Calvinism,[31] attacked Bull in print.[32]

Other published attacks on Bull included some from Nonconformists. John Tombes, Baptist and high Calvinist, answered Bull in Latin, coupling Bull with Baxter and citing William Pemble as an authority.[33] Joseph Truman, ejected for Nonconformity after the Restoration and a friend of Baxter,[34] offered a distinctly moderate Calvinist criticism of Bull in 1671. Truman had earlier written on the atonement, seeking to make the doctrine of Christ's satisfaction "more amiable," while criticizing the Antinomians. In his reply to Bull, Truman admitted that extreme Calvinists had so "grossly explained" "many Important Doctrines of the Reformed Churches . . . as to have ill Consequences following from them"; accordingly, "many Learned men, seeing the Intolerableness of such consequent Opinions" had denied important truths. A proper explanation of Reformed doctrine in the first place would have avoided this controversy. Truman then criticized Bull for a misleading exposition of St. Paul's teaching on grace, for reducing grace to nature, and for confusing sanctification with justification.[35] Bull's views were also rejected by Charles Gataker, a Cromwellian incumbent who eventually conformed after 1660; he was the son of Thomas Gataker, who had long before confuted Antinomianism. His essay on harmonizing Paul and James, Gataker asserted, had been completed before Bull's work was printed, but in "An Advertisement to the Candid Reader" Gataker noted that his conclusions were different from those of Bull's book. Gataker argued that it was Socinian to hold that Christ's work was merely exemplary and confirmatory of his message; Paul taught that only faith in Christ's atoning death brought justification, and St. James showed how the justified person was regenerated by grace in order to do good works.[36] Charles Gataker later wrote further on justification.[37]

Bull responded to the criticisms of Tully and Gataker in a further work and charged them with teachings that by consequence led to Antinomianism. But it was to Tully's accusation that Bull and those who agreed with him had departed from the true Reformed faith of the Church of England, substituting Socinian doctrine for it, that Bull reacted most vigorously, declaring that he would take his stand on the ancient fathers, with whom Calvin was at variance. Bull called Tully's defense of predestination no more than the ancient heresy of "the wretched monk" Gottschalk, revived by Calvin and others in the sixteenth century—it is a "grievous error," which such Protestant divines as Melancthon and Overall rightly rejected.[38]

Edward Fowler, the future bishop of Gloucester, was a Bedfordshire vicar in 1671 when he published *The Design of Christianity*, which was answered that same year by John Bunyan, then a resident of the county jail in Bedford. Fowler's book asserted that the design of the gospel and the end for which Christ came into the world was moral renewal and the imparting to humankind of a real righteousness. He complained of those presumably Antinomian persons who turned the grace of God into an occasion of wantonness and of those who understood God's decrees to be irrespective of human moral effort. Fowler defined justifying faith as including "a sincere resolution of obedience" to the precepts of the gospel and imputation as "dealing with sincerely righteous persons, as if they were perfectly so, for the sake and upon the account of Christ's righteousness." To think otherwise was to open the door to Antinomianism.[39]

To this bald moralism the author of *Pilgrim's Progress* responded vehemently. Bunyan, a Particular Baptist like Tombes who had controverted Bull, was distinctly a high Calvinist, with some Antinomian leanings and with many affinities to the theology of John Owen, for whom he had a high regard (Owen spoke favorably of him, too). Unconditional grace was central to Bunyan's thought. Bunyan feared the menace of Socinianism, regarded it as a denial of Christ's satisfaction, and was a strong predestinarian. The high Calvinist view that Christ suffered the identical penalty due to sinners was also shared by Bunyan.[40] It is no surprise that Fowler's ideas were to him no more than "heathenish" moralism, and he said so in his *A Defence of the Doctrine of Justification by Faith in Jesus Christ . . . Or, Mr. Fowler's Pretended Design of Christianity Proved To be Nothing More than to Trample under Foot the Blood of the Son of God; and the Idolizing of Man's Own Righteousness.* Bunyan, Dissenter from the established church though he was, nonetheless thought Fowler had lapsed from the "wholesome doctrine" of the Thirty-nine Articles and outlined his departures from them.[41] But the core of Bunyan's objection to Fowler was that he was a mere moralist who had cut the gospel of grace itself out of Christianity, making it an affair of nature and law, bereft of "coming to God by Christ," of "evangelical principles," of renewal by the Holy Spirit and the "new heart." Fowler's morality regarded as the design of Christianity was simply nature given divine assistance, Bunyan argued, whereas true gospel Christianity was not just a renewal of the fallen Adamic nature but the effectual giving, by predestinating grace, of a new spiritual life,[42] unknown to nature. Fowler's views were Socinian and Quaker, and Bunyan said Fowler himself would be as comfortable in Turkey as in a Christian land.[43]

Bunyan's intemperate reply was answered with further intemperance by Fowler the next year in *Dirt Wipt Off: Or a Manifest Discovery of the Gross Ignorance, Erroneousness and most Unchristian and Wicked Spirit of One John Bunyan, Lay Preacher in Bedford, which he hath Shewed in a Vile Pamphlet.* Complaining that Bunyan was "a very dirty creature" given to "brutish barkings," Fowler restated and defended his views, accusing his opponent of being "a Ranting Antinomian" for his wicked assertion that the holiness of the redeemed was that of Christ imputed to them. Indeed, Fowler focused upon Bunyan's doctrine of imputation with its high Calvinist corollaries, citing the Nonconformist Baxter as support for his own different understanding of imputation and justification.[44]

Compared to the still very scholastic approach of Bull in discussing theological questions, Fowler's approach smacked much more of the Latitudinarian spirit (Bunyan in fact called him "a glorious Latitudinarian"[45]) with its reduction of the Christian religion to some simple moral essentials. Consequently, the conflict between a theology exalting divine grace and one that expanded the realm of nature at the expense of grace became much sharper in the Fowler-Bunyan exchange than in the dispute of Bull with his opponents. Bunyan was less scholastic in his approach in answering Fowler than were Tully or Truman in confuting Bull, and in his reply can be seen the passionate predestinarian piety of the conventicle culture outraged at the declension from true Christianity of Anglican persecutors who claimed to be the arbiters of just which form of Christianity was to be validated by the power of the state. The sneers of Fowler and the narrow-mindedness of Bunyan seem the inevitable two sides of the embittered relations between the Church of England and Dissent after the brutality of the great ejection and the Clarendon Code.

A similar virulence ran through the next controversy over grace, which again tended to separate church from Dissent, this time revolving around the strictures of Samuel Parker against the Nonconformists. Parker, at the time of the controversy archdeacon of Canterbury, but later made bishop of Oxford by James II, by which time he was widely regarded as a wily defector to the Roman Catholicism of that monarch, was described by the "whiggish" though Anglican Gilbert Burnet as "a man that has no regard either to religion or virtue, but will accommodate himself to everything that may gratify either his covetousness or his ambition."[46]

The extreme Erastianism of Parker was evident in his attack upon the Dissenters. In the midst of his invective is to be found the argument that in religion all men should obey the government rather than disturb the peace. Especially liable to sedition, the greatest of evils, are religious fanatics, of whom Parker considered the English Dissenters to be particularly dangerous examples because of their Antinomian extremism.[47]

Parker's performance brought consternation to the Puritans, and John Owen first urged Baxter to reply and then answered Parker himself.[48] Owen's reply dealt mainly with the issues of conformity and toleration, which were the subject of Parker's diatribe, but also raised the same theological issue of Socinian moralism that kept recurring in Restoration religious debates. Among his reasons for dissent from the Church of England Owen included the point that the Dissenters were clinging fast to the truths of the Reformation, while many in the established church were declining from Reformation doctrine, denying original sin, denying the imputation of Christ's righteousness, and teaching justification by works. The real "dissenters" from the Church of England were those who, like Parker, rejected its established doctrines—a far greater dissent than that of Owen and his colleagues, who disagreed with the church over matters of discipline and liturgy.[49] Specifically, Owen charged Parker with teaching that grace and moral virtue were identical, a view Owen considered subversive of the Christian gospel. Parker, he observed, described Christianity without mention of either sin or redemption.[50]

In the next two years further writings of Parker attacked Owen caustically as "an enormous and irreclaimable offender," who could be dealt with only by strong rebukes.[51] The theology of grace was still not Parker's main subject, but rather what he took to be the Puritans' chief principle, "Insolence and Presumption against Princes," which should be punished "by the Pillory and the Whipping-Post."[52] Nonetheless Parker took up Owen's claim that there had been a declension in the Church of England from the doctrine of the Reformers. Parker asserted that there had been at the Reformation no intent to bring in any new doctrinal system but only to get rid of certain corruptions; the purpose of the Reformation was not "to exchange Thomas Aquinas his Sums for Calvin's Instructions, or Bodies of School-Divinity for Dutch Systems." He admitted that a proper Reformation was almost lost to "Calvinian rigours" through the work of the Puritans, but the church struggled against the false theology of "that proud and busie Man" Calvin. He topped off this argument by reviling the doctrine of predestination as an absurdity and berating the Marian martyrs as sufferers for the folly of supralapsarianism![53] Puritans teach justification by faith, he went on, as a cover for their licentiousness; without morals themselves, it is no wonder that they objected to the sound teaching that moral virtue and grace were the same. Parker added that none of the ancient church fathers ever distinguished between moral virtue and evangelical grace: such grace was nothing more to them than moral virtue heightened by the motives of the gospel. These ancient fathers, Parker continued, never taught their followers "to presume themselves into Salvation by a stout Belief," but "to purchase their future hopes by living up to the severest and most exalted doctrines of the Gospel." Parker agreed with Owen's charge that he had reduced religion to morality: "The Christian Institution is not for the substance of it any new Religion, but only a more perfect digest of the Eternal Rules of Nature and Right Reason." Jesus came into the world not to give any new moral teachings, but "only" to restore "the old Rule of Nature from the evil customs of the world, and to reinforce their Obligation by endearing our duty with better Promises, and urging our Obedience upon severer Penalties." Even the sacraments have as their one purpose the improvement of morality. Faith is belief in the doctrines of the gospel.[54] Thus a Socinian moralism completely vulnerable to the later claim associated with the Deists that no revelation at all was needed as an addition to natural religion had appeared some twenty years before John Locke's *The Reasonableness of Christianity* opened itself up to such a conclusion. Parker stated the moralist view more baldly than Fowler had.

Robert Ferguson, later an assistant to John Owen in his London congregation and later also a plotter against the government, entered the debate in 1673 with *A Sober Enquiry into the Nature, Measure, and Principle of Moral Virtue*, which concentrated on Parker's view of grace. Noting that those of Pelagian tendency had ever reduced grace to a "Natural Power,"[55] Ferguson argued that humanity by its disobedience forfeited the covenant of works and lost the power to please God by moral virtue. Thus, after the fall, humankind was utterly unable to fulfill the moral obligations demanded by God and was liable to eternal punishment for such failure. But God's grace intervened in this impasse with a new covenant of faith and repentance, in which God himself supplied the grace for believing and repenting.[56] Far from being identical with moral virtue, gospel grace was, as for Bunyan, a new principle that, though it might take up into itself the demands of moral virtue, was far more, being the transformation of life through the gospel of Christ.

Another answer to Parker came from the poet and parliamentarian Andrew Marvell. A friend of both Owen and Baxter, Marvell evidently concluded that the scurrility of Parker could best be dealt with by making him appear foolish, and this was his aim in *The Rehearsal Transprosed*, published in 1672. Marvell's satire, passing the licenser only through the personal intervention of the king, continually referred to Parker as "Bayes," a ludicrous and quarrelsome poet who appeared as a character in the duke of Buckingham's play *The Rehearsal*, and retold the life story of Parker in mock heroic, emphasizing his "lycanthropic" madness. Determined to be "a madman in print," part of his madness was to become a theological Don Quixote, "busied at present in vanquishing the Calvinists of Germany and Geneva." Marvell expressed the hope that by his example young clerics would beware henceforth "of overweening Presumption and preposterous Ambition." Imagining himself a wolf, and lacking cattle to ravage, Marvell went on, "you find him raving now against all the Calvinists of England, and worrying the whole Flock of them."[57]

Marvell was thoroughly aware of the theological dimensions of the dispute, and in spite of his warning never to "be grave with a Buffoon," he recurred seriously several times to the question of grace. Parker was abused for defending Bramhall, whom Marvell says made it his life work to substitute "Arminian tenets" for the "Calvinian doctrines" of the Church of England. That church, Marvell affirmed, was at its foundation

Reformed and Calvinist, and in traducing the doctrines of Calvin, Parker was forgetful that "most of our ancient, and many of the later Bishops nearer our times, did both hold and maintain those Doctrines." The new doctrines, he continued, began to come in just before the civil wars, borrowed by the "prelatists" from the Dutch Arminians, although clearly contrary to the received doctrine of the Church of England. It was only after these men had subverted the church that "the Calvinists were all studiously discountenanced." As for Parker's views about grace and moral virtue, Marvell added that if Parker were to become a bishop, "I am resolved instead of his Grace to call him alwayes his Morality," for Parker had "made the passage to Heaven so easie that one may fly thither without Grace." Parker, he noted further, made the way of salvation easier than the way of loyalty to an earthly ruler because only the latter involved for him an absolute submission.[58]

According to Burnet, Parker was humiliated by this response,[59] but he had his defenders. One of these, Richard Leigh, berated the Reformers, especially Calvin, and denounced Owen as a dangerous rebel.[60] Another, Edmund Hickeringill, a former Quaker who was later indicted for various infractions of the law, but was at the moment an Anglican incumbent, added Marvell to Owen as a desperate rebel and agreed with Parker that morality was the sum of Christianity, it being pure "enthusiasm" to think otherwise. Hickeringill described justification as a reward given by God to those who merited it by good works. He called Calvin a "knave" who taught sedition.[61]

Parker defended himself with *A Reproof to the Rehearsal Transprosed*, in which he asserted that the main principle of the Reformation in England had been the sovereignty of princes over their subjects rather than any new view of grace. Once more he said that grace and moral virtue were identical, remarking that Calvinist grace was "the Grace of Beggars and Bankrupts, that have the face to look demurely, and amuse us with talk of their intimate Communion with God, whilst their fingers are in our pockets, and their Daggers at our Throats."[62] But Marvell, too, had a rejoinder: justifying his raillery against Parker as directed against one who had wantonly sought to destroy the reputations of others and thus deserved the same himself, he turned to the theological issue with greater seriousness. Parker, Marvell averred, taught salvation by human effort alone, rejecting the grace of God. Addressing himself to Parker, he continued, "You run down and baffle that serious business of Regeneration, Justification, Sanctification, Election, Vocation, Adoption, which the apostle Paul hath . . . with so much labour illustrated and distinguished."[63]

John Owen played a major role in another controversy when, in 1673, a work written by him during the Interregnum, *Of Communion with God*, was attacked by the Anglican William Sherlock in *A Discourse concerning the Knowledge of Jesus Christ*. Owen's discourse had been a very warm, devotional treatment of the believer's communion with God, and to Sherlock, whose views depended on the earlier moralists and who was one of the leading Latitudinarians in the Church of England, this seemed a delusive fanaticism. Thus Sherlock presented a more "rational" account of the meaning of communion with God and Christ: to be "united to Christ," he said, signified "no more than to be a Christian, One, who belongs to that Society, whereof Christ is the Head." The Puritans and Dissenters, instead of being satisfied with this, "have advanced a kind of Amorous and Enthusiastick Devotion, which consists in a Passionate Love to the Person of Christ." This idea, however, falsely divided the person from the teaching of Christ, for the design of the Christian religion was obedience to Christ's law and the person of Christ is "excellent" in order that there might be a sanction for that law—"He came to be our Prophet and our Guide, to teach us by his precepts and his Life." Christ's death teaches the solemn obligation of morality, vindicating God's laws and securing pardon for the penitent. Salvation comes by believing and obeying the gospel of Christ, which consists of "the best Rules of Life." We are encouraged to follow these rules by "the most express Promises of a blessed Immortality." To know Christ is to be acquainted with the doctrine and religion he preached. Owen, however, taught that instead following Christ is having a "more intimate acquaintance with the Person of Christ," which means to Owen that Christ is our righteousness and that therefore we do not need to do anything good ourselves. Thus according to Sherlock Owen was teaching a dangerous religion of Christ's person as separate from his teaching.[64] As an indication of how remote the earlier Reformed theology of predestinarian grace was coming to seem to these new divines, it is interesting that Sherlock presented a rather fair statement of Owen's actual beliefs as though they were sufficiently absurd that their very recital would refute them: Owen, he says, teaches that "by trusting to the Expiation and Righteousness of Christ for Salvation, without doing any thing ourselves, we take care that God shall not be robbed of the glory of his free Grace by a Competition of any

Merits and Deserts of our own."[65] Nothing better illustrates the change
in theological assumptions after the Restoration than this treatment of
the great theological issues before the age of Cromwell as curious absurdities. In the earlier controversies with the Laudians, both sides had
accepted belief in a supernatural Christianity dealing with the soul's
relationship to God and argued whether that relationship was primarily
declared in the preaching of justification or nurtured in the sacramental
life of the church. But controversialists such as Fowler, Parker, and Sherlock took for granted the assumption that Christianity consisted of no
more than certain moral teachings plus revealed sanctions related to
those teachings. The path that led in England from Latitudinarianism to
Deism was already in full view in the 1670s.

In the rest of his work, Sherlock denied that there was any satisfaction
of God's justice in the atonement,[66] ridiculed the doctrine of election,
and asserted that the great error of the Calvinists was that they took
scriptural metaphors too literally. Christ did not come to "impute" righteousness but to exact it as the price of salvation; to be justified by faith is
to believe "those Revelations which Christ hath made of Gods will to
us." Christ loves those who obey him; we must be holy before our sins
can be forgiven, for sanctification precedes justification.[67] The gospel,
according to Sherlock, is that "God hath sent his own Son into the World
to make a plain, and easie, and perfect Revelation of his Will, to publishe
such a Religion, as may approve itself to our reason, and captivate our
Affections by its natural charms and beauties; and there cannot be a
greater injury to the Christian Religion, than to render it obscure and
unintelligible."[68]

Owen rallied to his own defense in amazement that anyone in the
Church of England would have so baldly set forth Socinian teachings,
denying what "hath been the doctrine of the church of England." Then
Owen quoted from Richard Hooker to show that Sherlock and not he
differed from the received faith of the Church of England, adding, "It is
evident that there is nothing concerning personal election, effectual vocation, justification by the imputation of the righteousness of Christ, participation of him, union of believers unto and with his person, derivation
of grace from him, etc., which are so reproached by our present author,
but they are asserted by this great champion of the church of England,
who undoubtedly knew the doctrine which it owned, and in his days approved."[69] Owen denied that he was guilty of "enthusiasm" and insisted
that scripture summons individuals to a personal acquaintance with

Christ. Owen defended the satisfaction of Christ against Sherlock's "Socinian" view of it and denied that he ever taught that by resting in Christ's righteousness one could ignore the commandments of Christ. It was plain to Owen that Sherlock was a "Pelagian." Even Robert Bellarmine was more orthodox concerning justification than Sherlock! "I do not know that ever I met with anything thus crudely asserted among the Quakers," declared Owen. "I never met with any who was so fearful and jealous lest too much should be ascribed in the matter of our salvation to Jesus Christ." Owen recorded his shock that the ancient doctrines of the Protestant faith were so lightly set aside and that the doctrine of God's eternal election and much else was traduced as fanaticism. Owen expressed doubt that such views could be openly "allowed to pass under the signature of public authority" in any other Christian country and marveled that it could occur in a land that had had such great theological teachers as Jewel, Whitgift, Abbot, Ussher, Hall, Prideaux, "and others innumerable."[70]

Sherlock answered Owen in 1675 with *A Defence and Continuation of the Discourse concerning the Knowledge of Jesus Christ*. He responded that he was arraigned by fanatics for the crime of preaching good works —"A strange and unpardonable crime, that a minister of the Gospel should preach up good Works!" Then he repeated many of his former ideas: that to know Christ was "to be acquainted with that Revelation which Christ hath made of Gods will to the world"; that obedience is necessary to entitle forgiveness; that justifying faith is a "firm and steadfast Assent to all the Revelations of the Gospel." He called Owen an Antinomian.[71] But Sherlock firmly denied being either Pelagian or Socinian. He also denied that he had departed seriously from the first teachings of the Church of England, saying only that if he had departed from them in some points, that was no crime for they were not infallible. The imputation of Christ's righteousness, he argued, was never taught in the English church.[72]

In the years immediately following Sherlock's initial attack on Owen, a number of contributions to the controversy came off the presses. Two Presbyterians, Vincent Alsop and Henry Hickman, attacked Sherlock as an Arminian and Socinian who was destroying the Protestant faith. Other attacks on Sherlock came from the pens of two other ejected ministers, Samuel Rolle and Thomas Danson,[73] as well as from a conforming layman but staunch Calvinist, Edward Polhill, and Owen's later assistant, Robert Ferguson. Hickman regarded Sherlock as an exponent of the "new divinity" of Socinus, defended Owen, noted Sherlock's departure from the Articles of the established church, criticized him for unfair statement of opposing views, but avoided defending any extreme Calvinist positions.[74] Polhill cried out concerning Sherlock's book that "when I read it, I thought my self in a new theological world; Believers appearing without their Head for want of a Mystical Union, strip'd and naked for lack of imputed Righteousness; the full treasures of Grace in Christ . . . emptied out of his person, and transfused into the doctrine of the Gospel; as if according to Pelagius all Grace were in doctrine only."[75] Ferguson approached the issue from a somewhat different angle, but one that showed considerable understanding of the new issues—he saw the debate with Sherlock to consist of difference over the extent of the use of reason, Sherlock maintaining in effect that reason was the true authority in religion.[76] Thomas Hotchkis, Anglican rector at Staunton, came to Sherlock's defense in a book that showed him worried about Antinomianism.[77] The argument was becoming very much one between church and Dissent. Anti-Calvinist views were now more firmly entrenched in the Church of England than they had ever been in Laudian days, and the form of the attack on Calvinism was more radical than that of Laud; it was part of a new approach to religious problems that can be seen in Latitudinarianism and later in Deism, both of which plainly called for a rational religion. To those who followed this new approach, Calvinism appeared as foolish fanaticism.

The Dissenters were alarmed by the seeming apostasy of the Church of England. John Owen, the most prominent of the high Calvinist theologians of the time, took this growing theological division between Anglicanism and Dissent over grace very seriously. To him it was rapidly becoming one of the chief reasons for dissent, though he always made it clear that this did not mean dissent from the traditional or sixteenth-century theology of the Church of England. His views were explicitly stated in the large work he wrote in defense of Dissent against Edward Stillingfleet, *The Inquiry concerning Evangelical Churches*:

A church that is filled with wranglings and contentions about fundamental or important truths of the gospel is not of choice to be joined unto. . . . And although . . . mutual forebearance is to be exercised, with respect unto a variety in apprehensions in some doctrines of lesser moment, yet the incursion that hath been made into sundry protestant churches, in the last and present age, of novel doctrines and opinions, with differences, divisions, and endless disputes which have ensued thereon, have rendered it very difficult to determine how to engage in complete communion with them; for I do not judge that any man is or can be obliged unto constant, total communion with any church. . . . wherein there are incurable dissensions about important doctrines of the gospel.[78]

Elsewhere in that same work he noted that although the Nonconformists agreed in the main doctrines of the faith with the Church of England, that agreement applied only to "doctrine as declared at the first reformation, and explained in the next age ensuing thereon." But, "If there be a change made in or of these doctrines, . . . by any in or of the Church of England, we profess our disagreement from them, and do declare that thereby the foundation of our communion with them is weakened, and the principal bond of it loosened."[79] And although the Thirty-nine Articles had been at their writing an adequate statement of the faith, Owen considered them inadequate in face of the threat of Arminianism and Socinianism and felt the Church of England was in need of "some more express testimony" against such errors.[80] In another work about dissent and toleration, Owen argued that though charity in differences of religion was desirable, it was not to be carried so far as "to lay aside the consideration of truth." That being so, he continued, it is necessary to dissent from the Church of England both in discipline and doctrine, for "there are daily inroads made upon the ancient doctrine of this church, and that without the least control from them who pretend to be the sole conservators of it," so that to conform to it would practically be to conform to Socinianism.[81]

Owen was sufficiently concerned about England's decay from the true religion of grace that in 1676 he published a work on *The Nature of Apostasy from the Profession of the Gospel,* an exposition of Hebrews 6:4–6. He was concerned not with the apostasy of rejecting Christianity altogether, but with a "partial apostasy" whereby the principles of evangelical truth and obedience were laid aside and various false doctrines substituted for them. Such apostasy continually plagues Christian faith and consists primarily of the exaltation of human self-sufficiency in place of God's grace. The main example of it had been the Roman apostasy from the faith of the earliest Christians, in which the "internal, effectual operations of the Spirit of Grace" were stifled by an emphasis upon "outward dispensations." But perhaps the most dangerous of doctrinal declensions had been that of Pelagianism, which over the long period of time had so subtly insinuated itself into the minds of men that "it continues to be no small part of that religion which the generality of Christians do at this day profess" and was currently making great advances. He cited the Arminianism of the Church of England as an example. But to this Arminianism, Owen continued, was now being added the "leprosy" of Socinianism, a far worse heresy, adding to Arminianism, among other things, the denial of Christ's satisfaction. Inroads had already been made in England by such false religion that the "use" of the "person of Christ" in religion was commonly decried and "justification by and upon our own obedience," as well as "regeneration as consisting only in the reformation of our lives" were openly taught. Socinianism, asserting the primacy of reason, denied all those doctrines that savor of mystery, such as predestination or the imputation of Christ's righteousness. The false moralists failed to understand that it is "grace, and the doctrine of it, as well as its power, that must put a stop to sin."[82]

Owen was not the only one who saw the difference between the established church and the Nonconformists as increasingly theological. The extent and virulence of the debate between church and Dissent suggested the same thing, as it increasingly came to be taken for granted that the Church of England was not Calvinistic and in that respect differed from Protestant Dissent. Assertions can be found almost at random in Anglican theological treatises and works of controversy directed against Dissenters which assumed the non-Calvinist character of the Church of England. Simon Patrick, elevated to the episcopate after the Glorious Revolution, for example, accused the Nonconformists of Antinomian excess and noted that it was a commonplace of Anglican theology that justification was by good works as well as faith.[83] Similarly, John Goodman, acknowledging that some Nonconformists made doctrine as well as discipline a matter of difference between themselves and the church, claimed that this was because they were trying to introduce the teaching of the Synod of Dort into it. "Must a novel Dutch Synod prescribe Doctrine to the Church of England, and outweight all Antiquity?" he asked. He considered antiquity antipredestinarian, except for St. Augustine, whose piety "was far more commendable than his Reason."[84] Richard Perrinchief argued more moderately that the differences between Calvinist and Arminian were such as the Church of England tolerated.[85]

Various theological treatises from the Nonconformists' side accentuated the theological issue as a point of division between church and Dissent. The Presbyterian Vincent Alsop, who had earlier rebutted Sherlock, defended the Synod of Dort against Goodman in 1678, arguing that until the time of Laud a theological system like that of Dort was generally held in the Church of England. But, as Baxter had argued long before, Alsop maintained that Dort's statement of predestinarian theology was essentially moderate and perfectly consonant with the Thirty-nine Articles, which creed he considered acceptable even to "the most rigid Calvinists," with whom he clearly did not class himself. But Alsop was less comfortable with stressing theological difference between church and Dissent than Owen had been and emphasized the closeness of Nonconformists to the official theological standards of the Church of England.[86] Thomas Manton, another Presbyterian, wrote a major work directed against Socinianism, but like the Anglican George Bull perceived that heresy as the denial of the Trinity and of the atonement of Christ.[87]

The Presbyterians, still hoping for comprehension within the establishment, and mainly promoting a more moderate Calvinism, were thus not among the most eager Dissenters to pursue theological polemics with Anglicans. But the Congregationalists and Particular Baptists were, because as high Calvinists their theological differences with the conformists were greater. They prospered in their "conventicle-culture" isolation from an establishment they found it useful to regard as apostate. John Owen, the leading theologian of high Calvinism, thought doctrinal differences had been added to other reasons for Nonconformity, and he continued to produce massive theological tomes in defense of Calvinism. The range of his theological concerns has been treated in chapter 4; but it is a further striking fact that so many of those who strongly assailed Arminian and Socinian error were connected in one way or another with Owen.

Among theological authors defending predestinarian grace who were connected to John Owen was Patrick Gillespie, a Scotsman who had collaborated with Cromwell and been a friend of Owen during the Interregnum. A preface by Owen graced his treatment of the covenant of redemption in 1677.[88] Another book on that subject, by the Congregationalist and strict Calvinist Samuel Petto,[89] received the endorsement of Owen as a sound exaltation of "the grace of God in the Covenant."[90] In a preface to a work by the ejected minister Bartholomew Ashwood, Owen remarked on the opposition lately made to the "mysteries of the gospel" and recommended Ashwood's book as giving testimony to the "free grace" of God in Christ.[91] Owen also wrote commendatory prefaces for such works as the Westminster divine and Cromwellian Independent William Bridge's *The Freeness of the Grace and Love of God to*

Believers, Stephen Lobb's *The Glory of Free Grace Displayed,* and John Ness's *Antidote to Arminianism,* published in 1671, 1680, and 1690, respectively. Owen's preface in the last appeared posthumously.

A very scholastic work defending the divine decrees of election and reprobation and the order of salvation flowing from them appeared from the pen of Edward Polhill, the layman who also attacked Sherlock, prefaced by Owen. Owen praised the work as useful in the defense of the faith against Quakers and "Papists" as well as Arminians and Socinians.[92] Another layman, Sir Charles Wolseley, a former member of Cromwell's council of state and presumably well known to Owen, assailed the Socinian view of justification by an inherent rather than imputed righteousness.[93] Yet another book bearing Owen's recommendation was *A Practical Discourse of God's Sovereignty* by Elisha Coles, a layman and a Congregationalist who had come into the favor of Thomas Goodwin at Oxford. Owen spoke in his preface of the Pelagianism that had long been making inroads on the theology of predestinarian grace.[94] Coles described his own work as an assault upon the opinion of "General Grace" by an assertion of the "invincible efficacie of Divine Grace" to particular persons, proceeding from God's sovereignty. Coles's book was built around the order of salvation, all of which flows out of election, and its treatment of predestination was characteristically high Calvinist.[95] Also like Owen writing with the Socinian menace in mind was Thomas Brooks, a former Cromwellian Independent, whose *A Golden Key to Open Hidden Treasures* was really a treatise on the atonement, propounding the view that the Socinian denial of a substitutionary atonement was a barrier to true faith and holiness. In high Calvinist fashion, Brooks employed many formulations to maximize the extent of Christ's sufferings, including the notion that he underwent the very penalty and curse due to sinners.[96] Finally, among these books by those related to Owen was a very practical exposition of the theology of grace from David Clarkson, who, late in Owen's life, had been his assistant in his London congregation. Avoiding scholastic logic and argumentative quibbling, Clarkson portrayed two versions of what Christianity might be: either a moralism or a religion of grace. But only in a religion of grace can there be a true salvation, for man by nature is powerless to aid himself. God's grace redeems persons through an order of salvation moving from election to glorification. The meaning of such a theology of grace is that "all is of Gift," and when moralism replaces this outlook, love and gratitude to God are stifled and the basis for holy obedience destroyed.[97]

Other defenders of the predestinarian theology of grace in the Restoration era were less obviously connected to Owen. Thomas Danson, a Nonconformist minister who had received preferment from Oliver Cromwell and who broke a lance against Sherlock in that controversy, defended the Reformed theology of justification in one work and the doctrine of the final perseverance of the elect in two others.[98] From Particular Baptist circles, though probably not by Bunyan as usually supposed,[99] came a defense of the doctrine of reprobation, which in spite of insisting that reprobates would "infallibly perish" expressed that teaching with a sensitive moderation.[100]

More important if less direct in their defense of grace than these occasional pieces were several elaborate works by the prodigiously learned Theophilus Gale. A pupil of Thomas Goodwin at Magdalen, Oxford, and an Independent, Gale was ejected from his Oxford posts at the Restoration and devoted his erudition thereafter to several of the more curious defenses of the predestinarian theology of grace that appeared in the later seventeenth century. One of these works was an inquiry into the Jansenists of France, prefaced by John Owen. Gale was sympathetic to the Jansenists, treating those heterodox Roman Catholics as crypto-Protestant in their Augustinianism.[101] But his more important work was his four-part *The Court of the Gentiles*, portions of which appeared throughout the 1670s. The purpose of the work was ostensibly to pursue exhaustively a theme appearing elsewhere in the scholarship of the century, which Gale claimed he gleaned first from Hugo Grotius: that all human wisdom and learning, including language, philosophy, and religion, were derived from the Old Testament and the "Jewish Church." The first part dealt with the Hebrew origin of all language and literature, the second traced the origin of all philosophy to Jewish wisdom, the third exposed the vanity of pagan philosophy, and the last part, "Of Reformed Philosophie," subdivided its material into moral philosophy and metaphysical philosophy before proceeding to a long treatment of "Divine Predetermination." Only on closer examination does the scope of this monumental work come clear: Gale was convinced that unaided human reason had never been able to find divine truth or truth at all on its own and therefore all that passed for reason and knowledge based on nature had really been derived from original revelation. On the other hand, insofar as such natural knowledge was corrupted, it was because of the perennial tendency of fallen human nature to assert its misguided self-sufficiency. Even within the citadel of Christian revelation that tendency had frequently reared its ugly head, Pelagianism, Arminianism, and most recently Socinianism being prime examples.[102] Thus his aim became contemporary, for he wanted to "beat down that fond persuasion" that the wisdom of the pagans was "the product of Natures Light," because he felt that there had lately been too much admiration of the powers of natural reason.[103] Granted the tendency of human pride since the fall, philosophy fell with Adam and had become "a common Strumpet, for carnal Reason to commit follie with," and ever since, "the lascivious wits of lapsed human nature" have gone "a whoring after Vain Philosophie."[104] The principal doctrine of such vain philosophy has ever been the freedom of the human will and an accompanying enhancement of human merit, Pelagianism being the inevitable philosophy of the natural man.[105] Thus his constructive fourth part was dedicated to a scholastic treatment of freedom, for the purpose of showing how God absolutely determined all things, yet without thereby being the author of sin.

But the Nonconformists themselves were divided over these same issues of grace into the high Calvinist Congregationalists and Particular Baptists and the moderate Calvinists, found mostly among the Presbyterians. In the debates between Dissenter and churchman that strayed into the area of the theology of grace, the moderate Calvinists often took a different tack from the high Calvinists, were more interested than the latter in minimizing the extent of the difference, and evidenced some tendencies in common with those accused of "Socinianizing" moralism. It was inevitable that a certain nervousness in the maintenance of a common front against Anglican moralists would erupt into theological misunderstandings and finally full-blown disputes between moderate and high Calvinists.

One of these disputes centered around John Howe. In 1677, that moderate Calvinist published a short letter that had been addressed to Robert Boyle under the title *The Reconcileableness of Gods Prescience of the Sins of Men, with the Wisdom and Sincerity of His Counsels*, in which he argued that God willed the salvation of all and that God would never predetermine persons to do things for which they would then be damned. In making these points, Howe also denigrated the scholastic approach, considering his subject too serious for the exercise of "scholastic wit."[106] Theophilus Gale, proud of having studied much in scholastic theology and already on record as against all Amyraldian or "semiarminian" modification of Calvinism, was unable in the fourth part of *The Court of the Gentiles* to let such error pass uncontested. Gale, burying Howe under quotations from Aquinas, Duns Scotus, and Francisco Suarez, claimed that Howe was a follower of the medieval scholastic Durandus of Saint Pourcain and took him to task for making God dependent upon the contingencies of human willing, which would, Gale alleged, rule out all God's "gratiose operations."[107] Howe defended himself in a postscript to his original letter, charged Gale with attacking a "Man of Straw," and again protested his dislike for quibbling arguments of this type.[108]

The quarrel did not rest there, for two more high Calvinists entered the fray in 1678. One, John Troughton, a scholar at Oxford when John Owen was vice-chancellor there and a blind Nonconformist who kept a conventicle, was also an opponent of Arminians and Socinians on justification. He published *A Letter to a Friend, touching Gods providence about sinful actions*, in answer both to Howe's original discourse and to his postscript.[109] The other came from Thomas Danson, who had already been in several theological debates, and who complained that Howe's words bordered "as near upon Arminianism as Scotland does upon England."[110] Danson disclosed the attitude of a high Calvinist to such betrayal: the "times" verged enough upon Socinianism as it was, without Howe ill-treating such a pious person as Gale; Howe had departed entirely from those true teachers Beza, Perkins, Pemble, and Twisse; as for guilt by association, Howe, Danson claimed, agreed with Baxter, Samuel Hoard, and John Goodwin. The consequence of the further spread of such notions, Danson thought, would be to open the door to atheistic and Epicurean denial of providence and the final usurpation of God's place by man.[111] Noteworthy in this discussion is how much predestination was taken as a part of a whole deterministic philosophy by its adherents and disconnected from soteriology, which was of course the scholastic tendency.

More divisive were the disputes, mainly between Presbyterian and Congregationalist Dissenters, over justification, imputation, and Antinomianism, with Richard Baxter again prominently in the center of the stage. In 1671, Baxter defended the Anglican Fowler against some of the strictures of Bunyan,[112] and in a joint Presbyterian-Congregationalist lecture at Pinner's Hall in London in 1672 under the terms of the indulgence of that year, Baxter managed again to offend strict Calvinists on the point of justification. Baxter continued to think that a tendency to Antinomianism made the Dissenters unnecessarily vulnerable to Anglican criticisms,[113] and after four Pinner's Hall lectures to clear up the matter Baxter was again accused of denying justification by the imputed righteousness of Christ, according to Calamy, London being rife with "Rumours of his preaching up Arminianism."[114] Baxter was constrained to write once more in self-defense, and again he multiplied distinctions in order to assert that although Christ purchased the benefits of the covenant of grace, persons must not minimize the duties incumbent upon them of obeying that covenant. But even in this attempt at vindicating his orthodoxy, Baxter went so far as to say that the real differences between Protestants and Rome were not over justification, but over false worship and papal power.[115] But while the Independents grumbled about Baxter's heterodoxy and his misuse of their joint lectureship, the Anglican conformist Thomas Tully, earlier an opponent of George Bull, fell upon Baxter. Tully said that Baxter taught the plainest justification by works and was thus at one with "Papists" and Socinians. Baxter's putative reconciling distinctions, Tully thought, were simply evasions that could never bring Baxter's doctrine into harmony with Reformed theology.[116]

Baxter continued to deal with these issues, however, in a manner offensive to high Calvinists, as is evident from his attempt at reconciliation, *Catholick Theologie: Plain, Pure, Peaceable: for the Pacification of the Dogmatical Word-Warriors*, in which he set out to reconcile the various points of view regarding predestination, original sin, imputation, and justification raised in the recent controversies. Farther down on the title page, Baxter noted that it was written for posterity, "when sad Experience hath taught men to hate Theological-Logical Wars" and to seek peace. In spite of that auspicious beginning, this book merely renewed the conflict. Baxter now avowed that his real work should be no longer to enter into theological debates but to seek peace and fellowship with other Christians.[117] Like Howe, he professed an abandonment of scholastic theology and argumentation and favored a more Latitudinarian outlook.

But the specter of Antinomianism was to reappear as a point of contention between the two main groups of Protestant Dissenters a few years later. This last phase of the Antinomian controversy came after the Toleration Act and lasted almost throughout the decade; it had the consequence of further dividing the two main bodies of English Protestant Dissent, leading the Presbyterians to take up a position much closer than ever to Arminianism and the Congregationalists to affirm more solidly than ever a high Calvinism verging on Antinomianism. The story has been told in detail before;[118] because it goes beyond the chronological scope of the present work, only a few salient elements relevant to what has preceded need be recounted here. The sermons of the old Antinomian Tobias Crisp were republished by his son Samuel Crisp in 1690 and triggered Richard Baxter's last outcry against that heresy, a Pinner's Hall lecture on 28 January 1690, in which the Crispian doctrine of imputation was condemned.[119] One year later Baxter was dead, and his place as the leading opponent of Antinomianism as a danger lurking within Dissent was taken by Daniel Williams, who became the pastor of a congregation of London Presbyterians. Although counseled by some to compromise and seek concord,[120] Williams got embroiled in dispute with the Congregationalists Thomas Cole, Isaac Chauncey, Nathaniel Mather, and Stephen Lobb. Lobb accused Baxter and Williams of a Socinian denial of Christ's satisfaction for sin[121] as well as of the true doctrine of imputation. By the end of 1694, the Presbyterians had withdrawn from the joint lecture at Pinner's Hall when Williams, John Howe, and William Bates set up a new lecture at Salter's Hall. The division over the theology of grace that underlay the differences between these two groups of Dissenters had worked a more complete rupture between them than ever before, though some measure of harmony was restored in the end of the last decade of the seventeenth century.[122] In the next century, the two groups furthered their divisions[123] and went their separate ways of Presbyterian accommodation to the spirit of the Age of Reason in contrast to the intransigent Calvinism of Congregationalists and Particular Baptists, some of whom pushed their Calvinism to that especially hardened form known as hyper-Calvinism.[124]

"Gracious" Piety

If the age of the Restoration was generally unreceptive to strict Calvinist theology, it was nonetheless a time for a great flowering of books of piety and devotion that explicated and applied personally the predestinarian theology of grace.[125] The tradition of the "spiritual writers" that stretched back to Elizabethan times was far from moribund and was developed between 1660 and 1690 in certain ways that mark that period as transitional between the Calvinist piety of the late sixteenth century and the evangelical piety of the eighteenth-century awakenings. Examination of late seventeenth-century devotional treatises with reference to their view of grace shows the same difference between moralistic Arminian piety and a piety centering on free grace that was evident from works of formal theology. A style of rational and moral piety based on more or less Arminian and even Pelagian assumptions thrived among Anglicans, often presented by its exponents as a distinct contrast to the "fanatical" piety of Calvinists, whom they considered responsible for the horrible excesses of the Interregnum years. This Latitudinarian piety with its tone of "sweet reasonableness" has appeared winsome to modern commentators, but Leonard J. Trinterud provides the reminder that it was also motivated by the needs of a particular class when he comments that "rational religion and the repression of troublemakers" was an Anglican desideratum in the years after the Restoration.[126] This tone of moderation in piety crept into the writings of the "Baxterians" and Presbyterians, too, but by and large on the level of piety and devotion their distance from Anglican Arminians and closeness to stricter Calvinists was more evident than in doctrinal debate. Presbyterians, high Calvinist Congregationalists, and Baptists continued to develop and express a piety revolving around divine grace in the order of salvation that revealed their continuity with Bucer and the other early reformers. High Calvinists wrote warmly personal works of devotion that belied the seemingly arid scholasticism of their systematic theological works, recalling once more the existential springs of "gracious" piety in religious experience and the ultimately secondary and functional character of their doctrinal definitions and polemics. Especially prominent in producing Calvinist books of devotion were many Dissenters who are difficult to classify as either Presbyterian or Congregationalist or who labored to mitigate the differences among the various factions of Nonconformists.

John Owen, John Bunyan, and other Dissenters had been bitterly assailed by conformist opponents for an "enthusiastic" zeal and fanatical piety insofar as they had insisted upon a very personal and emotional experience of union with Christ and the Holy Spirit. Arminian Anglican piety spoke of the believer's relationship to Christ and the Spirit in quite different tones, notably with restraint and externality as compared to more Calvinistic devotion, and with a distinct appeal to reason, sobriety, and moderation and, perhaps less admirably, to prudential and calculating motives. Restraint entailed avoidance of anything too personal or emotional, and the externality of this form of devotion was found in its preference for discussing the believer's relation to Spirit or Christ as a more formal and external relationship. This was sometimes reflected in the placing of piety in the context of the church as an institution. Thus Isaac Barrow's sermon on the Holy Spirit, delivered at Pentecost, stressed the Spirit's coming to the church as a whole and its indwelling in all the baptized.[127] When Jeremy Taylor preached on "The Spirit of Grace" he described "being in Christ" not chiefly as a personal union but as living a holy life of following Christ.[128] John Tillotson, eventually to be archbishop of Canterbury, described union with Christ as believing in him; there was no other "mystery" involved in that, he added, than there was in "becoming disciples of Christ and sincerely embracing his Doctrine." Grace was given to help in the following of Christ's commandments, but human effort was required, too.[129] The imitation of Christ coupled with the assurance that it was possible to live up to his commandments has been identified by J. Sears McGee as characteristic of Anglican piety.[130] Faith was treated in Anglican sermons in a manner consonant with that of the polemical moralists, as a basically cognitive act with moral consequences, the affective element being played down.[131]

Horton Davies has commented that in the Anglican devotion of this period, "enlightened self-interest is the sensible man's guide here to get the hereafter," and a sermon by George Bull identified the view that one should serve God apart from thought of reward as Antinomian fanaticism that undermined religion by denying to it the reasonable calculation of reward.[132] Three of Barrow's sermon titles suggest the prudential possibilities of this piety: "The Pleasantness of Religion," "The Profitableness of Godliness," and "The Reward of Honouring God."[133] And, of course, obedience to the authority of church and state as a religious duty was endlessly inculcated by Anglican authors.[134]

The devotional books that emanated from the circles of high Calvinism stood in the starkest contrast to those of the Anglican Arminians. They were characterized by a warm, emotional, and personal style that would not be expected in light of the abstractness and precision of their systematic works. But the complementing of scholastic theology with very emotional devotion had all along been characteristic of high Calvinism, for devotional writings and books of polemical theology were but two different means of promoting the same cause of salvation by grace alone. So rigid a scholastic as Twisse could pause to remind his readers that the end of predestination was holiness of life.[135] This Bucerian formula was a continuing motive for keeping piety and the abstract consideration of the divine decrees together. It has been seen earlier how commonly John Owen brought his theological discussions back to a similar point, and many of his most formidable polemical and theological writings have long portions of practical application. Thomas Goodwin's massive treatment of predestination is honeycombed with excursi dealing with matters of practical application, and much of it consisted of homiletical expositions of biblical passages that can only be described as "affectionate divinity." Stating the purpose of his inquiry into that difficult theological subject, Goodwin noted that because all saving grace is from election, an understanding of election is needful for piety; if piety is to be properly inculcated as a "new principle of holiness" that comes entirely from outside human beings by a supernatural divine agency, the nature of the divine decrees must be understood.[136] Many students of John Bunyan have found surprising the contrast between his rather dry works of theological argumentation and the lively piety of his allegories, but he shared that contrast with other high Calvinists.[137] The forbiddingly titled treatise of Particular Baptist provenance, *Reprobation Asserted*, was interested in that doctrine mainly as it applied to the conscientious inquiries of devout souls and was concerned with the operations of the grace of God in the human soul, not just in the divine choice considered abstractly.[138]

A recurrent theme of the Calvinistic devotional writings, especially prominent among high Calvinists after the Restoration, was the regeneration of the human soul by its union with Christ and the operation within it of the Holy Spirit. That high Calvinists should gravitate to such a teaching is not surprising because from the angle of piety this was a way of grounding religious experience in a supernatural divine grace to which every step of the Christian life could be referred as the agent. But this particularity of their devotional writings was also important in that very personal union with Christ and the indwelling of the Holy Spirit in the believer bridged the gap between the redemptive decrees and works of God and their termination in the actual believer, so that a way of thinking that seems to begin with very abstract and almost cosmic occurrences and transactions taking place far beyond history can be brought into connection with a very warm and personal piety of individuals in a particular local and historical community. This, too, would help explain the prominence of the work of the Holy Spirit in the theology of Owen and the frequency with which predestinarian spiritual writers produced treatises on the work of the Holy Spirit, Thomas Goodwin and Samuel Petto being others who wrote on that subject.[139]

Many of the shorter discourses of John Owen deal in one way or another with aspects of this inner renewal of persons by grace.[140] For Owen, "Christ is the centre of the mystery of the gospel," and Christ means grace given as a new principle in the regenerate, leading those "in Christ" to become "spiritually minded," their affections "changed, renewed, and inlaid with grace, spiritual and supernatural."[141] Stephen Charnock, an ejected minister who wrote a very scholastic work on the divine attributes and was a strong predestinarian, was also the author of a number of posthumously printed discourses on the subject of regenerating grace.[142]

The piety of John Bunyan's writings was of the same sort, but his work had an especially personal and existential flavor that is most prominent in his account of his own experience in *Grace Abounding*. Speaking of his own conversion, Bunyan said that "the Lord did also lead me into the mystery of union with the Son of God, . . . for if he and I were one, then his righteousness was mine, his merits mine." Later, as a preacher, Bunyan came to feel that "God led me into something of the mystery of union with Christ" whereby he could proclaim it with a greater understanding.[143] The very personal treatment of such a theme is echoed in several of the long conversations between pilgrims in *The Pilgrim's Progress*, as when Ignorance is rebuked for a mere "believing" in Christ "by faith and a sense of the need of Christ's personal righteousness to justify" before God or when the children of Christian and Christiana are catechized and repeat that the Holy Spirit saves by "illumination," "renovation," and "preservation."[144] Again on the level of personal experience, another Nonconformist autobiographer tells us that before conversion "The Holy Spirit of God I often derided," and "his gracious Operation in his Saints and Servants I often jeer'd and reproach'd" until God brought him to a state of grace by justification and adoption into Christ.[145]

Differing as sharply as they did on some matters of doctrine, the extent to which the Baxterian and Presbyterian divines stated the piety of grace in terms consonant with those of the stricter Calvinist Congregationalists is surprising. The perennial Baxterian fear of Antinomianism continued, and scattered assertions appear in the writings of Bates and Howe that smack of moralism,[146] but on the whole they, too, were concerned with a piety of gracious regeneration by supernatural agency, even though they avoided saying so in harsh predestinarian terms. Many of Baxter's devotional treatises long were favorites because they summoned persons to evangelical conversion.[147] In sermons on regeneration Howe complained that Christian "believing" was being given too attenuated a meaning by many. Bates made clear that only grace enabled persons to comply with the conditional terms of the gospel and described salvation by means of the timeworn Bucerian order of salvation.[148]

But the evident thirst of the devout for manuals of practical divinity outlining and applying the grace of God in salvation was also satisfied by a number of mostly Dissenting ministers who stood aloof from the high and moderate Calvinist parties, spending their efforts simply in the outlining of the steps of piety for all who would read. John Flavel and Joseph, William, and Richard Alleine may be taken as prime examples, but the multiplication of the names of such writers would not be a difficult task—Bartholomew Ashwood, David Clarkson, Walter Marshall, and perhaps even the conformist Edward Reynolds could be included.

After several years at Oxford, John Flavel became a Devonshire curate in 1650, was ejected in 1662, but remained in the area as an active preacher for most of the years until his death in 1691. A prolific author, he engaged briefly in controversy with the Baptists, but mainly wrote works of practical divinity. Most distinctive were those such as *Navigation Spiritualized* that found spiritual allegories in everyday activities.[149] Considered a Congregationalist, he sought harmony between his party and the Presbyterians and like the Baxterian Presbyterians felt strongly about the dangers of Antinomianism.[150] It is clear from his spiritual writings that he considered the process of justification and sanctification to be a work of divine grace, but he generally avoided putting this in terms of predestination. Christians, he hoped, would bury their animosities and pursue godliness, and through hundreds of pages of hortatory writing that is what Flavel did. In books bearing titles like his 1681 publication, *The Method of Grace in the Gospel Redemption*, he expounded a gracious union of the believer and the way that union sanctified.[151] Like the high Calvinists, he decried the growth of moralism: "It is much to be lamented, that many preachers in these days have hardly any other discourses in their pulpits than what we find in Seneca, Epictetus, Plutarch, or some such heathen moralist. Christ, the Holy Spirit, and (in a word) the gospel is not in their sermons." Yet unlike at least the high Calvinist John Bunyan he recommended the imitation of Christ as one of the main themes of a spiritual piety.[152]

A similar mediating position and concern with piety appeared in the work of the Alleine brothers, Richard and William. Born early in the century, in Somerset where his father was an incumbent rector, Richard Alleine received his university education at Oxford before the civil wars.

Holding Presbyterian views, he cooperated with the ecclesiastical system of the Commonwealth and was ejected after the Restoration. Not primarily a polemicist, he declared that he "would gladly spend his all upon those fundamental practical truths, in which all sincere Christians are agreed."[153] But those "fundamental practical truths," as he gave them exposition, were definitely of the sort that flowed out of the predestinarian piety of grace as it was applied to individual believers. His *Vindiciae Pietatis*, first printed in 1660, aimed, as the title page avowed, to vindicate godliness "from the Imputations of Folly and Fancy," which had scornfully been cast upon it, no doubt by moralists of the Anglican sort. True moral change, according to Richard Alleine, came from Christ transforming the heart and by walking in the Holy Spirit.[154] Other discourses of Richard Alleine bore the characteristic titles *Heaven Opened: Or, a Brief and plain Discovery of the Riches of Gods Covenant of Grace*, and *Instructions about heart-work . . . that we may live in the Exercise and Growth of Grace here, and have a comfortable Assurance of Glory to Eternity*, the last published posthumously, with a recommendation of it as a work of "practical godliness" by Samuel Annesley, one of the few Presbyterians who sided with the high Calvinists in the Antinomian quarrel after 1690.[155] William Alleine, Richard's younger brother, also an ejected minister, left behind at his death several discourses in the same vein,[156] and in an eschatological piece on the subject of the millennium, made the comment, compounded of frustration and wistfulness, that in the heavenly Jerusalem "the Doctrine of justification by free Grace, through the redemption that is in Jesus Christ will be fully cleared up, and all errours about it will vanish."[157]

Joseph Alleine was not related to William and Richard, except by marriage, for, a much younger man than they, he married Richard's daughter Theodosia in 1655. Educated at Oxford like the other Alleines, during the Cromwellian years he became an assistant at Taunton, Somerset, to the Presbyterian George Newton, receiving ordination from a Presbyterian classis. Ejected in 1662, he was several times thereafter imprisoned for illegal preaching, which impaired his health so that he died in 1668 at only thirty-four years of age. The evangelical zeal evident in his writings and his pastoral work, combined with his fortitude under persecution and his early death, made Joseph Alleine a heroic figure to his Dissenting posterity. Reputedly agreeing with the moderated Calvinism of Baxter,[158] Alleine was a warmly personal and passionate preacher and writer, and the frequent reprinting of his classic work, *An Alarme to*

Unconverted Sinners, posthumously published in 1671, testifies to his continuing popularity. In that work and other discourses printed after his death,[159] Joseph Alleine developed grace-centered piety in a number of ways that prefigure what have been taken to be the special concerns of the religiosity of the later evangelical awakenings: a conversion-centered, "second birth" piety becoming increasingly individualistic; an emphasis on personal evangelism and the need "to win Souls to Christ"; and an interest in foreign missions, pastoral visitation, and instruction of the young. Biographical reminiscences, partly written by his wife Theodosia and published after his death, portrayed him as the ideal pastor, laboring strenuously to bring God's grace into the individual lives of those under his spiritual direction.[160]

The conclusions to this chapter constitute a kind of epilogue to the whole. Having traced the vicissitudes of the Reformed theology of predestinarian grace down to nearly the end of the seventeenth century, it is apparent that a vast gulf separated the intellectual world of 1530 from that of 1690. The Reformed theology of predestinarian grace came into England from Continental sources as the latest theological innovation, with all the force of a revolutionary movement, which in many respects the Reformation was. But by the end of the next century, that same theology, much refined, systematized, and even ossified, was an embattled point of view, no longer at the center of the intellectual culture of the day. That fact became especially apparent in the controversies over grace after 1660. In the new intellectual landscape after 1690, the Reformed theology of predestinarian grace was rigid and defensive, about to give way to the vagaries of hyper-Calvinism as well as becoming the province of those who flourished only in sectarian isolation. In the eighteenth century, the Church of England pretty much abandoned Calvinism altogether and drifted along in the seas of Latitudinarian indifference and Erastian subjugation to the state.[161] Nor did the uneasy compromises of moderate Calvinism among the Presbyterians, as a theology, prove a very lasting holding point: Baxterians became Arminian and then Arian, as their opponents had warned.

But the piety of predestinarian grace fared better. Whether because of the very personal and emotional twists given it by stricter Calvinists or the ways in which moderate Calvinists showed it to be compatible with less rigid versions of Calvinist theology, and probably because of both, the piety of supernatural renovating grace acting upon the receptive individual for conversion and holiness continued to flourish in the English

Protestant world. Indeed, this piety underwent further transformations and had a surprising flowering in the eighteenth century, and the evangelical awakenings, in spite of their sometimes Arminian theological trappings (and they were more often Calvinistic, the Wesleys being more the exception than the rule among the evangelicals in this respect) should probably be regarded as being in more continuity with earlier English religion than is often supposed.[162] When George Whitefield complained that "Archbishop Tillotson knew no more of true Christianity than Mahomet,"[163] that was not a new theme, but the revival, albeit by a churchman, of an earlier tradition concerning the true nature of Latitudinarian religion that had been continuously nourished by Dissenting Calvinists, as well as a realization of how easygoing religion stood in the way of a "gracious" revival.

Conclusion ❖ Reflections on the Meaning of a Piety and Theology of Predestinarian Grace

The account and interpretation of the English theology of grace from 1525 to 1695 needs no summarizing conclusion; the main conclusions have been developed and stated in each chapter to emphasize patterns of consensus and change and the significance of the story told. But especially because of what will be to many readers the strangeness of the story, some attempt should be made to understand predestinarian grace in a broader and larger fashion, both as a chapter in the unfolding of the consciousness of Western humanity and as a religious phenomenon of remarkably gripping and pervasive power in the lives of many individuals. Occasional comments have been made about the historical importance of predestinarian thinking; perhaps a few further considerations of a functional sort will aid the understanding of its larger historical meaning. It has been repeatedly stated that predestination was rooted in a particular piety, or "way-of-being-religious"; some thoughts about this as a religious phenomenon may clarify such a piety.

Perhaps a consideration drawn from the sociology of knowledge will restore perspective. Peter Berger writes: "One of the fundamental propositions of the sociology of knowledge is that the plausibility, in the sense of what people actually find credible, of views of reality depends upon the social support these receive. Put more simply, we obtain our notions about the world originally from other human beings, and these notions continue to be plausible to us in a very large measure because others continue to affirm them."[1] Earlier in this century, the historian Carl Becker noted that "whether arguments command assent or not depends less upon the logic that conveys them than upon the climate of opinion in which they are sustained."[2] With such reminders, perhaps the modern student, by an effort of empathetic reconstruction of the past, can grant to predestinarian theology a plausibility for its time and place not unlike that which may well pertain to many of the confident assumptions of our own age. Such empathy is a useful preliminary for the two discussions that will follow, one raising the question of the social function in another age of a perception of reality alien to our own, and the other asking what was that "way-of-being-religious" that was encapsulated in notions of predestinarian grace.

Whatever else ideas and communal perceptions of reality are, they function in certain ways for the groups who adhere to them. Often they function in the more static fashion of providing internal sanctions for the maintenance of some established scheme of order, but at other times they seem to fulfill a more dynamic role, as older ideologies and frames of reference lose their plausibility and are replaced by others. Whether such changes occur because of changing social situations or whether changing situations result from changing ideas (it would be beyond the present purpose to engage in that discussion; though I suspect a richly complex interrelating of the two would come closest to the truth), the Reformation was a time of social and intellectual change, when ideas that had sustained age-old patterns of behavior were being challenged. Specifically, predestinarian thinking has been regarded as having functioned as an aid in the emergence of a more disciplined, middle-class society, as having abetted the transition from a more magical, supernaturalistic world view to one that accepted a greater degree of orderliness and rationality, and as having figured prominently in the movement from more concrete and material religious conceptions to more spiritual ones.

Christopher Hill has emphasized the first of these. He can speak, in Marxist and Hegelian fashion, of Calvinism in England having welded "revolutionary minorities into tight groups" and having "performed its historic task with the establishment of a society in which the protestant ethic prevailed." After this, according to Hill, it had outlived its usefulness for men of property and became a springboard for the more radical social ideas of dispossessed groups.[3] Such an approach is too neatly reductionist, but it does help explain the appeal of Calvinism to certain groups.

Why did predestinarian thinking loom so large in the Protestant Reformation and in the spread of Protestantism? Attention has recently been called to the very different mental universe medieval Christian folk inhabited, perhaps most pointedly by Carolly Erickson in her discussion of the "enchanted world."[4] In such a world, the suffusion of material things with supernatural powers and the possibility of the interruption of dependable regularity and order by the miraculous were assumed. Keith Thomas has claimed that "the Reformation period saw a new insistence upon God's sovereignty" and that the doctrines of God's omnipotence and providence replaced more varied and magical ideas about causality in the post-Reformation era.[5] Thus in combating the magical and sacramental perceptions of medieval Catholicism, the theology of the Reformation found providence and predestination especially useful weapons. Such a view fits with what Steven Ozment has stressed about the propaganda of early Protestantism and its bitter iconoclasm in assaulting an older religious order that located the divine in the physical objects of the cultus.[6]

To maintain that the Reformation was an effort to replace the more concretized and mechanical forms of religion calls attention to it as a movement toward more "inner" or spiritual religion. Recent scholarship has also seen this to be the case with the religious yearnings that preceded the Reformation at the end of the medieval era and even with the Catholic Counter-Reformation, which, seen in that light, has many functional parallels with the Protestant Reformation.[7] Long ago, Preserved Smith wrote:

> The shift of emphasis from the outer to the inner is traceable from the earliest age to the present, from the time when Homer delighted to tell of the good blows struck in fight to the time when fiction is but the story of an inner, spiritual struggle. The Reformation was one phase in this long process from the external to the internal. The debit and credit balance of outward work and merit was done away, and for it was substituted the nobler, or at least more spiritual and less mechanical, idea of disinterested morality and unconditioned salvation. The God of Calvin may have been a tyrant, but he was not corruptible by bribes.[8]

Setting aside the question of whether there is some ongoing movement of "history," such as this, Smith's argument does help in understanding predestination and the Reformation. For predestination is an astonishingly inward and spiritual doctrine. It bares the individual soul before God and strips away layers of concrete mediation between the soul and God. With one great sweep it could clear away the accumulated debris of religiosity, reducing religion to the essentials of the soul confronting God. No wonder that it had a perennial attraction for dissatisfied persons, from Wyclif to the Puritans, bent on purging the Christian community of ancient accretions.

But in this book I have argued all along that the notion of predestinarian grace was in some essential way a phenomenon of personal religious experience, not primarily an element in an intellectual system or a merely socially useful tool in the hands of particular social classes. Alfred

North Whitehead, following the thinking of Friedrich Schleiermacher, asserted that "the dogmas of religion are the attempts to formulate in precise terms the truths disclosed in the religious experience of mankind."[9] The theology of predestinarian grace was ultimately rooted in a particular piety or way-of-being-religious; it was the reflection of a religious experience. Speaking of Luther, though its application is valid more widely to Reformation predestinarians, Sheldon Shapiro notes that predestination was essentially an experience of grace and that therefore the person who held it "could contemplate with serenity the logical paradoxes of the idea of predestination."[10] Because this experience of grace, which entailed predestination, was so powerful, it had a logic, order, and beauty of its own that was difficult to grasp by an outsider, and, apparently, by modern persons. And thus, all the unfortunate consequences which outsiders saw entailed by predestination could be cheerfully ignored by its proponents. A comment by William James in *The Varieties of Religious Experience* is helpful: "One can never fathom an emotion or divine its dictates by standing outside of it. In the glowing hour of excitement, however, all incomprehensibilities are solved, and what was so enigmatical from without becomes transparently obvious. Each emotion obeys a logic of its own, and makes deductions which no other logic can draw."[11] At some point something like this has to be recognized by the modern investigator, or else an enormous episode in past human thinking will forever be elusive.

What are the elements of the religious experience of predestinarian grace? Phenomenologists of religion have stressed awe, terror, fear of the "sacred," or the sense of the "numinous" as the elemental stuff, the sui generis of religion; predestinarian grace as an experience, has precisely this ingredient, Rudolf Otto calling it "the numinous feeling in face of the mysterium tremendum."[12] Continuing his analysis of predestinarianism as a religious phenomenon, Otto notes that such awe quickly becomes a sense of dependence, "that self-abasement and the annulment of personal strength and claims and achievements in the presence of the transcendent" in which "the numen, overpoweringly experienced, becomes the all-in-all," disclosing the weakness of individual choice in opposition to the omnipotence of the will that "determines all."[13] Schleiermacher's famous definition of religion as the feeling of absolute dependence comes into service here also as a useful description of this kind of religious experience.

Awe and dependence can mean "the fear of the Lord," but in the experience of predestinarian grace they also conveyed, as a phenomenon of individual religious experience, an undergirding assurance. There remains a considerable difficulty in recognizing this, for predestination seems the opposite of such assurance. Already in the formulations of predestinarian thinking it has been seen how this was not the case, but can one get closer than that to the feeling-state of this predestinarian piety and explain it? First, if the human predicament is understood precisely as an experience of unfreedom and bondage, then a supernatural grace acting from beyond becomes the means of escape, and just as this seemed plausible to St. Augustine, so did it to the Puritan and English predestinarians. The state of godlessness was unfreedom, and total dependence on God provided the only solution; the natural state of humankind was that described in a totally different context by Oscar Wilde as characteristic of his fictional Dorian Gray: "There are moments . . . when the passion for sin, or what the world calls sin, so dominates a nature, that every fibre of the body, as every cell of the brain, seems to be instinct with fearful impulses. Men and women at such moments lose the freedom of their will."[14]

Predestination was comforting, then, because it meant that the awesome divine power that ruled over all rescued the sick soul from its pain. From that perspective, the claim to free will would have taken away all comfort by driving persons to despair of a salvation they were too weak to work out for themselves. Samuel Taylor Coleridge recognized this in his comments on Jeremy Taylor: "If ever book was calculated to drive men to despair, it is Bishop Jeremy Taylor's on Repentance. It first opened my eyes to Arminianism, and that Calvinism is practically a far, far more soothing and consoling system."[15] The Russian Orthodox theologian Nicholas Berdyaev, no friend to Calvinism or predestination, noted that "to acknowledge a degree of freedom of the will greater than Calvin or even St. Augustine allowed, provides no relief at all to the situation. Freedom of the will, in giving rise to sin, sets a trap in the interests of judgment and punishment."[16] Were this a theological book, Berdyaev's totally different approach to the problem might be pursued; but these references show that the usual assumption that a theology of the freedom of the will is more comforting is not necessarily correct.

The matter of assurance brings analysis of the social phenomenon and of the phenomenon of individual religious experience together. Sixteenth- and seventeenth-century persons seem to have been much worried by the problem of assurance and certainty.[17] The piety of predestinarian grace as an experience was particularly focused on providing assurance and certainty, as anxieties dissolved in the experience of being seized, in spite of one's unworthiness, as one of the chosen of that awesome yet gracious numen upon which one was totally dependent. It must be remembered that the powerful religious experience was always that of being chosen, not of being left out, and thus certainty and reassurance, not despair, were derived from the unique logic of this way-of-being-religious. Thus converged a particular theology of assurance and the recognizable need of a particular time and place for reassurance.

Perhaps a final word of a quite different sort, addressed to those who wrestle with this issue as a topic for theological reflection, will be appropriate. The pervasiveness of the piety of predestinarian grace and the persistence of its theological formulations over a long period of time should be a hint that although the formulations of the sixteenth- and seventeenth-century theologians are now probably beyond resuscitation, they were nonetheless related to important religious and theological intentions.[18]

Appendix ❖ The Covenant Theology

It will have been apparent to the reader that this study has by and large avoided discussion of the theology of the covenant in analyzing the theology of grace in English Protestantism. There are many reasons for this, not the least of which is that so much has already been written about it. But there are other reasons, and perhaps some explanation of them is appropriate, along with attention to the way what has preceded is related to covenant theology.

Covenantal thinking in English Protestantism has received a great deal of attention partly because it seems to have so many social and political ramifications. But in spite of its acknowledged importance as a theological organizing principle for English Protestants,[1] and its special usefulness as key to Protestant biblical interpretation, I have not found it as central an organizing principle for understanding the theology of grace as the Bucerian *ordo salutis*, granted the greater universality of that principle and its clear and explicit highlighting of unconditional predestination. But it must be added that the order of salvation could be coordinated very neatly with the covenant of grace, as it was by many English theologians.

Thus I also do not see the covenant theology as in any way seriously compromising a theology of unconditional predestination. Although it was for Perry Miller a consequence of the covenantal way of thinking that more and more scope was given to human responsibility, thereby subtly if not explicitly undermining unconditional predestination,[2] I have found little support for such a view. Although such supralapsarian Calvinists as William Twisse rejected the covenant scheme and sometimes predestinarian Antinomians ignored it, basically the Puritan covenant theologians, especially those identified as leaders of the movement by Perry Miller (e.g., Ames, Perkins, Preston, Sibbes) were all predestinarians and vigorous opponents of Arminianism. A covenantal approach does seem to erode predestinarian thinking, or at least appears as an instrument for avoiding it, among Arminian moralists such as Henry Hammond. The use of the covenant by Anglican anti-Calvinists is a story yet to be told, and one that might well be long. Richard Greaves has further clarified the relationship of covenant thinking to unconditional grace by identifying two strands of Protestant covenant thinking, one of which was more closely identified with Calvin than the other, and was followed by the mainstream of English Puritan theology, and another that had less room for Arminian implications.[3]

But if covenantal thinking had even the potential for derogating from the "grace alone" piety and theology of English Protestant thinkers, what accounted for its spread and popularity? Without exhausting the possibilities, several considerations come to mind. A covenant theology was distinctly a biblical theology, more closely following the Bible's own categories than some other options, and thus it is not suprising that covenant motifs were present in the theology of the early Reformation, claiming as it did to be returning to the pristine biblical faith. And later, as more Aristotelian and scholastic approaches grew stale, it must have retained its attractiveness as a fresh and patently biblical method for pursuing theological inquiry. It also had the merit of providing an explication, from the human and psychological side, of how persons were related to the divine initiative. On the level of piety it provided an excellent device for the explication of the devout life, and many "spiritual writers" employed it in that fashion.[4] And as an article by John von Rohr has shown, the covenant theme could be used (just as we have seen the elements of the *ordo salutis* being used) to cope with the very urgent need to find assurance of grace.[5]

Notes

Introduction

1. G. R. Elton in a review generally praises Patrick Collinson's *The Elizabethan Puritan Movement*, but faults it for too little attention to theology (*Historical Journal*, pp. 586–88).

2. William Haller, *The Rise of Puritanism*, pp. 83ff.; Alan Simpson, *Puritanism in Old and New England*, pp. 1–2, 39; Perry Miller's most extensive treatment of Puritan thought is in *The New England Mind: The Seventeenth Century*; John S. Coolidge, *The Pauline Renaissance in England*.

3. John F. H. New, *Anglican and Puritan*; J. Sears McGee, *The Godly Man in Stuart England*; see also Ronald J. Vander Molen, "Providence as Mystery, Providence as Revelation"; and Vander Molen, "Anglican against Puritan."

4. For example, see V. J. K. Brook, *A Life of Archbishop Parker*, pp. 103, 131, 143–44, 344–45; Wyndham M. Southgate, *John Jewel and the Problem of Doctrinal Authority*, pp. 31–32; John E. Booty, *John Jewel as Apologist of the Church of England*, p. 14; E. C. E. Bourne, *The Anglicanism of William Laud*, pp. 4, 77; Paul A. Welsby, *Lancelot Andrewes, 1555–1626*, pp. 4, 275. Patrick McGrath, *Papists and Puritans under Elizabeth I*, p. 13, on the other hand, calls the English church a *via media* only between different schools of Protestantism. Owen Chadwick, *The Reformation*, p. 211, suggested that the English compromise was between Lutheran and Reformed Protestantism; New, *Anglican and Puritan*, pp. 12, 108, uses the *via media* to describe an "unequivocally Protestant" settlement with Catholic undertones.

5. Basil Hall, "Puritanism," p. 295.

6. Peter Milward, *Religious Controversies of the Elizabethan Age*.

7. New, for example, finds the basis of Puritan and Anglican theological differences rooted in the very beginning of the Elizabethan period, insofar as Anglicanism retained a more medieval attitude toward such things as the nature of man and the sacraments than did Puritanism (*Anglican and Puritan*, pp. 12, 22, 71, 108). In complete opposition, Charles H. and Katherine George argue that no theological issues clearly divided Puritan from Anglican, but arrive at such a conclusion by citing "Puritan" and "Anglican" spokesmen from either end of their chronological spectrum, without awareness of changes in viewpoint (*The Protestant Mind of the English Reformation, 1570–1640*, p. 405). Both books fail to recognize that although "Puritanism" and "Anglicanism" scarcely existed as distinct entities in 1560, they gradually emerged as parties within the Church of England that came to have many differences by 1640, including some major points of theology. Charles H. George refined his analysis further in "Puritanism as History and Historiography," arguing that "Puritanism" as such is a faulty concept, whereas "Puritans," insofar as they stood for different things at different times, can hardly be regarded as constituting one single, clear-cut movement; "Anglicanism" he considers an "anachronism." Ian Breward, "The Abolition of Puritanism" discusses George's views and comes to some conclusions with which I would concur: that there is no doubt that, regarding Puritanism and Anglicanism, "there were theological tensions worth historical examination, without begging the question that there must be a distinctive puritan theology"; that it is unquestionable that Laud and his Puritan opponents differed over theological as well as other matters; and that a "continuity of religious experience and aspiration" brought together the various individuals called Puritans (pp. 26, 28, 29, 31). I would add that the "continuity of religious experience and aspiration" Breward cites eventually also involved a distinct theological tone and emphasis that sometimes spilled over into a different theological position from that of the conformist leadership in the Church of England. The Georges' work is also criticized in McGee, *Godly Man*, pp. 4–7. There is much validity to

his remarks that "quite aside from the question of whether there were substantial doctrinal differences between Anglicans and Puritans, the Georges' view badly underestimates the importance of differences in degrees of adherence to doctrines and in weight of emphasis upon doctrines" and "the absence of doctrinal disagreement on a number of important matters cannot in itself be regarded as proof that differences of emphasis did not fuel the fires of conflict" (pp. 4, 5).

Chapter 1

1. See, for example, the treatment of the various Protestant Eucharistic doctrines as they influenced the English Reformation in Horton Davies, *Worship and Theology in England from Cranmer to Hooker, 1534–1603*, pp. 76–84, 95–121.

2. See, for example, Wyndham M. Southgate, "The Marian Exiles and the Influence of John Calvin," pp. 148–52; O. T. Hargrave, "The Predestinarian Offensive of the Marian Exiles at Geneva," pp. 111–13.

3. With specific reference to predestination, I have already argued this in "The Doctrine of Predestination in the Early English Reformation," p. 201, n. 1, p. 202, n. 3. See also John Patrick Donnelly, *Calvinism and Scholasticism in Vermigli's Doctrine of Man and Grace*, p. 171.

4. For example, see Southgate, "Marian Exiles," p. 149; H. C. Porter, "The Anglicanism of Archbishop Whitgift," p. 133. James S. McEwen, *The Faith of John Knox*, pp. 64ff, 70, seems to want to clear even Calvin's disciple Knox of the imputation of teaching "Calvinist" predestination!

5. Leonard J. Trinterud, "The Origins of Puritanism," p. 37.

6. Gilbert W. Child, *Church and State under the Tudors*, p. 222; John Dowden, *Outlines of the History of the Theological Literature of the Church of England from the Reformation to the Close of the Eighteenth Century*, p. 64; C. D. Cremeans, *The Reception of Calvinistic Thought in England*, p. 120; Southgate, "Marian Exiles," p. 151; George Yule, "Theological Developments in Elizabethan Puritanism," p. 18; Ronald A. Marchant, *The Puritans and the Church Courts in the Diocese of York, 1560–1642*, p. 12; Everett H. Emerson, *English Puritanism from John Hooper to John Milton*, p. 27; Marshall M. Knappen, *Tudor Puritanism*, p. 78.

7. Trinterud, "Origins of Puritanism"; David Broughton Knox, *The Doctrine of Faith in the Reign of Henry VIII*, presents considerable evidence for this without distinguishing between Lutheran and Swiss influences; E. G. Rupp, *Studies in the Making of the English Protestant Tradition*, pp. 47ff.; William A. Clebsch, *England's Earliest Protestants, 1520–1535*, pp. 56, 68. Only Cremeans, *Calvinistic Thought*, p. 27, rejected a significant Swiss influence in the early English Reformation. James Kelsey McConica, *English Humanists and Reformation Politics under Henry VIII and Edward VI*, acknowledged the influence of Continental Protestants, but emphasized its humanist aspects, which was, however, only one part of their impact (pp. 237, 249–50); for McConica just about everything Protestant counts as "moderate" and "Erasmian." For alternatives to McConica, see John N. King, "Freedom of the Press, Protestant Propaganda, and Protector Somerset," pp. 4–5, and John K. Yost, "A Reappraisal of How Protestantism Spread during the Early English Reformation," pp. 438, 440.

8. Leonard J. Trinterud, ed., *Elizabethan Puritanism*, p. 303.

9. Frederick J. Smithen, *Continental Protestantism and the English Reformation*, documents Continental influence. Clebsch, *England's Earliest Protestants*, is of special importance for the shift of early English Protestants from Lutheran to Swiss models; see esp. pp. 68–69, 170, 199, 247; see also G. R. Elton, *Reform and Reformation*, p. 317. For the coming of the English bishops, especially Cranmer, under Swiss influence in their Eucharistic theology, see Davies, *Worship and Theology from Cranmer to Hooker*; see also W. Nijenhuis, *Ecclesia Reformata*, pp. 1–22. A case for Lutheran predominance in the English Reformation, at least before 1547, has been made, but not convincingly, in Neelak S. Tjernagel, *Henry VIII and the Lutherans*, p. 250: "During the reign of Henry VIII the

formative and determinative influence was that of Martin Luther and German Lutheranism." See also Cissie R. Bonini, "Lutheran Influences in the Early English Reformation," pp. 206–24. An excellent assessment of Continental influence in the English Reformation is Owen Chadwick, "The Sixteenth Century." For Swiss and Reformed influences, see Helmut Kressner, *Schweizer Ursprunge des Anglikanischen Staatskirchentums*; Melvyn E. Pratt, "Zwinglianism in England during the Reign of Elizabeth"; Robert D. Linder, "Pierre Viret and the Sixteenth-Century English Protestants," pp. 149–70; Constantin Hopf, *Martin Bucer and the English Reformation*; Hastings Eels, *Martin Bucer*, pp. 401–14; Patrick Collinson, "The Reformer and the Archbishop," pp. 305–30; Donnelly, *Calvinism and Scholasticism*, pp. 170–96; Charles H. Smyth, *Cranmer and the Reformation under Edward VI*, pp. 80–226.

10. Southgate, "Marian Exiles"; A. G. Dickens, *The English Reformation*, pp. 283–94; Richard Bauckham, "Marian Exiles and Cambridge Puritanism," pp. 137–48.

11. Jean Rilliet, *Zwingli*, p. 123; George R. Potter, *Zwingli*, pp. 323–25; G. W. Bromiley, ed., *Zwingli and Bullinger*, pp. 33–34; Heinrich Bullinger, *Commonplaces of Christian Religion*, fols. 104v, 106r, 135v, 144.

12. Louis Aubert, "L'Activité de Farel de 1550 à 1555," p. 640; Robert D. Linder, *The Political Ideas of Pierre Viret*, p. 34 n. 62, p. 36.

13. W. P. Stephens, *The Holy Spirit in the Theology of Martin Bucer*, pp. 23–24.

14. Donnelly, *Calvinism and Scholasticism*, pp. 123, 129, 130.

15. For the moderation of Calvin on predestination, see Edward A. Dowey, Jr., *The Knowledge of God in Calvin's Theology*, pp. 186–88, 209–17; François Wendel, *Calvin*, pp. 280–84; Brian G. Armstrong, *Calvinism and the Amyraut Heresy*, pp. 189–91.

16. Peter Martyr Vermigli, *The Common Places of the most famous and renowned Divine Doctor Peter Martyr*, pt. 3, p. 3.

17. Ibid.

18. Ibid., p. 4.

19. Stephens, *Holy Spirit in the Theology of Bucer*, p. 23 n. 1, pp. 37, 71, 261.

20. John Calvin, *Institutes of the Christian Religion*, 2:934–35, 960; Calvin, *Concerning the Eternal Predestination of God*, p. 134; see also Ronald S. Wallace, *Calvin's Doctrine of the Christian Life*, p. 199: "For Calvin, the whole purpose of our election is, indeed, our sanctification."

21. This is especially the case for Bucer; see Stephens, *Holy Spirit in the Theology of Bucer*, pp. 42, 46, 49ff.

22. Ibid., pp. 21–28, 38, 40; see also Joseph C. McLelland, "The Reformed Doctrine of Predestination according to Peter Martyr," pp. 261, 267; Donnelly, *Calvinism and Scholasticism*, pp. 133, 138.

23. *Common Places of Peter Martyr*, pt. 3, pp. 4–5.

24. Calvin, *Institutes*, 2:941, 971–73, 975–76.

25. John Scarisbrick, *Henry VIII*, p. 408.

26. Lacey Baldwin Smith, *Henry VIII*, pp. 119–20.

27. Lacey Baldwin Smith, *Tudor Prelates and Politics, 1536–1558*, argues that such bishops as Stephen Gardiner, Cuthbert Tunstall, and Edmund Bonner, who were somewhat touched by humanism and in favor of small reforms, as well as subservient to the monarch, gradually came to regard the breach with Rome as a mistake because of its too radical consequences; hence they resisted further reform under Edward VI and abetted the papal restoration under Mary Tudor.

28. Knox, *Doctrine of Faith*, pp. 1–78. See also Rupp, *English Protestant Tradition*, pp. 156–94.

29. William Tyndale, *Works*, 1:53.

30. Ibid., pp. 14, 56, 109; Tyndale, *An Answer to Sir Thomas More's Dialogue*, in *Works*, 3:174.

31. John Frith, *The Whole Workes*, pp. 83–90. Clebsch, *England's Earliest Protestants*, pp. 78–136, gives an account of Frith's career, as he does for the other early English Protestants considered here.

32. Robert Barnes, *A Supplicacion unto the most gloryous prynce Henry the viii*, sigs. N2ff., O2ᵛ, O3ᵛ.

33. George Joye, *George Joye Confuteth Winchesters False Articles*, fol. vi. For Joye, see Charles G. Butterworth and Allan G. Chester, *George Joye, 1495?–1553*.

34. Miles Coverdale, *A Confutacion of that treatise which one Iohn Standish made agaynst the protestacion of D. Barnes in the yeare 1540*, sigs. Bviiᵛ, Fviᵛ. For the dating of this work, see J. F. Mozley, *Coverdale and His Bibles*, p. 329.

35. Simon Fish, trans., *The Summe of the holye scrypture and ordynary of the Christen teaching*, sigs. Aii–Aiii.

36. Tyndale, *Works*, 1:15, 50, 53–54.

37. Ibid., p. 90.

38. Joye, *George Joye Confuteth Winchesters False Articles*, fol. xixᵛ; Joye, *The Refutation of the byshop of Winchesters derke declaration of his false articles*, fol. xlviiiᵛ.

39. William Turner, "To the Christen Reader," In *A Comparison betwene the Olde learnynge & the New*, p. 39, sig. (H)vi.

40. Coverdale, *Cofutacion*, sigs. Cii–Ciiiᵛ, Evi–Eviiᵛ, Fviʳ, Ii.

41. Tyndale, *Works*, 1:77.

42. Joye, *The Refutation of the byshop of Winchesters derke declaration*, fol. xliiᵛ; cf. also xlviiiʳ; Frith, *Whole Workes*, p. 10.

43. Trinterud, "Origins of Puritanism," pp. 38–40, 43–44; Trinterud, "A Reappraisal of William Tyndale's Debt to Martin Luther," pp. 33–34. Jens G. Moller, "The Beginnings of Puritan Covenant Theology," p. 52, says, "Tyndale's thinking becomes more and more pronouncedly ethical, to the extent of endangering his basically Reformed theology." An important discussion of the types of covenant theology in English Protestantism and their respective sources is Richard L. Greaves, "The Origins and Early Development of English Covenant Theology."

44. Perry Miller, "The Marrow of Puritan Divinity," in *Errand into the Wilderness*, pp. 48–98.

45. Clebsch, *England's Earliest Protestants*, pp. 3, 67, 87, 138, 154, 199, 247, 272, 276, 305, 314, 316–17.

46. This is apparent from the evidence of Miller's article; the theologians he designates as covenantal were also all strongly anti-Arminian. See also Norman Petit, *The Heart Prepared*, pp. 219–20. Greaves, "Origins of Covenant Theology," makes a distinction, with respect to the covenant and emphasis upon moral responsibility, between Zwingli and Calvin.

47. Tyndale, *Works*, 1:72; cf. also pp. 60, 71; ibid., 2:87, 193.

48. Ibid., 2:171; 3:36; Joye, *The Refutation of the byshop of Winchesters derke declaration*, fol. xlviiiᵛ.

49. Wallace, "Doctrine of Predestination," p. 201, n. 1.

50. Knox, *Doctrine of Faith*, p. 13.

51. Tyndale, *Works*, 1:110–11, 77, 90, 449.

52. Ibid., p. 89.

53. Frith, *Whole Workes*, pp. 83, 84.

54. Ibid., p. 84.

55. Ibid., pp. 17, 28, 55.

56. Ibid., pp. 91, 92, 95.

57. Tjernagel, *Henry VIII and the Lutherans*, pp. 13, 15–16, 19; Clebsch, *England's Earliest Protestants*, p. 69, disagrees, as do I.

58. Barnes, *Supplicacion*, sigs. P2, P3, o2ᵛ, P4ʳ.

59. William Roy, *The True beliefe*, sig. Cviiᵛ. Anthea Hume, "William Roye's 'Brefe Dialogue' (1527)," pp. 308–9, 317–18, demonstrates that this was the work of Bucer's associate Capito and that Roy seemed to have strengthened its statement of reprobation.

60. Fish, trans., *Summe of the holye scrypture*, sigs. Aiii–iv (of the prologue), fols. iv, xiᵛ, xxiʳ.

61. Joye, *The Refutation of the byshop of Winchesters derke declaration*, fol. xlixᵛ. Cf. Knox, *Doctrine of Faith*, p. 233: "Predestination was a cardinal doctrine for Joye."

62. John Bale, *The Image of bothe churches*, sig. OOvi^v, published in England after the death of Henry VIII, while Bale was an exile. See Leslie P. Fairfield, *John Bale*, p. 75.

63. Turner "To the Christen Reader," sigs. [H]i, [H]iii.

64. Lancelot Ridley, *A Commentary in Englyshe upon Sayncte Paules Epystle to the Ephesyans for the instruccyon of them that be unlerned in tonges*, sigs. Avii^r, Aviii^r, Bi.

65. John Fines, "A Register of Early British Protestants, 1520–1558," entry for "Garrett, Garard or Gerard."

66. Tyndale, *Works*, 3:192, cf. also pp. 39–40, 193; 2:122, 181; 3:429–32.

67. Barnes, *Supplicacion*, sig. O.

68. Coverdale, *Confutacion*, sigs. gv^r, gvi^r; Joye, *The Refutation of the byshop of Winchesters derke declaration*, fols. lv^r, lvii^r. Robert Barnes, in a letter of 1540, made similar charges against Gardiner (Hastings Robinson, ed., *Original Letters Relative to the English Reformation Written during the Reigns of King Henry VIII, King Edward VI, and Queen Mary*, pt. 2:616–17). In a rejoinder to Joye, Gardiner admitted that a certain kind of predestination was connected to God's general providence, but condemned Joye for teaching necessity and giving license to sin (*A Declaration of such articles as George Ioye hath gone about to confute as false*, fols. xxxii^v, xxxviii^r, xxxix^r, xl^r, xli^r, xliii^r). See also Knox, *Doctrine of Faith*, pp. 222, 224–25.

69. Charles Lloyd, ed., *Formularies of Faith Put Forth by Authority during the Reign of Henry VIII*, p. xxvi.

70. Ibid.

71. Ibid., pp. 359–63.

72. Smith, *Henry VIII*, p. 135.

73. Scarisbrick, *Henry VIII*, pp. 406–8.

74. *Miscellaneous Writings and Letters of Thomas Cranmer*, p. 95.

75. Robert Crowley, *The Confutation of XIII Articles, whereunto Nicholas Shaxton, late byshop of Salisburye subscribed and caused to be set forth in print the yere of our Lord mcxlvi, when he recanted in Smithfielde at London at the burning of mestres Anne Askue*, sigs. Hviii^v–Kviii^v.

76. Hugh Latimer, *Selected Sermons of Hugh Latimer*, pp. xv–xvi. See also Knox, *Doctrine of Faith*, p. 143.

77. *The byble, that is to say, al the holy scripture*, "prologue to Romans," esp. comment on Rom. 8–10; the topical table under "Fre chose or fre wyll," "Election," and "Predestination," gives summary statements followed by scriptural references. For the authority of this version see Rupp, *English Protestant Tradition*, p. 50. For the date and provenance of the annotations, see S. L. Greenslade, "English Versions of the Bible, 1525–1611," pp. 149–53.

78. For the character and complex bibliography of these works see T. H. L. Parker, ed., *English Reformers*, pp. 221–29.

79. Richard Taverner, *The Epistles and Gospelles with a brief Postyl . . . tyll Lowe Sonday*, fols. v^v, viii^v, xxxvii^v, lxvii^r, cxxx^r; Taverner, *The Epistles and Gospelles . . . tyll Advent*, fols. xix^v–xx, xl^v, lxvii; Taverner, *The Epistles and Gospelles . . . from Trinitie Sonday tyll Advent*, fols. xc, cxxxiiij.

80. *The Lamentacion of a synner, made by the moste vertuous Lady quene Catherine*, sigs. Cv, Cvi, Diii, Dv, Giii, Fv.

81. Karl Benrath, *Bernardino Ochino of Siena*, pp. 152–53, 163–64, 250–60. See also George H. Williams, *The Radical Reformation*, p. 633n.

82. *Certayne Sermons of the ryghte famous and excellente Clerk Master Bernardine Ochine*, sigs. Fvii, Fviii, Gvi^r, Hiii^v, Kvi^r–Kvii^r, Lvi^v, Lvii, Mi^r.

83. *Certayne Sermons, or homilies, appoynted by the kynges Maiestie, to be declared and redde . . .*, sigs. Biii^v–Ciii^v, Civ, Dii^r, Diii, Div^r, Ei^r, Hi^r. See also *Doctrine of Faith*, Knox, pp. 167–71.

84. *Certayne Sermons, or homilies*, sigs. Eiv–Giv.

85. Charles Hardwick, *A History of the Articles of Religion*, pp. 302–3.

86. Ibid., p. 303. For this important Augustinian concept and its later appearance, see St. Augustine, *Of the Gift of Perseverance*, 8, 16; *On the Spirit and the Letter*, 52–54, 57,

58, 59; *On Grace and Free Will*, 10, 31, 41, 43; Calvin, *Institutes*, 1:263–65; 2:957–58, 961, 981; Wendel, *Calvin*, pp. 281–82; Donnelly, *Calvinism and Scholasticism*, pp. 141–42; John S. Bray, *Theodore Beza's Doctrine of Predestination*, p. 117.
   87. Hardwick, *History of the Articles of Religion*, pp. 310–15.
   88. Porter, "The Anglicanism of Archbishop Whitgift," p. 133, speaking of the Thirty-Nine Articles, denies that they are "Calvinist" because reprobation is not mentioned; see also Smithen, *Continental Protestantism*, p. 187, and William P. Haugaard, *Elizabeth and the English Reformation*, pp. 261ff. But G. R. Elton calls them Calvinist rather than Lutheran (*Reform and Reformation*, p. 366), and considers article seventeen too predestinarian to be termed even "moderately Calvinist" (ibid., p. 251).
   89. Donnelly, *Calvinism and Scholasticism*, p. 176: "The definition itself of predestination in the articles seems nothing more than an expansion of the definition given by Martyr's tract on predestination which was written just about the same time."
   90. *A Short Catechisme, or playne instruction*, fols. xxxvii–xxxix, xliii.
   91. James A. Devereux, "Reformed Doctrine in the Collects of the First Book of Common Prayer."
   92. *The Catechism of Thomas Becon*, in *The Works of Thomas Becon*, 2:11–14.
   93. Becon, *Works*, 1:80–81, 72–73, 280.
   94. Ibid., 2:11, 221–22.
   95. Ibid., 3:316, 318, 608, 616. See Derrick S. Bailey, *Thomas Becon and the Reformation of the Church of England*, pp. 38, 105.
   96. Hugh Latimer, *Sermons of Hugh Latimer*, 1:305–6; 2:7, 147, 194, 206.
   97. For Latimer's maverick views on Christ's descent into hell, see Dewey D. Wallace, Jr., "Puritan and Anglican," pp. 258–59.
   98. Latimer, *Sermons*, 2:175; cf. 205.
   99. John Hooper, *Writings of Hooper*, 1:263–264; 2:225–26, 274.
   100. Ibid., 1:264.
   101. *Original Letters Relative to the English Reformation*, pt. 1, pp. 325–28. As a Marian exile, Traheron later published writings strongly affirming predestination: *An Exposition of a Parte of S. Iohannes Gospel made in sondrie readinges in the English Congregation at Wesel*, sigs. Fvi–vii[r]; *An Exposition of the 4. chap. of S. Joan's Revelation made by Bar. Traheron in sondrie Readings before his countre men in Germanie*, sigs. Dv[v], Dviii[v], Eii[r].
   102. *Original Letters Relative to the English Reformation*, pt. 2, p. 416.
   103. Hooper, *Writings*, 2:25.
   104. *A Worke of the predestination of saints wrytten by the famous doctor S. Augustine byshop of Carthage*, unpaginated epistle, "To the right vertuous Lady Anne, douchesse of Somerset."
   105. John Lamberd, *Of Predestination and Election made by Iohn Lamberd minister of the church of Elham*, sigs. Aii, Aiii, Bi, Ai [after completing B the signatures begin again with A].
   106. Crowley, *Confutation of XIII Articles*, sigs. Ji[v], Kvi[r], Kvii[r].
   107. Ibid., sig. Jiii[r].
   108. Anthony Gilby, *A Briefe Treatyse of Election and Reprobacion*, fol. 2[a], says that "whereas thre yeres agoe . . . I dyd write of this matter of election and reprobation, which is called predestination, in a certain Commentary upon the Prophete Malachy, by the occasion of this texte, 'I have loved Jacob and I have hated Esau,' . . . accomptyne thys doctrine so necessary, that upon all occasions it owght withe reverence to be uttered, to the glory of God."
   109. Alvin J. Beachy, *The Concept of Grace in the Radical Reformation*, demonstrates how far the radicals were from the magisterial Reformation in their ideas about grace (pp. 28, 34, 175–76).
   110. John Philpot, *The Examinations and Writings of John Philpot*, p. 46.
   111. Claire Cross, "Popular Piety and the Records of the Unestablished Churches, 1460–1660," pp. 269–92; see esp. p. 278, where opposition to predestination is attributed to the influence of Lollardy. Norman T. Burns, *Christian Mortalism from Tyndale to*

Milton, p. 111, relates the freewillers to Anabaptism and the Continent.

112. Joseph W. Martin, "English Protestant Separatism at Its Beginnings," pp. 56, 64, 72; Irvin B. Horst, *The Radical Brethren*, pp. 130–32, shows their similarity to the Anabaptists.

113. O. T. Hargrave, "The Freewillers in the English Reformation," pp. 278–80.

114. A. G. Dickens, *Lollards and Protestants in the Diocese of York, 1509–1558*, p. 22. Dickens also sees the predominant influence in such popular heresy as Lollard (pp. 51–52).

115. James E. Oxley, *The Reformation in Essex to the Death of Mary*, pp. 164–65, 192. Oxley's comment that the freewillers were laymen inclined to Lollardy *and "Calvinism"* (my italics) is odd.

116. Hargrave, "Freewillers in the English Reformation," pp. 271–73; Champlin Burrage, *The Early English Dissenters in the Light of Recent Research (1550–1641)*, 2:1–4.

117. *A Worke of the predestination of saints.*

118. Hargrave, "Freewillers in the English Reformation"; Burrage, *Early English Dissenters*, 1:51–53; John Strype, *Memorials of the Most Reverend Father in God Thomas Cranmer*, 2:502ff; Horst, *Radical Brethren*, pp. 122–36.

119. Nicholas Ridley, *The Works of Nicholas Ridley*, pp. 367–68.

120. Strype, *Memorials of Cranmer*, 2:505.

121. O. T. Hargrave, "The Doctrine of Predestination in the English Reformation," p. 117.

122. Philpot, *Examinations and Writings*, pp. 223–24, 270, 307.

123. John Bradford, *The Writings of John Bradford*, 2:170–71.

124. Ibid., p. 180.

125. Ibid.

126. Ibid., p. 195.

127. Ibid., 1:53, 65.

128. Ibid., pp. 76, 78. Cf. also pp. 311, 313–14.

129. Ibid., pp. 211, 216; 2:130.

130. Ibid., 1:212–13.

131. Ibid., p. 308.

132. Ibid.

133. Ibid., pp. 217–18, 251, 298, 301–5.

134. Ibid., 2:92.

135. Ibid., pp. 102, 113.

136. Lynn Baird Tipson, Jr., "The Development of a Puritan Understanding of Conversion," pp. 137, 139, reaches similar conclusions about Bradford.

137. John Strype, *Ecclesiastical Memorials Relating Chiefly to Religion, and the Reformation of it, and the Emergence of the Church of England, under King Henry VIII, King Edward VI, Queen Mary I*, 3, pt. 2, pp. 325–34.

138. Dan G. Danner, "Anthony Gilby," pp. 412–22, esp. 418.

139. As, e.g., Hargrave, "Predestinarian Offensive," pp. 122–23. The exiles seem to me to be the exponents of a predestinarian theology already formed in the earlier Reformation, as the evidence already presented in this chapter should establish; see also my "Doctrine of Predestination." Danner thinks Gilby's doctrine of predestination was developed before exile and apart from Calvin and that Gilby represented what had gone before in the English Reformation ("Anthony Gilby," pp. 416, 422).

140. See above, note 101, for exilic writings of Traheron mentioning predestination; two Frankfort exiles wrote to Bullinger complaining about the antipredestinarian "blasphemies" of a certain Justus Velsius (*Original Letters Relative to the English Reformation*, pt. 1:131–32).

141. John Scory, trans., *Two bokes of the noble doctor and B. S. Augustine thone entiteled of the Predestinacion of saintes, thother of perseverance unto thende, . . . very necessary for al tymes, but namely for oures, wherein the Papistes and Anabaptistes have revived agayne the wycked opinions of the Pelagians*, "Unto the Christian Reader," sigs. 4ʳ–5ʳ, 6ʳ, Ai. No facts of publication are given in the Folger Shakespeare Library copy

that I examined. *The Short-Title Catalogue* dates it "1556?" at London, and the *Dictionary of National Biography* simply says it was published between 1550 and 1560. The title page indicates that Scory was no longer bishop of Chichester; he was deprived in 1553, so it must have been after that; internal evidence in the epistle to the reader suggests that English Protestants were still undergoing persecution, therefore it must have been before the death of Mary; it could not have been published in England during the reign of Mary but must have been published abroad; and Scory did not go into exile immediately upon deprivation, but later in Mary's reign rather than sooner. The epistle to the reader is dated 1555, and he was in Geneva after 1556, so 1556 in Geneva is probably the best surmise.

142. The earliest edition of Whittingham's translation is not listed in the *Short-Title Catalogue*, which only lists its 1575 reprint by two London printers, D. Moptid and Iohn Mather. 1575 is a likely date for this reprint because it would have preceded Stockwood's 1576 translation of the later and fuller version of the original work by Beza and because its printers had not been active much before that. But it had been printed earlier at Geneva, probably in 1556 with Gilby's *Treatyse of Election and Reprobacion*, with which it continued to be associated in its various reprints. I have been unable to locate a copy of the earliest edition and so have been dependent upon the later printing.

143. Anthony Gilby, *A Briefe Treatyse of Election and Reprobacion wythe certane answers to the objections of the adversaries of this doctryne* (Geneva? 1556? Imprinted by James Poullain and Remy Houdouyn), fols. 2, 3. This first edition is very rare, although the Folger Shakespeare Library has a copy, and is not listed in the *Short-Title Catalogue*, except in its presumably 1575 London reprinting by Moptid and Mather.

144. Ibid., fol. 8.

145. Ibid., fols. 5, 13, 18, 21, 31.

146. Jasper Ridley, *John Knox*, p. 290.

147. Horst, *Radical Brethren*, pp. 115, 117–18; Hargrave, "Predestinarian Offensive," pp. 118–19; for Cooche see also Burrage, *Early English Dissenters*, 1:57–60; Horst, *Radical Brethren*, pp. 115–22.

148. John Knox, *An Answer to a Great Number of blasphemous cavillations written by an Anabaptist, and Adversarie to Gods eternal Predestination*, pp. 7, 8, 10–13.

149. Ibid., p. 22.

150. *The Geneva Bible*, New Testament fol. 70ᵛ, note on Rom. 2:6.

151. Ibid., New Testament, fol. 71ᵛ, note on Rom. 3:27.

152. Ibid., New Testament, fol. 73ʳ, notes on Rom. 8:2, 10, 12.

153. Ibid., New Testament, fol. 73ᵛ, note on Rom. 9:15.

154. Ibid., Old Testament, fol. 41ᵛ, note on Exod. 33:19.

Chapter 2

1. Nicholas Tyacke, "Puritanism, Arminianism and Counter-Revolution," p. 128.

2. Except perhaps for the adiaphoristic treatment of ceremonies in article thirty-four, the English Articles are prima facie Reformed. Even their Erastianism could as well be derived from Zurich as Wittenberg. The one bishop who would not sign them, Edward Cheyney, was considered a "Lutheran." William P. Haugaard considers them Reformed but leaning strongly in the direction of the Melancthonian type of Lutheranism (*Elizabeth and the English Reformation*, pp. 253–54). Those beginning with John Henry Newman who have regarded the articles as something other than Protestant must be assessed as totally ahistorical in their approach. Haugaard has exposed the fallacies of such arguments (pp. 267–68).

3. Richard W. Dixon, *History of the Church of England from the Abolition of the Roman Jurisdiction*, 5:109–10.

4. Thomas Harding, *A Confutation of a Booke Intituled an Apologie of the Church of England*, pp. 8, 134, 253; Reginald Pole, *A Treatise of Justification*, sig. **ivᵛ; Matthew Kellison, *A Survey of the New Religion Detecting Manie Grosse Absurdities which it*

Implieth, pp. 532, 536, 572, 577; A. D., *A Reply Made unto Mr. Anthony Wotton and Mr. John White Ministers*, pp. 159–71; Silvester Norris, *An Antidote or Soveraigne Remedie against the Pestiferous Writings of all English Sectaries*, pp. 198–227; *A Shorte Declaration of the Lives and Doctrinde of the Protestants and Puritans*, "Admonition to the Reader."

5. See below, pp. 00ff.

6. John Strype, *Annals of the Reformation and Establishment of Religion . . . during Queen Elizabeth's Happy Reign*, 1, pt. 1, pp. 494–98.

7. Robert Crowley, *The Confutation of XIII Articles*, sig. Jiiiʳ.

8. E.g., Haugaard, *Elizabeth and the English Reformation*, pp. 250, 261, 284.

9. John Calvin, *The Institutes of the Christian Religion*, 2:934, 941, 970; see also Edward A. Dowey, Jr., *The Knowledge of God in Calvin's Theology*, pp. 187–88, and Kilian McDonnell, *John Calvin, the Church, and the Eucharist*, pp. 169–70, 198; for the same motif in Bucer and Peter Martyr, see W. P. Stephens, *The Holy Spirit in the Theology of Martin Bucer*, p. 25, and John P. Donnelly, *Calvinism and Scholasticism in Vermigli's Doctrine of Man and Grace*, pp. 157–58.

10. Charles Hardwick, *A History of the Articles of Religion*, p. 312.

11. Ibid., pp. 300–303.

12. Edwin Sandys, *The Sermons of Edwin Sandys*, pp. 23–24; John Veron, *A Moste Necessary treatise of free will*; William Perkins, *The Workes of that famous and Worthy Minister of Christ in the University of Cambridge, Mr. William Perkins*, 1:558–59, 722–24; James Ussher, *An Answer to a Challenge made by a Jesuite in Ireland*, pp. 464–65; John Davenant, *Animadversions . . . upon a Treatise Intitled Gods Love to Mankinde*, pp. 12–13.

13. Haugaard, *Elizabeth and the English Reformation*, pp. 237, 276.

14. *Certaine Sermons or Homilies Appointed to be Read in Churches in the Time of Queen Elizabeth I: A Facsimile Reproduction of the Edition of 1623*, pp. 91–82 [second series of pagination].

15. Ibid., pp. 186–88, 258–59, 267–68.

16. Haugaard, *Elizabeth and the English Reformation*, pp. 278, 279; see also William P. Haugaard, "John Calvin and the Catechism of Alexander Nowell," pp. 50–65.

17. Alexander Nowell, *A Catechism written in Latin by Alexander Nowell*, pp. 181 (cf. also pp. 171, 174, 175), 179–81, 172.

18. John Northbrooke, *Spiritus est Vicarius Christi in Terra* (first printed in 1573), pp. 1–16; Edmund Bunny, *The Whole Sum of Christian Religion* (1576), sigs. Ci–Ciii, Dii; John Gibson, *An Easie Entrance into the Principall Points of Christian Religion* (1579), sig. Avi; Thomas Palfreyman, *The Treatise of Heavenly Philosophie* (1578), pp. 76, 81ff., 85, 105; Christopher Shutte, *A Compendious forme and summe of Christian doctrine* (1584), sig. B4; Alexander Gee, *The Ground of Christianity* (1584), pp. 63, 71, 96, 98; Henry Holland, *The Historie of Adam, or the foure-fold State of Man* (1606), p. 121; George Webbe, *A Briefe Exposition of the Principles of Christian Religion* (1612), sig. C5ʳ; Samuel Crooke, *The Guide unto True Blessednesse* (1613), pp. 60, 61, 81.

19. Bunny, *Sum of Christian Religion*, sigs. Avᵛ, Diᵛ; Gee, *Ground of Christianity*, p. 94; Crooke, *Guide*, p. 30.

20. Thomas Rogers, *The Catholic Doctrine of the Church of England*; for justification, see pp. 103–28. For "popery," see pp. 102, 104, 106, 110, 114, 115, 116, 122, 124, 127, 129–31, 139. For predestination, see pp. 142–58. Among his propositions are: "Not all men, but certain, are predestinate to be saved"; "In Christ Jesus, of the mere will and purpose of God, some are elected, and not others, unto salvation." For reprobation, see p. 145: "Err therefore do they which stand in opinion that Some are appointed to be saved, but none to be damned." See also Dewey D. Wallace, Jr., "Puritan and Anglican," p. 279.

21. John E. Booty, *John Jewel as Apologist of the Church of England*, p. 172, says that Jewel's doctrine was basically that of Peter Martyr. Wyndham M. Southgate's argument in *John Jewel and the Problem of Doctrinal Authority*, pp. 119, 145, that Jewel's theology was an example of a distinctly Anglican outlook because of its stress on reason and patristic authority is answered by Booty, pp. 136–37, 139–40, who denies that Jewel has a unique

emphasis on reason and the fathers. Jewel's appeal to patristic authority was fairly common in arguments against Roman Catholicism; Calvin relied heavily upon it in his *Reply to Sadoleto* and frequently recurred to it in the *Institutes*. Donnelly, *Calvinism and Scholasticism*, p. 175n. surmises that Jewel's patristic interest could easily be derived from the influence of Peter Martyr. For Grindal, see Patrick Collinson, "The Reformer and the Archbishop."

22. John M. Krumm, "Continental Protestantism and Elizabethan Anglicanism (1570–1595)," p. 29.

23. John Patrick Donnelly, "Italian Influences on the Development of Calvinist Scholasticism," pp. 88, 99; see also Donnelly, *Calvinism and Scholasticism*, p. 184: "The controversy at Strasbourg over predestination was of great importance because it established that Lutheranism and Calvinism would split henceforward over the theology of grace as well as over the eucharist, despite the fact that Luther and Calvin differed mainly in their emphasis on predestination." For further discussion of Lutheranism and predestination and one Lutheran theologian who came closer to the Reformed, see Robert Kolb, "Nikolaus Von Amsdorf on Vessels of Wrath and Vessels of Mercy."

24. James M. Kittelson, "Marbach vs. Zanchi," p. 34.

25. Philip Schaff, ed., *The Creeds of Christendom*, 1:306–7.

26. Hastings Robinson, ed., *The Zurich Letters (Second Series)*, 1:107–8, 185–86, 243; 2:99, 110–13. For further details on the English rejection of the Lutheran "Ubiquity," see W. Brown Patterson, "The Anglican Reaction."

27. Robinson, ed., *Zurich Letters*, 2:73, 102; 1:135; Cox quoted, ibid., p. 243. See also Patrick Collinson, *Archbishop Grindal*, pp. 41, 70.

28. V. J. K. Brook, *A Life of Archbishop Parker*, p. 271; Strype, *Annals of the Reformation*, 2:277–79, 284–85.

29. James Pilkington, *The Works of James Pilkington, Lord Bishop of Durham*, pp. 194–95, 673–78.

30. John Jewel, *The Works of John Jewel*, 2:933–34.

31. James Calfhill, *An Answere to the Treatise of the Crosse*, p. 350. This book was first published in 1565.

32. Matthew Hutton, *Brevis & dilucida explicatio*, pp. 1–43.

33. Gervase Babington, *A Sermon Preached at Paules Crosse*, pp. 5, 6, 8–9, 10, 17.

34. John Woolton, *The Christian Manual*, p. 29. This book was first published in 1576.

35. Richard Hooker, *A Learned Discourse of Justification, Works, and how the foundation of faith is overthrown*, p. 21.

36. Anthony Rudd, *A Sermon Preached before the Kings Maiestie at Whitehall upon the ninth of Februarie, 1605*, sig. D2ʳ.

37. Pilkington, *Works*, pp. 194–95; Jewel, *Works*, 2:933–34; Babington, *Sermon*, pp. 12, 20ff., 34. Quotations from Sandys, *Sermons*, pp. 257, 190; cf. p. 32. See also Calfhill, *Answere*, p. 350; Babington, *Sermon*, pp. 12, 20ff., 34; Thomas Cooper, *Certaine Sermons wherein is contained the Defense of the Gospell nowe preached, against such cavils and false accusations, as are objected . . . by the friends and favourers of the Church of Rome*, pp. 14, 17; Richard Curteys, *Two Sermons Preached by the reverend father in God the Bishop of Chichester*, sig. Aiiiᵛ.

38. Cooper, *Certaine Sermons*, p. 57; see also Sandys, *Sermons*, p. 95.

39. William Barlow, *A Defence of the Articles of the Protestants Religion*, p. 202.

40. Anthony Wotton, *An Answere to a Popish Pamphlet*, p. 44.

41. John Whitgift, *The Works of John Whitgift*, 1:188–89, 552.

42. Henoch Clapham, *A Manuell of the Bibles doctrine*, p. 139.

43. Albert Peel, ed., *Tracts Ascribed to Richard Bancroft*; A. F. Scott Pearson, *Thomas Cartwright and Elizabethan Puritanism, 1535–1603*, p. 407: "Even the adherents of the Bancroftian school acknowledged that the Puritans were in agreement with them on the fundamental points of doctrine."

44. Patrick Collinson, *The Elizabethan Puritan Movement*, p. 26; Roger B. Manning, *Religion and Society in Elizabethan Sussex*, p. xvi; J. Sears McGee, *The Godly Man in Stuart England*, pp. 4–5.

45. Hargrave, "The Predestinarian Offensive of the Marian Exiles at Geneva," pp. 122–23. For discussion of Hargrave's view, see chapter 1, above, note 139.

46. Irvin B.Horst, *The Radical Brethren*, pp. 112–15.

47. John Champneys, *The Harvest is at Hand*, sigs. Aiii^v, Av^r.

48. John Veron, *An Apology or defense of the Doctrine of Predestination*, fol. 15.

49. By O. T. Hargrave, "The Doctrine of Predestination in the English Reformation," pp. 207–9. The work refuted by Crowley was printed in 1631 as a major part of J. A., *An Historicall Narration of the Judgement of some most Learned and Godly English Bishops, Holy Martyrs, and Others . . . concerning God's Election.*

50. F. De Schickler, "Le Refugié Jean Véron, collaborateur des réformateurs anglais"; William M. Jones, "Uses of Foreigners in the Church of Edward VI," pp. 148–49.

51. John Veron, *A Fruteful treatise of Predestination and of the divine providence of god, with an apology of the same, against the swynyshe gruntinge of the Epicures and Atheystes of oure time*, quotations, sigs. Ciii^v–Civ^r of preface and fol. 8; see also fols. 12, 20–21, 31, 70.

52. John Veron, *A Moste Necessary treatise of free will, not onlye against the Papistes, but also against the Anabaptistes*, sigs. Av^v, Aii^v [second series of signatures].

53. Veron, *Apology*, fols. 28–29, 37, 42.

54. John Veron, *The Overthrow of the justification of workes and of the vain doctrine of the merits of men, with the true assertion of the justification of faith and of the good workes that procead or comte of the same*, sigs. Aii^v of preface, fols. 12, 37.

55. Christina H. Garrett, *The Marian Exiles*, pp. 137–38; Collinson, *Elizabethan Puritan Movement*, pp. 48–49, 77–78.

56. J. A., *An Historicall Narration*, p. 4. The title of the work was *The Copie of an Aunswere, made unto a certaine letter: wherein the Aunswerer purgeth himselfe and other, from Pelagius errours*, with no date or place.

57. Robert Crowley, *An Apologie, or Defence, of those Englishe Writers & Preachers which Cerberus the Three Headed Dog of Hell, chargeth wyth false doctrine, under the name of Predestination*, fols. 21, 29^v–30^r, 90.

58. Garrett, *Marian Exiles*, p. 157; Collinson, *Elizabethan Puritan Movement*, pp. 49–50, 76, 117; J. F. Mozley, *John Foxe and His Book*, pp. 63, 65, 74–75.

59. Walter Haddon and John Foxe, *Against Jerome Osorius Byshopp of Silvane in Portingall and against his slaunderous Invectives*, fols. 77, 79. At fol. 200^r, Foxe says that God rejected some "whom he would have damned," "vessels of wrath," "to shew forth his justice." See also John Foxe, *The Second Volume of the Ecclesiastical history, conteynyng the Actes and Monuments of Martyrs*, pp. 1840–42, where he refers to a decree of damnation and uses the examples of Esau and Saul, who were "refused"; and "ye see how faith in Christ, only and immediately, without any condition, doth justify us, being so linked with God's mercy and election, that wheresoever election goeth before, there faith in Christ must needs follow after." See also *Against Jerome Osorius*, fols. 131^r, 183^v, 189^v, 192^r, 193^v. There is frequent mention of God's grace in election in Foxe's *De Christo gratis justificante* (1583), published in 1694 in English translation as *Of Free Justification by Christ*, pp. 218, 219, 485. For other references to Foxe and predestination, see V. Norskov Olsen, *John Foxe and the Elizabethan Church*, p. 103 n. 8.

60. Collinson, *Elizabethan Puritan Movement*, pp. 101, 118–21, 138–39, 148, 150, 218–19, 233, 237–38, 248, 260, 263.

61. John Calvin, *Thirteene Sermons of Maister Iohn Calvine, Entreating of the Free Election of God in Iacob, and of reprobation in Esau*, sigs. B2^v, B1^v, A2^v, B1^r.

62. *A Parte of a Register, contayninge sondrie memorable Matters*, p. 534.

63. Theodore Beza, *A Briefe declaration of the Chiefe Poynts of Christian Religion*; a later version of this work, translated by John Stockwood, titled *The Treasure of Truth*, was published in 1576.

64. Thomas Cartwright, *A Confutation of the Rhemists Translation*, pp. 357–59, 680. Thomas Sampson, one of the vestiarian radicals, defined the church as the elect of God (*A Briefe Collection of the Church*, pp. 8–9).

65. Haugaard, *Elizabeth and the English Reformation*, pp. 277ff., 286–87.

66. Albert Peel, ed., *The Seconde Parte of a Register*, 1:197.

67. This is discussed later in this chapter.

68. *A Parte of a Register*, p. 345.

69. John Oliver Willyams Haweis, *Sketches of the Reformation and Elizabethan Age Taken from the Contemporary Pulpit*, pp. 95–96.

70. Edmund S. Morgan, *Visible Saints*, pp. 36–38, 42–43.

71. B. R. White, *The English Separatist Tradition*, pp. 54, 125–26, 168; but see also pp. 74–76, 128.

72. White denies any connection to the earlier "freewillers" (ibid., pp. 2–3). But later some Baptist Separatists were believers in free will, as will appear in chapter 3.

73. Albert Peel and Leland Carlson, eds., *The Writings of Robert Harrison and Robert Browne*, p. 137; Leland H. Carlson, ed., *The Writings of Henry Barrow*, p. 214. Even the discussion of the Christian life is mainly concerned with external matters (ibid., p. 570), and Henry Barrow could comment on "how corruptly Mr. Calvine thought of the church" (ibid., p. 317). A catechism by Robert Harrison is built almost entirely around man's obedience to God (Peel and Carlson, eds., *Writings of Robert Harrison and Robert Browne*, pp. 124ff.). Browne does refer to being redeemed "unto holiness" (ibid., p. 253). See also Leland H. Carlson, ed., *The Writings of John Greenwood*.

74. Patrick Collinson, "Towards a Broader Understanding of the Early Dissenting Tradition," p. 11.

75. William Haller, *The Rise of Puritanism*. The phrase is the title of his first chapter.

76. Leonard J. Trinterud, ed., *Elizabethan Puritanism*, p. 134.

77. Gordon S. Wakefield, *Puritan Devotion*, p. 111.

78. Irvonwy Morgan, *The Godly Preachers of the Elizabethan Church*, pp. 11, 15.

79. Thomas Tuke, "Translators Epistle upon Predestination," sigs. B2^v–B3^r.

80. Veron, *Fruteful Treatise*, sig. Cvii^v of preface; Field, in Calvin, *Thirteene Sermons*, sig. B2^r. John Knox, *An Answer to a Great Number of blasphemous cavillations*, p. 8; Babington, *Sermon*, p. 6.

81. Veron, *Fruteful Treatise*, fols. 8, 37; Rogers, *Catholic Doctrine*, p. 150.

82. Anthoney Maxey, *The Golden Chaine of Mans Salvation*, sig. A3^r.

83. John Downame, *The Christian Warfare*, p. 177.

84. Babington, *Sermon*, pp. 28–29; John Prime, *A Fruitefull and Briefe Discourse in Two Books*, pp. 45–46; Maxey, *Golden Chaine*, sigs. A3^r, D^2, D5^v–D6^r; Thomas Sparke, *A Short Treatise*, sig. Dv^v; Thomas Tuke, *The High-Way to Heaven*, passim; Perkins, *Workes*, 1: chart opposite p. 10, 2:607.

85. Downame, *Christian Warfare*, p. 177; Foxe, in Haddon and Foxe, *Against Jerome Osorius*, fol. 193^v; Foxe, *The Second Volume . . . conteynyng the Actes and Monuments*, pp. 1840–42.

86. Thomas Wilson, *Jacob's Ladder*, sig. a4^v.

87. Babington, *Sermon*, p. 34; Arthur Hildersam, *Lectures upon the Fourth of John*, p. 309 (these lectures were delivered long before publication in 1629).

88. Lynn Baird Tipson, Jr., "Invisible Saints," p. 469; Ian Breward, "The Significance of William Perkins," p. 122; Ernst Troeltsch, *Protestantism and Progress*, p. 62.

89. Samuel Hieron, *The Spirituall Sonne-Ship*, pp. 19–20; William Cowper, *Three Heavenly Treatises upon the Eight Chapter to the Romanes*, p. 449.

90. Rogers, *Catholic Doctrine*, p. 151, cf. p. 113; see also Sandys, *Sermons*, p. 185; George Gifford, *Foure Sermons upon Severall Partes of Scripture*, p. 34; Prime, *Fruitefull Discourse*, pp. 143ff.; Barlow, *Defence of the Articles*, pp. 12–13; Wotton, *Answere to a Popish Pamphlet*, p. 79; Perkins, *Workes*, 1:563; Hieron, *Spirituall Sonne-Ship*, p. 22; Miles Mosse, *Justifying and Saving Faith Distinguished from the faith of the Devils*, p. 37; Gervase Babington, *An Exposition of the Catholic Faith*, in *The Works of the Right Reverend Father in God Gervase Babington*, pp. 216–17; William Burton, *David's Evidence*, pp. 13–14, Henry Airay, *Lectures upon . . . Phillipians*, p. 403; Hildersam, *Lectures*, p. 308; Richard Rogers, *Seven Treatises, Containing such Direction as is Gathered out of the Holie Scriptures*, p. 2; John Rogers, *The Doctrine of Faith*, p. 35.

91. John Woolton, *A Newe Anatomie of the Whole Man*, fol. 39^v.

92. Downame, *Christian Warfare*, p. 191. See also Arthur Dent, *The Plaine Mans Pathway to Heaven*, p. 272; Samuel Gardiner, *A Dialogue or Conference . . . about the rites and ceremonies of the Church of England*, sig. A5ᵛ.

93. Dent, *Plaine Mans Path-way*, p. 271.

94. William Fulke, *A Comfortable Sermon of Faith, in Temptations and Afflictions*, sig. Eiiiᵛ.

95. Rogers, *Seven Treatises*, pp. 30, 84, 495.

96. Ibid., p. 47; John Downame, *A Treatise of Securitie*, pp. 85–86.

97. Babington, *Sermon*, p. 8; Prime, *Fruitefull Discourse*, p. 46; Downame, *Christian Warfare*, pp. 175, 199; Cowper, *Three Heavenly Treatises*, p. 19; Sparke, *Short Treatise*, sig. Av; Palfreyman, *Heavenly Philosophie*, p. 85; Anthony Anderson, *A Sermon of Sure Comfort*, p. 23; Maxey, *Golden Chaine*, sig. A4ʳ; Dent, *Plaine Mans Path-way*, pp. 310ff.; Perkins, *Workes*, 1:16, 24, 362, 2:60ff; Nicholas Byfield, *An Exposition upon Colossians*, p. 75; William Negus, *Mans Active Obedience*, p. 3; William Attersol, *A Commentarie upon the Fourth Booke of Moses, Called Numbers*, p. 86; George Gifford, *Certaine Sermons, upon Divers Texts of Holie Scripture*, p. 167; John Forbes, *A Treatise Tending to Cleare the Doctrine of Justification*, p. 3.

98. Prime, *Fruitefull Discourse*, p. 41; Downame, *Treatise of Securities*, p. 90; Sandys, *Sermons*, pp. 11, 21–22, 267–68; Gifford, *Certaine Sermons*, p. 166; Haddon and Foxe, *Against Jerome Osorius*, fol. 189ᵛ; Cowper, *Three Heavenly Treatises*, pp. 165, 235; Tuke, *High-Way to Heaven*, p. 7; Richard Cavendish, *The Image of Nature and Grace*, fols. 46ᵛ, 102f, 104ʳ; Attersol, *Commentarie upon Numbers*, p. 85; Samuel Hieron, *The Sermons of Master Samuel Hieron, Formerly Collected Together by Himselfe, and Published in one in His Life Time*, pp. 104, 154; Paul Baynes, *The Mirrour or Miracle of Gods Love unto the world of his Elect*, pp. 15–16.

99. Babington, *Sermon*, p. 19; Prime, *Fruitefull Discourse*, p. 55; Hieron, *Sermons*, p. 155; Tuke, *High-Way to Heaven*, p. 9; Tuke, "Translators Epistle upon Predestination," sig. B4ʳ; Sparke, *Short Treatise*, sig. Bivᵛ; Knox, *Answer*, p. 13; Wilson, *Jacob's Ladder*, sig. a6; Edward Dering, *M. Derings Workes*, sig. cc2ʳ of "Readings of M. Dering upon the Epistle to the Hebrues."

100. Prime, *Fruitefull Discourse*, p. 173.

101. Downame, *Christian Warfare*, pp. 148–49, 188, 261; Gifford, *Foure Sermons*, p. 45; Gifford, *Certaine Sermons*, p. 149; Dering, *M. Derings Workes*, sig. k5ᵛ of "Readings upon Hebrues."

102. Rogers, *Seven Treatises*, p. 25.

103. Knox, *Answer*, p. 10; Byfield, *Exposition upon Collossians*, p. 75; Tuke, *High-Way to Heaven*, pp. 9–10; Perkins, *Workes*, 1:291; Field, in Calvin, *Thirteene Sermons*, sig. B2ʳ; Elnathan Parr, *The Workes of that faithfull and Painefull Preacher, Mr. Elnathan Parr*, p. 88; Arthur Dent, *The Opening of Heaven gates*, pp. 89–90.

104. Babington, *Sermon*, p. 6.

105. Cowper, *Three Heavenly Treatises*, p. 370; Tuke, *High-Way to Heaven*, p. 8; Maxey, *Golden Chaine*, sig. A4ʳ; Samuel Gardiner, *The Foundation of the Faythfull, in a Sermon delivered at Paules Crosse*, sigs. A2ᵛ–A3ʳ; Veron, *Fruteful Treatise*, sigs. Civᵛ–Cvʳ.

106. Prime, *Fruitefull Discourse*, p. 58f. Gifford, *Certaine Sermons*, pp. 166–67; Downame, *Christian Warfare*, p. 176; Maxey, *Golden Chaine*, sigs. A5ᵛ, E5ᵛ; Palfreyman, *Heavenly Philosophie*, p. 85; Perkins, *Workes*, 1:356ff., 287ff.; Parr, *Workes*, pp. 86–87, 93; I. Anwick, *Meditations upon Gods Monarchie, and the Devill his Kingdome*, p. 32; William Burton, *Davids Thankes-giving*, pp. 29, 37; Robert Whittell, *The Way to the celestiall Paradise*, p. 57.

107. Downame, *Christian Warfare*, p. 310.

108. Cowper, *Three Heavenly Treatises*, p. 97; Field, in Calvin, *Thirteene Sermons*, sig. B2ʳ.

109. Bartimaeus Andrewes, *Certaine verie worthie, godly and profitable Sermons, upon the fifth Chapter of the Songs of Solomon*, p. 66. See also Haddon and Foxe, *Against Jerome Osorius*, fol. 202.

110. Richard Rogers, *Certaine Sermons*, p. 140; Gardiner, *Foundation of the Faythfull*, sig. D8ᵛ.

111. Downame, *Christian Warfare*, p. 189; Sparke, *Short Treatise*, sig. Aiiiᵛ.

112. Babington, *Sermon*, p. 2; Gee, *Ground of Christianity*, p. 96.

113. [John Bowle], *A Sermon Preached at Mapple-Durham in Oxfordshire*, p. 24.

114. Tuke, *High-Way to Heaven*, p. 36; Wilson, *Jacob's Ladder*, sig. a6ʳ.

115. Downame, *Christian Warfare*, pp. 274–75; see also Dering, *M. Derings Works*, sig. A6ʳ of "Godly Letters," sig. I1ʳ of "Readings upon Hebrues"; Thomas Wilson, *A Dialogue about Justification*, p. 7.

116. Downame, *Christian Warfare*, p. 284; Baynes, *Mirrour of Gods Love*, p. 9; Forbes, *Treatise*, pp. 8, 16.

117. Shutte, *Compendious forme*, sig. B2ᵛ. See also Babington, *Sermon*, p. 18.

118. *Lectures of I. B. upon the XII Articles of our Christian Faith, briefly set forth for the comfort of the godly*, sig. Fviiiᵛ; Shutte, *Compendious forme*, sig. C6; Eusebius Pagget, *Catechismus Latine*, p. 24; Henry Jacob, *A Treatise of the Sufferings and Victory of Christ, in the work of our Redemption*, pp. 4, 7, 16–17, 22, 33–34, 36, 37–38, 47, 73, 77–78. Bishop Thomas Bilson objected to this view in *The Survey of Christs Sufferings*, see esp. sigs. [A]3ʳ–[A]4ʳ and passim.

119. Wallace, "Puritan and Anglican," pp. 260–64, 284.

120. For this subject see Peter Toon, *The Emergence of Hyper-Calvinism in English Nonconformity, 1689–1765*.

121. Dering, *M. Derings Works*, sig. B1ʳ of "Godly Letters"; for a meditative focus on the cross, see Downame, *Christian Warfare*, p. 275; Rogers, *Seven Treatises*, p. 204; John Dod, *Seven Godlie and Fruitfull Sermons*, pp. 37, 40, 42; Richard Greenham, *The Works of the Reverend and Faithful Servant of Iesus Christ M. Richard Greenham*, pp. 364, 366–69, 694.

122. Haddon and Foxe, *Against Jerome Osorius*, fol. 200ʳ; Downame, *Christian Warfare*, p. 228; Cowper, *Three Heavenly Treatises*, p. 342; Prime, *Fruitefull Discourse*, p. 16, 37, 47; Hieron, *Sermons*, p. 425; Greenham, *Works*, p. 242; Perkins, *Workes*, 1:734–37; Thomas Barnes, *The Gales of Grace*, p. 64; Whittell, *Way to the celestiall Paradise*, p. 59.

123. Gifford, *Foure Sermons*, p. 121; Greenham, *Works*, p. 804; Dod, *Seven Godlie and Fruitfull Sermons*, pp. 3, 9–10; Woolton, *Newe Anatomie*, fol. 28; Andrewes, *Certaine Sermons*, p. 67; Thomas Morton, *A Treatise of the threefolde state of man*, p. 46; Rogers, *Certaine Sermons*, p. 131; Attersol, *Commentarie upon Numbers*, p. 86; Dent, *Plaine Mans Path-way*, pp. 14–16, 25; Tuke, *High-Way to Heaven*, p. 238; Barnes, *Gales of Grace*, pp. 6, 112; Thomas Wilson, *A Sermon on Sanctification or new Creation*, p. 24.

124. Morton, *Treatise of threefolde state*, p. 49.

125. Cavendish, *Image of Nature and Grace*, fol. 53ᵛ. For union with Christ, see Downame, *Christian Warfare*, pp. 308, 312; Woolton, *Newe Anatomie*, fol. 35; Sparke, *Short Treatise*, sig. Bviᵛ; Gardiner, *Foundation of the Faythfull*, sig. C3ᵛ; Laurence Chaderton, *An Excellent and godly sermon*, sig. Diiᵛ; Robert Horne, *Life and Death*, p. 274.

126. Gifford, *Foure Sermons*, pp. 34, 121; George Gifford, *A Treatise of True Fortitude*, sig. A5ᵛ; Sparke, *Short Treatise*, sig. Bvʳ; Greenham, *Works*, pp. 280, 364, 803–4; Dod, *Seven Godlie and Fruitfull Sermons*, p. 18; Gee, *Ground of Christianity*, p. 71; Dent, *Plaine Mans Path-way*, pp. 33, 277; Rogers, *Seven Treatises*, pp. 38, 40, 73, 75; Rogers, *Certaine Sermons*, p. 63; Palfreyman, *Heavenly Philosophie*, p. 83; Wilson, *Sermon on Sanctification*, pp. 24, 32; Haddon and Foxe, *Against Jerome Osorius*, fol. 145; Dering, *M. Derings Works*, sig. P2ᵛ of "Readings upon Hebrues"; Barnes, *Gales of Grace*, p. 6.

127. Wilson, *Sermon on Sanctification*, pp. 32–33.

128. Rogers, *Seven Treatises*, pp. 9, 39.

129. Cowper, *Three Heavenly Treatises*, p. 389.

130. Babington, *Sermon*, p. 32; Cavendish, *Image of Nature and Grace*, fol. 102ʳ; Sparke, *Short Treatise*, sig. Fiᵛ; Rogers, *Certaine Sermons*, p. 26; Attersol, *Commentarie upon Numbers*, p. 87; Wilson, *Dialogue about Justification*, p. 40; Rogers, *The Doctrine of*

Faith, pp. 46ff., 51; Horne, *Life and Death*, p. 208; Airay, *Lectures upon . . . Phillipians*, pp. 398–99.

131. Sandys, *Sermons*, p. 290.

132. Wilson, *Dialogue about Justification*, p. 30. See also Ezekiel Culverwell, *A Treatise of Faith*, p. 17.

133. Prime, *Fruitefull Discourse*, p. 117; see also Wilson, *Dialogue about Justification*, pp. 18–19; Gardiner, *Foundation of the Faythfull*, sig. C5ʳ; Negus, *Mans Obedience*, p. 28; Robert Allen, *The Doctrine of the Gospel*, p. 33.

134. Cowper, *Three Heavenly Treatises*, pp. 389–90; Babington, *Exposition of the Catholic Faith*, p. 242; John Foxe, *Of Free Justification by Christ*, p. 217; George Gifford, *A Godlie, zealous and profitable Sermon upon the second Chapter of St. Iames*, sig. B1ʳ; Prime, *Fruitefull Discourse*, p. 71; Airay, *Lectures upon Phillipians*, p. 678; Wotton, *Answere to a Popish Pamphlet*, pp. 113–14; Allen, *Doctrine*, pp. 37–38; Barlow, *Defence of the Articles*, p. 155; William Barlow, *An Answere to a Catholike English-man*, pp. 257–58; Forbes, *Treatise*, p. 65; John Randall, *The Necessitie of Righteousnes*, pp. 20–21.

135. Wilson, *Dialogue about Justification*, p. 93; Jewel, *Works*, 2:934; Hildersam, *Lectures*, sig. A2ʳ.

136. Palfreyman, *Heavenly Philosophie*, p. 93; Downame, *Christian Warfare*, p. 204; Gee, *Ground of Christianity*, pp. 100–101. See also Rogers, *Seven Treatises*, pp. 76, 189; Babington, *Sermon*, p. 16; Dering, *M. Derings Works*, sig. N8ʳ of "Readings upon Hebrues"; Fulke, *Comfortable Sermon of Faith*, sig. Fii; [Edward Dering and John More], *A Briefe and necessarie Catechisme or Instruction*, sig. B1ᵛ; Chaderton, *Excellent and godly sermon*, sig. Eviiiᵛ; Perkins, *Workes* 1:564; Forbes, *Treatise*, p. 137.

137. Downame, *Christian Warfare*, pp. 264, 271.

138. Gardiner, *Foundation of the Faythfull*, sig. C7ᵛ.

139. Prime, *Fruitefull Discourse*, pp. 162–63, 175; Rogers, *Seven Treatises*, p. 496; Gifford, *Foure Sermons*, p. 48; Sparke, *Short Treatise*, sig. Diiᵛ; Rogers, *Doctrine of Faith*, pp. 323ff.; Hildersam, *Lectures*, pp. 300–301; Gardiner, *Foundation of the Faythfull*, sigs. B2ᵛ, B3ᵛ. See also Dent, *Plaine Mans Path-way*, pp. 269–70.

140. Wotton, *Answere to a Popish Pamphlet*, p. 79.

141. Rogers, *Certaine Sermons*, p. 35; William Burton, *Davids Evidence*, p. 69. See also Babington, *Sermon*, p. 32; Gifford, *Godlie Sermon*, sig. Bii; Cowper, *Three Heavenly Treatises*, pp. 280ff.; Prime, *Fruitefull Discourse*, p. 142; Sandys, *Sermons*, pp. 281, 291; Gifford, *Certaine Sermons*, pp. 121, 135–36; Greenham, *Works*, p. 682; Tuke, *High-Way to Heaven*, p. 196; Randall, *Necessitie of Righteousnes*, p. 2.

142. Andrewes, *Certaine Sermons*, p. 65. See also Gifford, *Certaine Sermons*, p. 162; Tuke, *High-Way to Heaven*, p. 30; Babington, *Sermon*, p. 12; Cowper, *Three Heavenly Treatises*, p. 371; Palfreyman, *Heavenly Philosophie*, p. 76; Rogers, *Seven Treatises*, p. 502; Rogers, *Catholic Doctrine*, p. 144; Curteys, *Two Sermons*, sig. Aiiiᵛ, Anderson, *Sermon*, p. 23; Richard Crakanthorpe, *A Sermon of Sanctification*, p. 3.

143. Cowper, *Three Heavenly Treatises*, pp. 80, 395; see also Prime, *Fruitefull Discourse*, p. 177; Crakanthorpe, *Sermon of Sanctification*, p. 10.

144. Dod, *Seven Godlie and Fruitfull Sermons*, p. 15; Cowper, *Three Heavenly Treatises*, p. 40; Rogers, *Seven Treatises*, pp. 510ff.; Dent, *Plaine Mans Path-way*, p. 270; Perkins, *Workes*, 1:85–86.

145. Owen C. Watkins comments that the Puritans "completed" justification "with detailed studies of sanctification" (*The Puritan Experience*, p. 2).

146. Downame, *Christian Warfare*, pp. 231–32, 598.

147. Jewel, *Works*, 2:934; Dering, *M. Derings Works*, sig. L7ᵛ of "Readings upon Hebrues"; Sparke, *Short Treatise*, sigs. Aiiiʳ, Aviʳ; Tuke, *High-Way to Heaven*, p. 270; Anderson, *Sermon*, p. 25; Andrewes, *Certaine Sermons*, p. 65.

148. H. C. Porter, *Reformation and Reaction in Tudor Cambridge*, pp. 329–30; Walter H. Frere and Charles E. Douglas, eds., *Puritan Manifestoes*, p. 118; Peel, ed., *Second Parte of a Register*, 1:197. Porter's interpretation is different from mine.

149. Downame, *Christian Warfare*, pp. 656, 658–59, 661, 671. For perseverance in the

spiritual writers, including its relation to assurance, see Babington, *Sermon*, p. 33; Cowper, *Three Heavenly Treatises*, p. 30; Morton, *Treatise of threefolde state*, p. 22; Palfreyman, *Heavenly Philosophie*, p. 107; Gifford, *Foure Sermons*, p. 64; Anderson, *Sermon*, p. 24; Rogers, *Seven Treatises*, pp. 39, 44, 138, 500, 549; Jewel, *Works*, 2:933; Perkins, *Workes*, 1:291; Wotton, *Answere to a Popish Pamphlet*, p. 132; Greenham, *Works*, p. 245; Tuke, *High-Way to Heaven*, p. 58; Forbes, *Treatise*, p. 5; Gardiner, *Foundation of the Faythfull*, sig. A4ᵛ; Hieron, *Sermons*, p. 119; Horne, *Life and Death*, p. 208; Hildersam, *Lectures*, p. 306; Culverwell, *Treatise*, pp. 498, 504–5; William Fulke, *A Defence of the Sincere and True Translations of the Holy Scriptures*, p. 420; Burton, *Davids Thankes-giving*, p. 54.

150. Downame, *Christian Warfare*, p. 664.

151. Prime, *Fruitefull Discourse*, p. 192; Tuke, *High-Way to Heaven*, p. 300; Cowper, *Three Heavenly Treatises*, p. 371. See also Sparke, *Short Treatise*, sig. Dvᵛ.

152. Downame, *Christian Warfare*, pp. 58, 660; Prime, *Fruitefull Discourse*, pp. 160–61; Woolton, *Newe Anatomie*, pp. 40–41. Bryan W. Ball has commented on the connection of eschatology to soteriology in Puritan thought (*A Great Expectation*, pp. 47, 51).

153. William Haller, *Foxe's Book of Martyrs and the Elect Nation*, pp. 102–4.

154. *DNB*, 16:378.

155. Samuel Gardiner, *Dialogue*. Avoiding the raillery that often marred such productions, Gardiner calmly sought to persuade the erring to conformity.

156. *DNB*, 1:372–73; 3:564–65; 16:712; 9:813–14.

157. Besides his already cited preface to a translation of Calvin's sermons, Field translated from French *An Excellent Treatise of Christian Righteousness, Written First in the French Tongue by M. I. de l'Espine, & translated into English by I. Fielde, for the comfot of afflicted consciences . . . for establishing them in the true doctrine of Justification, as also for enabling them to confute the false doctrine of all Papistes and Heretickes in that poinct* (London, 1578).

158. Ronald A. Marchant, *The Puritans and the Church Courts in the Diocese of York, 1560–1642*, pp. 22, 24; Ogbu U. Kalu, "Bishops and Puritans in Early Jacobean England," p. 477.

159. Patrick Collinson, *A Mirror of Elizabethan Puritanism*, p. 2; Breward, "Significance of Perkins," pp. 114, 118–19; Richard A. Muller, "Perkins' *A Golden Chaine*."

160. I have argued this theory with special reference to George Gifford in Dewey D. Wallace, Jr., "George Gifford, Puritan Propaganda and Popular Religion in Elizabethan England," esp. pp. 34–46, 49, n. 108; for references to others besides Gifford, see p. 48, n. 107.

161. Rogers, *Seven Treatises*, sigs. A3ʳ, A5, A6ʳ, says that he wrote works of spiritual direction not only to make the Christian life more comforting to the devout, but also because "the Papists cast in our teeth, that we have nothing set out for the certaine and daily direction of a Christian," a charge Rogers considered false in the light of the many "catechisms, sermons, and other treatises" English Protestants had written.

162. In addition to some later works already cited, such as those by Culverwell, Thomas Barnes, and John Rogers, could be added the following: John Gibson, *The Sacred Shield of Al True Christian Souldiers* (1599); Thomas Cooper [not the bishop] *A Familiar Treatise, laying downe cases of conscience, furthering to Perseverance in sanctification* (1615); Robert Yarrow, *Soveraigne Comforts for a Troubled Conscience* (1619)—Yarrow stated that he wrote to make available the comforting aids of Perkins and Greenham, whose works were available only in expensive editions (sig. A6ᵛ); Henry Scudder, *The Christians Daily Walke in holy Securitie and Peace* (1628)—pp. 431–71 are an especially full discussion of predestination and assurance; Adam Harsnet, *A Touchstone of Grace . . . Laying downe infallible Evidences and markes of true Grace* (1630); John Preston, *The Breastplate of Faith and Love* (1630); John Ball, *A Treatise on Faith* (1631); Nathaniel Cole, *The Godly Mans Assurance; or a Christians certaine Resolution of his Owne Salvation* (1633); Robert Harris, *A Treatise of the New Covenant* (1634); William Whately, *The New Birth: or, a Treatise of Regeneration* (1635).

163. Thomas F. Merrill, ed., *William Perkins (1558–1602)*, p. ix, calls Perkins "the most famous and influential spokesman for Calvinism of his day."

164. John S. Bray, *Theodore Beza's Doctrine of Predestination*, pp. 12, 64. See also Brian G. Armstrong, *Calvinism and the Amyraut Heresy*, p. 37.

165. Donnelly, *Calvinism and Scholasticism*, p. 207. Armstrong, *Calvinism*, pp. 38–42, following Walter Kickel's influential study, *Vernunft und Offenbarung bei Theodor Beza* (1967), stresses the importance of Beza in Protestant scholasticism; but Bray, *Beza's Doctrine*, pp. 21, 131, 140, argues that Beza was less of a scholastic than usually supposed.

166. Peter Martyr's *Loci Communes* was printed in England in 1576 and 1583 and in English translation in 1583; Beza's little treatise on predestination appeared in English as *The Treasure of Trueth, touching the grounde worke of man his salvation* (1576); Ursinus's *Doctrinae Christianae Compendium* was printed in England in 1585 and 1586; *Zanchius his Confession of Christian Religion* (1599), included a treatment of predestination (pp. 384–90). Later, but belonging to the same scholastic genre, should be included such translations of Continental works as Amandus Polanus, *The Substance of Christian Religion* (1600, 1608), and *Treatise Concerning Gods eternal predestination* (1599), and Lucas Trelcatius, *A Briefe Institution of the Common Places of Sacred Divinitie* (1610), pp. 82–98 of which concern predestination.

167. Charles Partee, *Calvin and Classical Philosophy*, pp. 99, 111, 115; Quirinius Breen, "Humanism and the Reformation," pp. 155–56.

168. Donnelly, "Italian Influences," pp. 82, 84, 86, 88, 90; Donnelly, *Calvinism and Scholasticism*, pp. 185–90, 194, 202–4; Bray, *Beza's Doctrine*, pp. 121, 123, 126.

169. For Ramist logic generally, see Perry Miller, *The New England Mind: The Seventeenth Century*, pp. 111–53, 493–501; Walter Ong, *Ramus*.

170. Donnelly, *Calvinism and Scholasticism*, pp. 174–81; Wilbur Samuel Howell, *Logic and Rhetoric in England, 1500–1700*, pp. 206–7; Keith L. Sprunger, *The Learned Doctor William Ames*, pp. 14, 109–10, 129–30, 147; William Ames, *The Marrow of Theology*, p. 38; see also Matthew Nethenus, Hugo Visscher, and Karl Reuter, *William Ames*, pp. 71, 172, 182.

171. Miller, *New England Mind: The Seventeenth Century*, pp. 7, 116, 312; Samuel Eliot Morison, *The Intellectual Life of Colonial New England*, p. 43; Sprunger, *Learned Doctor Ames*, pp. 109, 129, 136; John F. Wilson, *Pulpit in Parliament*, pp. 139–40; John G. Rechtien, "Antithetical Literary Structures in the Reformation Theology of Walter Travers," pp. 51–60.

172. Bray, *Beza's Doctrine*, p. 69.

173. Dowey, *Knowledge of God in Calvin*, pp. 186–88; François Wendel, *Calvin*, pp. 263–84; McDonnell, *Calvin, Church, and Eucharist*, pp. 169–70, 198–200; Armstrong, *Calvinism*, pp. xvii, xix, 32–33.

174. Bray, *Beza's Doctrine*, pp. 70, 81, 87, 99, 129, 131; Armstrong, *Calvinism*, pp. 39–41; Richard A. Muller, "Perkins' *A Golden Chaine*," pp. 69–70; Donnelly, "Italian Influences," p. 98; Donnelly, *Calvinism and Scholasticism*, p. 124.

175. Veron, *Fruteful Treatise*, fols. 84ff.; Crowley, *Apologie*, fols. 36ᵛ, 61, 62f.; Dan G. Danner finds the treatment of predestination by Anthony Gilby, another Genevan exile, less soteriological in its orientation than that of Calvin ("Anthony Gilby," pp. 415–16).

176. Palfreyman, *Heavenly Philosophie*, pp. 74–109, see esp. p. 79.

177. Dudley Fenner, *Sacra Theologia, sive Veritas quae est secundum Pietatem*, fols. 4ᵛff.; Peter Milward erroneously identifies the 1599 *The Sacred Doctrine of divinity* as a translation of Fenner's book, though its preface disclaimed dependence upon Fenner (*Religious Controversies of the Elizabethan Age*, p. 81).

178. Wilson, *Jacob's Ladder*, pp. 1–9.

179. Forbes, *Treatise*, see esp. pp. 11, 20, 22.

180. Robert Hill, *Life Everlasting*, pp. 461, 520, 599, 612.

181. Breward, "Significance of Perkins," pp. 113–114, 122; Muller, "Perkins' *A Golden Chaine*," p. 80; Porter, *Reformation and Reaction*, p. 289; Donnelly, "Italian Influences," p. 99; Perkins, *Workes*, 1: chart opposite p. 10, pp. 17, 24, 16, 298. Beza, too, distinguished the decrees and their execution (Bray, *Beza's Doctrine*, p. 91).

182. Perkins, *Workes*, 1:sig. B2ʳ, pp. 107–8, 2:605. For the relation of Perkins to the Dutch controversy, see Carl Bangs, *Arminius*, pp. 206–21.

183. Some's *Questiones Tres* was published as an inclusion with Matthew Hutton, *Brevis & dilucida explicatio*; Some's viewpoint is summed up on p. 66: "Christus mortuus est efficaciter pro Electis tatum, adeoque non pro omnibus & singulis hominibus, sed in solis Electis." Beza had abandoned caution in affirming limited atonement (Bray, *Beza's Doctrine*, pp. 111–12).

184. This work was directed against the Catholic controversialist Thomas Stapleton and was printed in 1600.

185. Bray, *Beza's Doctrine*, p. 14.

186. Perkins, *Workes*, 1:105; see also 2:607.

187. Ibid., 1:105–7.

188. Ibid., p. 112.

189. Hill, *Life Everlasting*, p. 661.

190. Milward, *Religious Controversies*, pp. 1–8, lists all the titles in this controversy. Other examples are Lewys Evans, *The Castle of Christianitie, detecting the long erring estate as well of the Romaine Church, as of the Byshop of Rome*; John Knewstub, *An Aunsweare unto Certayne assertions, tending to Maintaine the Church of Rome to be the true and Catholique Church*; Oliver Carter, *An Answere made by Oliver Carter, Bachelor of Divinities*.

191. See above, chapter 1.

192. E.g., see Haddon and Foxe, *Against Jerome Osorius*, fol. 185; Sandys, *Sermons*, p. 24; Cavendish, *Image of Nature and Grace*, fols. 5off.; Crakanthorpe, *Sermon*, p. 25; William Sclater, *The Christians Strength*, p. 13.

193. Milward, *Religious Controversies*, p. 127; Donnelly, *Calvinism and Scholasticism*, p. 195; Tyacke, "Puritanism, Arminianism and Counter-Revolution," p. 125; H. R. Trevor-Roper, *Archbishop Laud, 1573–1645*, pp. 37–38, 50. See also Paul A. Welsby, *George Abbot*, pp. 34, 80.

194. John Rainolds, *Sex Theses de Sacra Scriptura et Ecclesia*, pp. 73ff.; John Rainolds, *The Summe of the Conference betweene John Rainoldes and John Hart*, pp. 709, 711–12; Fulke, *Defence*, pp. 340, 377, 386, 415, 420; William Whitaker, *A Disputation on Holy Scripture, against the Papists, especially Bellarmine and Stapleton*, p. 468; William Whitaker, *An Answere to the Ten Reasons of Edmund Campian the Jesuit*, pp. 37, 183ff., 193ff.; Perkins, *Workes*, 1:559, 561, 563–64, 567, 570, 574–75, 577, 612–14; Andrew Willet, *Limbomastix*, pp. 5–6; Andrew Willet, *Synopsis Papismi, That is, a Generall Viewe of Papistry*, pp. 553–57 (this work was greatly enlarged in subsequent editions); Thomas Bell, *The Survey of Popery*, pp. 354, 357–58, 362, 364, 366, 372; cf. also Bell, *The Catholique Triumph*, pp. 240, 242, 245–48; Barlow, *Defence of the Articles*, pp. 12–13, 109, 154–55; Barlow, *Answer*, deals mainly with the oath of allegiance, but touches on grace, pp. 257–58; John White, *The Way to the True Church*, pp. 256ff., 263–300; John White, *A Defence of the Way to the True Church*, pp. 208–40; Josias Nicholls, *Abraham's Faith*, pp. 151, 157, 163, 245ff.; Wotton, *Answere to a Popish Pamphlet*, pp. 103, 111–14; Anthony Wotton, *A Defence of Mr. Perkins Booke*, pp. 64–73; Thomas Gataker, *Jacobs Thankfulness to God for Gods Goodness to Jacob*, pp. 27–54; Robert Abbot, *A Defence of the Reformed Catholicke of M. W. Perkins, . . . The First Part*, pp. 40–41, 43ff., 46, 139; Robert Abbot, *The Second Part of the Defence of the Reformed Catholicke*, pp. 270–71, 379ff., 629ff.; Matthew Sutcliffe, *An Abridgement or Survey of Poperie* (the quotation is a chapter title); see also Oliver Ormerod, *The Picture of a Papist*. Pearson, *Cartwright and Puritanism*, pp. 362ff., considers Sutcliffe one of the principal anti-Puritan writers.

195. Perkins, *Workes*, 1:563–64, 567, 577, 598 f., 718; Willet, *Synopsis Papismi*, pp. 576, 581; Bell, *Survey of Popery*, pp. 362, 364, 366–67; Nicholls, *Abraham's Faith*, p. 163; Wotton, *Answere to a Popish Pamphlet*, pp. 113–14; Carter, *Answere*, p. 68, sigs. **3ᵛ–**4ʳ; Sandys, *Sermons*, pp. 289–90; Abbot, *Second Part of the Defence*, pp. 379ff., 629ff.

196. Barlow, *Answer*, p. 258; Barlow, *Defence of the Articles*, pp. 12–13.

197. Bell, *Survey of Popery*, p. 354; Wotton, *Answere to a Popish Pamphlet*, p. 103; Willet, *Synopsis Papismi*, p. 558.

198. Sandys, *Sermons*, p. 24; Evans, *Castle of Christianitie*, p. 63; Wotton, *Answere to a Popish Pamphlet*, p. 111; Nicholls, *Abraham's Faith*, p. 158; Bell, *Survey of Popery*, p. 358; Perkins, *Workes*, 1:559, 614, 730, 732; Whitaker, *Answere to Campian*, p. 37.

199. Nicholls, *Abraham's Faith*, pp. 157, 158; Wotton, *Answere to a Popish Pamphlet*, p. 111; Abbot, *Defence, First Part*, p. 139; Willet, *Synopsis Papismi*, p. 555.

200. See, for example, Harding, *Confutation*, fols. 61–62, 115, 126ᵛ; Kellison, *Survey of the New Religion*, pp. 442ff.; John Radford, *A Directorie Teaching the Way to the Truth in a Briefe and Plaine Discourse against the Heresies of this Time*, pp. 351–54, 356, 358, 361; Silvester Norris, *An Antidote or Treatise of Thirty Controversies*, devoted considerable attention to the theology of grace.

201. Tyacke, "Puritanism, Arminianism and Counter-Revolution," p. 128.

202. Attersol, *Commentarie upon Numbers*, p. 83 [87]; Sutcliffe, *Abridgement of Poperie*, p. 73; cf. also White, *Way to the True Church*, pp. 269, 278.

203. Haweis, *Sketches of the Reformation*, pp. 95–96.

204. Porter, *Reformation and Reaction*, p. 283.

205. Anthony Wood, *Athenae Oxonienses*, 1:579–80.

206. Antonio de Corro, *A Theological Dialogue*, fols. 29, 31, 31ᵛ, 79ʳ, 87ᵛ, 90ᵛ; Collinson, *Archbishop Grindal*, pp. 144–51; Paul J. Hauben, *Three Spanish Heretics and the Reformation*, pp. 6ff., 49, 80–81; A. Gordon Kinder, *Casiodoro De Reina*, pp. 82–92.

207. Richard Stuart, *Three Sermons Preached by the Reverend, and Learned, Dr. Richard Stuart . . . To which is added a Fourth Sermon, Preached by the Right Reverend Father in God Samuell Harsnett, Lord Archbishop of York*, pp. 133–34.

208. Ibid., pp. 134–36, 148–49, 155, 158, 163.

209. *DNB*, 9:52.

210. A detailed account of these incidents appears in Porter, *Reformation and Reaction*, pp. 315–90; see also John Strype, *The Life and Acts of John Whitgift, D.D.*, 2:227–314.

211. Porter, *Reformation and Reaction*, pp. 314, 344–45.

212. Ibid., pp. 345–50, 353–61; Whitgift, *Works*, 3:615. For Barrett's recantation, see William Prynne, *Anti-Arminianisme*, pp. 56–59.

213. Schaff, ed., *Creeds of Christendom*, 3:523–24.

214. Porter makes much of these modifications (*Reformation and Reaction*, pp. 367ff.), but they were completely acceptable to such stringent Calvinists as Some and Whitaker.

215. Whitgift, *Works*, 3:612–13.

216. Porter, *Reformation and Reaction*, pp. 376–77.

217. Andreas Gerardus, *A Special Treatise of Gods Providence*, pp. 380–81.

218. Porter, *Reformation and Reaction*, pp. 380–81, 387; Milward, p. 160.

219. Strype, *Life of Whitgift*, 2:303–4; Milward, *Religious Controversies*, p. 160.

220. Porter, *Reformation and Reaction*, pp. 285–86, 341–42, 398, 402; Paul A. Welsby, *Lancelot Andrews, 1555–1626*, pp. 43–44.

221. Porter, *Reformation and Reaction*, p. 410.

222. John Plaifere, *Appeal to Gospel for True Doctrine of Divine Predestination*, pp. 22–23.

223. Henry Hickman, *Historia Quinq-Articularis Exarticulata*, p. 502; William Barlee, *A Necessary Vindication of the Doctrine of Predestination, Formerly Asserted*, p. 26, refers to "Drunken Dick Thompson" as a notorious Arminian.

224. Thompson's work, published in the Netherlands in 1616 and reprinted in 1618, was entitled *Diatriba de amissione et intercisione gratiae et justificationis* and was answered by Robert Abbot in *De Gratiae et Perseverantia Sanctorum aliquot . . . Quibus accesit e jusdem in R. Thomsoni . . . Diatribam de amissione et intercisione* (1618).

225. Peter Heylyn, *Cyprianus Anglicus*, p. 122.

226. Mark H. Curtis, *Oxford and Cambridge in Transition, 1558–1642*, pp. 207, 213, 223–25; Peter Heylyn, *Historia Quinqu-Articularis*, p. 626.

227. William Barlow, "The Summe and Substance of the Conference held at Hampton

Court," pp. 180–81; Stuart Barton Babbage, *Puritanism and Richard Bancroft*, p. 94.

228. *Cygnea Cantio Guilielmi Whitakeri, hoc est, ultima illius concio ad clerum habita Cantabrigiae in templo Beatae Mariae, paulo ante mortem. Octob. 9. Dom. 1595* (1599); Milward, *Religious Controversies*, p. 161.

229. See the discussion of them as scholastics earlier in this chapter.

230. Andrew Willet, *Ecclesia Triumphans*, sig. A4. This was first published in 1603.

231. In an introductory preface to James Kimedonicus, *Of the Redemption of Mankind, Three Books*, sig. A2ᵛ. This publication defending limited atonement, a translation from Latin, included "A Booke of Gods Predestination," which vindicated, among other things, assurance of salvation and the propriety of preaching predestination (pp. 372ff., 391ff.).

232. Strype, *Life of Whitgift* 2:311–12.

233. Barlow, "Summe and Substance," p. 185.

234. Ibid., pp. 178, 180–81, 186.

235. William Sclater, *A Threefold Preservative against three dangerous diseases of these latter times*, sigs. B2ᵛ, D1, and passim; Gardiner, *Foundation of the Faythfull*, sig. 5; Perkins, *Workes*, 2:604.

236. Mosse, *Jutifying and Saving Faith*, p. 77; Airay, *Lectures upon . . . Phillipians*, pp. 293, 302.

237. Porter, *Reformation and Reaction*, pp. 287, 413; Porter's perspective is even clearer in his article, "The Anglicanism of Archbishop Whitgift," pp. 129–33. For a challenge to Porter's thesis that the Calvinist influence at Cambridge was only ephemeral, see Richard Bauckham, "Marian Exiles and Cambridge Puritanism," p. 137.

238. Collinson, "Towards a Broader Understanding," pp. 10–11.

239. See, e.g., Hauben, *Three Spanish Heretics*; Kinder, *Casidoro De Reina*, pp. 82–92; Herbert McLachlan, *Socinianism in Seventeenth-Century England*, pp. 4–9; Collinson, *Archbishop Grindal*, p. 144; references in Elisabeth G. Gleason, "On the Nature of Sixteenth Century Italian Evangelism."

240. Porter, *Reformation and Reaction*, pp. 352–53, 387; George H. Williams, *The Radical Reformation*, p. 752; *DNB* 16:442–43. W. Nijenhuis, "Adrianus Saravia"; A. W. Harrison, *Arminianism*, p. 128; see Mark Pattison, *Isaac Casaubon, 1559–1614*, pp. 221ff., 430; Bangs, *Arminius*, pp. 52, 54–55, 63, 71–72, 78, 128, 141, 198–99; see also Lambertus J. Van Holk, "From Arminius to Arminianism in Dutch Theology," p. 34; Armstrong, *Calvinism*, pp. 15, 120–27.

241. Owen Chadwick writes that "the advance of patristic scholarship befriended the conservative and traditionalistic elements everywhere in Protestantism; and nowhere more significantly than within the Church of England" (*The Mind of the Oxford Movement*, p. 17). For background, see pamphlet by S. L. Greenslade, *The English Reformers and the Fathers of the Church*; T. M. Parker claims that "much of the reaction to doctrinaire Calvinism can be traced to the spread of patristic studies in England" ("Arminianism and Laudianism in Seventeenth Century England," pp. 29–30).

242. Wallace, "Puritan and Anglican," pp. 273–77, 279.

243. Porter, *Reformation and Reaction*, pp. 386–88.

244. Marshall M. Knappen, ed., *Two Elizabethan Diaries by Richard Rogers and Samuel Ward*, pp. 125–26.

245. For the question of adiaphora in the English Reformation, see Ronald J. Vander Molen, "Anglican against Puritan," pp. 49, 51, 57.

246. Haugaard, *Elizabeth and the English Reformation*, pp. 181–82; G. R. Elton, *Reform and Reformation*, p. 367; F. W. Maitland, "The Anglican Settlement and the Scottish Reformation," p. 200.

247. Aspects of such an interpretation have been noted before: in their introduction, the editors, Rosemary O'Day and Felicity Heal, *Continuity and Change*, p. 15, note that the Puritans feared the retention of so much of the older church fabric because "the old organization could be employed for ends inimical to Calvinist theology, as well as Calvinist ritual." Long ago, Roland G. Usher argued that the reaction against Calvinist discipline helped lay the foundations for the outlook of the Anglican Arminians (*The Reconstruction of the English Church*, 2:267). F. W. Maitland also noted, "In controversy with the

Puritans the Elizabethan religion gradually assumed an air of moderation which had hardly belonged to it from the first" ("The Anglican Settlement and the Scottish Reformation," p. 208). John M. Krumm has observed that it was after the conflict between conformists and the Puritan Thomas Cartwright that Anglican authors became more wary of Genevan influences and more independent ("Continental Protestantism," p. 137).

248. Wallace, "Gifford, Propaganda and Popular Religion," pp. 34–39; for the background for such generalizations see Keith Thomas, *Religion and the Decline of Magic*, pp. 29ff., 70–77, 159–73, and Christopher Haigh, *Reformation and Resistance in Tudor Lancashire*, pp. 176–78, and passim.

249. Haigh, *Reformation and Resistance*, pp. 216–21, 269–94. See also Elliot Rose, *Cases of Conscience*, pp. 6, 16, 111–13.

250. Porter, *Reformation and Reaction*, pp. 285–86.

251. John Downe, *A Treatise of the True Nature and Definition of Justifying Faith*, sig. A2ᵛ, pp. 5–6, 9–10, 19, 69, 326ff.

252. L. S. Thornton, *Richard Hooker*, p. 59, and J. S. Marshall, *Hooker and the Anglican Tradition*, pp. 112–13, treat Hooker as "catholic" in his theology rather than Reformed, but the essentially Protestant cast of his mind and also that of Andrewes are vindicated in C. F. Allison, *The Rise of Moralism*, pp. 1–4, 27–30. It should be impossible to read Hooker's sermons, such as *A Learned and Comfortable Sermon of the certaintie and perpetuitie of faith in the Elect* or *A Learned Discourse of Justification, workes, and how the foundation of faith is overthrowne*, and not recognize how thoroughly rooted he was in the theology of the Protestant Reformation.

253. Welsby, *Lancelot Andrewes*, pp. 43–44; for the Latin text of Andrewes's remarks on the Lambeth Articles, see Lancelot Andrewes, *A Pattern of Catechistical doctrine, and Other Minor Works*, pp. 289–300.

254. Porter, *Reformation and Reaction*, pp. 410–11; see also *Articuli Lambethani*, pp. 41–55.

255. Richard Hooker, *Works*, 2:662–63. The difference of Hooker's views from Reformed orthodoxy on predestination is often exaggerated in relation to the quarrel with Travers, e.g., W. Speed Hill claims that Hooker set forth a doctrine of predestination at variance from that of Calvin because he did not believe that God caused evil, but surely Calvin denied that God caused evil ("The Evolution of Hooker's Laws of Ecclesiastical Polity," p. 124). Richard Bauckham, on the other hand, provides a careful analysis of just where Hooker stood against Travers ("Hooker, Travers and the Church of Rome in the 1580's," pp. 37–50).

256. Richard Hooker, *Of the Laws of Ecclesiastical Polity*, 1:153, 2:195–97, 228, 244. Though Hooker was greatly interested in the sacraments, it is difficult to see that he departed from the formulations of Calvin regarding them.

257. Ibid., 2:492, 523, 542.

258. Michael T. Malone argues for a greater closeness between the two on predestination than is usually supposed, but carefully notes the differences from scholastic Calvinism of Hooker's interpretation ("The Doctrine of Predestination in the Thought of William Perkins and Richard Hooker"). Cf. Gerald R. Cragg, *Freedom and Authority*, pp. 98, 100, where it is maintained that "Hooker did not represent a radical breach with many of the principles of Calvinist theology" but that "his work profoundly affected subsequent developments in English thought. It coalesced with a number of other influences to create a new temper and outlook."

259. John Donne, *The Sermons of John Donne*, 7:240–41, 3:177. Itrait Husain misunderstands Donne as more antipredestinarian than he was (*The Dogmatic and Mystical Theology of John Donne*, pp. 104–11).

Chapter 3

1. Notably in the older work by A. W. Harrison, *Arminianism*, pp. 122–56, but see also A. W. Harrison, "The Church of England Reaction from Calvinism in the Seventeenth

Century"; Godfrey Davies, "Arminian versus Puritan in England, ca. 1620–1640," which, however, treats Arminianism as chiefly a matter of ceremonial innovations accompanying the assertion of de jure episcopacy; Owen Chadwick, "Arminianism in England"; T. M. Parker, "Arminianism and Laudianism in Seventeenth-Century England," which tends to minimize the earlier Calvinist hegemony; Hillel Schwartz, "Arminianism and the English Parliament, 1624–1629"; and Nicholas Tyacke, "Puritanism, Arminianism and Counter-Revolution."

2. A. W. Harrison concluded that the predestinarian debate in England had "a larger share of responsibility for the civil war" than usually supposed ("Church of England Reaction," p. 216), but the recent article by Tyacke makes the best case for the importance of the Arminian controversy in England. I am in the strongest possible agreement with his conclusions that Arminianism in England represented an utterly radical theological innovation, that it isolated Calvinist Episcopalians who had hitherto represented the mainstream of Anglicanism, that it broke the main unity between Puritan and conformist leaving the Puritans as a whole more bitterly opposed to the established church than they had ever been, and that this theological division was significant enough to be a factor in the coming of civil war. Though without as full an awareness of the political background of these theological developments as that of Tyacke, I came to many of the same conclusions independently in my dissertation, "The Life and Thought of John Owen to 1660," pp. 90–92, 96–102.

3. Frederick Shriver minimizes the predestinarian issue in the king's condemnation of Vorstius and thinks Catholic attacks on Vorstius that linked James with him were crucial in the conflict ("Orthodoxy and Diplomacy," pp. 454–55; see Tyacke, "Puritanism, Arminianism and Counter-Revolution," pp. 132–24).

4. *King James I, His Majesties Declaration concerning His Proceedings with the States Generall of the United Provinces of the Low Countreys, in the Cause of D. Conradus Vorstius*, pp. 2, 20; Thomas Fuller, *Church History of Britain*, 3:249–52.

5. James I, *His Majesties Declaration*, pp. 15, 18, 33. Bertius later converted to Roman Catholicism.

6. *Memorials of Affairs of State in the Reigns of Q. Elizabeth and K. James I*, 3:451–52, 459–60.

7. Peter Heylyn, *Historia Quinqu-Articularis*, p. 632.

8. Parker, "Arminianism and Laudianism," p. 24.

9. Harrison, *Arminianism*, p. 141; Marshall M. Knappen, ed., *Two Elizabethan Diaries by Richard Rogers and Samuel Ward*, pp. 39, 44. The statement in *DNB* 8:20–21, that Goad adopted Arminianism while at Dort is, as far as I can tell, without foundation. A paper of his published posthumously showed him to have eventually softened his predestinarianism, but it was mainly a philosophical discussion of freedom and contingency (*A Disputation Partly Theological, Partly Metaphysical, concerning the Necessity and Contingency of Events in the World, in respect of God's Eternal Decree*, appended to [Laurence Womock], *The Result of False Principles . . . whereunto is added a learned Disputation of Dr. Goades*). See also John Platt, "Eirenical Anglicans at the Synod of Dort," which has a somewhat different view.

10. *The Collegiate Suffrage of the Divines of Great Britaine, Concerning the Five Articles controverted in the Low Countries*, pp. 4, 7–8, 22 ff., 124–26, 153 ff., 176.

11. Walter Balcanqual, *A Joynt Attestation, Avowing that the Discipline of the Church of England was not impeached by the Synod of Dort*, pp. 9–10.

12. John Hales, *Golden Remains of the Ever Memorable Mr. John Hales of Eton College*, pp. 12, 18, 24, 26, 31, of "Balcanqual's letters," bound with those of Hales from Dort.

13. *Calendar of State Papers Domestic, 1611–1618*, p. 504 (hereafter cited as *CSPD*); ibid., *1619–1623*, p. 49.

14. D. Harris Willson, *King James VI and I*, p. 400.

15. Kenneth Shipps, "The 'Political Puritan,'" p. 199; John Yates, *Gods Arraignment of Hypocrites*, p. 91.

16. Paul Baynes, *A Commentarie upon . . . Ephesians*, pp. 100–101, 103, 116, 155.

17. Thomas Bradwardine, *Thomae Bradwardini Archiepiscopi Olim Cantuariensis, De Causa Dei, Contra Pelagium*; CSPD, *1611–1618*, p. 526; CSPD, *1623–1625 with Addenda*, p. 553; Pierre Du Moulin, *The Anatomy of Arminianisme*; Joseph Hall, *Via Media: The Way of Peace*. In the Five Busy Articles, commonly known by the Name of Arminius, in Joseph Hall, *The Works of the Right Reverend Joseph Hall*, 9:490–98.

18. John White, *Two Sermons*, pp. 11–13; John Mayer, *Praxis Theologica*, pp. 163, 180–82; 49, 51–52 [second series of pagination]; Elnathan Parr, *The Grounds of Divinitie, Plainely discovering the Mysteries of Christian Religion*, pp. 290–320 (this was reprinted in 1615, 1625, and 1636); John Downame, *The Summe of Sacred Divinitie Briefly & Methodically Propounded*, pp. 60–64, 399, 419ff.; John Ball, *A Short Treatise Contayning All the Principall Grounds of Christian Religion*, esp. pp. 55–56; Christopher Sibthorp, *A Friendly Advertisement to the pretended Catholickes of Ireland*, pp. 153ff., 165–66, 181–83, 187–88; William Crompton, *Saint Austins Religion*, pp. 11–12, 141–42, 147, 150–51; Richard Bernard, *Rhemes against Rome*, pp. 310–12; John Bastwick, *Elenchus Religionis Papisticae*, pp. 194–98; Henry Burton, *Truth's Triumph over Trent*.

19. Richard Crakanthorpe, *A Sermon of Predestination, Preached at Saint Maries in Oxford*, sig. A², pp. 3, 5, 9, 13; Griffith Williams, *The Delights of the Saints*, pp. 6, 7, 68; Humphrey Sydenham, *Jacob and Esau*, pp. 5, 16, 18 (for Sydenham's royalism see DNB, 19:245–46); Robert Harris, *Gods Goodnes and Mercy*, p. 15.

20. For Andrewes and the Dutch Arminians, see *Memorials of Affairs of State*, 3:451–52, 459–60; Paul A. Welsby, *Lancelot Andrewes, 1555–1626*, pp. 167, 169; for Howson's censure, see Heylyn, *Historia Quinqu-Articularis*, pp. 631–32; for another version (or another incident), see William Prynne, *Anti-Arminianisme*, p. 252.

21. Tyacke, "Puritanism, Arminianism and Counter-Revolution," p. 130; see also Andrew Foster, "The Function of a Bishop," pp. 38–41.

22. Gerald E. Cragg, *Freedom and Authority*, p. 107.

23. Tyacke, "Puritanism, Arminianism and Counter-Revolution," p. 132.

24. Ibid., pp. 133–34.

25. Richard Montague, *A Gag for the New Gospell? No: A New Gagg for an Old Goose*, pp. 109–10, 119, 145, 148, 157, 179–80. For the identity of the Antichrist as a minor issue of the Arminian conflict, see Christopher Hill, *Antichrist in Seventeenth-Century England*, pp. 33–34, 37, 65.

26. John Cosin, *The Correspondence of John Cosin, D.D.*, p. 32. See also Richard Montague, *Appello Caesarem*, sigs. a1ᵛ–a2ʳ.

27. Peter Heylyn, *Cyprianus Anglicus*, pp. 130ff.

28. John Yates, *Ibis Ad Caesarem*; Henry Burton, *A Plea to An Appeale*, sig. ¶3ʳ; George Carleton, *An Examination of those Things Wherein the Author of the late Appeale holdeth the Doctrines of the Pelagians and Arminians to be the Doctrines of the Church of England*, sig. A3, pp. 1, 6–8; Daniel Featley, *Pelagius Redivivus*, passim, sigs. 6–8 of epistle dedicatory; Anthony Wotton, *A Dangerous Plot Discovered Wherein is Proved, that, Mr. Richard Montague Laboureth to Bring in the Faith of Rome*, pp. 3, 54ff.; Francis Rous, *Testis Veritatis* (a 1633 edition bore the title *The Truth of These Things*); Ezekiel Culverwell, *A Briefe Answere to Certaine Objections against the Treatise of Faith*, sigs. A8ᵛ, [B2].

29. Prynne, *Anti-Arminianisme*, pp. 114–20, 122, 125.

30. William Pemble, *Vindiciae Gratiae*, sigs. A2ᵛ–A4.

31. Ibid., pp. 17–18, 21–23, 29.

32. Adam Harsnet, *A Touchstone of Grace*, sig. A5ᵛ; John Doughty, *A Discourse concerning the Abstruseness of Divine Mysteries*, pp. 7, 11–13.

33. Irvonwy Morgan, *Prince Charles's Puritan Chaplain*, pp. 157–83, esp. p. 158.

34. Cosin, *Correspondence*, p. 42.

35. Heylyn, *Cyprianus Anglicus*, pp. 146–47.

36. John Cosin, "The Sum and Substance of the Conference Lately Had at York House concerning Mr. Montague's Books," pp. 21, 35–38, 63.

37. Samuel Clarke, *The Lives of Two and Twenty English Divines*, pp. 126–34, gives an account of Preston's remarks.

38. Schwartz, "Arminianism and the English Parliament," p. 55.

39. Wallace Notestein and Francis Relf, eds. *Commons Debates for 1629*, pp. 12–13.

40. Ibid., pp. 14–15.

41. Ibid., pp. 15–16.

42. Ibid., pp. 33–34.

43. John Cosin, *A Collection of Private Devotions*, included such offensive elements as prayer for the dead.

44. Notestein and Relf, eds., *Commons Debates for 1629*, pp. 100–101.

45. J. R. Tanner, *Constitutional Documents of the Reign of James I*, pp. 80–82.

46. Hardwick, *History of the Articles*, pp. 199–200.

47. William Prynne, *Canterburies Doome*, p. 159.

48. Hardwick, *History of the Articles*, pp. 201–2.

49. I. R., *The Spy*; *Collegiate Sufferage of the Divines of Great Britain*, published in Latin in 1626, 1627, and 1633.

50. Montague, *Appello Caesarem*, p. 26.

51. Christopher Potter, "His Own Vindication of Himselfe, by way of Letter unto Mr. V. touching the same points, Written July 7, 1629," p. 424. See also Christopher Potter, *A Sermon Preached at the Consecration of the Right Reverend Father in God Barnaby Potter*, pp. 66–67, 70.

52. *CSPD, 1638–1639*, pp. 279–80.

53. Heylyn, *Historia Quinqu-Articularis*, p. 634.

54. Henry Hickman, Πατρο σχολαστικο δικαιωσις, *or a Justification of the Fathers and Schoolmen*, sig. a1ᵛ.

55. Thomas Jackson, *Works*, 11:198, 209, 9:318ff., 10:554. These were all from his enormous *Commentaries on the Apostle's Creed*, which began publication in 1627.

56. Thomas Jackson, *A Treatise of the Divine Essence and Attributes*, sig. *3; see also Sarah Hutton, "Thomas Jackson, Oxford Platonist, and William Twisse, Aristotelian," pp. 640–41.

57. Samuel Hoard, *Gods Love to Mankind*, pp. 4, 10, 12, 14, 45, 91f.

58. Robert Shelford, *Five Pious and Learned Discourses*, pp. 58–60, 65–66, 71–72, 84, 107, 109, 133, 203–4.

59. William Milbourne, *Sapientia Clamitans, Wisdome Crying out to Sinners to returne from their evill wayes*, pp. 99–250, esp. 120–21, 142–43, 156–57, 205ff.

60. J. A., *An Historicall Narration of the Judgement of some most Learned and Godly English Bishops, Holy Martyrs, and Others*.

61. O. N., *An Apology of English Arminianisme or A Dialogue, betweene Iacobus Arminius . . . and Enthusiastus . . . Wherein Are defended the Doctrines of Arminius touching Free will, Predestination, and Reprobation*.

62. Tyacke, "Puritanism, Arminianism, and Counter-Revolution," p. 133.

63. James Heywood and Thomas Wright, *Cambridge University Transactions during the Puritan Controversies of the Sixteenth and Seventeenth Centuries*, 2:309, 393–95.

64. Tyacke, "Puritanism, Arminianism, and Counter-Revolution," p. 133.

65. Samuel Rawlinson Gardiner, *History of England from the Accession of James I to the Outbreak of the Civil War, 1603–1642*, 8:133.

66. Hickman, *Justification of the Fathers and Schoolmen*, sigs. b4ʳ–b5ʳ.

67. Anthony Wood, *The History and Antiquities of the University of Oxford*, 2:354–55, 382; Heylyn, *Cyprianus Anglicus*, p. 203.

68. William Laud, *An Historical Account of all Material Transactions Relating to the University of Oxford, From Archbishop Laud's Being Elected Chancellor to the Resignation of that Office*, p. 182.

69. Wheare was a friend of Francis Rous and had been tutor to John Pym (*DNB* 20: 1343–44).

70. Ibid., 6:1162–63.

71. Potter, "His Own Vindication of Himselfe," pp. 412–21, 427, 429. See also Herbert J. McLachlan, *Socinianism in Seventeenth-Century England*, pp. 59–60.

72. Wood, *History and Antiquities of Oxford*, 2:372–73.

73. Ibid., pp. 373–80, 422–23.

74. Ibid., pp. 382–83.

75. Laud, *Historical Account*, p. 182.

76. Wood, *History and Antiquities of Oxford*, 2:415–16.

77. Robert Baillie, *Laudensium Autokatakrisis*, pp. 10–11; Prynne, *Canterburies Doome*, p. 167.

78. Laud, *Historical Account*, pp. 15, 117. See W. R. Fryer, "The 'High Churchmen' of the Earlier Seventeenth-Century," pp. 110–11.

79. Heylyn, *Cyprianus Anglicus*, p. 202.

80. William Laud, *The History of the Troubles and Tryall of the Most Reverend Father in God and Blessed Martyr, William Laud, Lord Archbishop of Canterbury*, p. 371.

81. Prynne, *Canterburies Doome*, p. 177.

82. Ibid., p. 171.

83. W. Huntley, *A Breviate of the Prelates intolerable usurpations, both upon the King's Prerogative Royale, and the Subjects Liberties*, p. 163.

84. Laud, *Troubles and Tryall*, pp. 14, 16, 90, 352–53, 503.

85. Prynne, *Canterburies Doome*, p. 178; see also Baillie, *Laudensium Autokatakrisis*, p. 15.

86. W. J. Sparrow-Simpson, *Archbishop Bramhall*, pp. 35–47, exaggerates Ussher's eventual compliance with Bramhall; see also R. Buick Knox, *James Ussher*, pp. 18–21, 44ff.; Richard Parr, *The Life of the Most Reverend Father in God, James Usher, Late Lord Arch-Bishop of Armagh*, pp. 30–32.

87. James Ussher, *Gotteschalci, et Praedestinatianae controversiae ab eo Motae, Historia*.

88. Heylyn, *Cyprianus Anglicus*, p. 204. Downame's work was *A Treatise of the Certainty of Perseverance* (1631). Another work by Downame of that same year, *The Covenant of Grace or an Exposition upon Luke 1./73. 74. 75* (1631), also dealt with the controversial points, arguing that those who are truly redeemed in Christ's death are eventually justified, sanctified, and glorified, and thus that Christ cannot have died for all and again maintaining the indefectible final perseverance of the elect (pp. 40, 41, 46, 76–78, 193).

89. Parr, *Life of Ussher*, pp. 394, 399–400, 436.

90. Ibid., pp. 46–52, 433, 434, 477.

91. G. D. Henderson, "Arminianism in Scotland," pp. 493–95; Robert Baillie, *The Letters and Journals of Robert Baillie*, 1:149–50; Baillie, *Laudensium Autokatakrisis*, pp. 11ff.

92. William Guild, *An Antidote against Poperie*.

93. For example, in such an older essay as Davies, "Arminian versus Puritan."

94. For incidents of protest, see Cosin, *Correspondence*, pp. 161ff.; Heylyn, *Cyprianus Anglicus*, pp. 162ff., 244ff., 265ff., 295ff., 343, 378.

95. Laud, *Troubles and Tryall*, p. 38.

96. Potter, "His Own Vindication of Himselfe," pp. 420–21. See Fryer, "'High Churchmen,'" p. 107.

97. Roland G. Usher, *The Reconstruction of the English Church*, 2:268; see also Wilbur K. Jordan, *The Development of Religious Toleration in England from the Accession of James I to the Convention of the Long Parliament (1603–1640)*, pp. 115–16.

98. H. R. Trevor-Roper, *Archbishop Laud, 1573–1645*, p. 141; Cosin, *Correspondence*, p. 163.

99. A. S. P. Woodhouse, ed., *Puritanism and Liberty, Being Army Debates (1647–1649) from the Clarke Manuscripts*, p. [54], argued that the Arminian reaction against the doctrine of predestination represented "a shift towards a rational theology and a humanistic, even humanitarian, religion," but I find such a judgment untrue of the Laudians, whose dogmatic sacramentalism was no more liberal than Puritanism and Calvinism (see also Christopher Hill, *Milton and the English Revolution*, p. 272), though applicable to a growing Latitudinarian school that began with Hales and Chillingworth, continued through the Cambridge Platonists, and then became widespread in Restoration

Anglicanism as will be shown in chapter 5. For their rejection of Calvinism, see Cragg, *Freedom and Authority*, pp. 246–47; James Hinsdale Elson, *John Hales of Eton*, pp. 74–84, 107–8; Robert R. Orr, *Reason and Authority*, p. 60, with a bibliography of the extensive material about Chillingworth, much of it fairly recent; for the differences of at least Hales from Laud, see Elson, pp. 121–22. Robert Baillie recognized a difference between types of supporters of Arminianism when he commented that the English Arminians (by which he meant mainly the Laudians) inclined to "popery" whereas the Dutch ones inclined to "Socinianism" (*Scotch Antidote against the English Infection of Arminianism*, p. 18; cf. p. 20: "A British Arminian with the ancients will abhore the Extravagancies of Vorstius and Socinus, yet their heart is hot and inflamed after the abominations of Rome").

100. Tyacke, "Puritanism, Arminianism and Counter-Revolution," p. 130. See the remarks of John F. H. New: "Arminianism in England may well have developed directly from an expanded conception of the grace that comes with the sacraments" (*Anglican and Puritan*, p. 78), and Frederick E. Pamp, Jr.: "The necessary preface to the restoration of a sacramental form and operation to the Church of England was the reassertion of a theology which allowed of freedom of the will" ("Studies in the Origins of English Arminianism," p. 426).

101. Cosin, *Correspondence*, pp. 42–43.

102. C. F. Allison, *The Rise of Moralism*, pp. 47–48, 54–56, 58–59, 60–61.

103. See Hill, *Antichrist in Seventeenth-Century England*, pp. 33–40.

104. Cosin, "Sum and Substance of the Conference," p. 29.

105. Wotton, *Dangerous Plot Discovered*, pp. 54ff.; George Downame, *A Treatise of Justification*, pp. 1–5.

106. Baillie, *Letters and Journals*, 1:149.

107. Baillie, *Laudensium Autokatakrisis*, p. 34; *CSPD, 1640–1641*, p. 277; Laud, *Troubles and Tryall*, p. 369.

108. Robin Clifton, "Fear of Popery," pp. 144–67.

109. Carleton, *Examination*, pp. 11–12.

110. Michael McGiffert, ed., *God's Plot*, p. 73.

111. Richard Sibbes, *The Complete Works of Richard Sibbes*, 1:388.

112. Mark H. Curtis, *Oxford and Cambridge in Transition, 1558–1642*, p. 222.

113. John Davenport, *Letters of John Davenport*, pp. 23–24.

114. Richard Baxter, *Reliquae Baxterianae*, pt. 2, p. 149.

115. Quoted in James F. MacLear, "The Puritan Party, 1603–1643," pp. 129–30.

116. Fuller, *Church History of Britain*, 3:307.

117. Daniel Neal, *The History of the Puritans, or Protestant Nonconformists*, 1:368.

118. Perry Miller, *Orthodoxy in Massachusetts, 1630–1650*, p. 45.

119. *DNB*, 5:551; Fuller, *Church History of Britain*, 3:365–68.

120. Neal, *History*, 1:467; Prynne, *Canterburies Doome*, pp. 165–66; T. F. Kinloch, *The Life and Works of Joseph Hall*, pp. 32–33; Parr, *Life of Ussher*, p. 436.

121. John Davenant, *Animadversions . . . upon a Treatise intitled Gods love to Mankind*, pp. 4, 5, 16.

122. Ibid., p. 523.

123. Lawrence Stone has argued that the alienation of significant groups from the established political and religious institutions had much to do with the coming of revolution (*The Causes of the English Revolution, 1529–1642*, pp. 57, 103). Examination of religious questions has shown how profound such alienation could be. See also Collinson, *Archbishop Grindal*, p. 291; Brian Manning, "Religion and Politics"; Peter Laslett, *The World We Have Lost*, pp. 172–75.

124. Rosalie Colie, for example, thought that when the Puritans called the bishops "Arminians" it had "little doctrinal accusation" (*Light and Enlightenment*, p. 15); Charles H. George and Katherine George, too, in *The Protestant Mind of the English Reformation, 1570–1640*, minimized the specifically theological in all of this, as earlier noted (Introduction, note 7), and William M. Lamont, denies that there was a sustained

attack on Calvinism at all and remarks that "the whole concept of Predestination has been overworked" (*Godly Rule, Politics and Religion, 1603–1660*, p. 65).

125. For details, consult A. G. Matthews, *Walker Revised*, e.g., pp. 43, 47, 48, 55, 58, 87, 147, 166, 250, 302.

126. Robert Lord Brooke, *A Discourse Opening the Nature of that Episcopacie, which is exercised in England*, pp. 88 [132], 92 [136].

127. Edmund Calamy, *Gods Free Mercy to England*, p. 20.

128. Ibid., pp. 19–21; Edmund Calamy, *Englands Looking-Glasse, Presented in A Sermon, Preached before the Honourable House of Commons . . . December 22, 1641*, pp. 17, 40; Cornelius Burges, *The First Sermon, Preached to the Honourable House of Commons Now Assembled in Parliament at their Publique Fast, Novemb. 17, 1640*, sig. A4ʳ, p. 49; Stephen Marshall, *A Sermon Preached before the Honourable House of Commons Assembled in Parliament, At Their Publique Fast, November 17, 1640*, sig. A3ʳ.

129. John Gauden, *The Love of Truth and Peace*, pp. 30–37. For Gauden's role in *Eikon Basilike*, see *Eikon Basilike*, Philip A. Knachel, ed., pp. xxvii–xxxii.

130. Ethyn W. Kirby, "Sermons before Commons, 1640–1642," p. 547.

131. Oliver Cromwell, *The Writings and Speeches of Oliver Cromwell*, 1:128–29.

132. Thomas Harbie, *Divi Arminij Mactatorum Renata, et Renovata Petitio*; Robert Baillie, *An antidote against Arminianism*; his *Scotch Antidote* was published in 1652. For background, see F. N. McCoy, *Robert Baillie and the Second Scots Reformation*, p. 76; John Ball, *A Treatise of the Covenant of Grace*.

133. John Owen, *The Works of John Owen, D.D.*, 10:6–7, 11, 13, 53, 57, 73, 80, 94–97, 122–23.

134. Baillie, *Letters and Journals*, 2:325.

135. See, for example, John H. Leith, *Assembly at Westminster*, pp. 88–89.

136. Stephen Bredwell, *Detection of Ed. Glovers hereticall confection, lately contrived and proferred to the Church of England, Under the name of a present Preservative*, pp. 17, 91, 96–97. I was unable to locate Glover's book. See also Henry Martyn Dexter, *The Congregationalism of the Last Three Hundred Years, as Seen in its Literature*, p. 86.

137. As cited in Miller, *Orthodoxy in Massachusetts*, p. 97.

138. William L. Lumpkin, ed., *Baptist Confessions of Faith*, p. 100; John Smith, *The Works of John Smith*, 2:682, 733–35.

139. Thomas Helwys, *A Short and Plaine Proofe*, sigs. A2ᵛ, A3ʳ, A4, A7ᵛ, B1–2.

140. E.g., Lonnie D. Kliever, "General Baptist Origins"; Murray Tolmie, *The Triumph of the Saints*, p. 70; Michael R. Watts, *The Dissenters*, p. 46.

141. John Murton, *A Description of what God hath predestined concerning man, in his Creation, Transgression, and Regeneration*; Cragg, *Freedom and Authority*, p. 236.

142. Henry Ainsworth, *A Seasonable Discourse, or, A Censure upon a Dialogue of the Anabaptists, intituled, A Description of what God hath Predestinated concerning man*, pp. 1, 3, 12–13, 18–19, 26, 29–30.

143. John Robinson, *A Defence of the Doctrine Propounded by the Synode at Dort*, sig. A2, p. 130.

144. A. C. Underwood, *A History of the English Baptists*, p. 51; Tolmie, *Triumph of the Saints*, pp. 71–72.

145. Tolmie, *Triumph of the Saints*, p. 72.

146. Underwood, *English Baptists*, pp. 71–72; Alan Betteridge, "Early Baptists in Leicestershire and Rutland," pp. 354, 356; Tolmie, *Triumph of the Saints*, pp. 77–78.

147. Francis Duke, *The Fulnesse and Freenesse of Gods Grace in Jesus Christ*, p. 113; John Horn, *The Open Door for Mans Approach to God* (Horn probably was a clerical incumbent at Lyn, Norfolk); Thomas Moore, *The Universality of God's Free-Grace*, p. 1; Henry Denne, *Antichrist Unmasked in Three Treatises*.

148. Harrison says that Goodwin first taught Arminianism in 1638 (*Arminianism*, p. 151).

149. George Walker, *Socinianisme in the Fundamentall Point of Justification Discovered, and Confuted*, p. 6. Wotton's memory was defended by his son, who in 1641 published

anonymously *Mr. Anthony Wotton's Defence*. Walker responded by publishing earlier correspondence between himself and Wotton in his *A True relation of the chiefe passages betweene Mr. Anthony Wotton, and Mr. George Walker, in the yeare of our Lord, 1611*, where Wotton is charged with "Arminian trickes" (p. 17). See McLachlan, *Socinianism*, pp. 45–49.

150. "The Brownists' Paternoster," p. 37; Baxter, *Reliquae Baxterianae*, pt. 1, p. 53; Owen, *Works*, 10:156.

151. Francis Cheynell, *The Rise, Growthe, and Danger of Socinianisme*, pp. 43, 55, 62.

152. Ephraim Pagitt, *Heresiography*, pp. 102ff., 110–11.

153. Thomas Edwards, *The First and Second Part of Gangraena*, p. 74.

154. John Stalham, *Vindiciae Redemptionis*, pp. 15, 32, 78.

155. Samuel Rutherford, *Christ Dying and Drawing Sinners to Himselfe*, pp. 372–73, 432.

156. Moore, *Universality of God's Free-Grace*, p. 1.

157. Owen, *Works*, 10:150, 186, 205–6, 412.

Chapter 4

1. For the later history of Antinomianism, see Peter Toon, *The Emergence of Hyper-Calvinism in English Nonconformity, 1689–1765*, pp. 49–66.

2. William Haller treats the Antinomians Dell and Saltmarsh as examples of lay religiosity tending to "liberty" (*Liberty and Reformation in the Puritan Revolution*, pp. 198ff.); Gertrude Huehns treats it as a form of perfectionist libertarianism with strongly political overtones (*Antinomianism in English History with Special Reference to the Period 1640–1660*, pp. 12, 48–49); Christopher Hill goes rather far with the heresiographers in thinking that the Antinomians truly acted lawlessly—Antinomianism is for him the reflection of a lower-class "protest" sensibility using religious language to express its outlook (*The World Turned Upside Down*, pp. 153, 160, 173, 271); a psychological interpretation of Antinomianism appears in Emery Battis, *Saints and Sectaries*, p. 56; A. L. Morton regards Antinomianism as mainly political in its import, and seems to think that Antinomians rejected predestination altogether for a "free grace" which he misunderstands as universal grace; thus he can see Antinomianism as a "positive weapon against the hypocritically righteous, the Calvinist elect" rather than a narrowing of the circle of the "elect" (*The World of the Ranters*, pp. 50, 98, 117).

3. Perry Miller, *The New England Mind: From Colony to Province*, pp. 59–61; Edmund S. Morgan, *The Puritan Dilemma*, pp. 136–39; Norman Petit, *The Heart Prepared*, pp. 125–57; David D. Hall, ed., *The Antinomian Controversy, 1636–1638*, pp. 12ff., shifts the focus of interpretation from the problem of preparation to the problem of assurance.

4. This is true of Toon, *Hyper-Calvinism*; C. F. Allison, *The Rise of Moralism*, pp. 168–72; Ernest F. Kevan, *The Grace of Law*, p. 24. Richard L. Greaves, "The Origins and Early Development of English Covenant Theology," distinguishes two strands of thinking about the covenant in reformed theology, one of which might be understood as leading to "preparationism" and the other to Antinomianism.

5. William K. B. Stoever, *'A Faire and Easie Way to Heaven,'* esp. pp. 96, 102–3, 113.

6. Hall, *Antinomian Controversy*, pp. 202ff., 216, 301f., 356, 364; Norman T. Burns, *Christian Mortalism from Tyndale to Milton*, pp. 69–70.

7. Kevan, *Grace of Law*, p. 26.

8. Peter Gunter, *A Sermon Preached in the Countie of Suffolke, before the Clergie and Laytie, for the discoverie and confutation of certain strange, pernicious, and Hereticall Positions, publikely delivered, held, and maintayned, touching Justification, by a certain factious Preacher of Wickam Market, in the said Countie, by which, divers, especially of the Vulgar, farre and neare, were greatly seduced*, pp. 2–6, 59.

9. Huehns, *Antinomianism*, pp. 64–65; Kevan, *Grace of Law*, p. 26; DNB, 6:336–37.

10. John Eaton, *The Honey-Combe of Free Justification by Christ alone*, sig. B1, p. 147.

11. Ibid., pp. 25, 150, 185f., 206–7, 212, 235, 241ff., 286, 307.

12. Ibid., pp. 121, 123, 145.

13. Ibid., pp. 38, 68, 362, 365.

14. Ibid., pp. 7, 41, 47, 138, 142, 257, 321, 343, 371.

15. Ibid., pp. 430, 432, 435.

16. Ibid., p. 406.

17. Hall, *Antinomian Controversy*, pp. 202–3, 222–23, 226, 228, 237, 239, 278, 302–3, 337, 352, 382; Stoever connects Anne Hutchinson with earlier English sectarian Antinomianism ('A Faire and Easie Way to Heaven,' pp. 165–69).

18. Hall, *Antinomian Controversy*, pp. 43ff., 84–86, 98, 127–28, 139, 160–61, 380, 382, 398–99, 402.

19. John Saltmarsh, *Free Grace*, p. 210; an opponent referred to "Luther, whom they most magnifie" (Stephen Geree, *The Doctrine of the Antinomians by Evidence of Gods Truth, plainely Confuted*, sig. b4ʳ).

20. Saltmarsh, *Free Grace*, sig. A5ʳ, pp. 7, 31–32, 34, 40, 47, 55, 62, 85, 128, 155.

21. Ibid., p. 57.

22. John Saltmarsh, *The Fountaine of Free Grace Opened by Questions and Answers*, p. 20; Eaton, *Honey-Combe of Free Justification*, p. 121.

23. Saltmarsh, *Fountaine*, sig. A2ʳ, p. 2.

24. Saltmarsh, *Free Grace*, pp. 85, 129; Eaton, *Honey-Combe of Free Justification*, sig. B2ᵛ, pp. 7, 41, 47, 343, 371.

25. Richard Baxter, *Admonition to Mr. William Eyre*, sigs. A2ʳ, A4, p. 15; Herbert Thorndike, *An Epilogue to the Tragedy of the Church of England*, pt. 1, p. 14.

26. Eaton, *Honey-Combe of Free Justification*, p. 270; Saltmarsh, *Fountaine*, pp. 2, 22–23.

27. See chapter 3, above, n. 31.

28. Hall, *Antinomian Controversy*, p. 410.

29. Ibid., pp. 202, 263–64.

30. Toon, *Hyper-Calvinism*, pp. 28, 82; Allison, *Rise of Moralism*, pp. 171–72; Kevan, *Grace of Law*, p. 26; Geree, *Doctrine of the Antinomians*, reproduces Crisp's views in refuting them.

31. Murray Tolmie, *Triumph of the Saints*, p. 109.

32. John Simpson, *The Perfection of Justification maintained against the Pharisee*, pp. 20, 27, 56–57, 61–62, 65, 71, 200–201, 211, 213.

33. William Eyre, *Justification without Conditions*, sigs. A2, B6ᵛ, pp. 2, 5–7, 43–45, 128ff., 261ff.

34. Ibid., preface by Owen.

35. John Owen, *The Works of John Owen, D.D.*, 12:602, 604, 611.

36. Richard Baxter, *An Unsavoury Volume of Mr. Jo. Crandon's Anatomized*, sig. I2, pp. 15–18.

37. Geree, *Doctrine of the Antinomians*, sigs. A2ᵛ, B2ᵛ; see Anthony Burgess, *The True Doctrine of Justification Asserted and Vindicated from the Errors of Papists, Arminians, Socinians, and more especially Antinomians*, sig. A3.

38. Thorndike, *Epilogue*, pt. 1, pp. 11, 13.

39. Herbert Thorndike, *Just Weights and Measures*, pp. 55–56, 72.

40. Laurence Womock, *The Examination of Tilenus before the Triers*, sig. [A10ᵛ]; Thomas Pierce, *The Divine Purity Defended*, p. 128; Henry Hammond, Χάρις Καὶ εἰρήνη: *Or a Pacifick Discourse of Gods Grace and Decrees*, sig. A3ʳ.

41. John Plaifere, *Appeal to Gospel for True Doctrine of Divine Predestination*, pp. 1, 38ff.

42. [William Sancroft], *Fur Predestinatus*, sig. A2.

43. Brian G. Armstrong, *Calvinism and the Amyraut Heresy*, p. 62; A. W. Harrison, *Arminianism*, p. 109.

44. Womock, *Examination of Tilenus*, sig. A8ᵛ, pp. 19, 24, 30, 68, 84, 85, 124.

45. Laurence Womock, *The Result of False Principles*.

46. Thomas Pierce, *The Divine Philanthropie Defended*, p. 15.

47. Henry Hickman, Πατρο-σχολαστικο-δικαιωσις, *A Justification of the Fathers and Schoolmen*, p. 109.
48. *DNB*, 15:1146–48, where he is identified simply as "controversialist."
49. Thomas Pierce, *A Correct Copy of Some Notes concerning Gods Decrees, Especially of Reprobation*, pp. 32, 36, 41, 66, 68–69.
50. Pierce, *Divine Philanthropie*, p. 7.
51. Pierce, *Divine Purity*, sig. A4ᵛ, pp. 32, 100, 228.
52. Pierce, *Divine Philanthropie*, sig. A3ᵛ; *Divine Purity*, sig. A2ᵛ.
53. Pierce, *Divine Purity*, pp. 7ff., 20, 49.
54. Pierce, *Divine Philanthropie*, p. 15.
55. The other work was *The Self-Revenger Exemplified in Mr. William Barlee*; see, e.g. sig. *3ᵛ.
56. Thomas Pierce, αὐτοκατακρισις, *Self-Condemnation, Exemplified in Mr. Whitfield, Mr. Barlee, and Mr. Hickman*, p. 138.
57. Hickman, *Justification of the Fathers*, p. 7.
58. Calvinists had earlier complained of Bramhall's Arminianism (Francis Cheynell, *The Rise, Growthe, and Danger of Socinianisme*, p. 36; Robert Baillie, *Laudensium Autokatakrisis*, p. 15).
59. John Bramhall, *Castigations of Mr. Hobbes His Last Animadversions in the case concerning Liberty, and Universal Necessity*, pp. 6, 22; Bramhall, *The catching of Leviathan, or the Great Whale*, sig. Gg 7ʳ.
60. Bramhall, *Castigations of Mr. Hobbes*, pp. 256, 282. Hobbes cited the authority of Dort and the Reformed theologians for liberty and necessity as reconcilable (ibid., p. 279).
61. Bramhall, *Catching of Leviathan*, sigs. Gg5ᵛ, Gg3ʳ. See W. B. Glover, "God and Thomas Hobbes"; Leopold Damrosch, Jr., "Hobbes as Reformation Theologian."
62. Robert S. Bosher, *The Making of the Restoration Settlement*, p. 36. John W. Packer, *The Transformation of Anglicanism, 1643–1660: With Special Reference to Henry Hammond*, is an appreciative assessment of Hammond.
63. Hammond, *Pacifick Discourse*, sig. A4, pp. 5, 7, 64, 66; quotation on p. 25.
64. Isaac Walton, in *The Lives of John Donne, Sir Henry Wotton, Richard Hooker, George Herbert, & Robert Sanderson*, p. 386.
65. Womock, *Examination of Tilenus*, sigs. A5ᵛ–A6ʳ, p. 123.
66. Thorndike, *Epilogue*, 2:534.
67. *The Just Mans Defence*, translated by Tobias Conyers, sigs. A4ʳ, a1ᵛ.
68. [Peter Bertius], *The Life and Death of James Arminius, and Simon Episcopius*, preface by J. K.
69. Pierce, *Divine Philanthropie*, pp. 13–14.
70. Ibid., pp. 119–20, 130; Pierce, *Divine Purity*, p. 26; Pierce, *Self-Condemnation*, pp. 39, 63–64.
71. Pierce, *Divine Purity*, p. 27; Pierce, *Self-Condemnation*, p. 18.
72. Womock, *Examination of Tilenus*, p. 123.
73. Pierce, *Divine Philanthropie*, p. 51; to the same author's *Self-Condemnation* is appended an attack on Baxter for his criticisms of Grotius; Henry Hammond wrote in defense of Grotius, *A Second Defence of the Learned Hugo Grotius*, pp. 1, 2, 5, 11, and *A Continuation of the Defence of Hugo Grotius*, pp. 2, 13, 14, 18, 22, 28.
74. Pierce, *Divine Philanthropie*, p. 51.
75. Pierce, *Self-Condemnation*, pp. 63–64; Pierce, *Divine Philanthropie*, p. 51; Pierce, *Divine Purity*, p. 122.
76. E.g., Pierce, *Correct Copy*, pp. 29–30; Pierce, *Self-Revenger*, p. 155; Pierce, *Divine Philanthropie*, p. 51.
77. Hammond, *Pacifick Discourse*, passim.
78. Ibid., pp. 9–10. The assertion, however, comes from one of Sanderson's letters.
79. Allison, *Rise of Moralism*, p. 67. Allison's purpose was not to provide a historical context and explanation for the theological shift he detected, but as an analysis of the theological views of those he studied, his book is very acute. I would only disagree with his opinion (p. 194) that Anglican theologians generally accepted gratuitous justification until

1640, which seems to overlook the direction in which Laudian Arminianism was tending. J. Sears McGee has a similar approach to these Anglican divines (*The Godly Man in Stuart England*, p. 209). Many of the studies of individual divines of the period, however, overlook the extent of their departure from previous Anglican theology, e.g., Packer, *Transformation of Anglicanism*, Hugh Ross Williamson, *Jeremy Taylor*. Frank L. Huntley outlines Taylor's rejection of predestination and original sin for which he, too, was called a Socinian (*Jeremy Taylor and the Great Rebellion*, pp. 58–61, 79–94).

80. Pierce, *Divine Purity*, sig. A2ᵛ; Pierce, *Correct Copy*, p. 36.

81. Thorndike, *Epilogue*, pt. 2, p. 497.

82. Ibid., pt. 1, 97.

83. Ibid., pt. 2, pp. 595, 659; Thorndike, *Just Weights and Measures*, p. 73.

84. Thorndike, *Just Weights and Measures*, pp. 63–64.

85. Henry Hammond, *A Practical Catechisme*, pp. 37–39.

86. Allison, *Rise of Moralism*, pp. 119–21, 123, 133, 137.

87. Thorndike, *Just Weights and Measures*, pp. 65–66. To vindicate himself from the charge of Socinianism, George Bull wrote his enormous work on the Nicene Creed, an effort that must be seen as a diversionary tactic.

88. Thorndike, *Just Weights and Measures*, pp. 90, 138–39.

89. Ibid., pp. 125–30, 149; but see also David B. McIlhiney, "The Protestantism of the Caroline Divines."

90. Gerald R. Cragg, ed., *The Cambridge Platonists*, p. 8.

91. Rosalie Colie, *Light and Enlightenment*, p. x and passim.

92. Frederick J. Powicke, *The Cambridge Platonists*, pp. 54–59.

93. Cragg, ed., *Cambridge Platonists*, pp. 39, 41–43, 46–47.

94. Powicke, *Cambridge Platonists*, pp. 110–12.

95. Cragg, ed., *Cambridge Platonists*, pp. 9–10. But More's synergism was more complex than a mere moralism (Aharon Lichtenstein, *Henry More*, pp. 86–87).

96. Powicke, *Cambridge Platonists*, pp. 134, 141.

97. Peter Sterry, *A Discourse of the Freedom of the Will*, sig. b1ᵛ, pp. 32, 84, 31, 121. See also D. P. Walker, *The Decline of Hell*, pp. 106–8.

98. John Goodwin, Ἐιρηνομαχια: *The Agreement and Distance of Brethren*, pp. 2, 5, 9, 19, 21, 31, 32, 66–67.

99. John Goodwin, Ἀπολύτρωσις Ἀπολυτρώσεως, *or Redemption Redeemed*, sigs. A4ʳ, c3ʳ, a1ʳ, pp. 45, 66, 156–57, 170, 172, 386, 389, 555ff.

100. John Goodwin, *Triumviri*, pp. 47–48, 247.

101. Christopher Hill, *Milton and the English Revolution*, pp. 272–73.

102. Edward Choune, *A Whip for the Lecturers of Lewis, and for all Those Presbyterians, and others of the Clergy which maintain that damnable opinion of absolute Reprobation*, seems to be the work of an only slightly educated layman who is certainly no Quaker although irate at "jugling priests" for teaching absolute reprobation (sig. A2ʳ, pp. 6, 10, 25).

103. E.g., John Horne, identified as a parish incumbent in Lyn, Norfolkshire, and Thomas Moore were alluded to as "Freewillers" and "Independents" in a Quaker diatribe of 1659 (George Whitehead and George Fox, *A Brief Discovery of the Dangerous Principles of John Horne and Thomas Moore*, title page). Tobias Conyers, an Arminian, though he conformed in 1661, was earlier considered an Independent (A. G. Matthews, *Calamy Revised*, p. 132). See also B. S. Capp, *The Fifth Monarchy Men*, pp. 175, 179, 181.

104. George Fox, *The Journal of George Fox*, pp. 299–300.

105. John Stalham, *The Reviler Rebuked*, sig. e1ᵛ.

106. Melvin Endy, *William Penn and Early Quakerism*, pp. 164–65.

107. Hill, *Milton and the English Revolution*, pp. 4, 5, 8, passim; Don M. Wolfe, *Milton in the Puritan Revolution*; Hugh M. Richmond, *The Christian Revolutionary*.

108. John Milton, *De Doctrina Christiana*, pp. 25, 89, 337–39; Milton's treatise was probably completed no later than early in the Restoration era (Maurice Kelley, *This Great Argument*, p. 23).

109. Goodwin, *Redemption Redeemed*, p. 515.

110. Ibid., p. 178. For Cameron, see Armstrong, *Calvinism*, pp. 42–70.
111. Pierce, *Self-Revenger Exemplified*, p. 90.
112. Armstrong, *Calvinism*, pp. 121–27, 132–33, 264–69.
113. Benjamin B. Warfield, *The Westminster Assembly and Its Work*, pp. 130–44; see also A. F. Mitchell and John Struthers, eds., *Minutes of the Sessions of the Westminster Assembly of Divines*, pp. 150ff., 159ff.
114. Mitchell and Struthers, eds., *Minutes*, pp. 160–62.
115. Thomas Gataker, *A Mistake, or Misconstruction Removed*, p. 3, sig. A2ᵛ; reprinted in 1652 as *Antinomianism Discovered and Confuted*.
116. Ibid., pp. 17, 25.
117. [Thomas Bakewell], *The Antinomians Christ Confounded, and the Lords Christ Exalted*, sig. A1ʳ.
118. Geree, *Doctrine of the Antinomians*, sig. A3ʳ.
119. [Bakewell], *Antinomians Christ Confounded*, pp. 2, 5, 11, 19; Anthony Burgess, *The True Doctrine of Justification Asserted, and Vindicated, from the Errors of Papists, Arminians, Socinians, and more especially Antinomians*, p. 16; Benjamin Woodbridge, *Justification by Faith*, pp. 11ff., passim; John Eedes, *The Orthodox Doctrine concerning Justification by Faith Asserted and Vindicated*, passim; Geree, *Doctrine of the Antinomians*, p. 34.
120. Gataker, *Mistake*, p. 4; cf. also Benjamin Woodbridge, *The Method of Grace in the Justification of Sinners*, sig. A4ʳ.
121. Gataker, *Mistake*, pp. 11, 37.
122. [Bakewell], *Antinomians Christ Confounded*, pp. 12–13; Geree, *Doctrine of the Antinomians*, p. 50.
123. John Benbridge [Bainbridge], *Christ Above All Exalted*, sig. A3, pp. 4, 5, 13, 16.
124. Gataker, *Mistake*, p. 40.
125. [Bainbridge], *Christ Exalted*, pp. 19, 38–39; Geree, *Doctrine of the Antinomians*, pp. 128–29; Gataker, *Mistake*, p. 37.
126. Gataker, *Mistake*, pp. 11, 15; Geree, *Doctrine of the Antinomians*, pp. 29, 72, 76; [Bakewell], *Antinomians Christ Confounded*, pp. 7, 5.
127. Gataker was attacked by George Walker as a Socinian when Gataker defended the memory of Anthony Wotton against similar charges by Walker (George Walker, *A True relation of the chiefe passages betweene Mr. Anthony Wotton, and Mr. George Walker, in the yeare of our Lord, 1611*, pp. 2–4, 27).
128. Woodbridge, *Method of Grace*, sigs. A3ᵛ, A4ᵛ–a1ʳ. Both the Scotsman Baillie and the Independent John Owen called Baxter an Amyraldian (Owen, *Works*, 10:479; Irvonwy Morgan, *The Nonconformity of Richard Baxter*, p. 77; see also A. W. Harrison, *Arminianism*, pp. 111, 161).
129. Pierce, *Self-Revenger*, p. 90.
130. Richard Baxter, *Reliquae Baxterianae*, pt. 1, p. 107.
131. Richard Baxter, *Aphorisms of Justification*, pp. 96, 100–108.
132. Ibid., pp. 111, 123–24.
133. Ibid., pp. 125–26, 289–93.
134. Baxter, *Reliquae Baxterianae*, pt. 1, p. 107.
135. Owen, *Works*, 10:431, 435–36.
136. Eedes, *Orthodox Doctrine*, passim.
137. Eyre, *Justification without Conditions*, sig. A2; cf. sig. A6ᵛ.
138. John Crandon, *Mr. Baxter's Aphorisms Exorcised and Anthorized*, sigs. A2ᵛ–3ʳ, A6ʳ, B3ᵛ, B4.
139. Baxter, *Reliquae Baxterianae*, pt. 1, p. 110.
140. Richard Baxter, *Confession of His Faith*, pp. 190–91; *The Reduction of a Digressor, or Rich. Baxter's Reply to Mr. George Kendall's Digression*, pp. 89–91, 139; *Admonition to Eyre*, sigs. A2ʳ, A4, p. 15; *Unsavoury Volume*, pp. 15–18.
141. Baxter, *Confession*, p. 1.
142. Baxter, *Reliquae Baxterianae*, pt. 1, p. 107.
143. Ibid., p. 111.

144. Baxter, *Confession*, p. 33.

145. Ibid., pp. 34–35, sig. A4^r.

146. Baxter, *Reduction of a Digressor*, sig. A3^r.

147. Richard Baxter, *Confutation of a Dissertation . . . Written by...Colvinus*, sigs. 11 [sic], 3^r.

148. E.g., the remark that the purpose of Christ's redeeming work was "to make man fit for Gods Approbation and Delight" (Baxter, *Confession*, sig. A4^r).

149. Robert Baillie, *Letters and Journals of Robert Baillie*, 3:304.

150. There is a thorough treatment of Baxter's views on justification in Allison, *Rise of Moralism*, pp. 154ff.. Allison concluded that his views were "remarkably like those of Taylor, Thorndike, and Hammond" (pp. 157–58) and not unlike those of the Council of Trent (p. 163).

151. Richard Baxter, *The Grotian Religion Discovered, At the Invitation of Mr. Thomas Pierce in his Vindication*, sigs. *3^v, a1^r, A2^v; cf. Baxter, *Confession*, pp. 23, 26.

152. Baxter, *Grotian Religion*, sig. A3, p. 103.

153. Ibid., sigs. A4^r, C5^r, B8^r.

154. Henry Hickman, Ποθεν ζιζανια, *refutatio Tileni; Justification of the Fathers; A Review of the Certamen Epistolare Betwixt Pet. Heylin D. D. and Hen. Hickman B.D. Wherein the exception of the Dr. against Mr. H's arguments are all taken off, and our first Reformers proved not to hold with the Arminians. Also a Reply to Mr. Pierce.*

155. Hickman, *Justification of the Fathers*, sig. A5^v; *Review of the Certamen Epistolare*, sigs. A4^v, A5^r, pp. 40, 158.

156. Hickman, *Justification of the Fathers*, sig. A3^v. Baxter also alluded to Taylor's view of original sin (*Grotian Religion*, sig. A4^r); cf. Huntley, *Jeremy Taylor*, pp. 58–61, 79–94.

157. Henry Hickman, *Historia Quinq-Articularis Exarticulata*, sigs. A3^v, A4^r; Hickman, *Justification of the Fathers*, sig. A3r.

158. Hickman, *Review of the Certamen Epistolare*, pp. 74–75, 118–19.

159. Ibid., sig. A5^r.

160. Hickman, *Justification of the Fathers*, pp. 33–34.

161. Hickman, *Review of the Certamen Epistolare*, pp. 16, 67, 72, 77, 85–86; cf. *Historia Quinq-Articularis*, p. 456, where he rejected supralapsarianism.

162. Hickman, *Review of the Certamen Epistolare*, p. 93; in his *Historia Quinq-Articularis*, p. 474, he praised Amyraut.

163. Hickman, *Review of the Certamen Epistolare*, pp. 15, 79.

164. Ibid., p. 48.

165. Ibid., pp. 40, 42–43, 57–58, 105–6, 118–19, 138; Hickman, *Justification of the Fathers*, sigs. A3^r, a8^v, b1^v, b2, c1^r.

166. Henry Hickman, *Plus Ultra*, pp. 2–3.

167. Hickman, *Historia Quinq-Articularis*, sig. A3.

168. A healthy confusion about the relationship between party names and the advocacy of different clear-cut polities was introduced by J. H. Hexter's article, "The Problem of the Presbyterian Independents"; see also C. Gordon Bolam, Jeremy Goring, H. L. Short, and Roger Thomas, *The English Presbyterians*, p. 47; for Baxter's views on polity, see ibid., pp. 48, 54, 61–62, and James C. Spalding, "The Demise of English Presbyterianism, 1660–1760," p. 65.

169. James C. Spalding and Maynard F. Brass, "Reduction of Episcopacy as a Means to Unity in England, 1640–1662"; George R. Abernathy, Jr., *The English Presbyterians and the Stuart Restoration, 1648–1663*, pp. 7a, 13b, 31b, 60b, 61b, 65a; Walter G. Simon, "Comprehension in the Age of Charles II"; Spalding, "Demise of English Presbyterianism," pp. 67, 70–71.

170. Bolam et al., *English Presbyterians*, pp. 95, 116, 118, 121; Simon, "Comprehension in the Age of Charles II," pp. 442–43; Spalding, "Demise of English Presbyterianism," pp. 64–72; Bosher, *Restoration Settlement*, p. 118.

171. Spalding, "Demise of English Presbyterianism," pp. 78–80; Bolam et al., *English Presbyterians*, pp. 169, 172, 186–87, 205, 221, 232; Olive M. Griffiths, *Religion and*

Learning, pp. 94–150; J. Hay Colligan, *The Arian Movement in England*, pp. 30–31, 45–47, 59, 93, 104.

172. Edmund Calamy, *Englands Looking-Glasse, Presented in a Sermon Preached before the Honourable House of Commons . . . December 22, 1641*, p. 61.

173. G. Lyon Turner, "The Religious Condition of London in 1672 as Reported to King and Court," p. 198.

174. Bosher, *Restoration Settlement*, pp. 118–19; Hugh Martin, *Puritanism and Richard Baxter*, p. 50.

175. Edward Reynolds, *The Sinfulnesse of Sinne*, pp. 118, 199–200; Edward Reynolds, *A Sermon Touching the Peace and Edification of the Church*, pp. 19–24, 28, 32.

176. Elnathan Parr, *The Grounds of Divinitie, Plainely Discovering the Mysteries of Christian Religion*, pp. 291, 300, 307–8, 310–12, 318ff.

177. Joseph Hall, *The Works of the Right Reverend Joseph Hall*, 9:497–98, 509; John Davenant, *Animadversions . . . upon a Treatise intitled Gods Love to Mankind*, pp. 4, 5, 7, 23ff. John Owen, a high Calvinist, thought Davenant unsound on the doctrine of the atonement (Owen, *Works*, 10:432).

178. Spalding and Brass, "Reduction of Episcopacy," p. 417, 423–25; Richard Parr, *The Life of the Most Reverend Father in God, James Usher*, pp. 9–10.

179. E.g., Robert Dixon, who published a fairly Reformed treatment of *The Doctrine of Faith, Justification, and Assurance*, which referred to "miserable comforters" who drive souls to despair with their words about reprobation (pp. 16–17).

180. Herbert J. McLachlan, *Socinianism in Seventeenth-Century England*, pp. 163ff., 195ff.; William Twisse, *The Doctrine of the Synod of Dort and Arles, reduced to the practise*, p. 36; George Walker, *Socinianisme in the Fundamental Point of Justification Discovered, and Confuted*, pp. 2–5, 166–67.

181. Francis Cheynell, *Chillingworthi Novissima*, sigs. G4, G2ᵛ, B4ᵛ. Earlier Cheynell had cited Chillingworth as evidence that Laud was consciously patronizing Socinianism even though Laud himself was a "papist" (*The Rise, Growthe, and Danger of Socinianisme*, pp. 28, 72).

182. Francis Cheynell, *A Copy of Some Papers Past at Oxford, Betwixt the Author of the Practicall Catechisme, and Mr. Ch.*, p. 20.

183. Walker, *True Relation*, pp. 4, 25. Walker had worked out a genealogy of the heresy whereby Socinus had gotten his ideas from Abelard and Servetus, Anthony Wotton from Socinus (in spite of Wotton's reputation as anti-Arminian!), and John Goodwin from Wotton (Walker, *Socinianisme*, pp. 5–6).

184. Richard Resbury, *The Lightess-Starre*; Owen, preface to Eyre, *Justification without Conditions*.

185. Owen, *Works*, 12:592, 602, 604, 607, 611.

186. George Kendall, *Sancti Sanctiti*, sig. T1ᵛ, argued that in a certain sense God knew the elect as justified before time; Richard Lewthwat, *Vindiciae Christi et Obex Arminiano*, p. 25, affirmed that the elect are "just" in the sight of God prior to the entry of grace into the soul.

187. George Kendall, Θεοκρατία: *Or a Vindication of the Doctrine Commonly Received in the Reformed Churches concerning Gods Intentions of Special Grace and Favour to his Elect in the Death of Christ*, sig. ***1ʳ.

188. William Twisse, *A Discovery of Dr. Jackson's Vanity*; *Vindiciae gratiae*; *A Treatise of Mr. Cottons, Clearing Certaine Doubts concerning Predestination*, sigs. A3ᵛ–4ʳ; for Twisse's Aristotelianism, see Sarah Hutton, "Thomas Jackson, Oxford Platonist, and William Twisse, Aristotelian," pp. 649–51.

189. Twisse, *Doctrine of the Synod of Dort*, p. 18.

190. Twisse, *Treatise of Mr. Cottons*, preface, sig. A3ʳ.

191. William Twisse, *The Riches of Gods Love Unto the Vessels of Mercy, Consistent with His Absolute Hatred or Reprobation of the Vessels of Wrath*, sig. ¶4, pp. 5–7, 133.

192. George Kendall, *Fur Pro Tribunali*.

193. Richard Resbury, *Some Stop to the Gangrene of Arminianism*, pp. 67, 68, 78.

194. William Barlee, *Praedestination, as before privately, so now at last openly defended*

against Post-destination, pp. 18, 20–21, 28, 92–93, 159, 225; Barlee, *A Necessary Vindication of the Doctrine of Predestination, Formerly Asserted*, sigs. Aa2ᵛ, Bb1ʳ, Bb4ʳ, Mm3ʳ.

195. Thomas Whitfield, *The Doctrines of the Arminians and Pelagians truly stated and Clearly answered* (1651).

196. Thomas Whitfield, *A Vindication of the Doctrine of Gods Absolute Decree, and of Christs Absolute and Special Redemption*, p. 1.

197. Ibid., pp. 10, 40–41, 51, 54–55.

198. Toon, *Hyper-Calvinism*, p. 65.

199. Thomas Goodwin, *A Discourse of Election, of the Free and Special Grace of God Manifested Therein*, pp. 84–87, 90–94, 125–49, 238.

200. Even a spy book of 1663 noted that they often met together, G. Lyon Turner, "Williamson's Spy Book," pp. 249, 253.

201. Baxter, *Reliquae Baxterianae*, pt. 2, p. 199.

202. Wood, *Athenae Oxoniensis*, 3:1058, where Tully and Barlow are cited in quoted correspondence as champions against Socinianism and other heresies.

203. Dewey D. Wallace, Jr., "The Life and Thought of John Owen to 1660," pp. 13–15; Barlow's theology is considered in Allison, *Rise of Moralism*, pp. 141–44.

204. Richard L. Greaves, "John Bunyan's Holy War and London Nonconformity," p. 159.

205. For the conservative Independents, see Wallace, "Life and Thought of John Owen," pp. 195–201; for their program for the Cromwellian church, see ibid., pp. 203–5; see also Sarah G. Cook, "The Congregational Independents and the Cromwellian Constitutions." Stalham, Eyre, and Resbury are usually included among the lists of Independents ejected at the Restoration (R. Tudur Jones, *Congregationalism in England, 1662–1962*, pp. 49, 61). Brooks, often associated with Owen and Thomas Goodwin in common schemes, showed himself to be anti-Arminian in *Heaven on Earth*, pp. 30, 34.

206. Twisse, *Riches of Gods Love*, prefatory letter by Owen, sig. 1v.

207. Barlee, *Praedestination*, sig. A1ᵛ.

208. Crandon, *Mr. Baxter's Aphorisms*, sig. A1ᵛ.

209. Among works prefaced and recommended by Owen were Theophilus Gale, *The True Idea of Jansenisme, Both Historick and Dogmatick* (1669); William Bridge, *The Freeness of the Grace and Love of God to Believers* (1671); Edward Polhill, *The Divine Will Considered in its Eternal Decrees and Holy Execution of Them* (1673); Samuel Petto, *The Difference between the Old and New Covenant* (1674); James Durham, *The Law Unsealed* (1677); Patrick Gillespie, *The Ark of the Covenant Opened* (1677); Bartholomew Ashwood, *The Best Treasure* (1681); Elisha Coles, *A Practical Discourse of God's Sovereignty* (1685).

210. Wallace, "Life and Thought of John Owen," pp. 298–308.

211. John Hill, "The Diaries of John Hill," pp. 209–11, 221; Samuel Eliot Morison, *Harvard College in the Seventeenth Century*, p. 391n. See the tributes in Peter Toon, *God's Statesman*, pp. 173–74.

212. Toon, *God's Statesman*, pp. 14, 40, notes the importance to Owen of refuting Arminianism, but generally gives little attention to his theology.

213. John Owen, *Pneumatalogia, or a Discourse concerning the Holy Spirit* (London, 1674).

214. E.g., John Owen, *Of Communion with God the Father, Son, and Holy Ghost* (1657); *Christologia, or a Declaration of the Person of Christ* (1679); *Meditation and Discourses on the Glory of Christ* (1684); *The Grace and Duty of Being Spiritually Minded* (1681); *A Treatise of the Dominion of Sin and Grace* (1688); *Gospel Grounds and Evidences of the Faith of God's Elect* (1695). All are included in Owen, *Works*.

215. Owen, *Works*, 12:115, 116, 129, 131.

216. Ibid., 10:454; 11:126, 130–31, 143; 12:555.

217. Ibid., 10:227, 291, 457.

218. Ibid., pp. 205–6.

219. Ibid., pp. 560, 584–87.

220. Ibid., pp. 498–99, 505–6.
221. Ibid., pp. 507, 508, 512, 514, 516–17.
222. Ibid., pp. 556–57, 560.
223. Ibid., 12:411, 542–43.
224. Ibid., pp. 430–55, 485–92.
225. Ibid., pp. 508–48.
226. Ibid., 10:441; cf. also 438, 447.
227. See Toon, *Hyper-Calvinism*, pp. 55–58.
228. Owen, *Works*, 11:125; 12:563, 574, 597, 599–600.
229. Ibid., 12:597–600.
230. Ibid., 5:3–6, 65, 68, 372.
231. Ibid., pp. 20, 31, 44–45, 73, 127.
232. Ibid., 9:26.
233. Ibid., 13:415; cf. also 2:200.
234. Ibid., 12:6.
235. Ibid., 1:52, 81, 139–40, 169–72.
236. Ibid., 1:41–44, 287, 302.
237. Ibid., 1:39, 41.
238. Ibid., 1:77.
239. G. F. Nuttall, in *The Holy Spirit in Puritan Faith and Experience*, has treated the idea of the Spirit as a means to understanding Puritanism (p. viii) and regards Quakerism as a further step from the Puritan theology of the Spirit (pp. 26–27). But if Puritan interest in the doctrine was mainly a function of the theology of grace and was used to oppose a self-reliant moralism, perhaps the connections are less close. Some recent studies have emphasized the rational moralism of early Quakerism and its distance from such things as Antinomianism, e.g., Endy, *William Penn*, pp. 6–7, 9, 164, 244–45, 255.
240. Owen wrote against the Quakers in *Pro Sacris Scripturis Adversus Fanaticos* (1658); as did other conservative Independents, for example, John Stalham, *The Reviler Rebuked* (1657); John Stalham, *Contradictions of the Quakers* (1655); John Stalham, *Marginal Antidotes* (1657); Francis Harris, *Some Queries Proposed to the Consideration of . . . Quakers* (1655); Thomas Danson, *The Quaker Folly Made Manifest* (1659).
241. *A Discourse of the Work of the Holy Spirit in Prayer* (1682); *Two Discourses concerning the Holy Spirit and His Work: the one of the Spirit as Comforter; the other, as He is the Author of Spiritual Gifts* (1693).
242. Owen, *Works*, 3:5.
243. Ibid., pp. 9–10, 23, 27.
244. Ibid., pp. 217, 219, 221, 223–24, 244–45, 248–49, 482, 493, 502–4, 516, 522–23, 568, 593.

Chapter 5

1. Gerald R. Cragg, *From Puritanism to the Age of Reason*, pp. 13, 30.
2. Paul Hazard, *The European Mind (1670–1715)*, p. 445.
3. C. John Sommerville, "Religious Typologies and Popular Religion in Restoration England," p. 35.
4. H. R. Trevor-Roper, *Archbishop Laud, 1573–1645*, pp. 429–30. For a different view, see Robert S. Bosher, *The Making of the Restoration Settlement*, pp. 278–79. See also the interesting revisionist work by I. M. Green, *The Re-establishment of the Church of England, 1660–1663*, pp. 22–24.
5. Leonard J. Trinterud, "A.D. 1689," p. 29.
6. Peter Gay, *The Enlightenment*, 2:12: "The most powerful agent in the recovery of nerve was obviously the scientific revolution."
7. Richard S. Westfall, *Science and Religion in Seventeenth-Century England*, pp. 141–42.
8. Barbara J. Shapiro, *John Wilkins, 1614–1672*, pp. 62–63.

9. *DNB*, 13:974.

10. C. Gordon Bolam, Jeremy Goring, H. L. Short, and Roger Thomas, *The English Presbyterians*, p. 105.

11. Walter Simon, *The Restoration Episcopate*, p. 32.

12. Shapiro, *John Wilkins*, p. 226; see Paul E. More and Frank L. Cross, *Anglicanism*, pp. 291, 301f.; C. F. Allison, *The Rise of Moralism*, pp. 149–50, considers Barrow less of a moralist than Hammond and Taylor.

13. Cragg, *From Puritanism to the Age of Reason*, pp. 23–30, uses Sanderson as an example of moderate, Arminian Anglicanism becoming Latitudinarianism.

14. For Latitudinarianism, see ibid., pp. 61–86.

15. *DNB*, 10:562–63.

16. Frederick J. Powicke, *The Cambridge Platonists*, p. 95.

17. See, e.g., his discourse on "The Carnality of Religious Contention" in John Howe, *The Works of the Rev. John Howe, M.A., with Memoirs of His Life, by Edmund Calamy, D.D.*, pp. 461ff.

18. For example, in part 1 of his *The Living Temple*, ibid., pp. 7–55.

19. A. G. Matthews, *Calamy Revised*, p. 261.

20. William Bates, *The Whole Works of the Rev. W. Bates*, 4:332–33. Baxter had called attention to the pastoral difficulties of the doctrine of reprobation in 1671 in *God's Goodness Vindicated*.

21. Ibid., 3:5, 419–20; 1:261.

22. Ibid., 4:294, where Boyle is praised for his study of God in nature; Bates's *Considerations of the Existence of God and the Immortality of the Soul, . . . To which is now added, The Divinity of the Christian Religion, Proved By the Evidence of Reason, and Divine Revelation, For the Cure of Infidelity* (1676), is an example of natural theology and the "evidences" argument and even anticipates Paley's use of the human eye's intricacy as evidence of design (*Works*, 1:16). Baxter developed a natural theology in his *The Reasons of the Christian Religion*.

23. Theodosia Alleine, *The Life and Death of That Excellent Minister of Christ Mr Joseph Allein*, p. 57.

24. Jones, *Congregationalism in England*, pp. 71–74.

25. A. C. Underwood, *A History of the English Baptists*, pp. 105, 222. Murray Tolmie, *The Triumph of the Saints*, p. 62, notes the closeness of Tombes to the ecclesiastical views of the Cromwellian Independents. Richard Greaves, in his introduction to John Bunyan, *The Doctrine of the Law and Grace Unfolded and I Will Pray with the Spirit*, p. xxiv, connects Tombes's theology with that of Owen, Thomas Goodwin, and Samuel Petto.

26. Among other Anglican leaders called Socinians by opponents were John Wilkins (Shapiro, *John Wilkins*, p. 66), Edward Stillingfleet (Robert Todd Carroll, *The Common-Sense Philosophy of Religion of Bishop Edward Stillingfleet, 1635–1699*, pp. 48, 53–54), and, much later, John Tillotson (S. C. Carpenter, *Eighteenth-Century Church and People*, p. 65).

27. Allison, *Rise of Moralism*, pp. 132, 137.

28. George Bull, *Harmonia Apostolica*, pp. 28, 150.

29. Allison, *Rise of Moralism*, pp. 132, 137.

30. Ibid., p. 122. Allison (pp. 141–43) summarizes two letters Barlow wrote when a bishop, in which he argued that the imputation of Christ's righteousness to the believer was necessary for true justification; these were published in 1701 as *Two Letters Written by the Rt. Rev. Dr. Thomas Barlow*.

31. Anthony Wood, *Athenae Oxoniensis*, 3: col. 1056.

32. Thomas Tully, *Justification Paulina Sine Operibus* (1674).

33. John Tombes, *Animadversiones in Librum Georgii Bulli Cui titulum fecit Harmonia Apostolica*, sig.*2.

34. Matthews, *Calamy Revised*, p. 495.

35. Joseph Truman, *The Great Propitiation*, pp. 1, 70; Joseph Truman, *An Endeavor to Rectifie Some Prevailing Opinions Contrary to the Doctrine of the Church of England*, sig. A2ᵛ, pp. 2–3, 128–29, 259, 261–62, 270.

36. Charles Gataker, *The Way of Truth and Peace*, pp. 68–69.

37. Charles Gataker, *Ichnographia doctrinae de justificatione Secundum S. Scripturas* (1681); *Justificatio gratuita, sive Doctrina justificationis* (1685).

38. George Bull, *Examen Censurae*, pp. 74, 228, 230, 231, 234, 237, 245, 327, 329, 336–38.

39. Edward Fowler, *The Design of Christianity*, pp. 213–14, 217, 220–22, 262.

40. Richard L. Greaves, *John Bunyan*, pp. 23, 34, 38, 39, 51–52, 81, 98–99; John Brown, *John Bunyan*, pp. 241, 366, 368.

41. John Bunyan, *A Defence of the Doctrine of Justification*, pp. 220, 267.

42. Ibid., pp. 225, 226, 228, 230, 235, 238–39, 247, 250, 252, 256, 260, 263.

43. Ibid., pp. 232, 236, 268–69.

44. Edward Fowler, *Dirt Wipt Off*, sigs. A2ʳ, A4ʳ, pp. 6, 11, 13–14, 17, 40, 42, 49, 63–64, 66, 73ff.

45. Bunyan, *Defence of Justification*, p. 258.

46. Gilbert Burnet, *A Supplement to Burnet's History*, p. 216.

47. Samuel Parker, *A Discourse of Ecclesiastical Polity*, pp. 136, 144–45, 155, 210–12, 279, 286, 290. It has been claimed that Archbishop Sheldon's views were unleashed through Parker, his chaplain (Victor D. Sutch, *Gilbert Sheldon*, p. 109).

48. Baxter refused to answer Parker, pleading that "I had above all men been oft enough searched in the malignant fire," but did not approve of Owen's entry into the quarrel because he considered him, as one of the chief Cromwellians, to be too vulnerable (*Reliquae Baxterianae*, pt. 3, p. 42).

49. John Owen, *The Works of John Owen*, 13:354–55, 501; the title of Owen's rejoinder was *Truth and Innocence Vindicated; in a Survey of A Discourse Concerning Ecclesiastical Polity, and the Authority of the Civil Magistrate over the Consciences of Subjects in Matters of Religion*.

50. Owen, *Works*, 13:414, 417–18, 420, 424–25, 431.

51. [Samuel Parker], "Preface Shewing What Grounds there are of Fears and Jealousies of Popery," in John Bramhall, *A Just Vindication of himself and Episcopal Clergy, from the Presbyterian Charge of Popery*, sigs. c3ᵛ, b8ʳ.

52. Samuel Parker, *A Defence and Continuation of the Ecclesiastical Polity*, pp. 81, 88, 144.

53. Ibid., pp. 131, 658, 663, 666, 670–73; cf. [Parker], "Preface Shewing What Grounds," sig. a6.

54. Parker, *Defence and Continuation*, pp. 132, 134, 304–22.

55. Robert Ferguson, *A Sober Enquiry into the Nature, Measure, and Principle of Moral Virtue*, pp. 250–51.

56. Ibid., pp. 121–23, 126, 129, 132–35, 154.

57. Andrew Marvell, *The Rehearsal Transprosed*, pp. 61–62, 66–67, 69.

58. Ibid., pp. 37, 68–69, 70, 76, 135, 298; John M. Wallace, *Destiny His Choice*, p. 193, considers Marvell, as I do, to have been serious about his theological commitment to moderate Calvinism, in spite of his bantering tone.

59. Gilbert Burnet, *Burnet's History of His Own Time*, 1:467.

60. Richard Leigh, *The Transproser Rehears'd*, pp. 21, 126.

61. *DNB*, 9:797–800; Edmund Hickeringill, *Gregory, Father Greybeard*, pp. 6, 24, 71–73, 80, 252–53.

62. Samuel Parker, *A Reproof to the Rehearsal Transprosed*, pp. 16, 47–48, 52, 57.

63. Andrew Marvell, *The Rehearsal Transpros'd: The Second Part*, pp. 28, 30–31, 272–74, 276, 321.

64. William Sherlock, *A Discourse concerning the Knowledge of Jesus Christ*, pp. 7–8, 11–12, 15, 18–19, 21, 23–24, 33, 38.

65. Ibid., p. 35.

66. See also Edward Stillingfleet, *A Discourse concerning the True Reason of the Suffering of Christ* (1668); and *A Discourse Concerning the Doctrine of Christ's Satisfaction* (1697).

67. Sherlock, *Discourse*, pp. 28, 36, 67, 83, 247, 157, 211, 217, 253.

68. Ibid., p. 121.

69. Owen, *Works*, 2:278–80, 285.

70. Ibid., pp. 286–87, 292, 303–21, 336, 339.

71. William Sherlock, *A Defence and Continuation of the Discourse concerning the Knowledge of Jesus Christ*, pp. 6–7, 19, 26, 165, 312ff., 353.

72. Ibid., pp. 198ff., 202, 209–10, 273.

73. Vincent Alsop, *Antisozzo; or Sherlocismus Enervatus* (1675); Samuel Rolle, *Justification Justified* (1674); Thomas Danson, *A Friendly Debate between Satan and Sherlock* (1674).

74. Henry Hickman, *Speculum Sherlockianum*, pp. 6, 24, 29, 55–56.

75. Edward Polhill, *An Answer to the Discourse of Mr. William Sherlock*, "To the Reader."

76. Robert Ferguson, *The Interest of Reason in Religion*, "To the Reader"; pp. 165ff.

77. Thomas Hotchkis, *A Discourse concerning the Imputation of Christ's Righteousness to Us, and our Sins to Him*, passim, especially introductory epistle; he was more cautious than Sherlock and might almost be classed a moderate Calvinist.

78. Owen, *Works*, 15:340.

79. Ibid., p. 345.

80. Ibid., pp. 356–57.

81. Ibid., p. 67.

82. Ibid., 7:35, 52–53, 57, 60, 70–71, 73–78, 121, 123, 130–33, 153–55.

83. Simon Patrick, *A Friendly Debate between a Conformist and a Nonconformist*, pp. 12–14.

84. John Goodman, *A Serious and Compassionate Inquiry*, pp. 3, 6–8.

85. Richard Perrinchief, *Indulgence Not Justified*, p. 38.

86. Vincent Alsop, *Melius Inquirendum . . . St. Augustine, the Synod of Dort, and the Articles of the Church of England, in the Quinquarticular points, vindicated*, pp. 35–36, 48–51, 53.

87. Thomas Manton, *Christ's Eternal Existence, and the Dignity of His Person Asserted and Proved. In Opposition to the doctrine of the Socinians* (1685).

88. Owen, "To the Reader," in Patrick Gillespie, *The Ark of the Covenant Opened: Or, a Treatise of the Covenant of Redemption . . . The Second Part*.

89. Greaves, *John Bunyan*, p. 117.

90. Owen, untitled preface to Samuel Petto, *The Difference between the Old and New Covenant*.

91. Owen, "To the Reader," in Bartholomew Ashwood, *The Best Treasure*.

92. Edward Polhill, *The Divine Will Considered in its Eternal Decrees and Holy Execution of Them*, sigs. A2, A7.

93. Sir Charles Wolseley, *Justification Evangelical*, pp. 2–4, 20, 53ff.

94. Owen, untitled preface to Elisha Coles, *A Practical Discourse of God's Sovereignty*.

95. Coles, *Practical Discourse*, his own preface, and pp. 2, 3, 41, cf. also pp. 62, 66, 69.

96. Thomas Brooks, *A Golden Key to Open Hidden Treasures*, preface, pp. 203–8, 370–72.

97. David Clarkson, *A Discourse of the Saving Grace of God*, sigs. B4ᵛ, B6ʳ, pp. 2, 4, 27–29, 30, 48, 57, 58–59, 61–62, 65.

98. Thomas Danson, *A Friendly Conference between a Paulist and a Galatian, in defence of the Apostolic Doctrine of Justification of Faith without works* (1694); *Vindiciae Veritatis, or an Impartial Account of two late Disputations between Mr. Danson and Mr. Jeremiah Ives, Upon the question, viz. Whether the Doctrine of some true Believers, final Apostacy, be true or not?* (1672); Κλητοὶ Τετηρημένοι, *or the Saints Perseverance asserted and vindicated* (1672).

99. Richard L. Greaves, "John Bunyan and the Authorship of 'Reprobation Asserted,'" pp. 126–31; but see Paul Helm, "John Bunyan and 'Reprobation Asserted,'" pp. 87–93.

100. *Reprobation Asserted*, p. 26.

101. Theophilus Gale, *The True Idea of Jansenisme, Both Historick and Dogmatick*, p. 97, passim.

102. Theophilus Gale, *The Court of the Gentiles*, pt. 1, sig. *2, passim.

103. Ibid., pt. 1, sig. [*4].

104. Ibid., pt. 2, sig. a2.

105. Ibid., pt. 3, sigs. A3–4; for Gale as educator, see J. W. Ashley Smith, *The Birth of Modern Education*, pp. 41–46.

106. Howe, *Works*, pp. 117–18, 115, 123.

107. Gale, *Court of the Gentiles*, pt. 4, bk. 3, sig. A2ᵛ, pp. 143, 149; bk 2, pp. 522–23.

108. Howe, *Works*, p. 128.

109. John Troughton, *Lutherus Redivivus: Or the Protestant Doctrine of Justification by Faith Onely, Vindicated. And a Plausible Opinion of Justification by Faith and Obedience proved to be Arminian, Popish, and to lead Unavoidably unto Socinianism* (1677). Baxter complained of unfair criticism from Troughton in 1690 (Matthews, *Calamy Revised*, p. 494). John Troughton, *A Letter to a Friend, touching Gods providence about sinful actions. In answer to a letter entituled, The reconcilableness of Gods prescience, etc. and to the postscript of that letter* (1678).

110. Thomas Danson, *De Causa Dei*, p. 121.

111. Ibid., sigs. A2ʳ, A4ᵛ, A3ᵛ, pp. 44, 104–5, 110, 122.

112. Richard Baxter, *How Far Holiness is the Design of Christianity* (1671).

113. C. E. Whiting, *Studies in English Puritanism from the Restoration to the Revolution, 1660–1688*, p. 500.

114. Edmund Calamy, the younger, *An Abridgement of Mr. Baxter's History of His Life and Times, with an Account of the Ministers, etc. who Were Ejected or Silenced after the Restoration of King Charles II* 1:335.

115. Richard Baxter, *An Appeale to the Light, or, Richard Baxter's Account of Four Accused Passages of a Sermon*, pp. 1–5.

116. Thomas Tully, *A Letter to Mr. Richard Baxter*, pp. 4, 5, 14, 17.

117. Richard Baxter, *Catholick Theologie*, preface.

118. J. Hay Colligan, "The Antinomian Controversy"; Olive M. Griffiths, *Religion and Learning*, pp. 95–105; Peter Toon, *The Emergence of Hyper-Calvinism in English Nonconformity, 1689–1765*, pp. 49–66.

119. Toon, *Hyper-Calvinism*, pp. 49–50.

120. Among them were John Howe (Bolam et al., *English Presbyterians*, p. 108); and T. Beverley, *A Conciliatory Judgment concerning Dr. Crisp's Sermons, and Mr. Baxter's Dissatisfactions in Them*, p. 3, who both honored Crisp's memory and termed Baxter an "excellent" minister, comparing them together to Paul and James (p. 10); see also Toon, *Hyper-Calvinism*, p. 53.

121. Toon, *Hyper-Calvinism*, p. 53; Colligan, "Antinomian Controversy," p. 395.

122. Toon, *Hyper-Calvinism*, p. 53.

123. E.g., by the Presbyterian penchant for Arianism, see Griffiths, *Religion and Learning*, pp. 106–50; J. Hay Colligan, *The Arian Movement in England*; Roger Thomas, "The Non-Subscription Controversy amongst Dissenters in 1719"; Duncan Coomer, *English Dissent under the Early Hanoverians*, pp. 63–78.

124. See Toon, *Hyper-Calvinism*, passim.

125. Most discussion of Restoration Dissent concentrates on issues of toleration and comprehension and life under persecution; but Gerald R. Cragg, *Puritanism in the Period of the Great Persecution, 1660–1688*, pp. 128–55, has a fine general description of Dissenting piety; C. John Sommerville, *Popular Religion in Restoration England*, has attempted a quantitative analysis of Restoration works of devotion; see also Gordon S. Wakefield, *Puritan Devotion*, and Horton Davies, *Worship and Theology in England from Andrewes to Baxter and Fox, 1603–1690*, chapter 3.

126. Trinterud, "A.D. 1689," p. 41.

127. Isaac Barrow, *The Works of Isaac Barrow, D.D.*, 2:137–49.

128. Jeremy Taylor, *The Whole Works of the Right Rev. Jeremy Taylor*, 4:333–35, 348, 351.

129. Irene Simon, ed., *Three Restoration Divines, Barrow, South, Tillotson*, 2:543, 591–92, 593.

130. J. Sears McGee, *The Godly Man in Stuart England*, pp. 107–10, 113.
131. Simon, ed., *Three Restoration Divines*, 1:401, 404, 407, 411–12, 420–22, 429–30.
132. Davies, *Worship and Theology*, p. 115; George Bull, *The Works of George Bull*, pp. 346, 351–52, 357–58, 366; cf. also pp. 7–9.
133. Barrow, *Works*, 1:1–31.
134. Ibid., p. 8; McGee calls attention to the frequency and importance of this theme in Anglican thought (*Godly Man*, pp. 100, 106, 146, 151, 169).
135. William Twisse, *The Riches of Gods Love*, pp. 4, 36, 130, 236, 256.
136. Thomas Goodwin, *A Discourse of Election*, pp. 5, 9–10.
137. See Greaves, *John Bunyan*, p. 11.
138. *Reprobation Asserted*, e.g., p. 22.
139. Thomas Goodwin, *The Work of the Holy Spirit in Our Regeneration*; William Clagett, *A Discourse concerning the Operations of the Holy Spirit*; Samuel Petto, *The Voice of the Spirit, or an Essay towards a Discoverie of the Witnessings of the Spirit* (1654); according to G. F. Nuttall, *The Holy Spirit in Puritan Faith and Experience*, p. 14, the sermons of Richard Sibbes were important in directing Puritan attention to the Holy Spirit.
140. John Owen, *A Practical Exposition upon Psalm CXXX; Wherein the Nature of the Forgiveness of Sin is Declared* (1668); *The Nature, Power, Deceit, and Prevalency of the Remainders of Indwelling Sin in Believers* (1668); *The Grace and Duty of Being Spiritually Minded* (1681); *A Treatise of the Dominion of Sin and Grace* (1688).
141. Owen, *Works*, 6:157–60, 208–9, 270f., 403, 547, 647.
142. Stephen Charnock, *The Works of the Late Learned Divine Stephen Charnock, B.D.*, 2:1–169, 180–81.
143. John Bunyan, *Grace Abounding*, pp. 73, 86.
144. John Bunyan, *The Pilgrim's Progress*, pp. 274–75, 387ff.
145. George Trosse, *The Life of the Reverend Mr. George Trosse, Written by Himself and Published Posthumously according to his Order in 1714*, pp. 72, 133; Trosse completed his account in 1693 and was a Presbyterian.
146. E.g., Bates, *Works*, 1:470.
147. E.g., *The Saints' Everlasting Rest* (1650); *A Call to the Unconverted* (1658); *The Divine Life* (1664).
148. Howe, *Works*, p. 883; Bates, *Works*, 4:159.
149. For an account of Flavel's activities, see Edward Windeatt, "Devonshire and the Indulgence of 1672"; pp. 161–68 deal mainly with Flavel.
150. *The Whole Works of the Reverend Mr. John Flavel, Late Minister of the Gospel at Dartmouth in Devon*, 1:473; 4:333–47.
151. Ibid., 2:106, 110ff., 163ff., 227ff., 440ff., 458ff., 483ff.
152. Ibid., 4:409; 3:18ff. Bunyan had argued against Fowler that Christ did not set himself up for an example but that his life was principally a "legal obedience" fulfilled for sinners (Bunyan, *Defence of Justification*, pp. 264–65).
153. Richard Alleine, Χειροθεσία Τοῦ Πρεσβυτεροῦ, *or a Letter to a Friend; tending to prove, . . . That Ordination by Presbyters is Valid*, sig. A3.
154. Richard Alleine, *Vindiciae Pietatis*, pp. 6, 151.
155. Richard Alleine, *Instructions about heart-work*, Annesley's preface.
156. William Alleine, *Several Discourses on the unsearchable Riches of Christ*.
157. William Alleine, *The Mystery of the Temple and City Described*, pp. 56–57. Wing STC mistakenly attributed this to William Allen, vicar of Bridgewater, but Calamy the younger (*An Abridgement*, 2:263) says that Alleine wrote on the millennium, and many parallels of tone and specific ideas between this and William Alleine's *Several Discourses* prove it to be his work.
158. Alleine, *Life and Death of Joseph Alleine*, p. 57.
159. One early form of the Alarm appeared as *A Sure Guide to Heaven; or An Earnest Invitation to Sinners to turn to God*; also from Alleine there was *Remaines of that Excellent Minister of Jesus Christ, Mr. Joseph Alleine . . . All tending to promote Real Piety*.

160. One of the discourses in the *Remaines* was entitled "A Serious Call to Christians to win Souls to Christ"; see also Alleine, *Life and Death of Joseph Alleine*, pp. 48–49, 50, 63, and passim.

161. A good book on the subject, Norman Sykes, *Church and State in England in the Eighteenth Century*, pp. 412–14, 419–22, considers the complacency of the English church in that period to be often overstated.

162. The older book by John H. Overton, *The Evangelical Revival in the Eighteenth Century*, pp. 44–45, recognized the Puritan views of the atonement and Holy Spirit in evangelicalism; William R. Cannon, *The Theology of John Wesley*, pp. 68, 77–78, saw Wesley's theological discovery as that of grace alone; Robert C. Monk, *John Wesley's Puritan Heritage*, traced the influence of the Puritans on Wesley; Bernard Semmel, *The Methodist Revolution*, on the other hand, has interpreted Wesley as more on the side of rationalistic moralism and the perennial Anglican fear of Antinomian disorder.

163. Stuart C. Henry, *George Whitefield*, pp. 107, 135.

Conclusion

1. Peter Berger, *A Rumor of Angels*, pp. 42–43.
2. Carl L. Becker, *The Heavenly City of the Eighteenth-Century Philosophers*, p. 5.
3. Christopher Hill, *Milton and the English Revolution*, p. 270; Christopher Hill, *The World Turned Upside Down*, p. 276; see also Christopher Hill, *Society and Puritanism in Pre-Revolutionary England*, pp. 509–10.
4. Carolly Erickson, *The Medieval Vision*, pp. 3–28. See also Marc Bloch, *Feudal Society*, 1:82–83.
5. Keith Thomas, *Religion and the Decline of Magic*, pp. 79, 111.
6. Steven E. Ozment, *The Reformation in the Cities*, pp. 42–46, 164–66.
7. Jean Delumeau, *Catholicism between Luther and Voltaire*, pp. 8–9, 161.
8. Preserved Smith, *The Social Background of the Reformation*, p. 262.
9. Alfred North Whitehead, *Religion in the Making*, p. 58.
10. Sheldon Shapiro, "Quelques réflexions sur la signification psychologique de la prédestination dans la Réforme," p. 826 (my translation).
11. William James, *The Varieties of Religious Experience*, p. 260.
12. Rudolf Otto, *The Idea of the Holy*, p. 88.
13. Ibid., p. 89.
14. Oscar Wilde, *The Picture of Dorian Gray*, p. 210.
15. Quoted in C. F. Allison, *The Rise of Moralism*, p. 94.
16. Nicholas Berdyaev, *Truth and Revelation*, p. 121.
17. Delumeau, *Catholicism between Luther and Voltaire*, p. 126; Carl Bridenbaugh, *Vexed and Troubled Englishmen, 1590–1642*, p. 276; for one aspect of this, see Henry G. Van Leeuwen, *The Problem of Certainty in English Thought, 1630–1690*.
18. Predestination has been discussed in something like this light in B. A. Gerrish, *Tradition and the Modern World*, pp. 99–150, esp. 138–40.

Appendix

1. Some have considered its importance exaggerated, e.g., John F. H. New, *Anglican and Puritan*, p. 93: "Covenant theology does not seem to loom so large in English Puritan thought as has been suggested."
2. Miller, "The Marrow of Puritan Divinity," pp. 73, 79, 82.

3. See also Richard L. Greaves, "John Bunyan and Covenant Thought in the Seventeenth Century," pp. 151–69.

4. A fine example of this can be found in Robert Harris, *A Treatise of the New Covenant*, pp. 479–595, where the covenant is related to grace, the divine initiative (pp. 484f., 504), regeneration by the Holy Spirit (pp. 515ff., 523–24) and assurance (p. 502).

5. John von Rohr, "Covenant and Assurance in Early English Puritanism," pp. 195–203.

Bibliography

Primary Sources

A., J. *An Historicall Narration of the Judgement of some most Learned and Godly English Bishops, Holy Martyrs, and Others . . . concerning God's Election.* London, 1631.

Abbot, Robert. *A Defence of the Reformed Catholicke of M. W. Perkins, lately-deceased, against the bastard Counter-Catholicke of D. Bishop, The First Part.* London, 1606.

————. *The Second Part of the Defence of the Reformed Catholicke.* London, 1607.

Ainsworth, Henry. *A Seasonable Discourse, or, A Censure upon a Dialogue of the Anabaptists intituled, A Description of what God hath Predestinated concerning man.* 1623. Reprint, London, 1644.

Airay, Henry. *Lectures upon . . . Phillipians.* London, 1618.

Alleine, Joseph. *Remaines of that Excellent Minister of Jesus Christ, Mr. Joseph Alleine . . . All Tending to promote Real Piety.* London, 1674.

————. *A Sure Guide to Heaven: Or An Earnest Invitation to Sinners to turn to God.* London, 1691.

Alleine, Richard. *The Godly Mans Portion and Sanctuary: Being a Second Part of Vindiciae Pietatis.* London, 1663.

————. *Heaven Opened: Or, a Brief and plaine Discovery of the Riches of Gods Covenant of Grace.* London, 1665.

————. *Instructions about heart-work . . . that we may live in the Exercise and Growth of Grace here, and have a comfortable Assurance of Glory to Eternity.* 2d ed. London, 1684.

————. *Vindiciae Pietatis: Or, A Vindication of Godlinesse, In the greatest Strictness and Spirituality of it, from the Imputations of Folly and Fancy.* London, 1676.

————. *Χειροθεσία Τοῦ Πρεσβυτερού, or a Letter to a Friend; tending to prove . . . that Ordination by Presbyters is valid.* London, 1661.

Alleine, Theodosia. *The Life and Death of that Excellent Minister of Christ Mr. Joseph Allein.* London, 1677.

Alleine, William. *The Mystery of the Temple and City Described.* London, 1697.

————. *Several Discourses on the unsearchable Riches of Christ.* Bristol, 1697.

Allen, Robert. *The Doctrine of the Gospel.* London 1606.

Alsop, Vincent. *Antisozzo; or Sherlocismus Enervatus.* London, 1675.

————. *Melius Inquirendum . . . St. Augustine, the Synod of Dort, and the articles of the Church of England, in the Quinquarticular points, vindicated.* London, 1678.

Ames, William. *The Marrow of Theology.* Edited and translated by John D. Eusden. Boston: Pilgrim Press, 1968.

Anderson, Anthony. *A Sermon of Sure Comfort.* London, 1581.

Andrewes, Bartimaeus. *Certaine verie worthie, godly and profitable Sermons, upon the fifth Chapter of the Songs of Solomon.* London, 1583.

Andrewes, Lancelot. *A Pattern of Catechistical Doctrine, and Other Minor Works.* In *Works,* vol. 6. Oxford: J. H. Parker, 1846.

Anwick, I. *Meditations upon Gods Monarchie, and the Devill his kingdome.* London, 1587.

Articuli Lambethani. London, 1651.

Ahswood, Bartholomew. *The Best Treasure: Or the Way to be Made Truly Rich.* London, 1681.

Attersoll, William. *A Commentarie upon the Epistle of Saint Paul to Philemon.* London, 1612.

————. *A Commentarie upon the Fourth Booke of Moses, Called Numbers.* London, 1618.

Babington, Gervase. *A Sermon Preached at Paules Crosse.* London, 1591.

————. *The Works of the Right Reverend Father in God Gervase Babington*. London, 1615.

Baillie, Robert. *An Antidote against Arminianism*. London? 1641.

————. *A Dissuasive from the Errours of the Time*. London, 1645.

————. *Laudensium Autokatakrisis: The Canterburians Self Conviction*. N.p., 1641.

————. *The Letters and Journals of Robert Baillie*. Edited by David Laing. 3 vols. Edinburgh: Robert Ogle, 1841–42.

————. *Scotch Antidote against the English Infection of Arminianism*. London, 1652.

Benbridge [Bainbridge], John. *Christ Above All Exalted*. London, 1645.

[Bakewell, Thomas.] *The Antinomians Christ Confounded, and the Lords Christ Exalted*. London, 1644.

Balcanqual, Walter. *A Joynt Attestation, Avowing that the Discipline of the Church of England was not impeached by the Synod of Dort*. London, 1626.

————. *The Image of bothe churches*. London, 1548.

Ball, John. *A Short Treatise Contayning All the Principall Grounds of Christian Religion*. London, 1635.

————. *A Treatise of the Covenant of Grace*. London, 1645.

————. *A Treatise on Faith*. London, 1631.

Barlee, William. *A Necessary Vindication of the Doctrine of Predestination, Formerly Asserted*. London, 1658.

————. *Praedestination, as before privately, so now at last openly defended against Post-destination. In Correpterie Correction, given in by way of answer to A (so called) correct copy of some notes concerning Gods Decrees, Especially of Reprobation; published the last summer, by Mr. T. P.*. London, 1656.

Barlow, William. *An Answer to a Catholike English-man*. London, 1609.

————. *A Defence of the Articles of the Protestants Religion*. London, 1601.

————. "The Summe and Substance of the Conference held at Hampton Court." In *A History of Conferences connected with the Revision of the Book of Common Prayer*, edited by Edward Cardwell. Oxford: The University Press, 1849.

Barnes, Robert. *A supplicacion unto the most gloryous prynce Henry the viii*. London, 1534.

Barnes, Thomas. *The Gales of Grace: Or the Spirituall Winde: Wherein the Mysterie of Sanctification is Opened and Handled*. London, 1622.

Barrow, Isaac. *The Works of Isaac Barrow, D.D.* 3 vols. New York, 1845.

Bastwick, John. *Elenchus Religionis Papisticae. In quo probatur: Neque Apostolicam, Neque Catholicam*. London, 1627.

Bates, William. *The Whole Works*. Edited by W. Farmer. 4 vols. London, 1815.

Baynes, Paul. *A Commentarie upon the First Chapter of the Epistle of Saint Paul, Written to the Ephesians*. London, 1618.

————. *The Mirrour or Miracle of Gods Love unto the world of his Elect*. London, 1619.

Baxter, Richard. *Admonition to Mr. William Eyre*. London, 1654.

————. *Aphorisms of Justification*. London, 1649.

————. *Apology against the Modest Exceptions of Mr. T. Blake. And the Digression of Mr. G. Kendall*. London, 1654.

————. *An Appeale to the Light, or, Richard Baxter's Account of Four Accused Passages of a Sermon*. London, 1674.

————. *Catholick Theologie: Plain, Pure, Peaceable: For Pacification of the Dogmatical Word-Warriours*. London, 1675.

————. *Confession of His Faith*. London, 1655.

————. *Confutation of a Dissertation . . . Written by . . . Colvinus*. London, 1654.

————. *The Grotian Religion Discovered, At the Invitation of Mr. Thomas Pierce in His Vindication. With a Preface, vindicating the Synod of Dort from calumnies of the New Tilenus*. London, 1658.

————. *The Reduction of a Digressor, or Rich. Baxter's Reply to Mr. George Kendall's Digression*. London, 1654.

_____. *Reliquae Baxterianae*. Edited by Matthew Sylvester. London, 1696.

_____. *An Unsavoury Volume of Mr. Jo Crandon's Anatomized*. London, 1654.

Becon, Thomas. *The Works of Thomas Becon*. Edited by John Ayre. 3 vols. Parker Society, vols. 2–4. Cambridge: At the University Press, 1842–44.

Bell, Thomas. *The Catholique Triumph*. London, 1610.

_____. *The Downfall of Popery*. London, 1605.

_____. *The Survey of Popery*. London, 1596.

Bernard, Richard. *Rhemes against Rome*. London, 1626.

[Bertius, Peter.] *The Life and Death of James Arminius, and Simon Episcopius . . . Both of them Famous Defenders of the Doctrine of Gods Universal Grace and Sufferers for it*. London, 1672.

Beverley, T. *A Conciliatory Judgment concerning Dr. Crisp's Sermons, and Mr. Baxter's Dissatisfactions in Them*. London, 1690.

Beza, Theodore. *A Briefe declaration of the Chiefe Poynts of Christian Religion*. London, 1575?

_____. *The Treasure of Trueth, touching the grounde worke of man his salvation*. London, 1576.

Bilson, Thomas. *The Survey of Christs Sufferings*. London, 1604.

[Bowle, John.] *A Sermon Preached at Mapple-Durham in Oxfordshire*. London, 1616.

Bradford, John. *The Writings of John Bradford*. Edited by Aubrey Townsend. 2 vols. Parker Society, vols. 5, 6. Cambridge: At the University Press, 1848, 1853.

Bradwardine, Thomas. *Thomae Bradwardini Archiepiscopi Olim Cantuariensis, De Causa Dei, Contra Pelagium, et de Virtute Causarum, Ad Suos Mertonenses, Libri Tres*. London, 1618.

Bramhall, John. *Castigations of Mr. Hobbes His Last Animadversions in the case concerning Liberty, and Universal Necessity*. London, 1658.

_____. *The catching of Leviathan, or the Great Whale. Demonstrating, out of Mr. Hobs his own Works, that no man who is thoroughly an Hobbist, can be a good Christian, or a good Common-Wealths man . . . Because his Principles are not only destructive to all Religion, but to all Societies*. London, 1658.

_____. *A Just Vindication of himself and Episcopal Clergy, from the Presbyterian Charge of Popery*. London, 1672.

Bredwell, Stephen. *Detection of Ed. Glovers hereticall confection, lately contrived and proffered to the Church of England, under the name of a present Preservative*. London, 1586.

Bridge, William. *The Freeness of the Grace and Love of God to Believers*. London, 1671.

Brooke, Lord Robert. *A Discourse Opening the Nature of that Episcopacie, which is exercised in England*. London, 1642.

Brooks, Thomas. *A Golden Key to Open Hidden Treasures*. London, 1675.

_____. *Heaven on Earth: Or a Serious Discourse touching a wel-grounded Assurance*. London, 1654.

"The Brownists' Paternoster." *Congregational Historical Society Transactions* 5 (1911):34–39.

Bull, George. *Examen Censurae; or An Answer to Certain Strictures . . . on a Book Entitled Harmonia Apostolica . . . To which is Added an Apology for the Harmony and its Author, In Answer to the Declamation of T. Tully*. 1675. Reprint, Oxford: J. H. Parker, 1844.

_____. *Harmonia Apostolica: Or Two Dissertations; in the former of which the Doctrine of St. James on Justification by Works is explained and Defended; in the latter, The Agreement of St. Paul with St. James is clearly Shewn*. 1669–70. Reprint, Oxford: J. H. Parker, 1844.

_____. *The Works of George Bull*. Edited by Edward Burton, Vol. 1. Oxford: University Press, 1846.

Bullinger, Heinrich. *Commonplaces of Christian Religion*. London, 1572.

˜unny, Edmund. *The Whole Sum of Christian Religion*. London, 1576.

Bunyan, John. *A Defence of the Doctrine of Justification by Faith in Jesus Christ*. In *The Works of John Bunyan*, edited by Henry Stebbing, 4:220–69. New York: Johnson Reprint, 1970.
———. *The Doctrine of the Law and Grace Unfolded and I Will Pray with the Spirit*. Edited by Richard Greaves. Oxford: Clarendon Press, 1976.
———. *Grace Abounding*. New York: Dutton, 1976.
———. *The Pilgrim's Progress*. Edited by Roger Sharrock. Baltimore: Penguin Books, 1965.
Burges, Cornelius. *The First Sermon, Preached to the Honourable House of Commons Now Assembled in Parliament at their Publique Fast, Novemb. 17, 1640*. London, 1641.
Burgess, Anthony. *The True Doctrine of Justification Asserted, and Vindicated, from the Errors of Papists, Arminians, Socinians, and more especially Antinomians*. London, 1648.
Burnet, Gilbert. *Burnet's History of His Own Time*. Edited by Osmund Airy. 2 vols. Oxford: Clarendon Press, 1897.
———. *A Supplement to Burnet's History*. Edited by H. Foxcroft. Oxford: Clarendon Press, 1902.
Burton, Henry. *A Plea to an Appeale*. London, 1626.
———. *Truth's Triumph over Trent: The unreconcilable opposition betweene the Apostolicke Church of Christ, and the Apostate Synagogue of Antichrist, in the maine and fundamentall Doctrine of Justification*. London, 1629.
Burton, William. *Davids Evidence*. N.p., 1592.
———. *Davids Thankes-giving*. London, 1602.
Byfield, Nicholas. *An Exposition upon . . . Collossians*. London, 1615.
Calamy, Edmund. *Englands Looking-Glasse, Presented in a Sermon Preached before the Honourable House of Commons . . . December 22, 1641*. London, 1642.
———. *Gods Free Mercy to England. In a Sermon Preached before the Honourable House of Commons, Feb. 23, 1641*. London, 1642.
Calamy, Edmund, the Younger. *An Abridgement of Mr. Baxter's History of His Life and Times, with an account of the Ministers, etc., who were Ejected or Silenced after the Restoration of King Charles II*. 2 vols. London, 1713.
Calendar of State Papers Domestic.
Calfhill, James. *An Answere to the Treatise of the Crosse*. Edited by Richard Gibbings. Parker Society, vol. 11. Cambridge: At the University Press, 1846.
Calvin, John. *Concerning the Eternal Predestination of God*. Translated by J. K. S. Reid. London: James Clarke, 1961.
———. *The Institutes of the Christian Religion*. Edited by John T. McNeill, translated by Ford Lewis Battles. 2 vols. Philadelphia: Westminster Press, 1970.
———. *Thirteene Sermons of Maister Iohn Calvine, Entreating of the Free Election of God in Iacob, and of reprobation in Esau*. London, 1579.
Carleton, George. *An Examination of those Things Wherein the Author of the late Appeale holdeth the Doctrines of the Pelagians and Arminians to be the Doctrines of the Church of England*. London, 1626.
Carlson, Leland H., ed. *The Writings of Henry Barrow, 1587–1590*. London: George Allen & Unwin, 1962.
———. *The Writings of John Greenwood*. London: George Allen & Unwin, 1962.
Carter, Oliver. *An Answere made by Oliver Carter, Bachelor of Divinitie: unto Certaine Popish Questions and Demaundes*. London, 1579.
Cartwright, Thomas. *A Confutation of the Rhemists Translation*. N.p., 1618.
Cavendish, Richard. *The Image of Nature and Grace*. London, 1574.
Certaine Sermons or Homilies Appointed to be Read in Churches in the Time of Queen Elizabeth I: A Facsimile Reproduction of the Edition of 1623. Scholars Facsimiles and Reprints, 1969.
Certayne Sermons, or homilies, appoynted by the kynges Maiestie, to be declared and

redde, by all Persones, Vycars, or Curates, every Sonday in their Churches, where they have Cure. London, 1547.

Chaderton, Laurence. *An Excellent and godly Sermon.* London, 1578.

Champneys, John. *The Harvest is at Hand.* London, 1548.

Charnock, Stephen. *The Works of the Late Learned Divine Stephen Charnock, B.D.* 2 vols. 2d ed. London, 1699.

Cheynell, Francis. *Chillingworthi Novissima: Or, the Sicknesse, Heresy, Death, and Buriall of William Chillingworth.* London, 1644.

———. *A Copy of Some Papers Past at Oxford, Betwixt the Author of the Practicall Catechisms, and Mr. Ch.* London, 1647.

———. *The Rise, Growthe, and Danger of Socinianisme.* London, 1643.

Choune, Edward. *A Whip for the Lecturers of Lewis, and for all those Presbyterians, and others of the Clergy which maintain that damnable Opinion of absolute Reprobation.* London, 1657.

Clagett, William. *A Discourse concerning the Operations of the Holy Spirit.* London, 1680.

Clapham, Henoch. *A Manuell of the Bibles doctrine.* London, 1606.

Clarke, Samuel. *The Lives of Two and Twenty English Divines.* London, 1660.

Clarkson, David. *A Discourse of the Saving Grace of God.* London, 1688.

Cole, Nathaniel. *The Godly Mans Assurance; or a Christians certaine Resolution of his Owne Salvation.* London, 1633.

Coles, Elisha. *A Practical Discourse of God's Sovereignty.* 1678. Reprint, London, 1685.

The Collegiate Suffrage of the Divines of Great Britaine, concerning the Five Articles controverted in the Low Countries. Which Suffrage was by them delivered in the Synod of Dort, March 6, Anno 1619. London, 1629.

Cooper, Thomas. *Certaine Sermons wherein is contained the Defense of the Gospell nowe preached against such cavils and false accusations, as are objected . . . by the friends and favourers of the Church of Rome.* London, 1580.

———. *A Familiar Treatise, laying downe cases of conscience, furthering to Perseverance in sanctification.* London, 1615.

Corro, Antonio de. *A Theological Dialogue. Wherin the Epistle of S. Paul the Apostle to the Romanes is expounded.* London, 1575.

Cosin, John. *A Collection of Private Devotions.* London, 1627.

———. *The Correspondence of John Cosin, D.D.* Surtees Society, vol. 52. London: Blackwood & Sons, 1869.

———. "The Sum and Substance of the Conferences Lately Had at York House Concerning Mr. Montague's Books." In *The Works of John Cosin,* 2:17–81. The Library of Anglo-Catholic Theology. Oxford: J. H. Parker, 1845.

Coverdale, Miles. *A Confutacion of that treatise which one Iohn Standish made agaynst the protestacion of D. Barnes in the yeare 1540.* Zurich, 1541.

Cowper, William. *Three Heavenly Treatises upon the Eight Chapter to the Romanes . . . wherein the Counsaile of God Concerning Mans Salvation is so Manifested.* London, 1609.

Cragg, Gerald R., ed. *The Cambridge Platonists.* New York: Oxford University Press, 1968.

Crakanthorpe, Richard. *A Sermon of Predestination, Preached at Saint Maries in Oxford.* London, 1620.

———. *A Sermon of Sanctification.* London, 1608.

Crandon, John. *Mr. Baxter's Aphorisms Exorized and Anthorized.* London, 1654.

Cranmer, Thomas. *Miscellaneous Writings and Letters of Thomas Cranmer.* Edited by John E. Cox. Parker Society, vol. 16. Cambridge: At the University Press, 1846.

Crompton, William. *Saint Austins Religion: Wherein is Manifestly Proved out of the Works of that Learned Father that he dissented from Poperie and agreed with the Religion of the Protestants contrary to that Impudent, Erroneous, and Slanderous Position of the Bragging Papists of Our Times.* London, 1625.

Cromwell, Oliver. *The Writings and Speeches of Oliver Cromwell.* Edited by W. C. Abbott. 4 vols. Cambridge, Mass.: Harvard University Press, 1937.

Crooke, Samuel. *The Guide unto True Blessednesse: Or, a Body of the Doctrine of the Scriptures.* London, 1613.

Crowley, Robert. *An Apologie, or Defence, of those Englishe Writers & Preachers which Cerberus the Three Headed Dog of Hell, chargeth wyth false doctrine, under the name of Predestination.* London, 1566.

_____. *The Confutation of XIII Articles, whereunto Nicholas Shaxton, late byshop of Salisburye subscribed and caused to be set forth in print the yere of our Lord mcxlvi, when he recanted in Smithfielde at London at the burning of mestres Anne Askue.* London, 1548.

Culverwell, Ezekiel. *A Briefe Answere to Certaine Objections against the Treatise of Faith.* London, 1626.

_____. *A Treatise of Faith.* 1623. Reprint London, 1633.

Curteys, Richard. *Two Sermons Preached by the reverend father in God the Bishop of Chichester.* London, 1576.

D., A. *A Reply Made unto Mr. Anthony Wotton and Mr. John White Ministers.* N.p., 1612.

Danson, Thomas. *De Causa Dei: Or a Vindication of the Common Doctrine of Protestant Divines, concerning Predetermination from the Invidious Consequences with which it is burdened by Mr. John Howe, in a late Letter and Postscript, of God's Prescience.* London, 1678.

Davenant, John. *Animadversions . . . upon a Treatise intitled Gods Love to Mankind.* Cambridge, 1641.

Davenport, John. *Letters of John Davenport.* Edited by Isabel M. Calder. New Haven: Yale University Press, 1937.

Dell, William. *Several Sermons and Discourses.* London, 1652.

Denne, Henry. *Antichrist Unmasked in Three Treatises . . . The Drag-net of the Kingdom of Heaven.* London, 1646.

Dent, Arthur. *The Opening of Heaven gates: Or the Ready way to everlasting life.* 2d edition. London, 1611.

_____. *The Plaine Mans Path-way to Heaven.* London, 1601.

Dering, Edward. *M. Derings Workes.* London, 1597.

_____. *Two Godly Sermons.* London, 1590.

[Dering, Edward, and More, John.] *A Briefe and necessarie Catechisme or Instruction, very needfull to be known of all Householders.* London, 1597.

Dixon, Robert. *The Doctrine of Faith, Justification, and Assurance.* London, 1668.

Dod, John. *Seven Godlie and Fruitfull Sermons.* London, 1614.

Donne, John. *The Sermons of John Donne.* Edited by George R. Potter and Evelyn M. Simpson. 10 vols. Berkeley: University of California Press, 1957.

Doughty, John. *A Discourse concerning the Abstruseness of Divine Mysteries.* Oxford, 1628.

Downame, George. *The Covenant of Grace. Or An Exposition Upon Luke 1.* Dublin, 1631.

_____. *A Treatise of Justification.* London, 1633.

Downame, John. *The Christian Warfare.* London, 1604.

_____. *The Summe of Sacred Divinitie Briefly & Methodically Propounded.* London, 1630.

_____. *A Treatise of Securitie.* London, 1622.

Downe, John. *A Treatise of the True Nature and Definition of Justifying Faith.* London, 1635.

Duke, Francis. *The Fulnesse and Freenesse of Gods Grace in Jesus Christ.* London, 1642.

Du Moulin, Pierre. *The Anatomy of Arminianisme.* London, 1620.

Durham, James. *The Law Unsealed.* Glasgow, 1677.

Eaton, John. *The Honey-Combe of Free Justification by Christ alone.* London, 1642.

Edwards, Thomas. *The First and Second Part of Gangraena.* London, 1646.

Eedes, John. *The Orthodox Doctrine concerning Justification by Faith Asserted and Vindicated.* London, 1654.

Eikon Basilike. Edited by Philip A. Knachel. Ithaca: Cornell University Press, 1966.

Eliot, Sir John. *Sir Iohn Eliot His Grave and learned Speech Spoken in the High Court of Parliament Desiring an orderlie Proceeding in Eikon Basilike.* Edited by Philip A. Knachel. Ithaca: Cornell University Press, 1966. ·

Evans, Lewys. *The Castle of Christianitie, detecting the long erring estate as well of the Romaine Church, as of the Byshop of Rome.* London, 1568.

Eyre, William. *Justification without Conditions.* 1653. Reprint, London, 1695.

Featley, Daniel. *Pelagius Redivivus. Or Pelagius Raked Out of the Ashes by Arminius and His Schollers.* London, 1626.

Fenner, Dudley. *Sacra Theologia, sive Veritas quae est secundum Pietatem.* Geneva, 1586.

Ferguson, Robert. *The Interest of Reason in Religion.* London, 1675.

———. *A Sober Enquiry into the Nature, Measure, and Principle of Moral Virtue.* London, 1673.

Fish, Simon, trans. *The Summe of the holye scrypture and ordynary of the Christen teaching.* Antwerp? 1535.

Flavel, John. *The Whole Works of the Reverend Mr. John Flavel, Late Minister of the Gospel at Dartmouth in Devon.* 8 vols. Paisley, 1770.

Forbes, John. *A Treatise Tending to Cleare the Doctrine of Justification.* Middleburgh, 1616.

Fowler, Edward. *The Design of Christianity.* London, 1676.

———. *Dirt Wipt Off: Or a Manifest Discovery of the Gross Ignorance, Erroneousness and most Unchristian and Wicked Spirit of One John Bunyan.* London, 1672.

Fox, George. *The Journal of George Fox.* Edited by Rufus M. Jones. New York: Capricorn Books, 1963.

Foxe, John. *The Second Volume of the Ecclesiastical history, conteynyng the Actes and Monuments of Martyrs.* London, 1570.

———. *De Christo gratis justificante.* London, 1583.

———. *Of Free Justification by Christ.* A translation from the Latin. London, 1694.

Frere, Walter H., and Douglas, Charles E., eds. *Puritan Manifestoes.* London: Church Historical Society, 1952.

Frith, John. *The Whole Workes.* In *The Whole Works of W. Tyndall, Iohn Frith and Doct. Barnes, Three Worthy Martyrs, and Principal Teachers of this churche of England collected and compiled in one Tome together.* London, 1573.

Fulke, William. *A Comfortable Sermon of Faith, in Temptations and Afflictions.* London, 1574.

———. *A Defence of the Sincere and True Translations of the Holy Scriptures into the English Tongue, against the Cavils of Gregory Martin.* Edited by C. H. Hartshorne. Parker Society, vol. 17. Cambridge: At the University Press, 1843.

Fuller, Thomas. *Church History of Britain.* Edited by J. Nichols. 3 vols. London: Thomas Tegg, 1842.

Gale, Theophilus. *The Court of the Gentiles.* Oxford, 1672.

———. *The True Idea of Jansenisme, Both Historick and Dogmatick.* London, 1669.

Gardiner, Samuel. *A Dialogue or Conference . . . about the rites and ceremonies of the Church of England.* London, 1605.

———. *The Foundation of the Faythfull, In a Sermon delivered at Paules Crosse.* London, 1611.

Gardiner, Stephen. *A Declaration of such articles as George Ioye hath gone about to confute as false.* London, 1546.

Gataker, Charles. *The Way of Truth and Peace: Or, A Reconciliation of the holy Apostles, S. Paul and S. James, concerning Justification,* added to Thomas Gataker, *An Antidote against Errour, concerning Justification.* London, 1670.

Gataker, Thomas. *Jacobs Thankfulness to God for Gods Goodnesse to Jacob Wherein also the Popish Doctrine of Mans Merit is Discussed.* London, 1624.

———. *A Mistake, or Misconstruction Removed. (Whereby little difference is pretended to have been acknowledged between the Antinomians and Us.) And, Free Grace, As it is held forth in Gods Word . . . shewed to be other then is by the Antinomian party in these times maintained.* London, 1646.

Gauden, John. *The Love of Truth and Peace. A Sermon Preached before the Honourable House of Commons assembled in Parliament, Novemb. 29, 1640.* London, 1641.

Gee, Alexander. *The Ground of Christianity.* London, 1584.

The Geneva Bible: A Facsimile of the 1560 Edition. Madison: University of Wisconsin Press, 1969.

Gerardus, Andreas. *A Speciall Treatise of Gods Providence . . . Hereunto is added an appendix of certaine Sermons and Questions as they were uttered and disputed ad clerum in Cambridge.* N.p., 1588?

Geree, Stephen. *The Doctrine of the Antinomians by Evidence of Gods Truth plainely Confuted.* London, 1644.

Gibson, John. *An Easie Entrance into the Principall Points of Christian Religion, verie short and plaine for the simpler sorte.* London, 1579.

———. *The Sacred Shield of Al True Christian Souldiers.* London, 1599.

Gifford, George. *Certaine Sermons, upon Divers Textes of Holie Scripture.* London, 1597.

———. *Foure Sermons upon Severall Partes of Scripture.* London, 1598.

———. *A Godlie, zealous, and profitable Sermon upon the second Chapter of St. Iames.* London, 1582.

———. *A Sermon on the Parable of the Sower.* London, 1582.

———. *A Short Catechisme for Householders.* London, 1583.

———. *A Treatise of True Fortitude.* London, 1594.

Gilby, Anthony. *A Briefe Treatyse of Election and Reprobacion wythe certane answers to the objections of the adversaries of this doctryne.* Geneva?, 1556.

———. *A Commentarye upon the Prophet Mycha.* N.p., 1551.

Gillespie, Patrick. *The Ark of the Covenant Opened: Or, A Treatise of the Covenant of Redemption . . . The Second Part.* London, 1677.

Goodman, John. *A Serious and Compassionate Inquiry.* London, 1674.

Goodwin, John. ἀπολύτρωσις ἀπολυτρώσεως *or Redemption Redeemed.* London, 1651.

———. Εἰρηνόμαχια: *The Agreement and Distance of Brethren: Or a Brief Survey of the Judgment of Mr. J. G. and the Church of walking with him.* London, 1652.

———. *Impedit ira animum, or Animadversions upon Some of the Looser and Fouler Passages in a written Pamphlet.* N.p., 1641.

———. *Imputation Fidei. Or a Treatise of Justification.* London, 1642.

———. *Triumviri: Or, the Genius, Spirit, and Deportment of the Three Men, Mr. Richard Resbury, Mr. John Pawson, and Mr. George Kendall, in their late Writings against the Free Grace of God in the Redemption of the World.* London, 1658.

Goodwin, Thomas. *A Discourse of Election, of the Free and Special Grace of God Manifested Therein; the Absoluteness and Unchangeableness of His Decrees; And Their Infallible Accomplishment.* In *The Works of Thomas Goodwin, D.D.,* vol. 9, Edinburgh: James Nichol, 1864.

Gouge, Thomas. *The Surest and Safest Way of Thriving.* London, 1676.

Greenham, Richard. *The Works of the Reverend and Faithful Servant of Iesus Christ M. Richard Greenham.* London, 1612.

Guild, William. *An Antidote agaynst Poperie.* Aberdeen, 1639.

———. *A Compend of the Controversies of Religion.* Aberdeen, 1627.

Gunter, Peter. *A Sermon Preached in the Countie of Suffolke, before the Clergie and Laytie, for the discoverie and confutation of certain strange, pernicious, and Hereticall Positions, publikely delivered, held, and maintayned, touching Justification, by a certain factious Preacher of Wickham Market, in the said Countie, by which, divers, especially of the Vulgar, farre and neare, were greatly seduced.* London, 1615.

Haddon, Walter, and Foxe, John. *Against Jerome Osorius Byshopp of Silvane in Portingall and against his slaunderous Invectives: An Aunswere Apologeticall.* Translated by James Bell. London, 1581.

Hales, John. *Golden Remains of the Ever Memorable Mr. John Hales of Eton College.* London, 1659.

Hall, David D., ed. *The Antinomian Controversy, 1636–1638: A Documentary History.* Middletown: Wesleyan University Press, 1968.

Hall, Joseph. *The Works of the Right Reverend Joseph Hall.* Edited by Philip Wynter. 10 vols. Oxford: At the University Press, 1863.

Hammond, Henry. Χάρις καὶ εἰρήνη: *Or a Pacifick Discourse of Gods Grace and Decrees.* London, 1660.

────. *A Continuation of the Defence of Hugo Grotius.* London, 1657.

────. *A Practical Catechisme.* Oxford, 1646.

────. *A Second Defence of the Learned Hugo Grotius.* Oxford, 1655.

Harbie, Thomas. *Divi Arminij Mactatorum Renata, et Renovata Petitio. Or the Arminian Priests Last Petition for their former formalitie, and ancient Innovation, both in Church and Common-weale.* London, 1642.

Harding, Thomas. *A Confutation of a Book Intituled An Apologie of the Church of England.* Antwerp, 1565.

Harris, Robert. *Gods Goodnes and Mercy, Layd Open in a Sermon Preached at Pauls Crosse on the Last of June, 1622.* London, 1622.

────. *A Treatise of the New Covenant.* In *The Workes of Robert Harris.* London, 1635.

Harsnet, Adam. *A Touchstone of Grace, Discovering the differences betweene true and counterfeit Grace: Laying downe infallible Evidences and markes of true Grace.* London, 1630.

Helwys, Thomas. *A Short and Plaine proofe by the Word and Workes of God that Gods decree is not the cause of anye Mans sinne or condemnation.* N.p., 1611.

Heylyn, Peter. *Aerius Redivivus: Or, the History of the Presbyterians.* Oxford, 1670.

────. *Cyprianus Anglicus: Or the History of the Life and Death, of the Most Reverend and Renowned Prelate William by Divine Providence, Lord Archbishop of Canterbury.* London, 1671.

────. *Historia Quinqu-Articularis: Or a Declaration of the Judgement of the Western Churches, and more Particularly of the Church of England; in the Five Controverted Points, Reproached in these Last Times by the Name of Arminianism.* Reprinted in *The Historical and Miscellaneous Tracts of the Reverend and Learned Peter Heylyn D.D. Now Collected into one Volume.* London, 1681.

Hickeringill, Edmund. *Gregory, Father Greybeard.* London, 1673.

Hickman, Henry. *Historia Quinq-Articularis Exarticulata; or Animadversions on Dr. Heylin's Quinquarticular History.* N.p., 1673.

Πατρο-σχολαστικο-δικαιωσις, *or a Justification of the Fathers and Schoolmen, shewing that they are not Selfe-condemned for denying the Positivity of Sin.* Oxford, 1659.

────. *Plus Ultra: Or Englands Reformation, Needing to be Reformed.* London, 1661.

────. Πόθεν ζιζανια, *refutatio Tileni.* Oxford, 1659.

────. *A Review of the Certamen Epistolare betwixt Pet. Heylin D.D. and Hen. Hickman B.D. Wherein the exception of the Dr. against Mr. H's arguments are all taken off, and our first Reformers proved not to hold with the Arminians. Also a Reply to Mr. Pierce.* London, 1659.

────. *Speculum Sherlockianum: Or a Looking-glass in which Admirers of Mr. Sherlock may behold the Man, as to his Accuracy, Judgment, and Orthodoxy.* London, 1674.

Hieron, Samuel. *The Sermons of Master Samuel Hieron, Formerly Collected Together by Himselfe, and Published in His Life Time.* London, 1624.

────. *The Spirituall Sonne-ship: As It hath beene collected out of I Iohn 3.1.* London, 1611.

Hildersam, Arthur. *Lectures upon the Fourth of John.* London, 1629.

Hill, John. "The Diaries of John Hill." *Transactions and Collections of the American Antiquarian Society* 3 (1857):109–316.

Hill, Robert. *Life Everlasting: Or the True Knowledge of One Jehovah, Three Elohim, and Jesus Emmanuel: Collected out of the Best Modern Divines.* Cambridge, 1601.

His Majesties Declaration concerning His Proceedings with the States Generall of the United Provinces of the Low Countreys, in the Cause of D. Conradus Vorstius. London, 1612.

Hoard, Samuel. *Gods Love to Mankind. Manifested, By Dis-proving his Absolute Decree for their Damnation.* London, 1633.

Holland, Henry. *The Historie of Adam, or the foure-fold State of Man.* London, 1606.

Hooker, Richard. *A Learned and Comfortable Sermon of the certaintie and perpetuitie of faith in the Elect.* Oxford, 1612.

———. *A Learned Discourse of Justification, Works, and how the foundation of faith is overthrown.* Oxford, 1612.

———. *Of the Laws of Ecclesiastical Polity.* 2 vols. London: J. M. Dent, 1907.

———. *Works.* 2 vols. Oxford: Clarendon Press, 1890.

Hooper, John. *Writings of Hooper.* Edited by Samuel Carr and Charles Nevinson. 2 vols. Parker Society, vols. 20, 21. Cambridge: At the University Press, 1843, 1852.

Horne, John. *The Open Door for Mans Approach to God.* London, 1650.

Horne, Robert. *Life and Death: Foure Sermons.* London, 1613.

Hotchkis, Thomas. *A Discourse concerning the Imputation of Christ's Righteousness to Us, and our Sins to Him.* London, 1675.

Howe, John. *The Works of the Rev. John Howe, M.A., with Memoirs of His Life, by Edmund Calamy, D.D.* London, 1834.

Humfrey, John. *Peaceable Disquisitions.* London, 1678.

Huntley, W. *A Breviate of the Prelates intolerable usurpations, both upon the King's Prerogative Royale, and the Subjects Liberties.* N.p., 1637.

Hutton, Matthew. *Brevis & dilucida explicatio, verae, certae, & consolationis plenae doctrinae, De Electione, Praedestinatione ac Reprobatione.* Amsterdam, 1613.

Jackson, Thomas. *A Treatise of the Divine Essence and Attributes.* London, 1628.

———. *Works.* 12 vols. Oxford: Oxford University Press, 1844.

Jacob, Henry. *A Treatise of the Sufferings and Victory of Christ in the Work of our Redemption.* N.p., 1598.

James. I, King. *His Majesties Declaration concerning His Proceedings with the States Generall of the United Provinces of the Low Countreys, in the Cause of D. Conradus Vorstius.* London, 1612.

Jeanes, Henry. *A Vindication of Dr. Twisse.* Oxford, 1653.

Jewel, John. *The Works of John Jewel.* Edited by John Ayre. 4 vols. Parker Society, vols. 23–26. Cambridge: At the University Press, 1845–50.

Joye, George. *George Joye Confuteth Winchesters False Articles.* Wesill in Cliefeland, 1543.

———. *The Refutation of the byshop of Winchesters derke declaration of his false articles, once before confuted by George Ioye.* N.p., 1546.

The Just Mans Defence or, The Declaration of the Judgement of James Arminius. Translated by Tobias Conyers. London, 1657.

Kellison, Matthew. *A Survey of the New Religion, Detecting Manie Grosse Absurdities which it Implieth.* Douay, 1603.

Kendall, George. *Sancti Sanciti. Or the Common Doctrine of the Perseverance of the Saints . . . Vindicated from the attempts lately made against it, by Mr. John Goodwin.* London, 1654.

———. θεοκρατιά: *Or, a Vindication of the Doctrine Commonly Received in the Reformed Churches concerning Gods Intentions of Special Grace and Favour to his Elect in the Death of Christ.* London, 1653.

Kimedonicus, James. *Of the Redemption of Mankind, Three Books.* Translated by Hugh Ince. London, 1598.

King, John. *Lectures upon Ionas, Delivered at Yorke in the yeare of our Lorde 1594.* Oxford, 1597.

Knappen, Marshall M., ed. *Two Elizabethan Diaries by Richard Rogers and Samuel Ward.* Gloucester: Peter Smith, 1966.

Knewstub, John. *An Aunsweare unto Certayne assertions, tending to Maintaine the Church of Rome to be the true and Catholique Church.* London, 1579.

Knox, John. *An Answer to a Great Nomber of blasphemous cavillations written by an Anabaptist, and Adversarie to Gods eternal Predestination.* Geneva, 1560.

Lamberd, John. *Of Predestination and Election made by Iohn Lamberd minister of the church of Elham.* Canterbury, 1550.

La Place, Peter. *A Treatise of the Excellencie of a Christian man.* Translated by L. Tomson. London, 1589.

Latimer, Hugh. *Selected Sermons of Hugh Latimer.* Edited by Allan G. Chester. Charlottesville: University Press of Virginia, 1968.

————. *Sermons of Hugh Latimer.* Edited by George E. Corrie. 2 vols. Parker Society, vols. 27, 28. Cambridge: At the University Press, 1844, 1845.

Laud, William. *An Historical Account of all Material Transactions Relating to the University of Oxford, from Archbishop Laud's Being Elected Chancellor to the Resignation of that Office.* In *The Works of the Most Reverend Father in God William Laud, D.D.* Vol. 5. Oxford: J. H. Parker, 1853.

————. *The History of the Troubles and Tryall of the Most Reverend Father in God and Blessed Martyr, William Laud, Lord Arch-Bishop of Canterbury. Wrote by Himselfe, during his Imprisonment in the Tower.* London, 1695.

Leigh, Richard. *The Transproser Rehears'd.* Oxford, 1673.

Lesse, Nicholas, trans. *A Worke of the predestination of saints wrytten by the famous docyor S. Augustine byshop of Carthage, . . . Item, another worke of the sayde Augustine, entytuled of the vertu of perseverence To thend.* London, 1550.

Lewthwat, Richard. *Vindiciae Christi et Obex Errori Arminiano: A Plea for Christ, and Obstruction to the First Passage, Whereat the Errors of Arminius Steal into the Hearts of Men.* London, 1655.

Lloyd, Charles, ed. *Formularies of Faith Put Forth by Authority during the Reign of Henry VIII.* Oxford: The University Press, 1856.

Lobb, Stephen. *A Report of the Present State of the Differences in Doctrinals, between Some Dissenting Ministers in London.* London, 1697.

Lumpkin, William L., ed. *Baptist Confessions of Faith.* Chicago: Judson Press, 1959.

McGiffert, Michael, ed. *God's Plot: The Paradoxes of Puritan Piety, Being the Autobiography and Journal of Thomas Shepard.* University of Massachusetts Press, 1972.

Marshall, Stephen. *A Sermon Preached before the Honourable House of Commons Assembled in Parliament, at Their Publique Fast, November 17, 1640.* London, 1641.

Marvell, Andrew. *The Rehearsal Transprosed: Or, Animadversions upon a Late Book.* London, 1672.

————. *The Rehearsal Transpros'd: The Second Part.* London, 1673.

"Matthew's Bible." *The byble, that is to say, al the holy scripture.* 1551.

Maxey, Anthony. *The Golden Chaine of Mans Salvation.* London, 1610.

Mayer, John. *Praxis Theologica: Or, the Epistle of the Apostle St. Iames Resolved, Expounded, and Preached upon by way of Doctrine and Use.* London, 1629.

Memorials of Affairs of State in the Reigns of Q. Elizabeth and K. James I. Collected (chiefly) from the Original Papers of the Right Honourable Sir Ralph Winwood. 3 vols. London, 1725.

Milbourne, William. *Sapientia Clamitans, Wisdome Crying out to Sinners to returne from their evill wayes: Contained in Three pious and learned Treatises.* London, 1638.

Milton, John. *De Doctrina Christiana.* Translated by C. R. Sumner. In *The Works of John Milton,* edited by J. H. Hanford and W. H. Dunn, vol. 14. New York: Columbia University Press, 1933.

Mitchell, A. F., and Struthers, John, eds. *Minutes of the Sessions of the Westminster Assembly of Divines.* Edinburgh: William Blackwood & Sons, 1874.

Montague, Richard. *Appello Caesarem.* London, 1625.

————. *A Gag for the New Gospell? No: A New Gagg for an Old Goose.* London, 1624.

Moore, Thomas. *The Universality of Gods Free-Grace.* London, 1646.

More, Paul Elmer, and Cross, Frank Leslie, eds. *Anglicanism: The Thought and Practice of the Church of England, Illustrated from the Religious Literature of the Seventeenth Century.* London: S.P.C.K., 1957.

Morton, Thomas. *A Treatise of the threefolde state of man.* London, 1596.

————. *Two Treatises concerning Regeneration.* London, 1613.

Mosse, Miles. *Justifying and Saving Faith Distinguished from the faith of the Devils.*

Cambridge, 1614.

Murton, John. *A Description of what God hath predestined concerning man, in his Creation, Transgression, and Regeneration. As also an Answere to John Robinson, touching Baptisme.* N.p., 1620.

Musculus, Wolfgangus. *Common Places of Christian Religion.* London, 1563.

N., O. *An Apology of English Arminianisme or A Dialogue, betweene Iacobus Arminius . . . and Enthusiastus . . . Wherein Are defended the Doctrines of Arminius touching Free will, Predestination, and Reprobation: The said Doctrines being maintained & taught by many of the most learned Protestants of England, at this present time.* St Omer? 1634.

Negus, William. *Mans Active Obedience: Or the Power of Godlines.* London, 1619.

Nicholls, Josias. *Abraham's Faith: That is, the olde Religion. Wherein is Taught, that the Religion Now Publikely taught and defended by order in the Church of England, is the onely true Catholicke, auncient, and unchangeable faith of Gods elect.* London, 1602.

Norris, Silvester. *An Antidote or Soveraigne Remedie against the Pestiferous Writings of all English Sectaries.* N.p., 1615.

———. *An Antidote or Treatise of Thirty Controversies: With a large Discourse of the Church.* N.p., 1622.

Northbrooke, John. *Spiritus est Vicarius Christi in Terra. The poore mans Garden, wherein are Flowers of the Scriptures, and Doctours, verie necessarie and profitable for the simple and ignorant people to reade.* London, 1582.

Notestein, Wallace, and Relf, Francis, eds. *Commons Debates for 1629.* Minneapolis: University of Minnesota Press, 1921.

Nowell, Alexander. *A Catechism written in Latin by Alexander Nowell, Dean of St. Paul's: Together with the Same Catechism Translated into English by Thomas Norton.* Edited by G. E. Corrie. Parker Society, vol. 32. Cambridge: At the University Press, 1853.

Ochino, Bernardino. *Certayne Sermons of the ryghte famous and excellente clerk Master Bernardine Ochine.* London, 1550.

Ormerod, Oliver. *The Picture of a Papist: Or a Relation of the damnable heresies, detestable Qualities and diabolicall Practices of sundry heretics in former ages, and of the Papists in this age.* London, 1606.

Owen, John. *The Works of John Owen, D.D.* Edited by William H. Goold. 24 vols. London and Edinburgh: Johnstone and Hunter, 1850–55.

Pagget, Eusebius. *Catechismus Latine.* London, 1585.

Pagitt, Ephraim. *Heresiography: Or, a description of the Heretickes and Sectaries of these latter times.* London, 1645.

Palfreyman, Thomas. *The Treatise of Heavenly Philosophie.* London, 1578.

Parker, Samuel. *A Defence and Continuation of the Ecclesiastical Polity.* London, 1671.

———. *A Discourse of Ecclesiastical Polity.* London, 1670.

———. *A Reproof to the Rehearsal Transprosed.* London, 1673.

Parr, Catherine. *The Lamentacion of a synner, made by the moste vertuous Lady quene Catherine.* London, 1548.

Parr, Elnathan. *The Grounds of Divinitie, Plainely discovering the Mysteries of Christian Religion.* London, 1615.

———. *The Workes of that faithfull and Painefull Preacher, Mr. Elnathan Parr.* 3d ed. London, 1632.

Parr, Richard. *The Life of the Most Reverend Father in God, James Usher, Late Lord Arch-Bishop of Armagh.* London, 1686.

A Parte of a Register, contayninge sondrie memorable Matters. Middleburgh, 1593.

Patrick, Simon. *A Friendly Debate between a Conformist and a Nonconformist.* London, 1669.

Pawson, John. *A Brief Vindication of Free Grace.* London, 1652.

Peel, Albert, ed. *The Seconde Parte of a Register, Being a Calendar of Manuscripts under that Title Intended for Publication by the Puritans about 1593,* 2 vols. Cambridge: At the University Press, 1915.

———. *Tracts Ascribed to Richard Bancroft*. Cambridge: Cambridge University Press, 1953.

———, and Carlson, Leland, eds. *The Writings of Robert Harrison and Robert Browne*. London: George Allen Unwin, 1953.

Pelling, John. *A Sermon of the Providence of God*. London, 1607.

Pemble, William. *Vindiciae Gratiae: A Plea for Grace Wherein the maine sinewes of Arminius doctrine are cut asunder*. 1627. Reprint, London, 1629.

Perkins, William. *A Christian and Plaine Treatise on the Manner and Order of Predestination*. London, 1606.

———. *The Workes of That Famous and Worthy Minister of Christ in the University of Cambridge, Mr. William Perkins*. 3 vols. Cambridge: 1612, 1613.

Perrinchief, Richard. *Indulgence Not Justified*. London, 1668.

Petto, Samuel. *The Difference between the Old and New Covenant*. London, 1674.

Philpot, John. *The Examinations and Writings of John Philpot, Archdeacon of Winchester: Martyr, 1555*. Edited by Robert Eden. Parker Society, vol. 34. Cambridge: At the University Press, 1842.

Pierce, Thomas. αὐτοκατάκρισις, *or, Self-Condemnation, Exemplified in Mr. Whitfield, Mr. Barlee, and Mr. Hickman*. London, 1658.

———. *A Correct Copy of Some Notes concerning Gods Decrees, Especially of Reprobation*. London, 1655.

———. *The Divine Philanthropie Defended . . . In Vindication of some Notes concerning Gods Decrees, Especially of Reprobation*. London, 1657.

———. *The Divine Purity Defended: Or Vindication of some Notes concerning God's Decrees, Especially of Reprobation*. London, 1657.

———. *The Self-Revenger Exemplified in Mr. William Barlee*. London, 1658.

Pilkington, James. *The Works of James Pilkington, Lord Bishop of Durham*, Edited by James Scholefield. Parker Society, vol. 35. Cambridge: At the University Press, 1842.

Plaifere, John. *Appeal to Gospel for True Doctrine of Divine Predestination*. London, 1651.

Polanus, Amandus. *The Substance of Christian Religion*. London, 1600.

Pole, Reginald. *A Treatise of Justification. Found among the Writings of Cardinal Pole of blessed memorie*. Louvain, 1569.

Polhill, Edward. *An Answer to the Discourse of Mr. William Sherlock*. London, 1675.

———. *The Divine Will Considered in its Eternal Decrees and Holy Execution of Them*. London, 1673.

[Ponet, John.] *A Short Catechisme, or playne instruction*. London, 1553.

Potter, Christopher. "His Own Vindication of Himselfe, by Way of Letter unto Mr. V. touching the same points, written July 7, 1629." In J. Plaifere, *Appeal to the Gospel for True Doctrine of Divine Predestination*. London, 1651.

———. *A Sermon Preached at the Consecration of the Right Reverend Father in God Barnaby Potter*. London, 1629.

Preston, John. *The Breastplate of Faith and Love*. London, 1630.

———. *The Position of John Preston concerning the Irrestibleness of Converting Grace*. London, 1654.

Prime, John. *A Fruitefull and Briefe Discourse in Two Bookes: The One of Nature, The Other of Grace*. London, 1583.

Prynne, William. *Anti-Arminianisme; Or the Church of England's Old Antithesis to New Arminianisme*. London, 1630.

———. *Canterburies Doome: Or the First Part of a Complete History of the Commitment, Charge, Tryall, Condemnation, and Execution of William Laud*. London, 1646.

R., I. *The Spy: Discovering the Danger of Arminian Heresie and Spanish Trecherie*. Strasbourg, 1628.

Radford, John. *A Directorie Teaching the Way to the Truth in a Brief and Plaine Discourse against the Heresies of this Time*. N.p., 1605.

Rainolds, John. *Sex Theses de Sacra Scriptura et Ecclesia*. London, 1580.

———. *The Summe of the Conference betweene John Rainoldes and John Hart: Touching the Head and the Faith of the Church*. London, 1584.

Randall, John. *The Necessitie of Righteousnes*. London, 1622.

Reprobation Asserted: Or the Doctrine of Eternal Election and Reprobation Unfolded and Explained in Eleven Chapters. 2d ed. London, 1696.

Resbury, Richard. *The Lightless-Starre: Or Mr. John Goodwin Discovered a Pelagio-Socinian*. London, 1652.

_____. *Some Stop to the Gangrene of Arminianism*. London, 1651.

Reynolds, Edward. *A Sermon Touching the Peace and Edification of the Church*. London, 1638.

_____. *The Sinfulnesse of Sinne*. London, 1632.

Ridley, Lancelot. *A Commentary in Englyshe upon Sayncte Paules Epystle to the Ephesyans for the instruccyon of them that be unlerned in tonges*. N.p., 1540.

Ridley, Nicholas. *Works*. Edited by Henry Christmas. Parker Society, vol. 39. Cambridge: At the University Press, 1841.

Robinson, Hastings, ed. *Original Letters Relative to the English Reformation Written during the Reigns of King Henry VIII, King Edward VI, and Queen Mary*. 2 pts. Parker Society vol. 53. Cambridge: At the University Press, 1846, 1847.

_____. *The Zurich Letters (Second Series): Comprising the Correspondence of Several English Bishops and Others with some of the Helvetian Reformers, during the Reign of Elizabeth*. 2 vols. Parker Society, vols. 51, 52. Cambridge: At the University Press, 1842, 1845.

Robinson, John. *A Defence of the Doctrine Propounded by the Synode at Dort: Against John Murton*. N.p., 1624.

Rogers, John. *The Doctrine of Faith: Wherein are practically handled twelve principall points, which explaine the Nature and Use of it*. 1627. Reprint, London, 1633.

Rogers, Richard. *Certaine Sermons*. London, 1612.

_____. *Seven Treatises, Containing such Direction as is gathered out of the Holie Scriptures . . . in the Which . . . true Christians may learne how to lead a godly and comfortable life every day*. London, 1603.

Rogers, Thomas. *The Catholic Doctrine of the Church of England: An Exposition of the Thirty-Nine Articles*. Edited by J. J. S. Perowne. Parker Society, vol. 40. Cambridge: At the University Press, 1854.

Rollock, Robert. *A Treatise of Gods Effectual Calling*. London, 1603.

Rous, Francis. *Testis Veritatis*. London, 1626.

_____. *The Truth of These Things*. London, 1633.

Roy, William. *The True beliefe in Christ and his sacramentes, set forth in a Dialoge*. 1527. Reprint, 1550.

Rudd, Anthonie. *A Sermon Preached before the Kings Maiestie at Whitehall upon the ninth of Februarie, 1605*. London, 1606.

Rutherford, Samuel. *Christ Dying and Drawing Sinners to Himselfe*. London, 1647.

Saltmarsh, John. *The Fountaine of Free Grace Opened by Questions and Answers*. London, 1645.

_____. *Free Grace: Or the Flowings of Christs Blood Freely to Sinners*. 1645. Reprint, London, 1661.

Sampson, Thomas. *A Briefe Collection of the Church*. London, 1581.

[Sancroft, William.] *Fur Praedestinatus: Sive, Dialogismus Inter quendam Ordinis Praedicantium Calvinistam & Furem ad laquem damnatum habitus*. London, 1551.

Sandys, Edwin. *The Sermons of Edwin Sandys*. Edited by John Ayre. Parker Society, vol. 41. Cambridge: At the University Press, 1841.

Schaff, Philip, ed. *The Creeds of Christendom*. 3 vols. New York: Harper and Brothers, 1919.

Sclater, William. *The Christians Strength*. Oxford, 1612.

_____. *The Sick Souls Salve*. Oxford, 1612.

_____. *A Threefold Preservative against three dangerous diseases of these latter times*. London, 1610.

Scory, John, trans. *Two bokes of the noble doctor and B. S. Augustine thone entiteled of the*

Predestinacion of saintes, thother of perseverance unto thende, . . . very necessary for al tymes, but namely for oures wherein the Papistes and Anabaptistes have revived again the wycked opinions of the Pelagians. Geneva? 1556?

Scudder, Henry. *The Christians Daily Walke in holy Securitie and Peace.* London, 1628.

Shelford, Robert. *Five Pious and Learned Discourses.* Cambridge, 1635.

Sherlock, William. *A Defence and Continuation of the Discourse concerning the Knowledge of Jesus Christ.* London, 1675.

———. *A Discourse concerning the knowledge of Jesus Christ.* 1674. 3d ed., London, 1678.

A Shorte Declaration of the Lives and Doctrinde of the Protestants and Puritans. Rouen, 1615.

Shutte, Christopher. *A Compendious forme and summe of Christian doctrine.* London, 1584.

Sibbes, Richard. *The Complete Works of Richard Sibbes.* Edited by A. B. Grosart. 7 vols. Edinburgh: James Nichol, 1862–64.

Sibthorp, Christopher. *A Friendly Advertisement to the pretended Catholickes of Ireland.* Dublin, 1622.

Simon, Irene, ed. *Three Restoration Divines, Barrow, South, Tillotson: Selected Sermons.* 2 vols. in 3. Paris: Société d'Edition "Les Belles Lettres," 1967, 1976.

Simpson, John. *The Perfection of Justification maintained against the Pharisee.* London, 1648.

Smith, John. *The Works of John Smith.* Edited by W. T. Whitley. 2 vols. Cambridge: At the University Press, 1915.

Sparke, Thomas. *A Short Treatise, very comfortable for all those Christians that be troubled and disquieted in theyr consciences with the sight of their own infirmities: Wherein is shewed how such may in their own selves finde whereby to assure them of their free election, effectual vocation, and justification.* London, 1580.

Stalham, John. *The Reviler Rebuked: Or, a Re-inforcement of God.* London, 1657.

———. *Vindiciae Redemptionis.* London, 1647.

Sterry, Peter. *A Discourse of the Freedom of the Will.* London, 1675.

Stoughton, Thomas. *A Generall Treatise against Poperie.* Cambridge, 1598.

Strype, John. *Annals of the Reformation and Establishment of Religion . . . during Queen Elizabeth's Happy Reign.* 4 vols. Oxford: Clarendon Press, 1824.

———. *Ecclesiastical Memorials Relating Chiefly to Religion, and the Reformation of it, and the Emergence of the Church of England, under King Henry VIII, King Edward VI, Queen Mary I.* 3 vols. Oxford: Clarendon Press, 1822.

———. *The Life and Acts of John Whitgift, D.D.* 4 vols. Oxford: Clarendon Press, 1822.

———. *Memorials of the Most Reverend Father in God Thomas Cranmer.* 2 vols. Oxford: Clarendon Press, 1840.

Stuart, Richard. *Three Sermons Preached by the Reverend, and Learned, Dr. Richard Stuart . . . To which is added a fourth Sermon, Preached by the Right Reverend Father in God Samuell Harsnett, Lord Archbishop of York.* London, 1658.

Sutcliffe, Matthew. *An Abridgement or Survey of Poperie.* London, 1606.

Sydenham, Humphrey. *Jacob and Esau: Opened and Discussed by Way of Sermon at Pauls Crosse.* London, 1626.

Tanner, J. R. *Constitutional Documents of the Reign of James I.* Cambridge: Cambridge University Press, 1930.

Taverner, Richard. *The Epistles and Gospelles . . . from Trinitie Sonday tyll Advent.* London, 1540.

———. *The Epistles and Gospelles . . . tyll Advent.* London, 1540.

Taverner, Richard. *The Epistles and Gospelles with a Brief Postyl . . . tyll lowe Sonday.* London, 1540.

Taylor, Jeremy. *The Whole Works of the Right Rev. Jeremy Taylor.* 10 vols. London, 1848.

Thorndike, Herbert. *An Epilogue to the Tragedy of the Church of England: The Theological Works of Herbert Thorndike.* Vol. 3, parts 1 and 2. 1651. Reprint, Oxford, 1851.

———. *Just Weights and Measures: That is, The present State of Religion.* London, 1662.

Tombes, John. *Animadversiones in Librum Georgii Bulli Cui titulum fecit Harmonia Apostolica.* Oxford, 1676.

Traheron, Bartholomew. *An Exposition of the 4. chap. of S. Joan's Revelation made by Bar. Traheron in sondrie Readinges before his countre men in Germanie.* Zurich, 1557.

———. *An Exposition of a Parte of S. Iohannes Gospel made in sondrie readinges in the English Congregation at Wesel . . . now published against the wicked enterprises of new sterte up Arians in Englande.* N.p., 1557.

Trelcatius, Lucas. *A Briefe Institution of the Common Places of Sacred Divinitie.* London, 1610.

Trinterud, Leonard J., ed. *Elizabethan Puritanism.* Oxford: Oxford University Press, 1971.

Trosse, George. *The Life of the Reverend Mr. George Trosse, Written by Himself, and Published Posthumously according to his Order in 1714.* Edited by A. W. Brink. Montreal: McGill–Queen's University Press, 1974.

Truman, Joseph. *An Endeavour to Rectifie Some Prevailing Opinions, Contrary to the Doctrine of the Church of England.* London, 1671.

———. *The Great Propitiation: Or, Christs Satisfaction, and Man's Justification by it, Upon His Faith.* London, 1669.

Tuke, Thomas. *The High-Way to Heaven: Or, the Doctrine of Election, Effectual Vocation, Iustification, Sanctification, and eternal Life.* London, 1635.

———. "Translators Epistle upon Predestination." In William Perkins, *A Christian and Plaine Treatise of the Manner and Order of Predestination.* London, 1606.

Tully, Thomas. *A Letter to Mr. Richard Baxter Occasioned by several injurious Reflexions of His upon a Treatise entituled Justificatio Paulina.* Oxford, 1675.

Turner, William. "To the Christen Reader." In *A Comparison betwene the Olde learnynge & the New, Translated out of latin in English by Wyliam Turner.* Southwerke, 1537.

Twisse, William. *A Discovery of Dr. Jackson's Vanity.* Amsterdam? 1631.

———. *The Doctrine of the Synod of Dort and Arles, reduced to the practise.* N.p., 1650.

———. *The Riches of Gods Love unto the Vessels of Mercy, Consistent with His Absolute Hatred or Reprobation of the Vessels of Wrath.* Oxford, 1653.

———. *A Treatise of Mr. Cottons, Clearing Certaine Doubts concerning Predestination. Together with an Examination Thereof.* London, 1646.

———. *Vindiciae gratiae.* Amsterdam, 1632.

Tyndale, William. *Works.* Edited by Henry Walter. 3 vols. Parker Society, vols. 42–44. Cambridge: At the University Press, 1848–50.

Ussher, James. *An Answer to a Challenge made by a Jesuite in Ireland.* Dublin, 1624.

———. *Gotteschalci, et Praedestinatianae controversiae ab eo Motae Historia.* Dublin, 1631.

Vermigli, Peter Martyr. *The Common Places.* London, 1583.

Veron, John. *An Apology of defence of the Doctrine of Predestination.* London, 1561.

———. *A Fruteful treatise of Predestination and of the divine providence of god, with an apology of the same, against the swynyshe gruntinge of the Epicures and Atheystes of oure time.* London, 1563.

Walker, George. *Socinianisme in the Fundamentall Point of Justification Discovered, and Confuted.* London, 1641.

———. *A True relation of the chiefe passages betweene Mr. Anthony Wotton, and Mr. George Walker, in the yeare of our Lord, 1611.* London, 1642.

Walker, Williston, ed. *The Creeds and Platforms of Congregationalism.* 1893. Reprint, Boston: Pilgrim Press, 1960.

Walton, Isaac. *The Lives of John Donne, Sir Henry Wotton, Richard Hooker, George Herbert & Robert Sandevon.* London: Oxford University Press, 1927.

Webbe, George. *A Briefe Exposition of the Principles of Christian Religion.* London, 1612.

Whately, William. *The New Birth: Or, A Treatise of Regeneration.* London, 1635.

Whitaker, William. *An Answere to the Ten Reasons of Edmund Campian the Jesuit.* London, 1606.

———. *A Disputation on Holy Scripture, against the Papists, especially Bellarmine and Stapleton.* Translated and edited by William Fitzgerald. Parker Society, vol. 45. Cambridge: At the University Press, 1849.

White, John. *A Defence of the Way to the True Church*. London, 1614.

———. *Two Sermons*. London, 1615.

———. *The Way to the True Church*. London, 1608.

Whitehead, George, and Fox, George. *A Brief Discovery of the Dangerous Principles of John Horne and Thomas Moore*. London, 1659.

Whitfield, Thomas. *A Vindication of the Doctrine of Gods Absolute Decree, and of Christs Absolute and Special Redemption, to those Objections that are brought against them by Mr. Tho: Pierce*. London, 1657.

Whitgift, John. *The Works of John Whitgift*. Edited by John Ayre. 3 vols. Parker Society. vols. 46–48. Cambridge: At the University Press, 1851–53.

Whittell, Robert. *The Way to the celestiall Paradise*. London, 1620.

Willet, Andrew. *Ecclesia Triumphans: That is, the Ioy of the English Church*. Cambridge, 1614.

———. *Limbomastix: That is, A Canvise of Limbus Patrum*. London, 1604.

———. *Synopsis Papismi, That is, A Generall Viewe of Papistry: Wherein the whole mysterie of Iniquitie, and summe of anti-christian doctrine is set down, which is maintained this day by the Synagogue of Rome*. London, 1592.

Williams, Griffith. *The Delights of the Saints. A Most Comfortable Treatise*. London, 1622.

Wilson, Thomas. *A Dialogue about Justification*. London, 1611.

———. *Jacobs Ladder: Or A Short Treatise Laying Forth distinctly the severall degrees of Gods eternall Purpose*. London, 1611.

———. *A Sermon on Sanctification or new Creation*. London, 1611.

Wolseley, Sir Charles. *Justification Evangelical*. London, 1677.

Womock, Laurence. *The Examination of Tilenus before the Triers; In order to his intended settlement in the office of a Publick Preacher in the Common-wealth of Utopia. Whereunto are annexed the Tenets of the Remonstrants touching those five Articles Voted, Stated and imposed, but not disputed at the Synod of Dort*. London, 1658.

———. *The Result of False Principles . . . whereunto is added a learned Desputation of Dr. Goades*. London, 1661.

Wood, Anthony. *Athenae Oxoniensis*. Edited by Philip Bliss. 4 vols. Oxford, 1813–20.

———. *The History and Antiquities of the University of Oxford*. Edited by J. Gutch. 3 vols. Oxford, 1791–96.

Woodbridge, Benjamin. *Justification by Faith: Or a Confutation of that Antinomian Error, That Justification is before Faith*. London, 1653.

———. *The Method of Grace in the Justification of Sinners*. London, 1653.

Woolton, John. *The Christian Manuell*. Parker Society, vol. 49. Cambridge: At the University Press, 1951.

———. *A Newe Anatomie of the Whole Man, as well of his body, as of his Soule: . . . in his first creation, corruption, regeneration, and glorification*. London, 1576.

Wotton, Anthony. *An Answere to a Popish Pamphlet*. London, 1605.

———. *A Dangerous Plot Discovered Wherein is Proved, that, Mr. Richard Montague Laboureth to Bring in the Faith of Rome*. London, 1626.

———. *A Defence of Mr. Perkins Booke, Called a Reformed Catholicke*. London, 1606.

Yarrow, Robert. *Soveraigne Comforts for a Troubled Conscience*. 1619. Reprint, London, 1634.

Yates, John. *Gods Arraignement of Hypocrites: With an Inlargement concerning Gods Decree in Ordering Sinne*. Cambridge, 1615.

———. *Ibis Ad Caesarem: Or a Submissive appearance before Caesar; In Answer to Mr. Mountagues Appeale*. London, 1626.

Zanchi, Jerome. *Zanchius his Confession of Christian Religion*. Cambridge, 1599.

Secondary Sources

Abernathy, George R., Jr. *The English Presbyterians and the Stuart Restoration, 1648–1663. Transactions of the American Philosophical Society*, n.s., vol. 55, pt. 2. Philadelphia: American Philosophical Society, 1965.

Addison, J. T. "Anglican Thought, 1559–1667." *Historical Magazine of the Protestant Episcopal Church* 22 (1953):348–69.

Allison, C. F. *The Rise of Moralism: The Proclamation of the Gospel from Hooker to Baxter*. London: S.P.C.K., 1966.

Armstrong, Brian G. *Calvinism and the Amyraut Heresy: Protestant Scholasticism and Humanism in Seventeenth-Century France*. Madison: University of Wisconsin Press, 1969.

Ashley Smith, J. W. *The Birth of Modern Education: The Contribution of the Dissenting Academies, 1660–1800*. London: Independent Press, 1954.

Aubert, Louis. "L'Activité de Farel de 1550 à 1555." In *Guillaume Farel, 1489–1565: Biographie nouvelle écrite d'après les documents originaux par un groupe d'historiens, professeurs et pasteurs de Suisse, de France et d'Italie*. Paris: Editions Delachaux and Niestle, 1930.

Babbage, Stuart Barton. *Puritanism and Richard Bancroft*. London: S.P.C.K., 1962.

Bailey, Derrick Sherwin. *Thomas Becon and the Reformation of the Church of England*. Edinburgh: Oliver & Boyd, 1952.

Ball, Bryan W. *A Great Expectation: Eschatological Thought in English Protestantism to 1660*. Leiden: E. J. Brill, 1975.

Bangs, Carl. *Arminius: A Study in the Dutch Reformation*. Nashville: Abingdon Press, 1971.

Barbour, Hugh. *The Quakers in Puritan England*. New Haven: Yale University Press, 1964.

Battis, Emery. *Saints and Sectaries: Anne Hutchinson and the Antinomian Controversy in the Massachusetts Bay Colony*. Chapel Hill: University of North Carolina Press, 1962.

Bauckham, Richard. "Hooker, Travers and the Church of Rome in the 1580's." *Journal of Ecclesiastical History* 29 (1978):137–48.

———. "Marian Exiles and Cambridge Puritanism: James Pilkington's 'Halfe a Score.'" *Journal of Ecclesiastical History* 26 (1975):137–48.

Beachy, Alvin J. *The Concept of Grace in the Radical Reformation*. Nieuwkoop: B. deGraaf, 1977.

Becker, Carl L. *The Heavenly City of the Eighteenth-Century Philosophers*. 1932. Reprint, New Haven: Yale University Press, 1959.

Benrath, Karl. *Bernardino Ochino of Siena: A Contribution towards the History of the Reformation*. Translated by Helen Zimmern. New York: Robert Carter and Brothers, 1877.

Berdyaev, Nicholas. *Truth and Revelation*. Translated by R. M. French. New York: Harper and Brothers, 1953.

Berger, Peter. *A Rumor of Angels: Modern Society and the Rediscovery of the Supernatural*. Garden City: Doubleday and Company, 1969.

Betteridge, Alan. "Early Baptists in Leicestershire and Rutland." *Baptist Quarterly* 25 (1974): 354–78.

Bloch, Marc. *Feudal Society*. Translated by L. A. Manyon. 2 vols. Chicago: University of Chicago Press, 1971.

Bolam, C. Gordon; Goring, Jeremy; Short, H. L.; and Thomas, Roger. *The English Presbyterians: From Elizabethan Puritanism to Modern Unitarianism*. Boston: Beacon Press, 1968.

Bonini, Cissie Rafferty. "Lutheran Influences in the Early English Reformation: Richard Morison Re-examined." *Archiv für Reformationsgeschichte* 64 (1973):206–24.

Booty, John E. *John Jewel as Apologist of the Church of England*. London: S.P.C.K., 1963.

Bosher, Robert S. *The Making of the Restoration Settlement: The Influence of the Laudians, 1649–1662*. New York: Oxford University Press, 1951.

Bourne, E. C. E. *The Anglicanism of William Laud*. London: S.P.C.K., 1947.

Bradbrook, Muriel C. *Andrew Marvell*. Cambridge: Cambridge University Press, 1940.
Bray, John S. *Theodore Beza's Doctrine of Predestination*. Nieuwkoop: B. De Graaf, 1975.
Breen, Quirinius. "Humanism and the Reformation." In Jerald C. Brauer, ed., *The Impact of the Church upon Its Culture*, pp. 145–71. Chicago: University of Chicago Press, 1968.
Breward, Ian. "The Abolition of Puritanism." *Journal of Religious History* 7 (1972):20–34.
———. "The Significance of William Perkins." *Journal of Religious History* 4 (1966):113–28.
Bridenbaugh, Carl. *Vexed and Troubled Englishmen, 1590–1642*. New York: Oxford University Press, 1968.
Bromiley, G. W., ed. *Zwingli and Bullinger*. Philadelphia: Westminster Press, 1953.
Brook, V. J. K. *A Life of Archbishop Parker*. Oxford, Clarendon Press, 1962.
Brown, John. *John Bunyan*. London: Hulbert Publishing Co., 1928.
Burns, Norman T. *Christian Mortalism from Tyndale to Milton*. Cambridge, Mass.: Harvard University Press, 1972.
Burrage, Champlin. *The Early English Dissenters in the Light of Recent Research (1550–1641)*. 2 vols. 1912. Rpt. New York: Russell and Russell, 1967.
Butterworth, Charles C., and Chester, Allan G. *George Joye, 1495?–1553*: A Chapter in the History of the English Bible and English Reformation. Philadelphia: University of Pennsylvania Press, 1962.
Cannon, William R. *The Theology of John Wesley*. Nashville: Abingdon Press, 1956.
Capp, B. S. *The Fifth Monarchy Men: A Study in Seventeenth-Century English Millenarianism*. Totowa, N.J.: Rowman and Littlefield, 1972.
Carpenter, S. C. *Eighteenth-Century Church and People*. London: John Murray, 1959.
Carroll, Robert Todd. *The Common-Sense Philosophy of Religion of Bishop Edward Stillingfleet, 1635–1699*. The Hague: Martinus Nijhoff, 1975.
Chadwick, Owen. "Arminianism in England." *Religion in Life* 29 (1960):548–55.
———. *The Mind of the Oxford Movement*. Stanford: Stanford University Press, 1960.
———. "The Sixteenth Century." In *The English Church and the Continent*, edited by C. R. Dodwell, pp. 60–72. London: Faith Press, 1959.
Chester, Allan G. *Hugh Latimer: Apostle to the English*. Philadelphia: University of Pennsylvania Press, 1954.
Child, Gilbert W. *Church and State under the Tudors*. London: Longman's, Green, & Co., 1890.
Clancy, Thomas H. "Papist-Protestant-Puritan: English Religious Taxonomy, 1565–1665." *Recusant History* 13 (1976):227–53.
Clebsch, William A. *England's Earliest Protestants, 1520–1535*. New Haven: Yale University Press, 1964.
Clifton, Robin. "Fear of Popery." In *The Origins of the English Civil War*, edited by Conrad Russell, pp. 144–67. London: Macmillan, 1973.
Colie, Rosalie L. *Light and Enlightenment: A Study of the Cambridge Platonists and the Dutch Arminians*. Cambridge: Cambridge University Press, 1957.
Colligan, J. Hay. "The Antinomian Controversy." *Congregational Historical Society Transactions* 6 (1915):389–96.
———. *The Arian Movement in England*. Manchester: Manchester University Press, 1913.
Collinson, Patrick, *Archbishop Grindal, 1519–1583: The Struggle for a Reformed Church*. Berkeley: University of California Press, 1979.
———. *The Elizabethan Puritan Movement*. Berkeley: University of California Press, 1967.
———. *A Mirror of Elizabethan Puritanism: The Life and Letters of 'Godly Master Dering.'* London: Dr. William's Trust, 1964.
———. "The Reformer and the Archbishop: Martin Bucer and An English Bucerian." *Journal of Religious History* 6 (1971):305–31.
———. "Towards a Broader Understanding of the Early Dissenting Tradition." In *The Dissenting Tradition: Essays for Leland Carlson*, edited by C. Robert Cole and M. C.

Moody, pp. 3–38. Athens: Ohio University Press, 1975.

Cook, Sarah Gibbard. "The Congregational Independents and the Cromwellian Constitutions." *Church History* 46 (1977):335–57.

Coolidge, John S. *The Pauline Renaissance in England*. Oxford: Clarendon Press, 1970.

Coomer, Duncan. *English Dissent under the Early Hanoverians*. London: Epworth Press, 1946.

Cragg, Gerald R. *Freedom and Authority: A Study of English Thought in the Early Seventeenth Century*. Philadelphia: Westminster Press, 1975.

————. *From Puritanism to the Age of Reason: A Study of Changes in Religious Thought within the Church of England, 1660–1700*. 1950. Reprint, Cambridge: Cambridge University Press, 1966.

————. *Puritanism in the Period of the Great Persecution, 1660–1688*. Cambridge: Cambridge University Press, 1957.

Cremeans, C. D. *The Reception of Calvinistic Thought in England*. Urbana: University of Illinois Press, 1949.

Cross, Claire. "Popular Piety and the Records of the Unestablished Churches, 1460–1660." In *The Materials, Sources and Methods of Ecclesiastical History, edited by Derek Baker*, 11:269–92. Oxford: Basil Blackwell, 1975.

Curtis, Mark H. *Oxford and Cambridge in Transition, 1558–1642*. Oxford: Clarendon Press, 1959.

Damrosch, Leopold, Jr. "Hobbes as Reformation Theologian: Implications of the Free Will Controversy." *Journal of the History of Ideas* 40 (1979):339–52.

Danner, Dan G. "Anthony Gilby: Puritan in Exile—A Biographical Approach." *Church History* 40 (1971):412–22.

Davies, Godfrey. "Arminian versus Puritan in England, ca. 1620–1640." *Huntington Library Bulletin* 5 (1934):157–79.

Davies, Horton. *Worship and Theology in England from Andrewes to Baxter and Fox, 1603–1690*. Princeton: Princeton University Press, 1975.

————. *Worship and Theology in England from Cranmer to Hooker, 1534–1603*. Princeton: Princeton University Press, 1970.

Dawley, Powell Mills. *John Whitgift and the English Reformation*. New York: Charles Scribner's Sons, 1954.

Delumeau, Jean. *Catholicism between Luther and Voltaire: A New View of the Counter-Reformation*. Translated by Jeremy Moiser. London: Burns and Oates, 1977.

De Schickler, F. "Le Refugié Jean Véron, collaborateur des réformateurs anglais." *Bulletin historique et littéraire*, Société de L'Histoire du Protestantisme Français, 39, 3d ser. (1890):437–46, 481–93.

Devereux, James A. "Reformed Doctrine in the Collects of the First *Book of Common Prayer*." *Harvard Theological Review* 58 (1965):49–68.

Dexter, Henry Martyn. *The Congregationalism of the Last Three Hundred Years as Seen in Its Literature*. New York: Harper & Brothers, 1880.

Dickens, A. G. *The English Reformation*. New York: Schocken Books, 1964.

————. *Lollards and Protestants in the Diocese of York, 1509–1558*. London: Oxford University Press, 1959.

Dixon, Richard W. *History of the Church of England from the Abolition of the Roman Jurisdiction*. 6 vols. Oxford: Clarendon Press, 1895–1902.

Donnelly, John Patrick. *Calvinism and Scholasticism in Vermigli's Doctrine of Man and Grace*. Leiden: E. J. Brill, 1976.

————. "Italian Influences on the Development of Calvinist Scholasticism." *Sixteenth Century Journal* 7 (1976):81–101.

Dowden, John. *Outlines of the History of the Theological Literature of the Church of England from the Reformation to the Close of the Eighteenth Century*. London: S.P.C.K., 1897.

Dowey, Edward A., Jr. *The Knowledge of God in Calvin's Theology*. New York: Columbia University Press, 1952.

Eels, Hastings. *Martin Bucer*. New Haven: Yale University Press, 1931.

Elson, James Hinsdale. *John Hales of Eton*. New York: King's Crown Press, 1948.

Elton, G. R. *Reform and Reformation: England, 1509–1558*. Cambridge, Mass.: Harvard University Press, 1977.

————. Review of *The Elizabethan Puritan Movement*, by Patrick Collinson. *Historical Journal* 11 (1968): 586–588.

Emerson, Everett H. "Calvin and Covenant Theology." *Church History* 25 (1956):136–44.

————. *English Puritanism from John Hooper to John Milton*. Durham: Duke University Press, 1968.

Endy, Melvin. *William Penn and Early Quakerism*. Princeton: Princeton University Press, 1973.

Erickson, Carolly. *The Medieval Vision: Essays in History and Perception*. New York: Oxford University Press, 1976.

Fairfield, Leslie P. *John Bale: Mythmaker for the English Reformation*. West Lafayette: Purdue University Press, 1976.

Fines, John. "A Register of Early British Protestants, 1520–1558." Unpublished Ms., used by permission of author.

Foster, Andrew. "The Function of a Bishop: The Career of Richard Neile, 1562–1640." In *Continuity and Change: Personnel and Administration of the Church of England, 1500–1642*, edited by Rosemary O'Day and Felicity Heal, pp. 33–54. Leicester University Press, 1976.

Fryer, W. R. "The 'High Churchmen' of the Earlier Seventeenth-Century." *Renaissance and Modern Studies* 5 (1961):106–48.

Gardiner, Samuel Rawlinson. *History of England from the Accession of James I to the Outbreak of the Civil War, 1603–1642*. 10 vols. London: Longmans, Green, and Company, 1903.

Garrett, Christina H. *The Marian Exiles: A Study in the Origins of Elizabethan Puritanism*. Cambridge: Cambridge University Press, 1938.

Gay, Peter. *The Enlightenment: An Interpretation*. 2 vols. New York: Alfred A. Knopf, 1969.

George, Charles H. "Puritanism as History and Historiography." *Past and Present* 41 (1968):77–104.

————, and George, Katherine. *The Protestant Mind of the English Reformation, 1570–1640*. Princeton: Princeton University Press, 1961.

Gerrish, B. A. *Tradition and the Modern World: Reformed Theology in the Nineteenth Century*. Chicago: University of Chicago Press, 1977.

Gleason, Elisabeth G. "On the Nature of Sixteenth Century Italian Evangelism: Scholarship, 1953–1978." *Sixteenth Century Journal* 9 (1978):22–23.

Glover, W. B. "God and Thomas Hobbes." *Church History* 29 (1960):275–97.

Greaves, Richard L. *John Bunyan*. Grand Rapids: Wm. B. Eerdmans, 1969.

————. "John Bunyan and the Authorship of 'Reprobation Asserted.'" *Baptist Quarterly* 21 (1965):126–31.

————. "John Bunyan and Covenant Thought in the Seventeenth Century." *Church History* 36 (1967):151–69.

————. "John Bunyan's Holy War and London Nonconformity." *Baptist Quarterly* 26 (1975):158–68.

————. "The Origins and Early Development of English Covenant Theology." *The Historian* 31 (1968):21–35.

————, ed. Introduction to John Bunyan, *The Doctrine of the Law and Grace Unfolded and I Will Pray with the Spirit*. Oxford: Clarendon Press, 1976.

Green, I. M. *The Re-establishment of the Church of England, 1660–1663*. Oxford: Oxford University Press, 1978.

Greenslade, S. L. *The English Reformers and the Fathers of the Church*. Oxford: Clarendon Press, 1960.

————. "English Versions of the Bible, 1525–1611." In *The Cambridge History of the Bible*. Vol. 3, *The West from the Reformation to the Present*, edited by S. L. Greenslade, pp. 141–74. Cambridge: Cambridge University Press, 1963.

_____. *The Work of William Tindale*. London: Blackie & Sons, 1938.

Griffiths, Olive M. *Religion and Learning: A Study in English Presbyterian Thought from the Bartholomew Ejections (1662) to the Foundation of the Unitarian Movement*. Cambridge: Cambridge University Press, 1935.

Haigh, Christopher. *Reformation and Resistance in Tudor Lancashire*. Cambridge: Cambridge University Press, 1975.

Hall, Basil. "Puritanism: The Problem of Definition." In *Studies in Church History*, edited by G. J. Cuming, 2:283–96. London: Thomas Nelson, 1965.

Haller, William. *Foxe's Book of Martyrs and the Elect Nation*. London: Jonathan Cape, 1963.

_____. *Liberty and Reformation in the Puritan Revolution*. New York: Columbia University Press, 1955.

_____. *The Rise of Puritanism*. New York: Columbia University Press, 1938.

Hardwick, Charles. *A History of the Articles of Religion: To Which is Added a Series of Documents, from A.D. 1536 to A.D. 1615; Together with Illustrations from Contemporary Sources*. London: George Bell & Sons, 1895.

Hargrave, O. T. "The Doctrine of Predestination in the English Reformation." Ph.D. dissertation, Vanderbilt University, 1966.

_____. "The Freewillers in the English Reformation." *Church History* 37 (1968):271–80.

_____. "The Predestinarian Offensive of the Marian Exiles at Geneva." *Historical Magazine of the Protestant Episcopal Church* (1973):111–23.

Harrison, A. W. *Arminianism*. London: Duckworth, 1937.

_____. *The Beginnings of Arminianism to the Synod of Dort*. London: University of London Press, 1926.

_____. "The Church of England Reaction from Calvinism in the Seventeenth Century." *Religion in Life* 13 (1944):213–24.

Hauben, Paul J. "A Spanish Calvinist Church in Elizabethan London, 1559–65." *Church History* 34 (1965):50–56.

_____. *Three Spanish Heretics and the Reformation*. Geneva: Libraire Droz, 1967.

Haugaard, William P. *Elizabeth and the English Reformation: The Struggle for a Stable Settlement of Religion*. Cambridge: Cambridge University Press, 1968.

_____. "John Calvin and the Catechism of Alexander Nowell." *Archiv fur Reformationsgeschichte* 61 (1970):50–66.

_____. "Katherine Parr: The Religious Convictions of a Renaissance Queen." *Renaissance Quarterly* 22 (1969):346–59.

Haweis, John Oliver Willyams. *Sketches of the Reformation and Elizabethan Age Taken from the Contemporary Pulpit*. London: William Pickering, 1844.

Hazard, Paul. *The European Mind (1670–1715)*. Translated by J. L. May. Cleveland: World Publishing Co., 1963.

Helm, Paul. "John Bunyan and 'Reprobation Asserted.'" *Baptist Quarterly* 28 (1979):87–93.

Henderson, G. D. "Arminianism in Scotland." *London Quarterly Review* 157 (1932):493–504.

Henry, Stuart C. *George Whitefield: Wayfaring Witness*. Nashville: Abingdon Press, 1957.

Hexter, J. H. "The Problem of the Presbyterian Independents." *American Historical Review* 44 (1938):29–40.

Heywood, James, and Wright, Thomas. *Cambridge University Transactions during the Puritan Controversies of the Sixteenth and Seventeenth Centuries*. Vol. 2. London: H. G. Bohn, 1854.

Hill, Christopher. *Antichrist in Seventeenth-Century England*. London: Oxford University Press, 1971.

_____. *Milton and the English Revolution*. 1977. Reprint, New York: Penguin Books, 1979.

_____. *Puritanism and Revolution: The English Revolution of the Seventeenth Century*. 1958. Reprint, New York: Schocken Books, 1964.

————. *Society and Puritanism in Pre-Revolutionary England.* 2d. ed. New York: Schocken Books, 1967.

————. *The World Turned Upside Down: Radical Ideas during the English Revolution.* New York: Viking Press, 1972.

Hill, W. Speed. "The Evolution of Hooker's Laws of Ecclesiastical Polity." In *Studies in Richard Hooker: Essays Preliminary to an Edition of His Works*, pp. 117–58. Cleveland: The Press of Case Western Reserve University, 1972.

Hopf, Constantine. *Martin Bucer and the English Reformation.* Oxford: Basil Blackwell, 1946.

Horst, Irvin B. *The Radical Brethren: Anabaptism and the English Reformation to 1558.* Nieuwkoop: B. de Graaf, 1972.

Howell, Wilbur Samuel. *Logic and Rhetoric in England, 1500–1700.* Princeton: Princeton University Press, 1956.

Huehns, Gertrude. *Antinomianism in English History.* London: Cresset Press, 1951.

Hume, Anthea. "William Roye's 'Brefe Dialogue' (1527): An English Version of a Strassburg Catechism." *Harvard Theological Review* 60 (1967):307–21.

Huntley, Frank Livingstone. *Jeremy Taylor and the Great Rebellion.* Ann Arbor: University of Michigan Press, 1970.

Husain, Itrait. *The Dogmatic and Mystical Theology of John Donne.* 1938. Reprint, Westport: Greenwood Press, 1970.

Hutton, Sarah. "Thomas Jackson, Oxford Platonist, and William Twisse, Aristotelian." *Journal of the History of Ideas* 39 (1978):635–52.

James, William. *The Varieties of Religious Experience.* New York: Collier Books, 1961.

Jarrott, C. A. L. "John Colet on Justification." *Sixteenth Century Journal* 7 (1976):59–72.

Jones, R. Tudur. *Congregationalism in England, 1662–1962.* London: Independent Press, 1962.

Jones, William M. "Uses of Foreigners in the Church of Edward VI." *Numen* 6 (1959):142–53.

Jordan, Wilbur K. *The Development of Religious Toleration in England from the Accession of James I to the Convention of the Long Parliament (1603–1640).* London: George Allen & Unwin, 1936.

————. *The Development of Religious Toleration in England from the Convention of the Long Parliament to the Restoration (1640–1660).* Cambridge, Mass.: Harvard University Press, 1938.

Kalu, Ogbu. "Bishops and Puritans in Early Jacobean England: A Perspective on Methodology." *Church History* 45 (1976):469–81.

Kelley, Maurice. *This Great Argument.* Princeton: Princeton University Press, 1941.

Kevan, Ernest F. *The Grace of Law: A Study in Puritan Theology.* London: Carey Kingsgate Press, 1964.

Kinder, A. Gordon. *Casiodoro De Reina: Spanish Reformer of the Sixteenth Century.* London: Tamesis Books, 1975.

King, John N. "Freedom of the Press, Protestant Propaganda, and Protector Somerset." *Huntington Library Quarterly* 40 (1976):1–9.

Kinloch, T. F. *The Life and Works of Joseph Hall.* London: Staples Press, 1951.

Kirby, Ethyn Williams. "Sermons before the Commons, 1640–1642." *American Historical Review* 44 (1939):528–48.

Kittelson, James M. "Marbach vs. Zanchi: The Resolution of Controversy in Late Reformation Strasbourg." *Sixteenth Century Journal* 8 (1977):31–44.

Kliever, Lonnie D. "General Baptist Origins: The Question of Anabaptist Influence," *Mennonite Quarterly Review* 36 (1962):292–321.

Knappen, Marshall M. *Tudor Puritanism: A Chapter in the History of Idealism.* Chicago: University of Chicago Press, 1939.

Knox, David Broughton. *The Doctrine of Faith in the Reign of Henry VIII.* London: James Clarke & Co., 1961.

Knox, R. Buick. *James Ussher: Archbishop of Armagh.* Cardiff: University of Wales Press, 1967.

Kolb, Robert. "Nikolaus Von Amsdorf on Vessels of Wrath and Vessels of Mercy: A Lutheran's Doctrine of Double Predestination." *Harvard Theological Review* 69 (1976):325–43.

Kressner, Helmut. *Schweizer Ursprunge des Anglikanischen Staatskirchentums.* Gutersloh: C. Bertelsmann Verlag, 1953.

Krumm, John M. "Continental Protestantism and Elizabethan Anglicanism (1570–1595)." In *Reformation Studies: Essays in Honor of Roland H. Bainton*, edited by Franklin H. Littell, pp. 129–44. Richmond: John Knox Press, 1962.

Lacey, Douglas R. *Dissent and Parliamentary Politics in England, 1661–1689.* New Brunswick: Rutgers University Press, 1969.

Lamont, William M. *Godly Rule, Politics and Religion, 1603–1660.* London: Macmillan, 1969.

Laslett, Peter. *The World We Have Lost: England before the Industrial Age.* 2d ed. New York: Charles Scribner's Sons, 1971.

Leith, John H. *Assembly at Westminster: Reformed Theology in the Making.* Richmond: John Knox Press, 1973.

Lichtenstein, Aharon. *Henry More: The Rational Theology of a Cambridge Platonist.* Cambridge, Mass.: Harvard University Press, 1962.

Linder, Robert D. "Pierre Viret and the Sixteenth-Century English Protestants." *Archiv fur Reformationsgeschichte* 58 (1967):149–70.

———. *The Political Ideas of Pierre Viret.* Geneva: Libraire Droz, 1964.

Little, David. *Religion, Order, and Law: A Study in Pre-Revolutionary England.* New York: Harper & Row, 1969.

McConica, James Kelsey. *English Humanists and Reformation Politics under Henry VIII and Edward VI.* Oxford: Clarendon Press, 1965.

McCoy, F. N. *Robert Baillie and the Second Scots Reformation.* Berkeley: University of California Press, 1974.

McDonnell, Kilian. *John Calvin, the Church, and the Eucharist.* Princeton: Princeton University Press, 1967.

McEwen, James S. *The Faith of John Knox.* London: Lutterworth Press, 1961.

McGee, J. Sears. "Conversion and the Imitation of Christ in Anglican and Puritan Writing." *Journal of British Studies* 15 (1976):21–39.

———. *The Godly Man in Stuart England: Anglicans, Puritans, and the Two Tables, 1620–1670.* New Haven: Yale University Press, 1976.

McIlhiney, David B. "The Protestantism of the Caroline Divines." *Historical Magazine of the Protestant Episcopal Church* 44 (1975):143–54.

McLachlan, Herbert J. *Socinianism in Seventeenth-Century England.* London: Oxford University Press, 1951.

Maclear, James F. "The Puritan Party, 1603–1643: A Study in a Lost Reformation." Ph.D. dissertation, University of Chicago, 1947.

Maclure, Millar. *The Paul's Cross Sermons, 1534–1642.* Toronto: University of Toronto Press, 1958.

McLelland, Joseph C. "The Reformed Doctrine of Predestination according to Peter Martyr." *Scottish Journal of Theology* 8 (1955):255–71.

Maitland, F. W. "The Anglican Settlement and the Scottish Reformation." In *Selected Historical Essays of F. W. Maitland*, edited by Helen M. Cam, pp. 152–210. Boston: Beacon Press, 1962.

Malone, Michael T. "The Doctrine of Predestination in the Thought of William Perkins and Richard Hooker." *Anglican Theological Review* 52 (1970):103–17.

Manning, Brian. "Religion and Politics: The Godly People." In *Politics, Religion, and the English Civil War*, edited by Brian Manning, pp. 82–123. London: Edward Arnold, 1973.

Manning, Roger B. *Religion and Society in Elizabethan Sussex: A Study of the Enforcement of the Religious Settlement, 1558–1603.* Bristol: Leicester University Press, 1969.

Marchant, Ronald A. *The Puritans and the Church Courts in the Diocese of York, 1560–1642.* London: Longmans, 1960.

Marshall, J. S. *Hooker and the Anglican Tradition*. London: Adam and Charles Black, 1963.

Martin, Hugh. *Puritanism and Richard Baxter*. London: SCM Press, 1954.

Martin, Joseph W. "English Protestant Separatism at Its Beginnings: Henry Hart and the Free-Will Men." *Sixteenth Century Journal* 7 (1976):55–74.

Matthews, A. G. *Calamy Revised*. Oxford: Clarendon Press, 1934.

————. *Walker Revised*. Oxford: Clarendon Press, 1948.

Merrill, Thomas F., ed. *William Perkins (1558–1602), English Puritanist*. Nieuwkoop: B. de Graaf, 1966.

Miller, Perry. "The Marrow of Puritan Divinity," *Errand into the Wilderness*. Cambridge, Mass.: The Belknap Press of Harvard University Press, 1956. pp. 48–98.

————. *The New England Mind: From Colony to Province*. 1953. Reprint, Boston: Beacon Press, 1961.

————. *The New England Mind: The Seventeenth Century*. 1939. Reprint, Boston: Beacon Press, 1961.

————. *Orthodoxy in Massachusetts, 1630–1650*. 1933. Reprint, Boston: Beacon Press, 1959.

Milward, Peter. *Religious Controversies of the Elizabethan Age: A Survey of Printed Sources*. Lincoln: University of Nebraska Press, 1977.

————. *Religious Controversies of the Jacobean Age: A Survey of Printed Sources*. Lincoln: University of Nebraska Press, 1978.

Moller, Jens G. "The Beginnings of Puritan Covenant Theology." *Journal of Ecclesiastical History* 14 (1963):46–67.

Monk, Robert C. *John Wesley's Puritan Heritage*. Nashville: Abingdon Press, 1966.

Morgan, Edmund S. *The Puritan Dilemma: The Story of John Winthrop*. Boston: Little, Brown and Company, 1958.

————. *Visible Saints: The History of a Puritan Idea*. 1963. Reprint, Ithaca: Cornell University Press, 1965.

Morgan, Irvonwy. *The Godly Preachers of the Elizabethan Church*. London: Epworth Press, 1965.

————. *The Nonconformity of Richard Baxter*. London: Epworth Press, 1946.

————. *Prince Charles's Puritan Chaplain*. London: George Allen & Unwin, 1957.

Morison, Samuel Eliot. *Harvard College in the Seventeenth Century*. Cambridge, Mass.: Harvard University Press, 1936.

————. *The Intellectual Life of Colonial New England*. 1936. Reprint, Ithaca: Cornell University Press, 1960.

Morton, A. L. *The World of the Ranters: Religious Radicalism in the English Revolution*. London: Lawrence and Wishart, 1970.

Mozley, J. F. *Coverdale and His Bibles*. London: Lutterworth, 1953.

————. *John Foxe and His Book*. London: S.P.C.K., 1940.

Muller, Richard A. "Perkins' *A Golden Chaine*: Predestinarian System or Schematized *Ordo Salutis?*" *Sixteenth Century Journal* 9 (1978):69–81.

Neal, Daniel. *The History of the Puritans, or Protestant Nonconformists: From the Reformation in 1617, to the Revolution in 1688*. 3 vols. London: Thomas Tegg and Son, 1837.

Nethenus, Matthew; Visscher, Hugo; and Reuter, Karl. *William Ames*. Translated by Douglas Horton. Cambridge, Mass.: Harvard Divinity School Library, 1965.

New, John F. H. *Anglican and Puritan: The Basis of Their Opposition, 1558–1640*. Stanford: Stanford University Press, 1964.

————. "The Whitgift-Cartwright Controversy." *Archiv fur Reformationsgeschichte* 59 (1968):203–12.

Nijenhuis, W. "Adrianus Saravia as an Eirenical Churchman in England and the Netherlands." In Derek Baker, ed., *Reform and Reformation: England and the Continent, c.1500–c.1750*, pp. 149–63. Oxford: Basil Blackwell, 1979.

————. *Ecclesia Reformata: Studies on the Reformation*. Leiden: E. J. Brill, 1972.

Nuttall, G. F. *The Holy Spirit in Puritan Faith and Experience*. Oxford: Basil Blackwell, 1946.
————. *Richard Baxter*. London: Thomas Nelson and Sons, 1965.
————. *Visible Saints: The Congregational Way, 1640–1660*. Oxford: Basil Blackwell, 1957.
O'Day, Rosemary, and Heal, Felicity, eds. *Continuity and change: Personnel and Administration of the Church of England, 1500–1642*. Leicester University Press, 1976.
Olsen, V. Norskov. *John Foxe and the Elizabethan Church*. Berkeley: University of California Press, 1973.
Ong, Walter. *Ramus: Method and the Decay of Dialogue: From the Art of Discourse to the Art of Reason*. Cambridge, Mass.: Harvard University Press, 1958.
Orr, Robert R. *Reason and Authority: The Thought of William Chillingworth*. Oxford: Clarendon Press, 1967.
Otto, Rudolf. *The Idea of the Holy*. Translated by J. W. Harvey. 1923. Reprint, New York: Oxford University Press, 1958.
Overton, John H. *The Evangelical Revival in the Eighteenth Century*. London: Longmans, Green and Company, 1907.
Oxley, James E. *The Reformation in Essex to the Death of Mary*. Manchester: Manchester University Press, 1965.
Ozment, Steven E. *The Reformation in the Cities: The Appeal of Protestantism to Sixteenth-Century Germany and Switzerland*. New Haven: Yale University Press, 1975.
Packer, John W. *The Transformation of Anglicanism, 1643–1660: With Special Reference to Henry Hammond*. Manchester: Manchester University Press, 1969.
Pamp, Frederick E., Jr. "Studies in the Origins of English Arminianism." Ph.D. dissertation, Harvard University, 1951.
Parker, T. H. L., ed. *English Reformers*. Philadelphia: Westminster Press, 1966.
Parker, T. M. "Arminianism and Laudianism in Seventeenth-Century England." In *Studies in Church History*, edited by C. W. Dugmore and Charles Duggan, 1:20–34. London: Thomas Nelson & Sons, 1964.
Partee, Charles. *Calvin and Classical Philosophy*. Leiden: E. J. Brill, 1977.
Patterson, W. Brown. "The Anglican Reaction." In *Discord, Dialogue, and Concord: Studies in the Lutheran Reformation's Formula of Concord*, edited by Lewis W. Spitz and Wenzel Lohff, pp. 150–165. Philadelphia: Fortress Press, 1977.
Pattison, Mark. *Isaac Casaubon, 1559–1614*. London: Longmans, Green & Co., 1875.
Pearson, A. F. Scott. *Thomas Cartwright and Elizabethan Puritanism, 1535–1603*. 1925. Reprint, Gloucester: Peter Smith, 1966.
Petit, Norman. *The Heart Prepared: Grace and Conversion in Puritan Spiritual Life*. New Haven: Yale University Press, 1966.
Pinto, Vivian De Sola. *Peter Sterry: Platonist and Mystic*. Cambridge: Cambridge University Press, 1934.
Platt, John. "Eirenical Anglicans at the Synod of Dort." In Derek Baker, ed. *Reform and Reformation: England and the Continent c. 1500–c. 1700*, pp. 221–43. Oxford: Basil Blackwell, 1979.
Porter, H. C. "The Anglicanism of Archbishop Whitgift." *Historical Magazine of the Protestant Episcopal Church* 31 (1962):127–41.
————. *Reformation and Reaction in Tudor Cambridge*. Cambridge: Cambridge University Press, 1958.
Potter, George Richard. *Zwingli*. Cambridge: Cambridge University Press, 1976.
Powicke, Frederick J. *The Cambridge Platonists*. London: J. M. Dent and Sons, 1926.
Pratt, Melvyn E. "Zwinglianism in England during the Reign of Elizabeth." Ph.D. dissertation, Stanford University, 1953.
Rechtien, John G. "Antithetical Literary Structures in the Reformation Theology of Walter Travers." *Sixteenth Century Journal* 8 (1977):51–60.
Richmond, Hugh M. *The Christian Revolutionary: John Milton*. Berkeley: University of California Press, 1974.

Ridley, Jasper. *John Knox*. New York: Oxford University Press, 1968.
Rilliet, Jean. *Zwingli: Third Man of the Reformation*. Translated by Harold Knight. London: Lutterworth, 1964.
Rose, Elliot. *Cases of Conscience: Alternatives Open to Recusants and Puritans under Elizabeth I and James I*. Cambridge: Cambridge University Press, 1975.
Rupp, E. G. *Studies in the Making of the English Protestant Tradition*. Cambridge: Cambridge University Press, 1947.
Scarisbrick, John. *Henry VIII*. Berkeley: University of California Press, 1969.
Schwartz, Hillel. "Arminianism and the English Parliament, 1624–1629." *Journal of British Studies* 12 (1973):41–68.
Semmel, Bernard. *The Methodist Revolution*. New York: Basic Books, 1973.
Shapiro, Barbara J. *John Wilkens, 1614–1672: An Intellectual Biography*. Berkeley: University of California Press, 1969.
Shapiro, Sheldon. "Quelques réflexions sur la signification psychologique de la prédestination dans la Réforme." *Revue d'histoire ecclésiastique* 68 (1973):823–32.
Shipps, Kenneth. "The 'Political' Puritan." *Church History* 45 (1976):196–205.
Shriver, Frederick. "Orthodoxy and Diplomacy: James I and the Vorstius Affair." *English Historical Review*, no. 336 (1970), pp. 449–74.
Simon, Walter G. "Comprehension in the Age of Charles II." *Church History* 31 (1962):440–48.
––––––. *The Restoration Episcopate*. New York: Bookman Associates, 1965.
Simpson, Alan. *Puritanism in Old and New England*. Chicago: University of Chicago Press, 1955.
Smith, Lacey Baldwin. *Henry VIII: The Mask of Royalty*. Boston: Houghton Mifflin, 1971.
––––––. *Tudor Prelates and Politics, 1536–1558*. Princeton: Princeton University Press, 1953.
Smith, Preserved. *The Social Background of the Reformation*. Part 2 of *The Age of the Reformation*. 1920. Reprint, New York: Collier Books, 1962.
Smithen, Frederick J. *Continental Protestantism and the English Reformation*. London: James Clarke & Co., 1927.
Smyth, Charles H. *Cranmer and the Reformation under Edward VI*. 1926. Reprint. Westport, Conn., Greenwood Press, 1970.
Sommerville, C. John. *Popular Religion in Restoration England*. Gainesville: University of Florida Press, 1977.
––––––. "Religious Typologies and Popular Religion in Restoration England." *Church History* 45 (1976):32–41.
Southgate, Wyndham M. *John Jewel and the Problem of Doctrinal Authority*. Cambridge, Mass.: Harvard University Press, 1962.
––––––. "The Marian Exiles and the Influence of John Calvin." *History* 27 (1942):148–52.
Spalding, James C. "The Demise of English Presbyterianism, 1660–1760." *Church History* 28 (1959):63–83.
Sparrow-Simpson, W. J. *Archbishop Bramhall*. London: S.P.C.K., 1927.
Sprunger, Keith L. "Ames, Ramus, and the Method of Puritan Theology." *Harvard Theological Review* 59 (1966):133–51.
––––––. *The Learned Doctor William Ames: Dutch Backgrounds of English and American Puritanism*. Urbana: University of Illinois Press, 1972.
Stephens, W. P. *The Holy Spirit in the Theology of Martin Bucer*. Cambridge: Cambridge University Press, 1971.
Stoever, William K. B. *'A Faire and Easie Way to Heaven': Covenant Theology and Antinomianism in Early Massachusetts*. Middletown: Wesleyan University Press, 1978.
Stone, Lawrence. *The Causes of the English Revolution, 1529–1642*. London: Routledge & Kegan Paul, 1972.
Sutch, Victor D. *Gilbert Sheldon: Architect of Anglican Survival, 1640–1675*. The Hague: Martinus Nijhoff, 1973.
Sykes, Norman. *Church and State in England in the Eighteenth Century*. 1934. Reprint, Hamden: Archon Books, 1962.

Thomas, Keith. *Religion and the Decline of Magic*. New York: Charles Scribners, 1971.

Thomas, Roger. "The Non-Subscription Controversy amongst Dissenters in 1719: The Salter's Hall Debate." *Journal of Ecclesiastical History* 4 (1953):162–86.

Thornton, L. S. *Richard Hooker: A Study of His Theology*. London: S.P.C.K., 1924.

Tipson, Lynn Baird, Jr. "The Development of a Puritan Understanding of Conversion." Ph.D. dissertation, Yale University, 1972.

―――. "Invisible Saints: The 'Judgment of Charity' in the Early New England Churches." *Church History* 44 (1975):460–71.

Tjernagel, Neelak Serawlook. *Henry VIII and the Lutherans: A Study in Anglo-Lutheran Relations from 1521–1547*. St. Louis: Concordia Publishing House, 1965.

Tolmie, Murray. *The Triumph of the Saints: The Separate Churches of London, 1616–1649*. Cambridge: Cambridge University Press, 1977.

Toon, Peter. *The Emergence of Hyper-Calvinism in English Nonconformity, 1689–1765*. London: The Olive Tree, 1967.

―――. *God's Statesman: The Life and Work of John Owen*. Grand Rapids: Zondervan, 1973.

Trevor-Roper, H. R. *Archbishop Laud, 1573–1645*. 2d ed. London: MacMillan and Co., 1962.

Trinterud, Leonard J. "A.D. 1689: The End of the Clerical World." In Winthrop Hudson and Leonard J. Trinterud, *Theology in Sixteenth and Seventeenth Century England, Papers Read at a Clark Library Seminar, February 6, 1971*, pp. 27–47. Los Angeles: William Andrews Clark Memorial Library, 1971.

―――. "The Origins of Puritanism." *Church History* 20 (1951):37–57.

―――. "A Reappraisal of William Tyndale's Debt to Martin Luther." *Church History* 31 (1962):24–45.

―――, ed. *Elizabethan Puritanism*. Oxford: Oxford University Press, 1971.

Troeltsch, Ernst. *Protestantism and Progress*. Translated by W. Montgomery. 1912. Reprint, Boston: Beacon Press, 1958.

Turner, G. Lyon. "The Religious Condition of London in 1672 as Reported to King and Court." *Congregational Historical Society Transactions* 3 (1907):192–205.

―――. "Williamson's Spy Book." *Congregational Historical Society Transactions* 5 (1912):242–58.

Tyacke, Nicholas. "Puritanism, Arminianism and Counter-Revolution." In *The Origins of the English Civil War*, edited by Conrad Russell, pp. 119–43. London: MacMillan, 1973.

Underwood, A. C. *A History of the English Baptists*. London: Carey Kingsgate Press, 1956.

Usher, Roland G. *The Reconstruction of the English Church*. 2 vols. New York: D. Appleton and Co., 1910.

Vander Molen, Ronald J. "Anglican against Puritan: Ideological Origins during the Marian Exile." *Church History* 42 (1973):45–57.

―――. "Providence as Mystery, Providence as Revelation: Puritan and Anglican Modifications of John Calvin's Doctrine of Providence." *Church History* 47 (1978):27–47.

Van Holk, Lambertus J. "From Arminius to Arminianism in Dutch Theology." In *Man's Faith and Freedom: The Theological Influence of Jacobus Arminius*, edited by G. O. McCulloh, pp. 27–45. New York: Abingdon Press, 1962.

Van Leeuwen, Henry G. *The Problem of Certainty in English Thought, 1630–1690*. The Hague: Martinus Nijhoff, 1963.

von Rohr, John. "Covenant and Assurance in Early English Puritanism." *Church History* 34 (1965):195–203.

Wakefield, Gordon S. *Puritan Devotion: Its Place in the Development of Christian Piety*. London: Epworth Press, 1957.

Walker, D. P. *The Decline of Hell: Seventeenth-Century Discussions of Eternal Torment*. Chicago: University of Chicago Press, 1964.

Wallace, Dewey D., Jr. "The Doctrine of Predestination in the Early English Reformation." *Church History* 43 (1974):201–15.

———. "George Gifford, Puritan Propaganda and Popular Religion in Elizabethan England." *Sixteenth Century Journal* 9 (1978):27–49.

———. "The Life and Thought of John Owen to 1660: A Study of the Significance of Calvinist Theology in English Puritanism." Ph.D. dissertation, Princeton University, 1965.

———. "Puritan and Anglican: The Interpretation of Christ's Descent into Hell in Elizabethan Theology." *Archiv für Reformationsgeschichte* 69 (1978):248–87.

Wallace, John M. *Destiny His Choice: The Loyalism of Andrew Marvell*. Cambridge: Cambridge University Press, 1968.

Wallace, Ronald S. *Calvin's Doctrine of the Christian Life*. Edinburgh: Oliver and Boyd, 1959.

Warfield, Benjamin B. *The Westminster Assembly and Its Work*. New York: Oxford University Press, 1931.

Watkins, Owen C. *The Puritan Experience*. London: Routledge & Kegan Paul, 1972.

Watts, Michael R. *The Dissenters: From the Reformation to the French Revolution*. Oxford: Clarendon Press, 1978.

Welsby, Paul A. *George Abbot: The Unwanted Archbishop, 1562–1633*. London: S.P.C.K., 1962.

———. *Lancelot Andrewes, 1555–1626*. London: S.P.C.K., 1958.

Wendel, François. *Calvin: The Origins and Development of His Religious Thought*. Translated by Philip Mairet. London: Collins, 1963.

Westfall, Richard S. *Science and Religion in Seventeenth-Century England*. 1958. Reprint, Ann Arbor: University of Michigan, 1973.

White, B. R. *The English Separatist Tradition: From the Marian Martyrs to the Pilgrim Fathers*. London: Oxford University Press, 1971.

———. "The Organization of the Particular Baptists, 1640–1660." *Journal of Ecclesiastical History* 17 (1966):209–26.

Whitehead, Alfred North. *Religion in the Making*. New York: MacMillan, 1930.

Whiting, C. E. *Studies in English Puritanism from the Restoration to the Revolution, 1660–1688*. London: S.P.C.K., 1931.

Wilde, Oscar. *The Picture of Dorian Gray*. New York: Modern Library, 1926.

Williams, C. H. *William Tyndale*. London: Thomas Nelson and Sons, 1969.

Williams, George H. *The Radical Reformation*. Philadelphia: Westminster Press, 1962.

Williamson, Hugh Ross. *Jeremy Taylor*. London: Dennis Dobson, Ltd., 1952.

Willson, D. Harris. *King James VI and I*. New York: Henry Holt and Co., 1956.

Wilson, John F. *Pulpit in Parliament: Puritanism during the English Civil Wars, 1640–1648*. Princeton: Princeton University Press, 1969.

Windeatt, Edward. "Devonshire and the Indulgence of 1672." *Congregational Historical Society Transactions*, no. 3 (July, 1902), pp. 159–70.

Wolfe, Don M. *Milton in the Puritan Revolution*. New York: Thomas Nelson and Sons, 1941.

Woodhouse, A. S. P., ed. *Puritanism and Liberty, Being Army Debates (1647–1649) from the Clarke Manuscripts*. Chicago: University of Chicago Press, 1951.

Yost, John K. "A Reappraisal of How Protestantism Spread during the Early English Reformation." *Anglican Theological Review* 60 (1978):437–46.

Yule, George. "Theological Developments in Elizabethan Puritanism." *Journal of Religious History* 1 (1960):16–25.

Zuck, Lowell H. "The Influence of the Reformed Tradition on the Elizabethan Settlement." *Concordia Theological Monthly* 31 (1960):215–26.

Index

Berkeley, Gilbert, 33
Bernard, Nathaniel, 93
Bernhere, Augustine, 21
Bertius, Peter, 80, 126, 220 (n. 5)
Beza, Theodore, 3, 129, 180; on predestination, 25; translated into English, 41, 206 (n. 142), 209 (n. 63); and scholasticism, 56, 57; influence in England, 57, 59; on reprobation, 60; criticized, 67, 124; on decrees of God, 215 (n. 181); on limited atonement, 216 (n. 183)
Bible, 15, 63, 107, 125, 178, 198. *See also* Geneva Bible
Bibliander, Andreas, 72
Biddle, John, 145, 151
Bilson, Thomas, 73, 212 (n. 118)
Bishops of the Church of England, 36, 160–61, 169; as spiritual writers, 53; and the spread of Arminianism, 105; and sectarian Arminians, 108. *See also* Episcopacy
"Bishop's Book," 14
Boethius, 130
Bondage of the Will, On the (Luther), 6, 34
Bonner, Edmund, 201 (n. 27)
Book of Common Prayer, 17
Book of Homilies, 16, 32
Booty, John E., 207–8 (n. 21)
Bosher, Robert S., 125
Bowle, John, 47–48, 53
Boyle, Robert, 179, 235 (n. 22)
Bradford, John, 20, 27, 38, 40, 71, 205 (n. 136); in controversy with the freewillers, 22–24; and the order of salvation, 44; on predestination as comforting, 47; as a spiritual writer, 53
Bradwardine, Thomas, 5, 82
Bramhall, John, 96, 124–25, 168, 228 (n. 58)
Bray, John S., 58, 215 (n. 165)
Brenz, Johann, 35
Brevis & dilucida explicatio, verae, certae, & consolationis plenae doctrinae De Electione, Praedestinatione ac Reprobatione (Hutton), 35
Breward, Ian, 45, 199 (n. 7)
Bridge, William, 149, 176
Bridges, Gabriel, 93
Briefe Answere to Certaine Objections against the Treatise of Faith, A (Culverwell), 85
Briefe declaration of the Chiefe Poynts of Christian Religion, A (Beza), 25, 206 (n. 142)
Briefe Treatyse of Election and Reproba-

cion . . . , A (Gilby), 26, 206 (nn. 142, 143)
Brooke, Robert Greville Lord, 87, 104
Brooks, Thomas, 149, 157, 161, 177, 233 (n. 205)
Brownists, 106, 210 (n. 73) *See also* Separatism
Bucer, Martin, xv, 3, 5, 85, 106, 183; on predestination, 6; on sanctification, 7, 9; in England, 15; John Bradford studies under, 20; Grindal his protégè, 33; on the order of salvation, 44; on election to holiness, 51, 118; ridiculed by *Fur Predestinatus*, 122
Buckeridge, John, 69, 83, 87
Buckingham, George Villiers first duke of, 87–88, 93
Buckingham, George Villiers second duke of, 168
Bull, George, 127, 162–64, 184, 229 (n. 87)
Bullinger, Heinrich, xv, 3, 6, 18, 33, 34, 35, 205 (n. 140)
Bullingham, Nicholas, 33
Bunyan, John, 161, 178, 180, 185–86, 235 (n. 152); controversy with Edward Fowler, 164–66
Burges, Cornelius, 96, 104
Burgess, Anthony, 137
Burnet, Gilbert, 166, 169
Burns, Norman T., 204–5 (n. 111)
Burton, Henry, 84–85
Burton, William, 51
Byfield, Nicholas, 54

Calamy, Edmund, 104, 133, 143
Calfhill, James, 35
Calvin, John, xv, 3, 25, 67, 118, 121, 126, 129, 164, 167, 169; on predestination, 4, 6, 31, 34–35; on sanctification, 7; and John Hooper, 18; defended by John Philpot, 20; followed in Nowell's Catechism, 32; influences Thomas Rogers, 33; translated by John Field, 41; on Christ's descent into Hell, 48; and scholasticism, 56; and humanism, 72; praised by John Donne, 78; and Thomas Hobbes, 125; and Moise Amyraut, 133; and covenant theology, 198; and Anthony Gilby, 205 (n. 139); and the church fathers, 207–8 (n. 21); criticized by Henry Barrow, 210 (n. 73); and Richard Hooker, 219 (nn. 255, 256, 258)
Calvinists and Calvinism, 4, 56, 72, 92, 119; in the Church of England, 36, 65,

Paul's Cross, 35, 66, 70, 80

Pelagianism, 27, 41, 72, 110, 124, 125,
140, 157, 179, 183; early English Protestants accuse Roman Catholics of,
13–14, 15; freewillers charged with, 21,
24; Roman Catholicism and Pelagianism
identified, 30, 33, 39, 40, 62, 64–65;
Arminians accused of, 60, 70, 83, 85, 94,
95, 97, 109; Robert Ferguson on, 168;
John Owen thinks Anglicans guilty of,
172, 174

Pelagius Redivivus (Featley), 85

Pemble, William, 86, 119, 124, 146, 163,
180

Perfectionist heresy, 38, 106

Perkins, William, 81, 82, 106, 125, 129,
214 (nn. 162, 163); both a scholastic
theologian and a spiritual writer, 55;
influenced by Petrus Ramus, 57; his
scholastic theology, 59–61; refutes
Roman Catholicism, 63; defends predestination, 69, 70; ridiculed, 122, 123

Perpetuity of Faythe, The (Some), 60

*Perpetuity of a Regenerate Mans Estate,
The* (Prynne), 85–86

Perrinchief, Richard, 175

Perseverance of the Saints, xii, 52–53, 101;
in the controversy over Richard Montague, 84, 85, 86, 88; George Downame
silenced for teaching, 97; denied by Edward Glover, 106; rejected by Anglicans,
126; defended, 141, 151, 178, 223 (n.
88). *See also* Falling from grace, possibility of

Peter, Hugh, 149

Petto, Samuel, 149, 157, 176, 185

Philpot, John, 20, 21, 22, 24

Pierce, Thomas: attacks Antinomians, 121;
attacks predestinarians, 123–25; cites
Philip Melancthon and John Overall,
126; on new Covenant, 127; favors
Amyraldism, 133; and Richard Baxter,
136, 139, 140; opposed by Henry
Hickman, 140

Pietas crucis, 49, 153

Piety of grace, xiii, xv, 90, 101, 191; in John
Bradford, 22–24; in the spiritual writers,
43–55 passim; held by episcopalians,
102; held by sectarian Arminians, 107; in
John Eaton, 115; and John Goodwin,
131–32; and Richard Baxter, 133; and
Henry Hickman, 141; and John Owen,
150; and Presbyterians, 161; and Dissenters, 162, 183; and John Bunyan, 165;
and high Calvinists, 184–86; and the Alleines, 188–89; its future, 189–90; its

meaning, 193–96; its relation to the
covenant, 198. *See also* Grace of God;
Theology of grace

Pilgrims Progress, The (Bunyan), 186

Pilkington, James, 33, 35

Pinner's Hall Controversy, 180–82

Plaifere, John, 122

Plea for Grace, A (Pemble), 86

Plotinus, 130

Pneumatalogia (Owen), 156

Polanus, Amandus, 215 (n. 166)

Polhill, Edward, 172–73, 177

Pompanazzi, Pietro, 57

Ponet, John, 17

"Popery," 100, 104, 105, 128, 224 (n. 99);
equated with Pelagianism, 33, 64, 65;
Richard Baxter accused of, 138

Porter, H. C., 71, 204 (n. 88)

Potter, Barnaby, 94

Potter, Christopher, 91, 94, 98

Practical Catechism (Hammond), 127

Practical Discourse of Gods Sovereignty, A
(Coles), 177

Praedestinatione, De (Pilkington), 35

*Praedestinationis Modo et Ordine et de
Amplificatione Gratiae Divinae* (Perkins),
60

Preaching: and Puritans, 30, 43, 75; of predestination, 42, 44, 91, 141, 218 (n.
231); and Anglicans, 75

Predestinarians, 96, 105, 106. *See also*
Anti-Arminians; Calvinists and Calvinism; Predestination

Predestination, xii, xiii, 8, 27, 36, 38, 71,
99, 100; its importance, 6; and
sanctification, 9; and assurance, 11; in
early English Protestantism, 11–13, 202
(n. 61); in the Edwardian Reformation,
15–19; in the controversy with the
freewillers, 20–23; and the Marian
exiles, 25, 204 (n. 108); defended by John
Knox, 26–27; after Elizabethan settlement, 29–35 passim; in the Thirty-nine
Articles, 31–32, 204 (nn. 88, 89);
Lutheran-Reformed differences over, 34;
and Anglican-Puritan differences, 37;
John Foxe on, 40, 209 (n. 59); and Nonconformists, 41; and Separatists, 42; to
be preached, 42, 44, 91, 141, 218 (n.
231); in order of salvation, 45; Ernst
Troeltsch on, 45; and assurance, 45–46;
is comforting, 47; in scholasticism, 58–
60, 215 (n. 166); in the theology of William Perkins, 59–61; in controversy with
Rome, 64; and Matthew Parker, 65; and
Antonio de Corro, 65–66; and Lambeth

Articles, 67; at Oxford, 68–69, 95; and foreknowledge, 73; and John Overall, Lancelot Andrews, and Richard Hooker, 76–77, 219 (n. 255); and English delegates at Dort, 81–82; Richard Crakanthorpe preaches on, 82–83; defended by William Prynne and William Pemble, 86; in York House Conference, 88; discussion concerning it forbidden, 90–91; defended by Archbishop Ussher, 97; attacked by Laudians, 101; defended by John Davenant, 104; discussed in Westminster Assembly, 106; criticized by Thomas Helwys, 107; in relation to Antinomianism, 113, 118, 119, 121–22; attacked by Anglicans, 121–28 passim; and the Cambridge Platonists, 129; rejected by John Goodwin, 130–31, and John Milton, 132; and moderate Calvinists, 134–35, 138–39, 140–42; Thomas Goodwin writes on, 148; affirmed by William Bates, 161; in the controversy with Samuel Parker, 167; and Socinianism, 175; defended by Vincent Alsop, 176; and providence, 180; Richard Baxter on, 181; Stephen Charnock a strong predestinarian, 186; avoided by John Flavel, 187; meaning of, 192–96; and covenant theology, 197; in George Joye, 202 (n. 61); and Lollardy, 204 (n. 111); and Benjamin Traheron, 204 (n. 101), 205 (n. 140); and Thomas Rogers, 207 (n. 20); and Thomas Goad, 220 (n. 9). *See also* Calvinists and Calvinism; Decrees of God; Election; Reprobation

Predestination and Election made by John Lamberd minister of the church of Elham, Of (Lamberd), 19

Preparation for grace, 114, 119, 132, 135, 226 (nn. 3, 4)

Presbyterians: against Antinomianism, 121; and Richard Baxter, 136, 139; and moderate Calvinism, 142–44; and high Calvinism, 149, 162; after the Restoration, 159, 160–61; and controversies with Anglicans, 172, 176; dispute with Congregationalists, 180–82; piety of, 183, 186–87; and John Flavel, 187; and the Alleines, 188

Preston, John, 87, 88

Prideaux, John, 69, 93–94, 97, 103, 172

Prime, John, 46, 53, 54

"Prophesyings," 55

Providence, 58, 180, 192–93, 203 (n. 68)

Prynne, William, 85–86, 96, 103

Pucci, Francesco, 72

Purgatory, 12, 14, 38

Puritans and Puritanism, xi, xv, 4, 108, 112, 140; differences from Anglicanism, xi–xii, xv–xvi, 54, 71, 101–2, 199–200 (n. 7), 218–19 (n. 247); and Tyndale's moralism, 10; and John Hooper, 18; and Anthony Gilby, 19; and Swiss theology, 28; and Calvinist theology, 29; and preaching, 30; and bishops of Church of England, 36; and grace, 37; and Separatists, 42; spread Protestant teachings, 43; and preaching, 43–44, 75; attacked, 53, 54, 83, 84, 90; and the order of salvation, 54; and logic of Ramus, 58; at Hampton Court Conference, 69; and Duke of Buckingham, 87; and Archbishop Laud, 95, 98, 100; and Arminianism, 101–2, 104; and Antinomianism, 113–14, 121; and covenant theology, 127, 198; and sectarian Arminians, 130–31; attacked by Peter Heylyn, 142; and the Restoration, 158; attacked by Samuel Parker, 166–67; on the Holy Spirit, 234 (n. 239); and John Wesley, 240 (n. 162). *See also* Congregationalists; Nonconformists and Nonconformity; Presbyterians

Pym, John, 85, 88, 222 (n. 69)

Quakers, 113, 132, 156, 165, 169, 172, 234 (nn. 239, 240)

Questions Tres: De Merito et Efficacia, Remissionis Peccatorum Per Fidem Certitudine ac Iustificantes fidei perseverantia (Some), 60

Radical Reformation: and Bernardino Ochino, 16; and freewillers, 20–21; and Antinomianism, 113; and grace, 204 (n. 109)

Rainolds, John, 62, 66, 68, 70

Ramus, Petrus, 57, 58

Randall, John, 54

Ranters, 131

Reason, 173, 175, 178–79, 183

Reconcileableness of Gods Prescience of the Sins of Men, with the Wisdom and Sincerity of His Counsels, The (Howe), 179

Recusancy, 75

Redemption Redeemed (Goodwin), 130

Reformation, 192; on the continent, xiv–xv, 3–4, 15, 142, 189, 198; in England, 5, 11, 28, 43, 70, 72, 73; in England, as viewed in later controversies, 99, 101, 128, 131, 166–67. *See also* Ed-